Shadow of a Mouse

The publisher gratefully acknowledges the generous support of the Institute for Scholarship in the Liberal Arts, College of Arts and Letters, University of Notre Dame

Shadow of a Mouse

Performance, Belief, and World-Making
in Animation

Donald Crafton

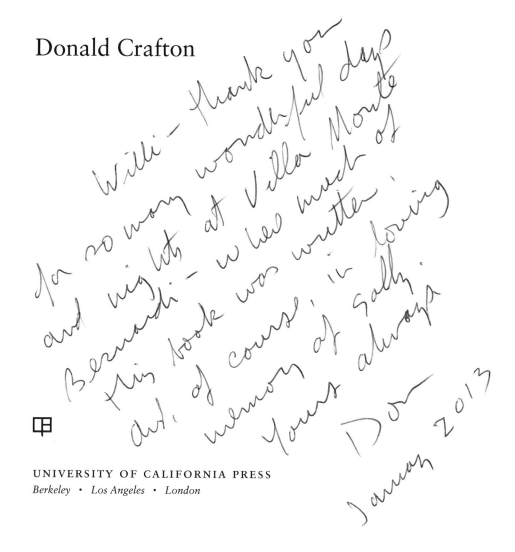

Willi — thank you
for so many wonderful days
and nights at Villa Monte
Bernardi — who had much of
this book was written —
and, of course, in loving
memory of Sally.
Yours always
Don
January 2013

UNIVERSITY OF CALIFORNIA PRESS
Berkeley • Los Angeles • London

University of California Press, one of the most
distinguished university presses in the United States,
enriches lives around the world by advancing
scholarship in the humanities, social sciences, and
natural sciences. Its activities are supported by the UC
Press Foundation and by philanthropic contributions
from individuals and institutions. For more
information, visit www.ucpress.edu.

University of California Press
Berkeley and Los Angeles, California

University of California Press, Ltd.
London, England

Library of Congress Cataloging-in-Publication Data

Crafton, Donald.
 Shadow of a mouse : performance, belief and
world-making in animation / Donald Crafton.
  p. cm.
 Includes bibliographical references and index.
 ISBN 978-0-520-26103-7 (cloth : alk. paper) —
ISBN 978-0-520-26104-4 (pbk. : alk. paper)
  1. Animated films—History and criticism.
2. Cartoon characters. 3. Motion picture
acting. 4. Characters and characteristics in motion
pictures. I. Title.
 NC1765.C73 2012
 791.43'34—dc23   2012005216

Manufactured in the United States of America

22 21 20 19 18 17 16 15 14 13
10 9 8 7 6 5 4 3 2 1

The paper used in this publication meets the minimum
requirements of ANSI/NISO Z39.48–1992 (R 2002)
(*Permanence of Paper*).

For Susan,
The Seraph

Contents

Illustrations

Preface

One wag suggested that I should call this book *After Mickey*. I suppose in some ways it does pick up where *Before Mickey,* a book I wrote decades ago, left off, with the coming of sound in animation and the beginnings of the studio era of Hollywood cartoons after 1928. But my intention wasn't to write a continuing chronicle of the studios; Mike Barrier and others have done a fine job of that. Since my original aim was to restrict myself to the understudied decade of the 1930s, *Before Bugs* might have been accurate. But as I watched the hundreds of films from the period in archives and those that are readily available on video (a small percentage of the cartoons actually released), I realized that the big stories were not limited to the advancement of the main studios and the growing competition with the Disney juggernaut, but they also included what these filmmakers were trying to accomplish and the ways audiences were responding. It became clear that the Hollywood animators were pursuing a shared goal: to create a new kind of film performance. Perhaps the title *After Before Mickey* might have captured the scope of my project, which deals with films made outside a set chronology and in some instances outside the studio system, but that would have been much too confusing.

Instead I have chosen *Shadow of a Mouse,* a title that alerts readers to what they're in for in the pages ahead while also satisfying my desire for suggestiveness. The mouse casting the shadow is Mickey and the animated populace that in the 1930s became increasingly corporeal on the screen, occupied illusionistic spaces, and responded to natural elements—lights and shadows. Indeed, along with the use of perspective, creating highlights and shadows became crucial to generating cartoon space.

The mouse also is The Mouse, *Variety*'s moniker for the whole Disney enterprise. Over the course of the 1930s, Walt Disney Productions became the most important cartoon studio—artistically, culturally, and financially—before or since. Disney's biography, his professional career, the reception and social impact of his studio's films, and the vicissitudes of the global businesses are central not only to animation history but also to America and the rest of the world. Nevertheless, in *Shadow of a Mouse,* I hope to peer around the hegemonic figure of the corporate rodent and pay more due to Disney's competitors that labored in the shadows, the Fleischers and Warners, of course, but also the other studios in the classic period. I also consider to some extent international and contemporary independent animators. This is a challenge. The Mouse's penumbra is so large and deep that it shades most everything. I have determined that it's not possible to write or converse about classic animation without acknowledging Disney's influence and contributions.

That cartoons are performances may seem either self-evidently so, or just as evidently balderdash, depending on one's attitude. I will not try to convince the reader of the former in these few sentences. For the present I'll simply point out that my conclusions relate to how cartoons got to be what they were, why they behaved according to the Disney norm or modified or resisted it, and why the films took on their forms and attitudes toward acting, toward theatricality, and toward audiences. My conclusions are speculative but not unempirical. They are based on my observations of cartoons' origins, industrial practices, and the development of techniques and themes. I reflect on their content and speculate about cartoons' reception by mass audiences. The time, the place, and the qualities of the makers and observers of these films were crucial to their performativity.

A *New Yorker* cartoon by Frank Cotham shows two barbarians in medieval warrior garb riding their horses across a plain.[1] A mounted tweed jacket–wearing, pipe-smoking, note-taking professor of barbarian studies follows them closely. Academic pretentiousness masquerading as disinterested analysis is being lampooned here, and the joke hits home. I know just how that professor feels because I, too, have been on the trail, attempting to extract academic rationality from something that is unruly, uncouth, and a bit threatening: the performativity, belief systems, and world-making of the book's subtitle.

The trek began when I was asked to present a keynote address to the Society for Animation Studies. In "Performance *in* and *of* Animation," I wanted to show that animation matters in film studies—not that anyone at that gathering needed convincing. Of course, the animated cinema's fascinating specialized technology, its unique properties as a kinetic graphic medium, and its ability to generate motion and evoke emotion have always been recognized. It was a form of expression that occupied superb craftspeople and served amazing artists. It evolved from storytelling forms, many with connections to mythology, fairy tales, and other ancient fictions, that provided outlets for the uncanny, the incoherent, and the just plain funny. Cartoons developed their own aesthetic norms that were understood and followed by vast audiences. They enjoyed reciprocity with—that is, they influenced and were influenced by—the non-animated cinema, stage presentations, comic strips, comic books, graphic novels, and modern art. Aside from these verities, though, I wanted to seize the opportunity to propose that we consider animated films as a cultural enterprise based on performativity.

The part of my claim that was more difficult to articulate, and therefore to accept, concerned the relationship of animation cinema to our non-animated film experience and, for that matter, to live performances. I maintained that, really, screen performances by cartoon actors were scarcely different from those by human movie actors. Since pursuing this line of reasoning, I am convinced that it is correct—but it is a denser, more complicated relationship than I initially had presumed.

There isn't much said here about computer animation, but not because it isn't performative. It is. The blockbuster features from Pixar and others have actually resuscitated classic performance styles. It's just that computer-generated imagery (CGI) is another immense project waiting to be tackled. I discuss only a couple of the innumerable historical and practicing European filmmakers who deserve attention and none of the Asian ones. Their performances often are radical departures from the Hollywood norm, especially when they revitalize traditions from local popular theatrical traditions and artistic techniques, puppetry, shadowgraphy, and vernacular graphic expressions such as graffiti and *manga*. Inevitably, these films are very different performance models and therefore topics to be pursued elsewhere. I also limit the discussion mainly to the short films made for domestic distribution through movie theaters rather than features or those made for television.

As a special category on the film program, cartoons may be subjected to all the critical approaches that have been developed in cinema studies.

Although the "film program" hasn't existed as an exhibition practice for decades outside some festival and nostalgic re-presentations, many of my propositions remain appropriate to the study of present-day animation. Writers on the medium may invoke the problematic distinction between its "realistic" and "artificial" aspects, argue for or against cartoons' ability to enlighten, educate, persuade, frighten, or corrupt viewers. They may debate the pros and cons of the medium's social influence, sketch its successes and failures as an industry and a business, extol it as a vehicle of personal expression by artists, poets, storytellers, and essayists. They delineate its aesthetic forms and structures as narrative constructions, as spectacle, as images of the mind, of race, of gender, of the subjectivity of the viewer in society, of the circumstances of production and reception. In short, any discourse about film in the past or future finds itself vibrant in arguments about animation. These are debates that inform media studies in general and—who knows?—may boomerang back on the discipline of performance studies.

Cartoons as performance art? In fact, this line of inquiry has the potential to swing the door open on a new way of contemplating animation and film as popular culture activities. Marvin Carlson (who was not addressing animation) provided a rationale when he wrote:

> Performance discourse and its close theoretical partner, "performativity," today dominate critical discourse not only in all manner of cultural studies, but also in business, economics, and technology. The rise of an interest in performance reflects a major shift in many cultural fields from the what of culture to the how, from the accumulation of social, cultural, psychological, political, or linguistic data to a consideration of how this material is created, valorized, and changed, to how it lives and operates within the culture, by its actions. Its real meaning is now sought in its praxis, its performance.[2]

We have every reason to extend this inquiry to the "how" of cultural productions of the past, of which animation was and is an important, albeit unsung, praxis.

If animation were performative, a "performance art" in the contemporary sense, it operated according to a peculiar aesthetic.[3] Defining *performance* has been nettlesome for performance theorists and philosophers precisely because the word has many meanings, uses, referents, and connotations. I try to narrow these meanings to make them specific to cartoons and retain some useful descriptors without sounding too pedantic. I regard performances as specific types of events, interactive behaviors, and actions.[4] It is curious that many contemporary definitions of performance are nearly all-inclusive and yet have seldom been applied to traditional media entertainment.[5] If, as the performance studies experts say, performances are ubiquitous, then why have they not attended more to mass-market performances such as popular film and classic animation?[6] Our look at movie cartooning as yet another variant of performance should have the side effect of bringing awareness to the performativity of other "popular" forms, such as mainstream cinema and television, video gaming, and online presentations. Although Betty Boop may not be as interesting in some respects as, let's say, Annie Sprinkle, she does bring her own unique attractions to the performance party. The means of her embodiment as a star has the potential to generate insights about Annie's performativity too.

The critic and social theorist Walter Benjamin would have appreciated the serendipity of the *New Yorker* cartoon and my quest. Mickey Mouse struck him as exemplifying a "new barbarism." He meant that in a good way; for him—at least in his early writing—cartoons provoked humanizing laughter. (Later he came to regard collective laughter as more ambivalent, a more complicated, possibly darker social performance.) Given his strong interest in animation, he too was a kind of professor of barbarian studies.

In my note-taking journey on the track of animation performativity, many institutions and individuals—alas, too many to list here in their entirety—have supported me. These include the students to whom I have professed my theories and who in turn have taught me about clarity, practicality, and common sense. Thank you.

My apologies to those who should be on this list, but whose help and influence I am temporarily forgetting. For their assistance, which ranges from the conversational to the physical to the practical and the massively inspirational, I am grateful to Richard Abel, Rick Altman, Dudley Andrew, Michael Barrier, Jerry Beck, Matthew Bernstein, Giannalberto Bendazzi, David Bordwell, Eileen Bowser, Neil Brand, Suzanne Buchan, Scott Bukatman, John Canemaker, Phil Carli, Jessica Chalmers, Chen Mei, Alan Cholodenko, Ian Christie, Jim Collins, Bob Cowan, Ton Crone, Scott Curtis, Harvey Deneroff, Julia Douthwaite, Erwin Feyersinger, Michael Friend, Michael Frierson, Agustín Fuentes, Kenneth Garcia, André Gaudreault, Aaron Gerow, Michael Geyer, Daniel Goldmark, Tom Gunning, Connie Harmacinski, Kevin Heffernan, Heather Hendershot, Kay Taylor Hightower, Peter Holland, Jan-Christopher Horak, Dorcas and Mike Hults, Ron Hutchinson, Alison Hrynyk, Henry Jenkins, Graham Jones, J.B. Kaufman, Charlie Keil, Melody Kesler, Frank Kessler, Clare Kitson, Mark Langer, Antonia Lant, Martin Marks, Paul

Matwiy, Richard May, Linda Harris Mehr, Annette Melville, Anthony Monta, Russell Merritt, J.J. Murphy, James Naremore, David L. Nathan, Cheryl and Bill Niehaus, Jan Olsson, Mark Pilkinton, Michael Pogorzelski, Ray Pointer, Dana Polan, Rick Prelinger, Christian Quendler, Christina Ries, David Robinson, Kevin Sandler, Hank Sartin, Katie Schildhouse (especially for her translations from Klingon), Sally and Willi Schmelzer, Georges Schwizgebel, J.J. Sedelmaier, David R. Smith, Murray Smith, Christine Sopczynski, Don Stelluto, Dan Streible, Randy Thom, Kristin Thompson, Lee Tsiantis, John Turner, Jon Vickers, John Welle, Paul Wells, Pamela Wojcik, and Virginia Wright Wexman.

For its institutional leadership and support, I am in debt to the Notre Dame Institute for Scholarship in the Liberal Arts under the aegis of Deans Christopher Fox, John McGreevy, and Mark Roche. In particular, ISLA provided a subvention for this book. The Notre Dame Office of Research directed by Robert Bernhard also contributed important publication subventions. My most thankful thank-yous go to the Academy of Motion Picture Arts and Sciences for an Academy Scholars grant. Not only did the generous support from this pioneering program give me substantial funding for a year of research, but the encouragement of Shawn Guthrie kept me on target as the project meandered through one distraction after another.

Mary Francis at the University of California Press has served as a helpful advisor to me. As an editor, she is a boon to the entire field of cinema studies.

To all the Craftons, Ron, Darlene, Ken, and Mark, mother Maxine, and my kids, Elise and Andy: big hugs for your patience and encouragement. Roberta and Charles Ohmer, I have appreciated our conversations about so many things, none having anything at all to do with animation.

Susan Ohmer originally suggested that I submit my proposal to the Academy Scholar program. Except for a brief period of total immersion into the world of Angry Birds, she has constantly guided and inspired me. My journey toward discovering animation performance began with her, and thanks to her it is far from finished.

Acknowledgments

This research and its publication were made possible in part by support from the Academy Foundation of the Academy of Motion Picture Arts and Sciences; the Institute for Scholarship in the Liberal Arts, College of Arts and Letters, University of Notre Dame; and the Office of the Vice President for Research, University of Notre Dame.

The author acknowledges the following institutions and publications for their kind permission to allow previously published material to be revised and reprinted. A version of chapter 1 was presented to the Society for Animation Studies at DreamWorks SKG, Glendale, California, September 28, 2002. Earlier versions of chapter 4 appeared as "Planes Crazy: Disney's Transformations of Pictorial Space," *Iconics/International Studies of the Modern Image 6* (2002), courtesy of the Japan Society of Image Arts and Sciences (JASIAS), and as "Planes Crazy: Transformations of Pictorial Space in 1930s Cartoons," *CiNéMAS* 15, nos. 2–3 (2005), courtesy of GRAFICS. An earlier version of chapter 5 appeared in Daniel Goldmark and Charlie Keil, eds., *Funny Pictures: Animation and Comedy in Studio-Era Hollywood* (Berkeley: University of California Press, 2011).

Introduction

Six Cartoon Conundra

Our most important aim is to develop definite personalities
in our cartoon characters. We don't want them to be just
shadows, for merely as moving figures they would provoke
no emotional response from the public.
—Walt Disney (1938)

Animated images surround us from our first waking moments, when
we see the digital hands on our alarm clocks, to bedtime, when we put
our screens to sleep. Most of the films discussed in this book are from
the days when animation was integral to the moviegoing experience.
We paid attention to them. They were designed to amuse or instruct
vast and diverse audiences, primarily in movie theaters. From the 1930s
through the 1950s, many of these short films were as popular as the
full-length features they accompanied. They were essential components
of the overall program, along with comedies, travelogues, two-reel dramas, and other "selected short subjects," as the radiant marquees beamed.

"Hollywood cartoon" signified a mode of production and was shorthand for an attitude, a certain style, a suite of techniques, specific types
of stories and reception expectations, and even a standard length of seven
minutes (give or take a couple). Giannalberto Bendazzi has surveyed
every country with a commercial film industry and discussed their animation studios and fledgling artisans.[1] There were also many filmmakers
outside the studios who tried their hand at making cartoons and animating objects. Though the examples in this book focus on short theatrical
American films made before World War II, one might just as readily pick
international cartoons from any period or works intended to be seen on
TV screens, cable networks, or computers. So we are not at all on the
track of "the golden age of Hollywood cartoons." If I seem to privilege
American animation from the 1930s and '40s, it's because that was

where and when the medium was acquiring its characteristic methods, forms, and content. North American audiences were consolidating their expectations and developing patterns of responsive behavior. It's also because, unlike international and independent animation, the historical product I discuss here is increasingly available in video formats and online. Nearly all the films mentioned in the book are available for the reader's corroboration, contemplation, and enjoyment.

Throughout this book I apply an organizing concept that relates some of these films to one another, to the mainstream productions of their time, and to works outside the system altogether. That concept is "animation performativity," or the aesthetic functioning of bodies in ways that cause events to happen onscreen, as well as the functioning of movie audience members as coanimators, as fellow performers of the films.

Whoa! Certainly we routinely accept (rightly or not) that the beings in a so-called live-action film are acting, that they are communicating and that we in the audience are responsive to them. But are cartoon actors acting in the same way? Their drawn or modeled figures are different biologically from those in live-action movies, but as screen performers, fundamentally they're the same. Welcome to the Tooniverse. It's a portal in the movie experience through which we may venture into realms similar to but different from the imagined ones in mainstream movies. These animated worlds and their inhabitants exist if viewers and animators believe they do. While the makers of Hollywood-style movies with humans try hard to construct worlds that facilitate the viewers' nearly total immersion in their fictions, until recently, with the advent of computer animation, animators did not attempt to make simulacra of live movies. Even Walt Disney always insisted that his artists preserve at least a small gap of implausibility to keep animatography distinct from cinematography.

I am focusing, more or less, on what I'm calling classic cartoons, those short films made by a few large-scale producers for theatrical distribution from 1928 through roughly the 1950s. Although most of my examples come from the seldom-studied 1930s, I also bring in animated performances from other times and places, especially in the coda, which branches further afield. Yes, there were the feature films that began with *Snow White and the Seven Dwarfs* in 1937; yes, there were the abstract films by Mary Ellen Bute, Len Lye, Norman McLaren, and Oskar Fischinger and the shadow films of Lotte Reiniger and the European avantgardists; yes, there were the rise and fall of big producers and directors.

There are monolithic concerns that could and should be examined in much more detail, such as the ethnic and class stereotyping rampant in cartoons. Complicated issues also surround gender and sexuality in animation production and representations. The relation of animation to nationality and national production, and the economics of cartoon distribution and exhibition, are some important histories and debates that deserve more scholarship as well. I hope that the principles of performance that I present here will be pertinent, albeit with some controversy, when those studies are done. In the meantime, it's becoming obvious that studying animation as performance forces us to reflect on the ramifications for non-animated films, live performances, computer-generated performances, and cyberperformers as well.

I am limiting the scope of this study to only a few conundra, or questions asked seriously that elicit playful answers. My intention is not to produce something like a history of cartoon acting, to write a unified theory of animation performance, or to provide hints on how to perform as an animator. The creative work that goes into cartooning, even in the most industrialized phases of the studio period, and the idiosyncratic applications by fans are so distinctive that all we might hope for would be high-confidence generalizations. I offer, instead, observations and propositions that weave in and out of the complexity of animation performativity.

The amorphous Tooniverse can't be charted with compass and square; we need tools suited to its unique navigational demands. Imagine it as a solar system. Performance is its sun, burning at its thermonuclear core, the source of its energy. This sun's gravity, which corresponds to the implied power structures in the films, orders but does not totally control the many planets in its sway. These planets are the different schools, methods, and styles of animated films, each with a different reflectivity, coefficient of mass, and flora and fauna and with a diverse population of toons. Our journey begins at the bright center and moves toward the periphery. Along the way we'll fly by a few planets, explore two or three in detail, and end up in the far reaches of the Tooniverse. At that distance, performance bends backward and performs its own beginning and end.

The chapters in part 1 apply selected concepts from performance studies. The first great conundrum of the (at least) six I'll consider is acting. Characters run the gamut from mere moving shapes to beings that we accept readily as sentient and desirable personalities. Then there are the effects of music, sound, choreography, and graphic design (or their lack) to measure. Perhaps the most important performative determinant, however, is the viewer's belief in the cartoon actors' ability to entertain and moviegoers' capability and willingness to give them license to do so.

Film theorists have traditionally ignored or disparaged acting in the movies. Beginning in the 1970s, however, as film scholars turned their attention to screen acting, theater theoreticians and practitioners were becoming excited about performance art and exploring the possibilities of adapting emerging theories in anthropology, ethnography, and sociology as practical methodologies and as the basis for new theory. These academics observed that most cultures use performances to organize society and everyday life, whether they are formal shows such as ceremonies and rituals, or informal ones, such as chanting, dancing, and playing. Performance studies as a discipline was born to cope with new concepts of performative experiences being identified in global cultures, in everyday life, in art, and has expanded like The Blob to bring into its maw a multitude of behaviors. Except animated cartoons. And, for that matter, film and television. At the same time, with only a few exceptions, scholars of film studies seemingly didn't know or didn't give a fig about contemporary "theatrical" performance theorizing. Strangely, performance studies and film acting studies alike have avoided the great puzzling lacuna that is animation performance.[2]

The first chapter introduces the Big Bang of animated cinema: how do cartoon performances exist at all? It's important to realize that cartoons are not records of performances, the way non-animated films may in part be, but rather they are performances themselves. Toon actors are clearly different from the human stars we know and love, and yet many viewers respond to them not only as performers on-screen but as objects of off-screen fandom as well. Today this is especially the case with the transnationally idolized heroes of Japanese animation, but earlier there was Felix the Cat, Betty Boop, Popeye, Tom and Jerry, the Flintstones, Simpsons, and South Park clans, and the inimitable Disney gang, each with their own devoted followers. Although each presents a fascinating special case, the principal challenge is to divine the different layers of performances in these films.

Keep in mind, though, that usually it's all about bodies. For most of its history, animation has been obsessed with representing the human form in extremis. Perhaps this was a reaction against lingering Victorian sentiments that abjured the human body or concealed/revealed it with artful irony. Perhaps animation was participating in the prurient potential of burlesque, boxing, and—let's be honest—academic painting and ballet. Whatever the origins of their work, filmmakers used animation as technique and as genre to make bodies dance, leap, float, and dive in a whimsical world with its own gravity. Animators also revel in their ability to distend, to fragment, and to expand and contract physiques, turning them inside out to show shocking and fascinating views of innards. They readily explore cavities in ways impossible for any porn star, sideshow attraction, or ecdysiast. Narration, spatialization, and musicalization in cartoons almost always back up body performance.

Audience members experience these performances (as we do those in all films) as separate activities, an immediate one happening on-screen and an extended one that encompasses everything that allows what happens to happen. Unlike most feature films in the classical mode, which try to entice moviegoers into their envelopes of fiction posing as fact, performance *in* animation is often more of a push-pull. The pushing-away aspect dazzles us with dynamic shapes, sounds, gags, and cartoony beings, but it's difficult to fully immerse ourselves there. At the same time, the compelling aspect of animation performance lures us into the film's rarified atmosphere where we participate in a fully fleshed-out sensual world. Walt Disney capitalized on this latter tendency and famously stressed the "plausible impossibility" of acting, the solidification of cartoon bodies, the construction of believable spaces and "personality." It was not that other producers didn't know how to combine believability with the impossible. Some tried to emulate him, some just didn't pursue the goal as doggedly as Disney did, and some didn't care.

In addition to the internal performances, we attend to the performance *of* animation, for example, when we discuss possible reasons the filmmakers decided to make their characters move in their on-screen environment in a certain way, or when we point out the preexisting ideas and conventions they brought to the work. We consider the technology that realizes it, and how the enjoyment, knowledge, and awareness of a film keep gestating inside our heads after the show is over.

I use the terms *figurative* and *embodied* to describe toon acting. I hope readers won't take these to be rigid antagonisms, because that would be plain wrong. Neither are they really on a continuum. Instead, think of them as controls that apply to various components of acting and that pertain not only to the on-screen performers but also to the actions and intentions of the animators, the contexts and traditions, and the mindsets and behaviors of the moviegoers. They are connected, of course, as when we crank up the brightness knob, the contrast and hue levels will go down.

I claim that moviegoers are coanimators because, at the basest material level, they fund the productions as consumers. Producers must anticipate their fickle taste to survive, but, more pertinently, they must recognize that audiences do much of the work with their personal and collective creative energy. Audiences also coanimate when they indulge their assumptions, exercise their imaginations, suspend disbelief up to a point, and fill in toons' personalities. The on-screen characters come to the user with "some assembly required." The fact is that the same process applies to "real" actors on film, especially stars. Human movie actors are as manufactured, as artificial, and as steeped in irony as toons. On-screen performers thus exploit the viewers' ability to hold contradictory attitudes, their capacity to immerse themselves in the character, the action, and the story while also keeping their distance. They respond viscerally to toons as stars while knowing they are not flesh and blood. We discuss some of the mechanisms that enable filmmakers and moviegoers to connect, for example, by re-performing or rehearsing shared knowledge and preconceptions. Sometimes animators take an existing performance and alter it to make it a new one, not unlike the way a DJ will select and sample music to create a new remix.

Now, toons are not living people, yet they exhibit agency and liveness just as human movie actors do. In chapter 2 I focus on the power relationships that are scripted by the animators but that to some extent develop outside their control. This is the second great conundrum: Why do toon actors and their performances seem live and present, despite our knowing that they are projected film frames of drawings or posed models? Animators may draw or mold their characters to move and speak in certain ways, but the characters then seem to acquire their own agency, that is, the ability to do things and influence others. I examine other entertainment forms, including puppets and animal and mechanical actors, to find analogous examples of agency.

By the same token, toons have liveness because they are media beings. The fact that they are projected audiovisual performers equates them with the actors in other movies, but this doesn't give them "real" life by some strange alchemy. Nevertheless, liveness, like agency, exists in the mind of the watcher as much as on the screen. I illustrate this argument with some unexpected examples, such as the player piano, which, like the cartoon actor, involves a performer's body that is both present and absent. We navigate into the central orb of cartoon performance by examining whether toons' combined agency, liveness, inherent campiness, and "personality" can make them stars and, if so, whether they are different from human movie stars.

In part 2 the voyage of discovery will take us to the planets ruled by historical contingency, vaudeville and pictorial space. I recount the generic development of "classical" animated cartoons to reveal animation's debt to the performances it inherited from the popular variety theater known as vaudeville in the United States, music hall in the United Kingdom, and variety in Europe. A third great conundrum is why animated cinema adopted its form, content, and presentation styles from vaudeville to begin with, and why such forms persisted well after the popular stage venues were gone. It seems that cartoons constitute a "memory palace" where the patterns of the presentations—the varied content of the shows, the gags, the democratic audience address, and the assumptions about the ethnicity, race, class, and gender of the crowds—were re-performed on film. Sometimes the references were specific, as when characters put on shows of their own within the cartoon story. Sometimes the films connected cartoon antics and stage performance by evoking a more generalized sense of the liveness and anarchy of the vaudevillesque experience. Denizens of the vaudeville stage, such as magicians and minstrels as well as hecklers in the audience, continued to influence cartoon comedy from the 1930s into the television era.

Although vaudeville was nearly defunct at the time, cartoons from the 1930s through the 1960s riffed on its memory. Adapting a concept from Mikhail Bakhtin and others, I explore the propensity of animators and the complicity of audiences to construct timescapes, that is, worlds imagined in the likeness of a particular time, place, and significance in history that are convincing in their details but patently fictional. Animation's preservation of minstrelsy and its insistence on highlighting bodily performance are examples of cultural timescapes that cartoons perpetuated.

In order for these performances to happen, there must be a unified space to accommodate them. Non-animated films (and animated object films) are created using camera lenses that have been crafted to deploy pictorial conventions such as perspective rendering, conventions that are traceable to the Renaissance (an exception is when filmmakers distort the scene as a special effect). The pictorial space in cartoons, however, including those shots that emulate lens effects, like simulated fisheye views, must be constructed entirely graphically. The fourth conundrum, the subject of chapter 4, is how animation space was constructed, why, and what its relationship to cartoon performance was. These conventions developed in tandem with the changes in character personification. Timescapes too may be "embodied" when they are populated with actors who need to move within them.

The changes in the look and feel of animation pictorialism in the 1930s were extraordinarily rapid, even faster than the commercial growth of computer animation in the 1980s and 1990s. (From the beginnings of theatrical computer animation, with John Lasseter's *The Adventures of André and Wally B.* in 1984, to Pixar's all-computer-animated feature *Toy Story* in 1995, there was a span of about eleven years. Compare this to the evolution of story, character construction, and spatial design from Disney's *The Merry Dwarfs,* in 1929, to *Snow White and the Seven Dwarfs,* in 1937, a span of about eight years.) Classic animation performance was constrained and partly defined by the photomechanical nature of the medium's production. The limitless space of the scenes contrasts paradoxically with the highly restrictive performative limitations imposed by the industrial process of cel animation. For example, prior to the late 1930s, two different spatial systems operated simultaneously in animated films: that of cels, on which flattened characters moved mostly laterally, and that of backgrounds, where depth was indicated with perspective lines and shading. Attempting to reconcile these separate spaces according to an expanding conception of performance was an objective of several major studios in the classical period. Whether that project ultimately helped or hurt the medium is one of the lively controversies in animation history.

It is here that my emphasis on shadows becomes a key concept in cartoon spatialization, for only volumes may cast shadows across the planes of their environment. Creating a Tooniverse with believable height, depth, and theatricality meant constructing scenes in which toons establish their presence by exhibiting weight and solidity in their enveloping worlds. Although I use the phrase *shadow of a mouse* in various metaphoric ways in this book, in chapter 4 I use it literally, since the Disney studio was the most motivated and most successful in defining visually credible worlds. They devised shadow treatments, among other techniques, to amplify their toons' solidity and to facilitate embodiment.

The interplanetary journey continues in part 3 with explorations of how animation came to be regarded as instrumental, that is, how publics came to conceive of cartoon performance as sanctioning some social behaviors and warning against others. Although these two chapters are at some distance from the center of our solar system's performative energy, that is, the theories relating to performance *in* and *of* animation presented at the book's beginning, the case studies remain fundamentally about performances as social, personal, collaborative artistic activities.

The fifth chapter deals with the conundrum of whether animated performance is socially benign or instrumental. It reveals that interpretations of the seminal Depression-era cartoon, Disney's *The Three Little Pigs,* were never cut-and-dried. From the outset there were those who saw it as a parable of how President Franklin Roosevelt's New Deal would bring an end to the Depression, and those who saw it as an affirmation of former president Herbert Hoover's politics of small government and self-reliant individualism. Although this disagreement could be considered a tempest in a teapot, the difference of opinion actually illuminates deeper fissures in the debate about the significance of cartoon reception that would spread to other manifestations of popular media culture such as comic books, rock music, television, video games, and social networking. That is, are cartoons instrumental performances that "infect" their viewers and inspire them to respond in predictable ways, or are they simple benign amusements that generate feel-good laughter, distraction, forgetfulness, and nothing more? Again, concepts of ritual and repetition from performance studies enable us to reconsider these films in a broader context. Are the animators (then and now) creating works intended to spread their intentions virally among those exposed to the films (a concept held by thinkers as divergent as Leo Tolstoy and the Frankfurt School)? Did animation's alleged transgressive qualities give it special status as a positive redemptive art form, or, conversely, did cartoons lull viewers into accepting the powerless status quo of their down-and-out lives as normal and immutable?

In chapter 6 the sun's rays of performativity reach the known edge of the solar system and, appropriately for the circular physics of animation, turn back to the beginning, which is the animated body. The conundrum here is why do many animated films pattern themselves on organic and biological models of process and sometimes seem obsessed with images of eating? This chapter is different from the others because it's primarily thematic, looking narrowly at one recurring constellation of images, sounds, and situations that I call the *digestion motif.* Although the chapter seems to be an explication of content more than theory, in fact, animators' ability to offer performances of the body—stretching, squashing, deforming, and dissecting it—have preoccupied them since the medium's beginnings.

I begin chapter 6 more or less where the previous chapter left off, with considerations of Hollywood films from the 1930s, but I quickly fly beyond. Its comes as no surprise that many cartoons released during the Great Depression would take advantage of stories of sumptuous eating and the threat of starvation as part of a dedicated platform to re-perform the personal and social anxieties of the time. Some of these films were classically instrumental, making implicit pleas for individual actions. Others, though, presented more darkly inflected stories of potential, or even probable, emaciation or death. I look at *Three Little Pigs* again, but this time from a different angle. Rather than examining its potential for social transformation through infectious laughter, I regard it as an invocation of primal fears. After all, it's a story of children (well, piglets) who are scared by and may be devoured by a wild animal. The animators of this and other films, especially recent ones, exploit the power of cinematic and toon embodiment to entertain, all the while shocking viewers with implicit or actual horrifying images of the body's interior, scenarios of outrageous edibility and corporeal defilement.

On these outer reaches of our argument lie such asteroidal filmmakers as Jan Švankmajer, Bill Plympton, and Blu. Although their hermetic animations are far from classic studio productions, they share a creatively morbid interest in extreme eating, penetrating the body with X-ray-like visions and flirting with cannibalism and self-cannibalism, also known as autophagy.

Why in the world would animators make films that re-perform the biological actions of bodies and flirt with taboos? Paraphrasing Mark Twain, I am gratified to be able to answer promptly. I don't know. The filmmakers themselves might not be able to answer such questions fully. We are free to speculate with the knowledge of cartoon performance that we will have amassed by that point in the book. I will suggest that a possible rationale might be found in the animators' traditional interest in bodies as contingent, malleable places that may be expanded, contracted, metamorphosed, and blown up at will. The cartoonists' technique of stretching and squashing the exterior of toons is also a prerogative to access, distort, and parody their insides. Even the practices of cycling—that is, creating the images and photographing them—and recycling—that is, washing and reusing the cels—echo the great circle of digestion and regeneration. Of special interest is the classic trope of the artwork rebelling against the animator, sparring with the creator before ultimately getting quashed and recycled. The traditional predilection of animation filmmakers to make cartoons that re-perform the making of cartoons reflects a profoundly organic comprehension of animation. Their films symbolize (or show) procreation, birth, growth, and death. They inflict upon us their visions of extreme eating, cannibalism, and autophagy.

Undoubtedly there are more than six great conundra concerning animation. Although it is the nature of these kinds of questions not to be fully answerable, I proceed with the confidence of my convictions and launch my effort to cross the solar system of performance. Watch out! The edges of the Tooniverse are slippery when wet.

PART ONE

Animation Performance

CHAPTER I

Performance *in* and *of* Animation

What is typically lost in discussions about animation is the fact that when you watch an animated film, the performance you're seeing is the one the animator is giving to you. If an animated character makes you laugh or cry, feel fear, anger, empathy, or a million other emotions, it is largely due to the work of these often unsung artists, who invest a lot of themselves in the creation of these indelible moments.

—Brad Bird

There's something about Betty. She is one of the earliest cartoon characters to be a fully fleshed-out being and the only classic toon star gendered as female (neither Minnie nor Daisy were leading ladies). Now, truth be told, Betty Boop can be a little annoying. Her high-pitched voice is a bit too squeaky. She and her playmates, Bimbo and Ko-Ko the Clown, behave like children when some adult judgment (and they seem to be adults) would make their lives easier. They are also unthinking colonialists and probably more than a little racist when they travel to exotic lands. Her sexy design is irritating to anyone with the least concern about reducing female identity to a sexual package: the gams, the short skirt showing a to-be-taken-off garter, the heart-shaped décolletage. As her theme song points out in regard to her unmentionable sexual charms, "Those eyes, that pretty nose,/Although aside from these/She's got so much of those!" Then there's her relation to "Uncle" Max, who plays her cartoonist-creator in the films where they appear together. She is vamping him, to be sure, and he clearly is besotted with her, living out the middle-age male sugar-daddy fantasy.

Betty, though "made of pen and ink," will indeed "win you with a wink." Despite her off-putting aspects, Betty Boop definitely had personality. Her cartoons, especially the piquant "pre-Code" ones made before 1934, appeal irresistibly. It is difficult not to respond to this drawing as a vivacious human female, despite her disproportionate, infantile head, chubby cheeks, and absurdly small lips. When she acts, she's lithe and loquacious. Her coo and her wink project knowledge of the ways of the world. She's been around. Yet she also has little-shopgirl innocence. You feel sorry for her because her clothing tends to drift away from her body and she has to fend off the grotesquely horny men (her bosses, the Old Man of the Mountain, etc.) who want to have at her virginal "boop-oop-a-doop." You want to know her better, befriend her, or more. A little Olympia. This might explain the presence of the hula-dancer Betty doll that for many years has occupied a spot on my bookshelf. In my imagination, she's more than a drawing, more than a collectible. She's one of my favorite actresses.

There's nothing weird about my mixed feelings about Betty. She isn't a fetishistic hallucination, a dream, or a delusion. Although I like the experience of encountering her in her own imaginary world, I also know that I can't walk up to her and tell her how neat or annoying she is. Boop's a fan object, not a real object. Still . . .

Animator, screenwriter, and director Brad Bird (*The Incredibles*, 2004; *Ratatouille*, 2007) knows what he's talking about. The implications of his lapidary observations in the epigraph above seem unassailable:

Animated films are performances.

Animated characters (whether Betty or Mr. Incredible) are actors who may convey strong emotions.

The audience responds emotionally to the acting.

The animated characters and therefore the emotions originate with the animators.

The animators create the performances and therefore are the "real" performers.

These observations are simple enough, but, like all things that we would rather think about as merely entertaining, animated film performances are far from simple. They're hard to make, even now with all our technological savvy, and they are products of the tentacular global media-culture industry. Cartoon stars rival human ones as recognizable celebrities and in the avidity of their fans. As do human stars, cartoon characters create a sense of being live and present in the film experience. The settings, landscapes, and stages they occupy are fictional worlds that we like to believe in, all the while knowing them to be fantastic.

In this chapter, I am interested especially in the ways in which animated beings such as Betty, Mickey, Popeye, and others are so easily rationalized as film performers. Admittedly this is counterintuitive. Although nothing is too outlandish, stunning, or hard to swallow for them, they still seem normal, like other screen actors. They just happen to be animated. Watching them, I enjoy a powerful sensation of recognition and a potent sense of their presence. They are drawings, but are they also movie stars? This dissonance is the most fundamental conundrum. How can inanimate drawings or objects act, or perform at all?

The first thing to point out is that Bird's comments refer to two aspects of performativity. The behaviors, actions, and expressivity of the actors, as well as the dramatic situations, narrative flow, plots, and depictions presented in the films, are part of the performance *in* animation. This is what happens in exhibition, that is, what we see being done on the screen. So Betty performs *in* the animation when she moves, acts, and dances the hula. Thus this performance is primarily audiovisual. It is an enacted event in a self-sufficient diegetic world. *In* animation, no performance occurs until the drawings, clay models, or whatever begin to move.

Bird points to viewers' emotional reactions as they experience watching the film in real time. But he also refers to the animators' earlier work of making the film, which involves the performance *of* animation. These are the continuously unfolding processes that begin before the film is made and continue after its first performance. What happens on the screen doesn't stay on the screen. For this reason, I agree with Bird that the animators' work is a performance, but I qualify it as a *conditional* performance, the condition being that the film will be completed and projected to its viewers. Alexander Sesonske got it right when he said,

> Neither these lively creatures [toons] nor their actions ever existed until they were projected on screen. Their projected world exists only *now*, at the moment of projection—and when we ask if there is any feature in which it differs from reality, the answer is, "Yes, every feature." . . . For there is no past time at which these events either did occur or purport to have occurred. Surely not the time the drawings were made, or the frames photographed; for the world I know and see had not yet sprung into existence then. It exists only now, when I see it; yet I cannot go to where its creatures are, for there is no access to its space from ours except through vision.[1]

The performance *in* the film, contrarily, is both a result and a springboard. It is dependent on, but separate from, the performance *of* animation, which comprises these conditional performances by the animators but also implicates the responsive performances by the viewers as their reflections, conversations, affection for the characters, and other reactions develop over time. In the case of Betty, we might also note the history of the Fleischer studio before the initiation of the character; the poaching of "real" performers' traits (those of Palace headliner Helen Kane, a.k.a. the Boop-Boop-a-Doop Girl, in particular); the history of representing and the reception of female entertainers; the techniques such as rotoscoping applied by the filmmakers; the distribution of economic power via film distribution; and the marketing and merchandizing juggernaut that produced the effigy on my bookshelf. Moreover, the elements of Betty's acting, the way she targets her performances to a vaudeville-like theater audience within the films, her interactions with "live" characters (including Max, her putative creator), and the setting of the animated character within the "real" world via photographic backgrounds are just a few streams that may contribute to Boop's incredibly dense performativity.

Thus the encompassing performance *of* animation refers to the whole contextual process from inception to its open end. Often it is known only by inferences, for instance, through speculation about what the animators were doing and why, and how audiences were responding. Performance isn't a sender-receiver communication model but rather a galaxy of relationships, many of which remain unknowable.

Bird's model places the site of performance solidly with the filmmakers (the original context for the quotation is an introduction to a book on acting for animators). That, however, is not the only option. I will stress the part that film viewers also play, inscrutable though it may be, since they must assent to the films' offers to perform—by paying attention, by "getting into" the show via laughter, singing along, or applauding, and by embracing the characters as show people. And by buying tickets and DVDs or subscribing to streaming services.

Bird notes that expressive communication is the major aim of cartoon performance. These performances are instrumental, meaning that they convey emotions. They are bound to specific times, places, and material conditions of production and circulation and so have an impact on their original audiences. But cartoons are also frameworks that fan backward, outward, and into the future. Historical consumers of these films, then as now, experience them within their own diverse and evolving understanding. The physical print of the film might be the same, but a cartoon viewed in wartime movie houses in 1942 was experienced far differently by those audiences, who likely viewed it as a performance of patriotism, than it is by today's audiences—especially students—who see the characters performing propaganda and racism.

From the standpoint of historical reception, these are entirely different performances of the same physical film.

Because acting is crucial, however, let's begin with Bird's concept of performance, which contains the most profound irony. Indeed, according to traditional theories of stage acting, dramatic irony is the basis of performance, since the actors, while performing, are not themselves but a believed-in character.[2] The Hamlet onstage is also the drama major down the hall. Experiencing a temporary forgetfulness, spectators may imagine, contradictorily but without great confusion or anxiety, that they're watching characters and not actors whose bodies just disappear. It's as though viewers are in two places simultaneously, within the fiction and outside it. Disney's characterizations depended on this classical model, which in fact is allegorized in *Dumbo* (Samuel Armstrong et al./ Disney, 1941). The elephant protagonist is convinced that a magic feather is the source of his flying power. It works *in* the performance because, in fact, he can fly when he holds it with his trunk. We moviegoers, thanks to our superior position inside the narration, know that Dumbo's ability derives from his pure soul and his aerodynamic ears, not from his magic feather. These two beliefs are equally valid, and yet they are incompatible (a stern ethical lesson that the film drives home at the end, opting for the nonmagical explanation). Similarly, we are aware that Betty behaves and enchants like a real actor. We also know that she is different from non-animated screen actors, although she herself seems to be unaware that she's not human.

The Disney animators often described Mickey Mouse and other characters as though they were people. A 1935 memo to the animators asked the question that was preoccupying the studio then, "What Makes and Breaks Personality"? The anonymous supervisor concluded that animal and inanimate objects had to be humanized, not just physically but mentally as well. Sounding like Soviet director Sergei Eisenstein, who had visited the studio, the author observed, "A memorable shock is produced by the mixture of the fantastic and *impossible with the believable.*" The studio was obviously wrestling with the problem of imparting credulity to its characters while retaining their cartoonish charms. The memo discussed Mickey's transformations in *Band Concert* (Wilfred Jackson/Disney, 1935) as an example of how only "a few human touches and minor traits can *vitalize* a general character into a personality." *Band Concert* demonstrated how Mickey's persistent conducting during a violent storm, as well as his oversize uniform with sleeves falling over his hands, "makes him living and unforgettable."[3] The film also demonstrated a foundational concept about animation performance: that it bears the marks of allegory, metaphor, and irony. Mickey's inept appearance is at odds with his masterful and unexpected talent as a conductor.

Perhaps most intriguing in Bird's observations is the issue of personal investment, implying both a psychological and ethical involvement of spectators in performance. What is the process that reifies the animators' feelings in their work so that audiences later will understand and feel those emotions on their own? For that matter, how do audiences invest themselves in the animation experience? What Bird describes initially seems to be a performative situation, but is it really?

One performance studies textbook offers this definition: "*Performative events* require a *performer*, a *text*, an *audience*, and a *context*. At the base of all definitions of the performer is a performer who is a human, whose instrument is his or her own body."[4] According to another definition, "a performance is an activity done by an individual or group in the presence of and for another individual or group."[5] Another scholar reflects that if we ask what makes performing arts performative, "I imagine the answer would somehow suggest that these arts require the physical presence of trained or skilled human beings whose demonstration of their skill is the performance."[6]

Yipe!

Stipulating that the performing agent must be a human body sharing a physical space with an attentive audience seems to nip in the bud the existence of performing cartoon characters made of drawings, objects, clay, or pixels. Yet Betty Boop is presented and accepted as a human performer.[7] She certainly seems to be performing "texts" for us, the audience, in a specific time and place (context). No one would disagree that she has definite skills and uses her body as an instrument. Too bad she's a toon, following the impeccable nomenclature for the animated laborers introduced in *Who Framed Roger Rabbit?* (Robert Zemeckis, 1988).[8]

Are toons human? *No*, because they do not have biological human bodies in our physical world. We can't physically feel them or interact with them. They may not—and usually do not—possess human form. They are works of fiction, like Captain Ahab. *Yes*, if "human" is a metaphor, an attitude, a belief, or a cognitive category whose boundaries are contingent on definitions and functions that we recognize as human. Of course Ahab is human, but the whale is not. Nevertheless, the protagonist effectively demonstrates the ability of people to see animals as embodying human conditions and behaviors. We easily impute humanness to Captain Ahab, but we also humanize Moby Dick the whale when we, sympathizing with Ahab, assign to it the human attributes of evil and bloodthirstiness.

From this we gather that equating "body" with "physically human" is too narrow; germs and splinters are foreign bodies, and there are bodies of stars, of essays, of legislatures. There are cultural beings embodied as human, such as Santa Claus and Mother Goose. Our pets, which for many of us are more like people than like animals, or Donald Duck, who is more human than he is duck, and toons all have personhood without being biologically human.[9] Although they are not lived bodies and may not have human forms, these characters coexist in our lived world thanks to the embodying function of various cognitive, anthropomorphic, and social processes. Then there's the pathetic fallacy.

Perceiving moving lines, colorful shapes, blobs of clay, piles of sand, furry puppets, and even plain forms in motion on-screen as animated bodies—of humans, animals, and any number of other beings—is a complex process. Cognitive psychologists, anthropologists, sociologists, art historians, cultural theorists, theologians, and the tweedy professoriat have advanced explanations. John Ruskin called it the pathetic fallacy. He was referring to the tendency of some writers to project feelings and interpretations onto inanimate objects and nature.[10] An old mill, for example, might also be the bosom of a sheltering home, and indifferent Nature or Hope might be immanent in a cloud formation. But he could just as easily have applied the term to animated matches, caricatured people and animals, or simple geometric shapes that move in certain ways. Especially if they are associated with stories, sound, and speech, animated characters may be arranged by filmmakers in ways that let us understand them as humorous (or sympathetic, disgusting, or threatening) humanoids (I give you *South Park*). Cartoons and their actors are as capable of supporting such projections as other media forms are, plus they carry forward a long tradition from popular graphic arts.[11]

Is Betty Boop a "performer?" Some theorists would have to veto Betty's performativity because of their requirement for human physical coexistence with a human audience. This goes beyond the fact that she happens to be black-and-white and two-dimensional. The living human requirement disqualifies non-animated mediatized expressions such as sound recordings, film, and radio and television broadcasts. Animated performances seem to fail the "live performer copresent with a live audience" test as well. This is not a coincidence, since the test's hidden agenda is to affirm the "intrinsic," "essential," "unique," and "live" properties of theater performance. But wait. Cinema does not fail the test if we simply stipulate that performers need not be human beings, and that the performers may have presence without being physically corporeal. More important than the humanity of the on-screen performer is that of the audience members. Animated films, like all entertainments, are made with the assumption that they will be viewed by some gathering of spectators and auditors. In the classic period of cartoons, this screening was in a movie theater, where a "living" human audience understood that a performance was in progress. The performativity occurs in the unfolding of the event for moviegoers, not in the "blood" of an actor.

The performativity of animation can't be separated from performance in non-animated cinema (the subject of lively ongoing discussions). The cartoon performance occurs in the real time and space of exhibition, but the performance *of* animation is a composite phenomenon of mind and material that happens in a common space to which animators and audiences have read-write access. I call this zone of fascination and fantasy the *Tooniverse*. Paradoxically it inducts and repels us while asserting and disavowing its existence by calling attention to its constructedness. No individual constituent (animation studios, material forces such as the motion picture distribution system, or audiences) is solely in control in this movie-made world, which resembles other ephemeral realms of art and culture, such as the worlds of theater, literature, and visual and sonic experience.[12] The Tooniverse is a collaborative construction because it's coanimated by the filmmakers and viewers.

Although ironic representation underlies all animation performance, there are different creative approaches to it. Bird is a proponent of what I'll call *embodied acting*. The popular wisdom is that it was introduced by Disney, after which it quickly replaced older styles of acting. Historically, this approach was influenced by the teaching of Stanislavsky and developed into "the Method," popular in 1950s stage and films. Embodied acting is still dominant today in feature animation. Actually, Brad Bird is one of its exemplars. Another approach, however, is *figurative acting*, which never disappeared and now thrives, especially in Japanese anime, in animated television series in the tradition of *Beavis and Butt-head, The Simpsons*, and *South Park*, and in much online animated work.

Disney, after he had begun espousing an embodied approach to screen acting, belittled what I'm calling the figurative approach as shallow or primitive. But figuration remained a potent alternative practice for developing personality. Even after Disney's forays into embodied personality animation had been critically acclaimed, "not everybody used it," as Chuck Jones observed. According to the famed Warner Bros. director, "I don't know how many ways there are to animate, but in our pictures, Bugs and Daffy and all our characters were defined by the movement. None of them are funny to look at if you've never seen them in movement. It's like good actors. Woody Allen or Charlie Chaplin aren't funny to look at, but they are funny by the way they move. That's the whole point about character animation. But that's one way of animating."[13] The figurative acting Jones describes emphasized movement that conveys signifying gestures and pantomime typical of broad humor and slapstick rather than emotive personality, character nuance, and emotional expression. The characters, often derived from comic art graphic traditions and from popular theater (vaudeville, burlesque, music hall), accentuated dynamism and immediate legibility. The embodied approach to acting, however, asks actors to look within themselves and use their own intense feelings to engender dramatic bodies for their audience. Actors develop a character, coming to understand its motives, life story, and psychology, in order to materialize it as something that observers will accept naturally, with barely a second thought.

FIGURATIVE PERFORMANCES

Figurative performance is extroverted. Characters behave as recognizable "types," marshaling a small range of instantly identifiable facial and body expressions. They rehearse their distinctive movements and characteristic gags in film after film. They elicit surprise and shock but mostly laughs as they move the gag-laden story along. We appreciate them as we understand clowns or slapstick comedians with distinctive yet familiar styles. James Naremore might agree that figurative acting is ostensive; performers display character by showing off.[14] These performances are formally presentational, meaning that the actors often face the audience and display their talent as though putting on a show. Cartoon characters convey thought and emotion through conventional distortions of their bodies, for example, by stretching and squashing themselves. Sometimes they feign actual presence in the movie theater, acknowledging the audience by gesturing, speaking, or singing to the "camera." The acting is skin deep. So throughout the 1930s, for instance, when characters shout, "Mammy," as they do countless times, everyone would have understood this as a reference to Al Jolson's minstrel singing. Such performances work against audiences ignoring the toons' constructedness and getting "into" the characters, which was a goal of embodied performance. Early cinema's exploitation of "attractions" and its affinity for slapstick relied more on what André Gaudreault calls *monstration* (being shown) than it did on narration (telling).[15] Tom Gunning's observation that early films "reach out and confront" spectators catches the dynamism of figurative performance's antiabsorption aesthetic.[16] Theorists of drama following Brecht, and of film following Eisenstein and Bresson, have promoted acting styles that were extroverted in this sense. Eisenstein was especially smitten by the figurative reflexivity and kinetic performance in these cartoons and rhapsodized about black-and-white "plasmatic" Mickey, who was always moving and morphing like an amoeba: "Here we have a being represented in drawing, a being of a definite form, a being which has attained a definite appearance, and which behaves like the primal protoplasm."[17]

In the early 1930s, the best-known animation actors were Mickey Mouse, Betty Boop, Popeye, and Farmer Al Falfa. Bosko, from Hugh Harman and Rudolf Ising at Schlesinger's, and Oswald, produced by Walter Lantz at Universal, rounded out the field. All became cartoon stars through their figurative performances. This was the tradition out of which Disney grew and against which he reacted. Most performances in these cartoons resembled gags that one might see in a comic strip, in a short film comedy, or live on the vaudeville stage, where such routines were, in Naremore's words, "threatening to disrupt coherence at every level of the performance, deriving laughter not only from the foolish inconsistency of the characters but from a split between actor and role."[18] Emotion and empathy, in this other concept of performativity, were less important than immediacy, surprise, visual gags, and witty repartee. Although it was all about performers' bodies and physicality, neither the animators nor their customers expected to learn anything about their toons' depth of being.

Not that animated performances in the figurative mode were bereft of emotion; they simply expressed it using different devices. Performances arising from even the most rigidly conventionalized forms may still convey feeling by way of vocabularies of masklike signs and gestures. *The Song of the Birds* (Dave Fleischer/Paramount, 1935), for example, uses emblematic displays and music to show the robin parents grieving over their wounded chick. Emotion is conveyed by a chorus of neighbor birds aligning in a semicircle around the parents and singing a

FIGURE 1. *The Song of the Birds* (1935). In figurative performance, grief is evoked by symbolic tableaux and music, not by expression. Original in color.

mournful song. It resembles a stage apotheosis (Figure 1). Embodied approaches, on the contrary, would try to invoke subjectivity, identification, and empathy to achieve the same empathetic response.

A Disney film in which the performance is mostly figurative is *The Moose Hunt* (Burt Gillett/Disney, 1932). Pluto, though he speaks in a human voice three times in the film, acts as a stereotypical dog doing his canine business, for example biting fleas, peeing inappropriately, and so on. In one scene he pretends that he has been shot by Mickey and winks at the film viewer to show us he's playacting. Distraught, Mickey, after miming his grief over Pluto in a very stagy fashion, looks at the audience and pleads to the "camera," asking, "Is there a doctor in the house?"[19] Elsewhere there are movie references, as when Mickey commands Pluto to "speak" and the dog drops to one knee and replies, "Mammy!" When Pluto ends his charade, he puckers his lips and says to Mickey, "Kiss me," evidently re-performing another movie line that audiences would have recognized but that is now lost in the fog of the past (is it Ronald Colman? John Gilbert? Garbo?). The characters draw attention to their roles as performers in a cartoon. In Mickey, viewers might have seen a hybrid of Charles Lindbergh, Douglas Fairbanks, and Buster Keaton.

The eponymous king in *King Neptune* (Burt Gillett/Disney, 1932) is a jolly, rotund protagonist who also was the archetype for Father Noah,

Old King Cole, King Midas, and Santa Claus in later movies. The supporting cast members are generic mermaids and pirates, including a stereotypical gay buccaneer in a lavender shirt. At this time the Disney studio's approach to acting was more or less similar to that of other studios. As Disney became more invested in alternative characterization strategies in the later 1930s, his actors drifted away from this figurative presentation. Accordingly, Eisenstein's ardor for Disney cooled as he perceived the new style to be less "plasmatic."[20]

Betty Boop was a most interesting amalgam of figurative and embodied performance. She isn't a completed character, but she does have a personal background, individuality, and some agency. Heather Hendershot has noted the bivalence and considers Betty simultaneously a "design motif" and a "designed product."[21] As a movie viewer, I have no difficulty in typecasting Betty as a starring coquette such as Colleen Moore, Clara Bow, Marilyn Monroe, Cameron Diaz, or Reese Witherspoon. Betty's acting, however, has few characteristics of the embodied style: her movements, gestures, and expressions are formulaic; she is not introspective; we don't bond with her as a thoughtful being. We are aware perhaps that she is a marketing franchise. Nevertheless, her performances generate a sense of presence. "Perhaps, at least to a certain degree," observes Joanna Bouldin apropos of Betty, "the material and sensuous connection between image and original is maintained in animation, albeit a complicated, morphed and multiplied connection."[22]

The wonderfully strange *Betty Boop's Rise to Fame* (Dave Fleischer/Paramount, 1934) illustrates those contradictory connections. A journalist comes calling on cartoonist Max (played by Max Fleischer) to interview the cartoon star. Max obligingly dips his pen into the inkwell and lightning sketches the animated flapper. Riding on his pen from paper to desktop, she subtly transforms from two to three dimensions (Figure 2). Betty introduces three scenes showing some of her star turns—actually, clips from two-year-old Paramount cartoons. When the show is over, she dives back into the inkpot and the reporter gets a splash in the eye.

Now, on the merely commercial level, one might dismiss the omnibus film as what the trade called a cheater, a clever if somewhat lazy attempt to pad a nine-minute cartoon with just a few minutes of new animation. This, however, would be a mistake. Typical of examples of figurative performativity, *Rise to Fame* replicates in its story line the process by which each subperformance develops from previous ones.

FIGURE 2. *Betty Boop's Rise to Fame* (1934). Max Fleischer draws Betty's shadow on the paper background. The shadow then separates and follows her as she enters Max's three-dimensional world.

Borrowing the Hollywood biopic form, it purports to show how the protagonist grew from her formative appearances on stage and screen into today's movie star. Her celebrity is signaled in several ways in addition to the film title. For instance, the reporter isn't interested in creator Max's life or remarkable talent, only in Betty's star story. She is a professional actor—a vaudevillian—whose job it is to sing, dance, play movie roles, and mold herself into a spectacle. The films she selects to document her "rise" are not titles that might have embodied an autobiographical legend based on her ethnic roots, such as *Minnie the Moocher* (Dave Fleischer/Paramount, 1931), in which we meet her immigrant parents, or *Any Rags* (Dave Fleischer/Paramount, 1932), in which we see her at home in a tenement.[23] Rather, Betty selects cartoons in which she's a chameleon-like showgirl. She shifts through identities in nested performances. We see Max's new performance (his creation of Betty), which enacts a story (the implied biography), and Betty's new performance, which encapsulates her old performances. Her distinctive character evolves as we get to know her through these concatenations of talents appropriate for an entertainer from the louche world of burlesque (and animated cartoons). If she were performing in the embodied style, we would have been invited to understand her as an autonomous being much as we would with other contemporary film stars. We might learn more about how her class or ethnicity influenced her behavior. We want to know why she's so attracted to the hula and African American jazz.

Betty is in part a star by association. She shows us how she is a figuration of "the star" by importing celebrity charisma into her Tooniverse. Her personality is an infectious composite of acquired details, more like a collection of poached traits than a complex expression of inner drives and motives. As a figure, she lacks an interior core of emotion or individual expressivity. She does her "imitations" stage act in clips from *Stopping the Show* (Dave Fleischer/Paramount, 1932) and successively appropriates the mannerisms, accents, and song stylings of Kane, of Ziegfeld Follies chanteuse Fanny Brice, and of the cabaret singer Maurice Chevalier, her fellow employee at Paramount.[24] It is the historicized performances in the old film clips that authenticate her current existence. *Rise to Fame* builds in plenty of pretend memories. The photographs of Brice and Chevalier speak to Betty in voices that sound like the originals, as though these recognizable "real" people remember and accept her as a "real" showbiz protégé.[25] In their conditional performance, the animators clearly assumed that their audiences would get the references.

The animators tried to excite their audiences by constructing worlds that acknowledged mainstream cinema but also retained vestigial connections to powerful traditions in live performance, with which their viewers were probably very familiar. Many pre–World War II audiences were as experienced as consumers of vaudeville and radio broadcasts as they were of the movies. (Max Fleischer, for example, was a popular radio personality.) Animators and audiences alike related to theaters as intermedial zones that combined stage acts, live music, and song with cinema, and where the boundaries defining film acting and between on- and offstage became blurred.

Animators used figuration to create the impression that cartoons were anticinema, or at least outside its rules. They mocked the movies and movie stars and poked reflexive fun at themselves as film workers. They relied on graphic conventions that put their toons' bodies through gyrations to show off their nonhuman anatomical rubbery quality, their imperviousness to physical attacks and dismemberment. Characters like Bosko masqued to an incessant visual rhythm syncopated to the jazzy sounds coming from the orchestra pit and early soundtracks. Eisenstein saw in such acting the potential for resisting Stanislavskian notions of embodiment (which he despised), and for world domination by Hollywood's brand of performativity and probably capitalism itself.

Alongside Disney's mid-1930s quest to endow cartoon characters with personality, individuated character, and what the animators liked to call the "illusion of life," other studios continued introducing characters that they hoped would compete with Mickey but also continued to produce figurative performances. For example, the gags with book and magazine titles and trade names that become animated caricatures, as in

Speaking of the Weather (Frank Tashlin/Schlesinger, 1937), expect the viewer to match the joke to the popular media image. The many caricatures in films such as *The CooCoo Nut Grove* (Friz Freleng/Schlesinger, 1936) referenced celebrities (such as bandleader Ben Bernie) and their parodies (Ben Birdie). Many of these persons have long since faded from the radar screen of popular culture, leaving the joke structures behind without the ironic force of the original star figurations.

Standardized character model sheets not only helped the animators working in the figurative mode to maintain a consistent look in scenes, but they also provided a formulary of poses and facial expressions. The studio apprentice system, whereby experienced animators taught standard practices to the newcomers, perpetuated ways of signifying character through pantomimed gestures that had been current for a century in theater and painting. The need to establish nonverbal techniques for expressing emotions and meaning was linked to the material circumstances of dramatic presentation. Without electric illumination of the stage or amplification of the voice, actors learned that they must communicate with their bodies. Furthermore, the range of these gestures had to be of a limited number and easily understood by audiences. Actors and theatergoers absorbed these somatic signs. As it had been practiced in gaslight melodrama, the actors move from pose to pose, conveying thoughts through conventional broad gestures of face and limbs. Audiences grasp the message by training or by intuition.

The name most often associated with this approach is François Delsarte. Many versions of his so-called system of expression were available to singers, actors, and public speakers.[26] These book illustrations linking poses and gestures to conventional meanings provided a ready reference for stock facial and bodily expressions. Artists of every stripe as well as silent filmmakers such as Griffith were steeped in these poses, which were a staple of theater acting. As the animation studios became industrialized, the model sheets that catalogued the characteristic poses, the roster of facial expressions, and each toon actor's "mouth chart" enabled clarity and consistency of acting. Ken Anderson, in a typical training session for Disney animators, would sketch the various faces associated with specific thoughts. If the filmmaker wanted the character to portray concentration, for instance, he would draw the brows furrowed and the eyelids down.[27]

The plasticity that Eisenstein admired so much in Mickey is actually a characteristic typical of figurative performance, in which the body creates its own expressive space. Betty, for instance, constantly goes in and

FIGURE 3. *Betty Boop's Rise to Fame* (1934), reprising *Betty Boop's Bamboo Isle* (1932). Her hula is so hot it wilts a flower.

out of temporal and dimensional zones as well as fictional spaces. When she and Max show us the paper cutouts representing the cartoons' "sets," the "fourth wall" becomes unstable and the viewer's engagement in the space is very confusing, moving from the photographic 3-D of Max's studio to 2-D background drawings and back to 3-D when the film within the film begins and the "sets" become the character's action space. Although Betty presents herself visually and verbally to the reporter and Max in his studio space, she also makes eye contact with "us" in the movie audience when she speaks to the "camera." When she's acting—that is, presenting herself as a professional performer—the display is frontal, with eye contact. It's very stagelike even when she's not actually on a stage. Like Betty herself, the films are coy (Figure 3). That lei lilting across her bare breasts is a voyeuristic temptation that never gives an unobstructed view of what lies beneath, and an emblem, perhaps, of films in the figurative mode. They promise to reveal more than they do, teasing viewers into thinking that they'll learn something about the protagonist, about cartoon stardom, and about the animation process itself. Instead, the animators lead us—without much resistance, it must be said—down a garden path of playful delusion.

Figuratively performing characters don't try to hide that they're manufactured beings; they are happy to show us the process of their making and how they got to be cartoons, often in a funny, self-mocking way.[28] *Making 'Em Move* (Harry Bailey and John Foster/Van Beuren,

FIGURE 4. *Making 'Em Move* (a.k.a. *In a Cartoon Studio*, 1931).
The toon animators merely sketch toon actors in sequential poses.

1931, rereleased as *In a Cartoon Studio*) is another cartoon that purports to tell all about cartoon performance. A curious woman (or is she
a cat?) wonders how animation is done. A wizened doorkeeper shows
us the "secret." Hilarious scenes of musical mayhem ensue as the
animal-animators madly manufacture the various phases of their
assembly-line product. The conceit is that the cartoonists are sketching
other cartoon beings performing, merely reproducing faithful views of
the living creatures in the other world they inhabit. The joke calls into
question animated embodiment.[29] (It also became the premise of *Who
Framed Roger Rabbit?*, in which the Tooniverse is the workers' literal-
ized ghetto, Toon Town.) One *Making 'Em Move* artist-character draws
a hula-dancing kitten that obligingly strikes a slightly different pose for
each drawing (Figure 4). When the sketchers' sheets are flipped they
synthesize an animated dance. A galloping movie camera films the pages
of drawings as the animator riffles them past the lens. A "live" band with
a phonograph needle hooked up to it scratches the soundtrack onto the
edge of the film stock. The characters are comedians without any depth
or subtlety of personality. The interest is in putting over the gag, showing their funny actions, and engaging in self-parody, not in setting forth
the toons' motivated behaviors.

In *A Cartoonist's Nightmare* (Jack King/Leon Schlesinger Studio,
1935), the animation studio is pictured as a crazy factory populated by
funny folks and caricatures (of the Schlesinger staff, perhaps). One

FIGURE 5. *A Cartoonist's Nightmare* (1935). The villain drags the animator into the space of the cel.

animator stays after hours and falls asleep working on the studio's newest character, Beans. In the cartoon in progress, a monster is chasing Beans, but in a stunning dream sequence the villain drags the animator into the cel (Figure 5). The bad guys of previous Schlesinger cartoons capture and torment him, singing, "The tables are turned and now you're in our clutches."[30] Beans rescues the animator by tossing him a pencil with which he can draw and erase his way out of trouble. This film is mostly a figurative performance. Beans is cute but has few personality features, and he declaims with standard cartoon poses and gestures. The villains—even more cookie-cutter—were actually drawings lifted from earlier films. There is a hint of the developing Disneyesque style detectable, perhaps, in the rounded, relatively individualized depiction of the animator. We are invited to enter the protagonist's inner life and share his subjectivity.[31]

Rather than providing insight into a character's psyche or suggesting a moral, the narratives of films adhering to the figurative approach make their points through repetition and symbolic visuals. Some prior state or activity comes around again as something new. So it makes sense for Betty to recycle her films; for the animators in the factory to turn the performances of toons into cycled toon drawings; for the sleeping animator to cast himself as the lead in the Beans cartoon he's working on. The more repetitions such as these that we experience, the more familiarity we have with the characters' uniqueness and personalities. Not only were such recurrences familiar and satisfying to moviegoers who expected such repetitions, but they also reflexively illustrate the notion of *re-performance,* which is crucial to figuration.

The term *re-performance* was inspired by performance theorist Richard Schechner's claim that all performances are "restored behavior." Discussing social practices and rituals, which include organized public performances such as plays, performance art, and films, he deploys a cinematic analogy: "Restored behavior is living behavior treated as a film director treats a strip of film. These strips of behavior can be rearranged or reconstructed; they are independent of the causal systems (social, psychological, technological) that brought them into existence. They have a life of their own. The original 'truth' or 'source' of the behavior may not be known, or may be lost, ignored, or contradicted—even while that truth or source is being honored and observed."[32]

Bracketing (until the next chapter) the term "living behavior," Schechner's points are salient for figurative performances in cartoons. He calls attention to the arbitrariness of the behaviors. Setting a behavior to music or filming it, for example, would be such a performative marker. Recurring performances in animation are meaningful as repetitions in and of themselves, not necessarily because they advance a narrative. They are "arrangements," that is, materials that have been transformed from ordinariness by repeating a prior behavior/performance with a different purpose, by declaring them to have a special significance, or by calling attention to their arranged status by framing, marking, or heightening them, or through other means. Schechner might describe the animators' use of repetition as a *rehearsal.*[33] "It is the work of rehearsals to prepare the strips of behavior so that when expressed by performers these strips seem spontaneous, authentic, unrehearsed."[34]

The idea of rehearsing in order to create the appearance that a behavior is unrehearsed describes another distinction between performance *in* and *of* animation. One of Schechner's conditions for a performance is that it is not extemporaneous original behavior or improvised gesturing but instead adheres to some agreed-upon map, scenario, or pattern. The conditional performance by the animators preparing the strips of behavior—that is, the stories, drawings, and mise-en-scène—makes the screen performance seem spontaneous, authentic, and unrehearsed, like any other screen performance. Nonetheless, the on-screen actions follow the templates designed by the animators. These "organized sequences of events, scripted actions, known texts, scored movements—exist separate from the performers who 'do' these behaviors."[35] In animation performances, everything that happens between "scored movements" and on-screen behavior is controlled and motivated; everything in a projected cartoon is a performance, Schechnerian restored behavior.[36] The performativity doesn't reside innately in making the drawings, in the drawings themselves, or in the reception, but it emerges during the screening as a cultural and aesthetic transaction, as well as what Bird alluded to as personal investment.

Re-performance in animation narratives was engineered into the technical basis of the medium. The process illustrated effectively in *Making 'Em Move* is a series of mechanical transpositions from hatching the idea, to slavishly copying the movements of the hula dancer, to photographing each drawing, to showing the finished cartoon to a rapt audience. It ends with the film fans' "reception," which consists of tearing down the movie screen. As it shows the production of drawings on the assembly line, the Van Beuren film not only capitalizes on the common animation technique of cycling, but it also demonstrates how it is done. Cycling is figurative because it re-performs the work of repeating, that is, it rephotographs the sequence of drawings. Its subject is itself.

The Fleischers' use of the rotoscope, their patented technology for tracing "live" cinema motion onto cels to produce animation drawings, is another example of what Schechner might call the "work of restoration." One kind of performance is transformed into another, as illustrated in *Rise to Fame*. Betty re-performs—"restores"—the hula scene that she first did in *Betty Boop's Bamboo Isle* (Dave Fleischer/Paramount, 1932) by reanimating it. The earlier film began with footage of the dancer Miri in a filmed hula performed by the Royal Samoans troupe.[37] In the rotoscoped segment, Betty reprises the dancer's movements. Backtracking, both the Betty-Miri films were mediatized reiterations of Miri's stage act, which re-performed an ethnic ritual with religious significance for native Hawaiians as a popular spectacle (that is, it expropriated it).[38]

Meanwhile, Betty "browns up" her body to resemble Miri's, her darkened skin thus transforming her dance into a race masquerade. It's the kind of body performance that David Graver calls the *group representative*, which is clearly figurative. These are corporeal identities that result from factors outside the actor, for instance, being "linked to race, class, or gender and constructed within the socio-historical discourse of culture."[39] The many performances of blackface and minstrelsy in classic animation are instances where the actor-toon is a race hieroglyph, either as a black or a nonblack masquerading as some other. In *Blue Rhythm* (Burt Gillett/Disney, 1931), Mickey and Minnie are shown to be either black or in blackface, and they are cast as group representatives of "Mammy singers" and southern black women blues singers (see Figure 15). We've already noted Betty's typage as a representative of various female bodies. Here, according to Graver, "the socio-historical body replaces character, and these theatrical representations are instrumental in defining the socio-historical bodies they display."[40] In Bouldin's words, "we experience the authentic flesh of Betty's animated body," but this body is a figure that is compounded from layers of rotoscopically restored behaviors.[41]

In a broader sense, restored behavior applies to the whole underlying concept of figurative performance. Each recursion transforms the underlying actions, events, and situations into something special, behaviors to note, spectacles to watch, in short, into things like movies and cartoons. Crucial to animation re-performance is the way classic cartoons referenced non-animated films but remained flagrantly off-center. Spaces in cartoons were seldom abstract patterns; usually they were landscapes or rooms. (In object animation, the spaces could be 3-D sets or the photographed physical environment.)[42] Although gravity was routinely defied in the actions performed, up was up and down generally remained down. Most importantly, the characters behaved as movie actors. Despite the glorification of the Tooniverse as an alternative world to Hollywood—and no one could deny that it was—the cartoonists nevertheless kept one eye on the forms of narrative and visual exposition and on the performative styles that were being practiced in the mainstream. This explains why even the looniest stories, the silliest cartoon images, and the most outré gags are still comprehensible as short movies.[43]

We may also explain the generic nature of classic studio animation as a function of re-performance. Schechner writes that restored behaviors, analogous to the infinite rehashing of animation stories, sources, and actions that recur in film after film, "can be worked on, stored and recalled, played with, made into something else, transmitted, and transformed. . . . Performance in the restored behavior sense means never for the first time, always for the second to *n*th time: twice-behaved behavior."[44] The nested performances within the performances in our samples attest that these are not random scenes but recursive events re-created for a purpose. Modestly, they were created to entertain and amuse us, but there was more. *Rise to Fame*, for example, might be seen as an observation about how cartoons capitalize on existing templates for their inspiration, genre formation, and the medium's rampant disregard for originality. The film also invites thoughts on how celebrity is established through the complicity of journalists, fan magazines, and voyeuristic moviegoers.

Because re-performance is by definition a second-order restatement of something else (the original performance), it's always figurative, with the components of its construction more or less discernible. Therefore, the restored behaviors in the films implicate the conditional performances of the animators at work and the audiences watching. This figural performativity invites readings of the films that point out the underpinnings of the industrial system constituting their material being. The stories similarly re-perform social structures and attitudes, such as patriarchy, family relationships, and sexual identities. As an illustration, the characters in these films are typecast according to their gender. Betty's animators use caricatural exaggeration of female sexuality to define her.[45] *Making 'Em Move* represents the female protagonist as a stereotypical curious feline. The animators in that film are all male, while the model for their drawings is a female to be looked at. The only female in *A Cartoonist's Nightmare* is Beans's mother, who enables his jailbreak by melodramatically delivering a cake with a file in it. Classic animation in the figurative mode generally treated women as, well, figures. Clearly Disney tried to break the mold with Snow White (whose design Betty Boop's designer Grim Natwick contributed to, ironically) and more individuated adolescent feature-film protagonists that appeared later. Eventually, perhaps because of oversaturation and marketing, these attempts became subsumed into the quintessential stereotype of femininity: "Disney princesses."

EMBODIED PERFORMANCES

Embodied acting is introverted. It is the philosophy and practice of creating imaginatively realized beings with individuality, depth, and internal complexity. The Disney studio pursued it as part of Walt's vision, no doubt, but it was also a means of differentiating their productions from those of others. Don Graham, the founder of Disney's in-studio art school for animators, provided a thumbnail history in which he claimed that cartoon acting developed only after the new technology of sound was mastered (by Disney, of course). He counted music as crucial, especially since the Disney sound films had little or no speech for the first two years. The goal was simply to create laughs in the audience by "the excitement of the action and sound." Graham observed that Minnie in *The Barn Dance* (Walt Disney, 1929) was the first character to develop a personality: "Precocious, like many little girls, Minnie had developed a little ahead of Mickey. In it she had acted like a little flirt." Mickey emerged in *The Plowboy* (Ub Iwerks/Disney, 1929), the first film in which he "ceased to be a mouse and became a person."[46]

The association with personality and sound is important, as is Graham's passing comment that cartoons didn't talk much. In fact, compared to other short films of the 1930s, although there was abundant singing and musical accompaniment in animation, there was surprisingly little dialogue. It was surprising because the voice is one of the most obvious ways to embody a character on-screen. Instead, animators turned their attention to bodily motion and gestures as ways to express personality. What Graham doesn't mention is that the new approach at Disney was motivated by a desire not only to innovate a new form, but also to compete with their personality-packed rival, Betty Boop. She was not necessarily a fully embodied character, but from 1931 to 1934 she could be found at the nearest Paramount theater displaying a believable, beguiling personality.

The story has been told and retold of characterization experiments with embodied acting in the Silly Symphonies, beginning with the individualized cast of *The Three Little Pigs* (Burt Gillett/Disney, 1933).[47] Jones put it succinctly: "It started with the three little pigs. Most people don't realize that *Three Little Pigs* in 1933 was the first picture with three characters that looked alike and were differentiated by the way they moved and the way they spoke. From that point on, acting came to animation."[48] Disney's animators in the 1930s set their sights on turning their cartoon characters into embodied actors. "It was the uppermost thing, and it all came about because Walt wanted to make the cartoon characters believable to the audience," said animator Wilfred Jackson a bit disingenuously. "Right from the start, he didn't want them to be just something moving around on the screen and doing funny things. He wanted the audience to care what happened to the characters, and to believe them as real beings, not just as a bunch of funny drawings."[49] Around 1934, the staff gradually began implementing the new approach. Former supervising animators Frank Thomas and Ollie Johnston recalled, "Several people at the studio enrolled in acting classes, seeking a greater understand of the disciplines of the theater."[50] Certainly much of this theatrical training would have been traditional and Delsartian. There is abundant evidence that Stanislavsky was also in the air at Disney.

This performance practice at the Disney studio had a specific theoretical underpinning in the lectures and writing of Konstantin Stanislavsky

(1863–1938).[51] Animators seized upon this approach at the same time it was catching on in Hollywood as their inspiration and guide to embodied animation.[52] Intended as a way to educate stage actors, the Stanislavsky method—later called "the Method"—emphasizes studying and "living" the role, incarnating the character by living it oneself. "An actor is under the obligation to live his part inwardly, and then to give to his experience an external embodiment," Stanislavsky wrote.[53] Conjured through techniques variously called *embodying, passage, ownership, engagement,* or *emergence,* this character was an epiphenomenon, a transcendental, phantasmagorical being.[54] From the audience member's perspective, attention shifts from the actor as a person on the stage or screen to the character "brought to life," a state implied by catchy expressions such as "Meryl Streep *is* Margaret Thatcher." This way of acting aimed to increase the degree of performance irony by decreasing the distance between the actors' stage presence and their embodied characters.

Animator Vlad "Bill" Tytla, for one, studied the book by Richard Boleslavsky, *Acting: The First Six Lessons,* published in 1933. Boleslavsky had trained under Stanislavsky at the Moscow Art Academy and taught "the system" at the school he founded in New York in 1923. His most famous graduates were Lee Strasberg and Stella Adler.[55] Meanwhile, Boleslavsky was directing pictures in Hollywood in the 1930s.[56] In November 1936, Walt Disney initiated weekly evening classes to begin the character studies for the *Snow White* feature. Describing these story sessions, Barrier writes, "The work . . . resembled a Stanislavski-style rehearsal, as Disney and his writers tried to get the action right, leaving the exact words till last. (In these transcripts, especially, story work on *Snow White* resembles the staging of a play more than the writing of one.)" Barrier commented on Tytla's animation of Grumpy: "This acting was, however, *cartoon acting,* and, as Tytla demonstrated, such acting could go well beyond what Boleslavsky and Stanislavski had in mind, and not just in the circumstances of its production. A method actor was supposed to make visible to his audience through his face and body the movement of his character's thoughts and emotions; the actor could not reveal his character through dialogue alone." Animator Marc Davis recollected of those days, "We would all study the acting of Laughton [probably a reference to Charles Laughton in *Les Misérables,* directed by Boleslavsky in 1935]. We all read Stanislavsky."[57] In Thomas and Johnston's memoir, the many references to animation acting frequently invoke Stanislavskian notions of embodiment without mentioning him by name. This approach was always contrasted to the older figurative style. For instance, they wrote:

> It seemed such a short time ago that [the artists] were animating spindly legged, weightless Mickeys and Minnies with their superficial little relationships. Occasionally there had been a glimmer of things to come in pictures like *Elmer the Elephant* and *Country Cousin,* where there had been a special character who had strong feelings about what was happening, but for the most part this was all new, and it seemed as though it had blossomed overnight. Now we sat entranced as Walt talked about these seven little men who were becoming as much flesh and blood as the person sitting next to us; and while the problems they faced in their make-believe world were extraordinary, we could grasp them and could feel them ourselves.[58]

What evidence within the films is there that the staff was experimenting with these typologies of performance, channeling their own thoughts, feelings, and emotions to round out their characters rather than applying some recurring graphic template (à la early Mickey)? From surviving transcripts of studio discussions, for example, we know that the Donald Duck character was planned with distinctive individual features. The memo on personality discerned that, in *Orphan's Benefit* (Burt Gillett/Disney, 1934) and *The Band Concert,* Donald presented "a memorable mixture of *physical* (walk, posture, fighting attitude, voice) and *mental* (conceit, arrogance, persistence, retaliation), of *general* and individual[,] of human and animal traits. All this rounded out combination makes for a rise of Duck's personality entrenched in the mind of millions." The integration of motion, gesture, and dialogue was not gratuitous but appeared on the screen to have been inner-directed. "All stages of Duck's conflict with orphans and with Mickey's band are well motivated; all his physical actions and pantomime reveal consistently Duck's character with new shades and individual touches in every picture."[59] These notes were addressed to a new breed of artisan, the "character animator," whose job it was not only to draw but also to articulate the acting basis for the performances within the increasingly industrialized process. One of them described the personality that he saw in the duck in 1936:

> There is nothing "half way" about Donald. He is either very angry or very happy and seldom stays in a neutral mood for long. He is a show-off, boastful and cocky[,] and is happy only when he is up to some mischief or is having his own way. If the least thing goes wrong or crosses him he flies into a rage out of all proportion to the situation. However, his bark is much worse than his bite. He seldom really advances toward a fight, but prefers to jump

around in one place and hurl violent threats. Once in a while, however, things overtake him, then he usually gets the worst of it. But no matter how beaten and torn he may be he retains his fighting spirit to the end.[60]

These beings are not diametrically opposed to the extroverted ones made using the figurative approach, whose exteriors correspond to a recognizable type or attribute. Nor are they superior to them, or an advanced evolution. The animators were just aiming for something different.

Disney personnel, with the sanction of the upper-level management, no doubt, tried to distance themselves from the earlier style of their own work and that of their competitors. Director Dave Hand advised young animators, "We have been pretty stock-minded in the past. We always made a walk in the same way. That is one thing Don [Graham's] action analysis classes are doing—at least did for me. A few years ago there were only two walks—a regular walk and a Felix walk. Then we began to think and now we find a walk for every different kind of person."[61] This, in fact, was one of Graham's refrains: that the animator must understand the character before drawing it. He insisted that movement was communicated not only in drawings and space but also through the artist's understanding of its feelings, motives, and emotions, which elicited empathy. He observed that when they were successful, animators could convey the paradoxical impression of realism combined with fantasy: "The characters still were cartoon drawings, with proportions far removed from real growth forms, yet their actions had a feeling of being *real*," he wrote, referring to *The Flying Mouse* (David Hand/Disney, 1934).

> This sense of reality in the action was pure illusion—but satisfying. It opened up a world of fantasy in which anything could happen—and still be real. Mice could fly; bats could sing songs. But such actions are *real* only within a framework of fantasy. A brilliant pantomimist through his human actions may convincingly suggest a bird flying or a fish swimming. Not one of his own body shapes resembles the bird or the fish; yet his actions are convincing and seem real. And so with all the cartoon characters. Their actions and their physical proportions are truly not real in a world sense, but they may be so animated as to *seem* real.[62]

Graham suggests here that cartoon characters may be what we would now call *avatars*, abstractions of external beings within the film. They may perform the animators or viewers as their proxies. Avatars don't necessarily resemble their original beings; in fact, they usually don't. Dumbo's companion, Timothy the mouse, for example, is our avatar because he's the source of our knowledge that Dumbo doesn't need the feather to fly. The presence of such stand-in characters on-screen facilitates moviegoers' participation in the performance, thus enabling it "to *seem* real."

Without knowing it, Graham was echoing the observations of French sociologist Marcel Mauss, who in a 1935 speech to a professional society identified the characteristic ways that humans moved as "techniques of the body." He was an early advocate of the view that bodies and their defining gestures are culturally constructed. Differences in walking and swimming are cultural, he maintained, and the activities vary among societies. They are based on biomechanical abilities, to be sure, but they are also learned behaviors that are passed around. One way he became aware of this was when, while hospitalized in New York, he noticed the nurses and girls walking in a distinctive way. He divined its origin: "At last I realized that it was at the cinema" that they had learned this walk. After repatriation, he saw the same phenomenon in France and realized that this "technique" had spread through cultural contact and "prestigious instruction," that is, learning from a trusted authority. "Returning to France, I noticed how common this gait was, especially in Paris; the girls were French and they too were walking in this way. In fact, American walking fashions had begun to arrive over here, thanks to the cinema."[63] Graham too based his teaching on observations of movements that could be extrapolated through imitation and transposed to forms other than the sources. We might say that Graham redefined observed bodies to produce cultural meanings from them. Hence the famous classes in which the animators sketched live animals, and the less famous sessions where the animators analyzed live-action films of human actors. He asked his artists to create what Mauss called a "social idiosyncrasy," deep-seated corporeal habits of movement, gesture, and behavior that come to typify a whole society, or, in the case of cartoons, whole species. As Mauss put it, "They are not simply a product of some purely individual, almost completely psychical arrangements and mechanisms."[64] For Graham's concept to work it had to be based on a similar belief that movements were transmutable, not simply from one society to another, but from one class of being (animal, human, imaginary) into human motion. His animators were trying to capture and re-perform these universally recognized somatic "techniques," effectively borrowing them from their owners. The moviegoers ultimately had to recognize that a character, let's say the Ugly Duckling, was believable and empathetic in part because when the drawings moved, the character swam like a duck.

Embodied performers have discernible interior as well as extrinsic traits—idiosyncrasies, Mauss might say. This *completed character,* as Graver described it, "is the body that Western audiences are trained to look for first and gaze at most intently. Its ready display of both inside and outside makes it a pleasing object of contemplation. This body can appear in paintings, novels, and film as readily as on the stage."[65] By the time of *The Flying Mouse,* Disney's embodied performance approach is apparent. The mouse protagonist's design, unlike Mickey's, is three-dimensional and less comic-strippy. (Mickey's iconic 2-D ears do not shift perspective, even when his head rotates.) The little mouse longs to fly. A fairy (apparently a cynical one) grants his wish—except that she gives him bat wings. The Faustian bargain results in banishment from the communities of bats and birds alike, as well as from his mouse family. The studio's self-analysis made it clear that personality drove the narrative: "*Flying Mouse* builds the initial situation and its consequences from the dominant characteristic [of the mouse] badly and blindly desiring to fly like a bird. The disastrous effect of the acquired wings—a complete isolation of the mouse and horrible companionship with the bats—is a *logical* inevitable result of the essential characteristics of the mouse."[66]

The Tooniverse here has been made habitable by the mouse, his friends, and his enemies. It's implied that a fictional world extends beyond the frame. The actors cast convincing shadows that situate them within their physical environment. The performers in *The Flying Mouse* speak natural-sounding dialogue and make eye contact with each other but never look at the film audience or acknowledge that there is one. We are privy to the motives, thoughts, and emotions of the protagonist through his humanoid facial expressions, full-body gestural acting, and the ability to eavesdrop on his thoughts. The actions are also believable because the plot motivates them. The main business is couched within a fairy's spell, setting it off as magic and subjective, giving us a glimpse into the youthful imagination of the mouse that wants to fly. When he tries out his leaf wings, crashes into a puddle, and his siblings laugh at him, we see pain, humiliation, inspiration, and resolve cross his face, with appropriate body language and music, all within the span of a couple of seconds (Figure 6). Graham taught that the timing and clarity of these communicative moments *in* the animation were part of the conceptualization *of* the work: "Gestures don't happen in animation; they are drawn purposefully." Terms implying three-dimensionality, like scene and staging, enter the studio's conversations. He acknowledged that the viewers' immediate acceptance of the scene was essential to embodi-

FIGURE 6. *The Flying Mouse* (1934). The mouse's movements and fleeting expressions convey its embodied emotions. Original in color.

ment. "First," Graham continued, "each [gesture] must be clearly staged or presented to the audience. If a gesture, no matter how subtle, is not grasped by the audience the whole scene and conceivably the whole picture may be lost."[67] A fully emotive, interiorized, transcendent body-technique of acting has emerged.

Walt Disney's comments in the sweatbox sessions with his animators reveal that he was deeply invested in achieving embodiment by hybridizing animal and human behaviors to achieve what Graver called a completed character—but Disney did not want it to be too complete. Watching a rough cut of the film that would be released as *Alpine Climbers* (1936), Disney told the director, Hand, "Where the eagle takes off, they get him too human, and he doesn't look funny. He should have done an eagle action that paralleled a human action instead of a human action. I think the public is used to and expects the cartoon to up and walk, but when you get the animal thing that gives you a parallel to something in the human, yet it has the animal to it, then it's funny." Disney here seems to anticipate what would be theorized decades later as the "uncanny valley."[68] This refers to the unpleasant eeriness felt when one is confronted with a replica that mimics its human analog too closely for comfort. As Disney put it intuitively, regarding Clara Cluck's operatic performance in *Mickey's Grand Opera* (Wilfred Jackson/Disney, 1936), the animal's body had to maintain sufficient distance from that of a human: "The funniest part of the old hen when she sings in the Opera picture is when she sounds like a hen. When she becomes too human she's not funny."[69] Eventually Disney conflated the embodied acting approach with narrative. "I look for a story with heart," he told Bob Thomas. "It should be a simple story with characters the audience really can care about. They've got to have a rooting interest. . . . Everything should be related to human experience in storytelling."[70]

Modern instruction for cartoonists routinely teaches them this style of character animation as acting. Animators perform movement to perform emotion. Ed Hooks tells students, "Humans empathize with emotion. The audience is why actors act and why you are animating in the first place. The goal of the animator is to expose emotion through the illusion of movement on screen. What the character is doing on a moment-to-moment basis is vitally important, the points of empathy with the audience involve emotion, how the character *feels* about what he is doing. Empathy is as essential to dynamic acting as oxygen is to water."[71] According to Bird, "If the public could watch the faces of the best animators when caught up in the act of drawing an emotional scene, they would see artists as fully invested *in the moment* as the best live actors. The difference is that an animator *stays* in that moment, often working for weeks to express an emotion his or her character takes only seconds to convey on-screen."[72]

It is evident from watching the Disney short films from the decade that the studio's vaunted push toward naturalism on all levels included efforts on the part of the animators to incarnate their nascent characters, find the right movements and expressions, and then get that interiority to emerge in their drawings. The thought process, reflected Graham, is the most important motivating force. Characters' actions must be generated by primary thoughts and feelings.[73] The catchall phrase for this aim in the studio was "personality," a performance that combined emotion and intellect:

> *Emotionally*—by arousing human appeal, *sympathy* or antagonism, by playing on spectator's feeling of justice or injustice, anxiety, satisfaction, etc.
>
> *Intellectually*—by bolstering the character, with *idea-theme*, revealed in the actions, feelings and attitudes of the character. Thus character acquires a deeper all human meaning for all nations and classes.[74]

The characters, as they give their performances as on-screen moving beings, act out the emotions and movements of the animators. As "Streep *is* Thatcher," the animators *are* the characters. They try to "live" them much as human actors, through study, rehearsal, and introspection, get into their roles. They clothe their characters in a vesture of psychology, personality, appearance, and body language. But, as the studio guidelines suggest, these character traits are not the animator's unique personality but a universalizing impulse that, rather immodestly, allows the animator's self-embodiment to inject into the films deeper meanings for humanity.

We are familiar with the anecdotes and funny photos of animators acting out parts, hamming it up for each other and studying themselves in mirrors to transmute their own mannerisms and expressions into their toons. According to Graham, Walt acted out every part in *Snow White* for his animators.[75] Disney also hired professional actors to perform the parts before film cameras as inspiration. Applying Naremore's terms, this facilitated the representational, mimetic, or naturalistic style of acting, which corresponds to what we're calling embodied.[76] Clearly, the animators imbibed deeply this philosophy of acting. Hand, supervising director of *Snow White,* recalled when asked by Michael Barrier about relying on formulas:

> Well, when you say "formulas," I know you don't mean a circle for a head or a pear-shaped body, you mean a formulized character, the characteristics in the character. We used to sit as a group, in the large sound stage we had at that time, and people would get up and act out their impression of a particular character. The most interesting thing to me in the whole studio is something that's quite hidden, to make a character come alive, be born. Come to life dimensionally, not the way some of it's done.

The studio concept of embodied animation here is building on the early convention of the animator's self-figuration in the film (the "hand of the artist" motif). But instead of overtly placing the filmmaker's avatar in the film as a participant, the animators are still present, though they are participating as embodied characters within the narrative. In the industrialized enterprise, of course, the unique animator has given way to the collective consciousness of the team, where each member contributed to defining a unified character. Hand continues, "Every key animator had to know that character, and it was a great deal of effort to get every animator to know the character completely. I don't know if you appreciate the amount of creative effort that comes out of an animator to make the character live a certain way. Not Mickey Mouse, Donald Duck, and Pluto; they had few subtle shades. These *Snow White* characters that actually have these little idiosyncrasies, little twists and turns and little walks. Every animator had to know how to do it."[77]

Disney's *Clock Cleaners* (Ben Sharpsteen/Disney, 1937) is a signal achievement of animated embodiment, not only because of its hilarious panache, but also because of its autocritique of that mode of production. The narrative is as simple as can be: three cleaners are maintaining a city clock, which responds to them as an antagonist. The film is structured with episodes showcasing each of the three protagonists, framed by introductory and concluding scenes. Each character begins his episode as a fully embodied, idiosyncratic being with a distinctive, recognizable personality and an inhabited body. Our impression is that they are at home performing the routine of their daily lives. Mickey Mouse is the efficient, assured foreman of the group. Donald Duck is an enthusiastic worker whose short temper quickly gets in the way of the job. Goofy is a nonchalant naïf going about obliviously. The quotidian story adds the dramatic ingredients of a recalcitrant nesting stork and the anthropomorphic clock with its own voice and personality. It's a unique performance of an incident that will only happen once in the lives of these characters, but their responses are consistent with their overarching behavioral styles.

Mickey first encounters the stork asleep on its nest. Though the mouse's simple face limits his expressivity, his supple body language makes up for it. He tries to evict the stork, but the big bird's weight is a match for Mickey's strength, and his whole body strains against the resistance. The stork turns the tables and ejects Mickey, who, reverting to his former figurative style, directs a silent plea toward the "camera" to give the audience a standard gesture of despair.

Donald's chore is to clean the clock's giant mainspring. It takes on a life of its own and pokes him with a steel prod. Donald objects with enraged repartee, and the spring, voiced by a mouth harp, responds metallically. Donald's pugilistic moves and salty language are manifestations of his hot-blooded temper. Finally, the spring flings him into a gear that transmits the rhythmic beat of the mechanism into his body, which uncontrollably ticks with every tock.

Goofy's job of dusting the bell is interrupted by the sculptural figures that signal the hour, Father Time and the Statue of Liberty. Suspicion dawns gradually on his limited mind, as if illustrating Graham's advice to the animators to picture thought. After a blow to the head by Lady Liberty's torch, he pumps himself back upright by pressing his hands down on the air. He then launches on a careening somnambulistic tour of the vertiginous exterior of the tower.

In addition to being hilarious, *Clock Cleaners* suggests that the studio knew what it had achieved in embodied performativity. The film acknowledges that quest by parodying the figurative approach. This is clearest in Goofy's encounter with the automatons, since those personifications have no personhood or interiority beyond what they allegorize. They are "animated," but in a very limited way, since they are only capable of tracking and raising or lowering their hammers. Ironically, Goofy, initially embodied, loses his self-animation as he skids across the beams in his coma. He becomes an automaton. Mickey and Donald both lose their agency as the stork and the mainspring, respectively, take control of their destinies.

The clockwork finally ingests all three cartoon heroes. They end up in the cogs of the same gear that had captured Donald and they share the same fate. The relentless rhythm of the mechanism takes over their bodies and, even after they're free from the spring's grasp, they continue into the finale, twitching to the clock's beat.

The story, then, shows neoteny, a reverse evolution from fully embodied to *dis*embodied characterizations. Mickey, Donald, and Goofy travel back to the days of figurative performance in cartoons. The system itself has become a figure for the clockwork industrialization of the animation process that asserts its own implacable regime under the ironically opposed signs of Time and Liberty.

Clock Cleaners also illustrates how interacting with their environment defines embodied characters, whose Tooniverse provides an imaginative setting for their behavior and reactions. Graver, who emphasizes the importance of embodiment as an aspect of theater's fictional world-making, describes the relationship between actors' interiority and their fit into an accommodating environment: "In looking for the worlds in which the actor establishes a corporeal existence we are looking for more than just worlds in which the actor has meaning. We are, rather, looking for worlds in which he or she has a body. More than just an object or image, a body has interiority, exteriority and autonomy. A body's interior hides its unseen, volitional mechanisms, the motivating forces that drive its observable behavior."[78]

The concept of embodiment as existence within a coherent fictional world is crucial to Disneyesque animation. The "action" is derived not only from moving the body in space, a main concern of figurative acting, but also from protecting the integrity of its somatic boundaries. This is the body that our cartoon heroes lose when the story line denies them their mastery inside the space of the clock. Sometimes this means preserving the body's outline (preventing it from stretching or being squashed into oblivion, for instance). At other times it's a question of keeping the body distinct from other animated forms in the scene, or of defining it as separate from or integrated within its graphic background.

Clock Cleaners also demonstrates how figurative and embodied performances do not inhabit opposite poles. Animators don't need to choose between their characters slipping on a banana peel or delivering a soliloquy: they can do both, to a degree. These films don't abjure the slapstick of figuration; rather, they incorporate it as an extension of character.

ANIMATION'S MANY BODIES

The animators and Graham were pursuing a Stanislavskian ideal of embodiment, trying to inject human thought, motion, and emotion into their formerly figurative hieroglyphs, but the result was more complicated than they intended. They constructed lifelike movements and gave their characters the illusion of sentience, free will, and human frailty without visible strings to the animators or their techniques. Inadvertently, though, they introduced ambiguity and increased the likelihood of unintentional meanings. The more the animators succeeded in vitalism, the less control they had over how the characters would be understood and used by the films' audiences. Indeed, we may read characterization against the grain. The situation approaches contemporary performance art inasmuch as character may be seen a vehicle for presenting the actor's body, as well as the other way around.[79] So viewers have the opportunity to reverse engineer cartoon characters to ascribe their own personalities, ideas, and meanings to them. This casts Bird's statement at the beginning of this chapter in a new light. We can see how his defense of animators as actors may be a reaction against the public's tendency to think that the cartoon characters' emotions are spontaneous, natural, and—the worst outcome from his point of view—completely autonomous from the animators' work. In fact, these performances are not antagonistic; they're mutually consensual.

The animators embody not only their characters but also their future viewers, since the goal of their conditional performance—the entire artistic and commercial point—is to entertain their customers. I, like most viewers, know that the performance I'm watching is a human-made creation, so, if I want, I may reflect on the filmmakers, on their lives as workers, as people, and as lived bodies. Viewers' and animators' embodiments are thus reciprocal, which is not to suggest that their intentions and interpretations are the same. This is why we recognize the presence behind the screen of such distinctive personalities as Otto Messmer, the Fleischers, Ub Iwerks, Chuck Jones, Frank Tashlin, Tex Avery, and others in the pantheon of cartoon auteurs without having met them. We grasp why it pleases fans to believe that "Uncle Walt" animated Mickey Mouse. We indulge in corporeal impressions of these animators' presence because they are being re-performed by their avatars.

In fact, embodiment isn't located in only one place or the other. It pertains to the viewers' presence in the fiction as much as to the animators or to the characters. Don't we routinely experience works of fiction, music, or games by being both immersed within them and yet disengaged? The performance participants' experience is what Schechner (in another context) calls the "me . . . not me" paradox.[80] On one hand, I have the strong sensation of *for-me-ness,* that the film was made with me in mind. I may enter "into" it, that is, into the Tooniverse. I become engaged in the story, laugh at the gags, and feel acrophobia on the dizzying heights of the cleaned clock. Part of "me" is up on the screen participating in the performance, at least as an active witness. It's the effect demonstrated in *A Cartoonist's Nightmare* when the animator hero, who is both my and the animator's avatar in the film, is grabbed by a cartoon villain and dragged into the film within the film. We see similar scenarios in *Sherlock Jr.* (Buster Keaton/Metro, 1924), *The Purple Rose of Cairo* (Woody Allen, 1985), and in the music video *Take On Me* (Steve Barron, animation by Michael Patterson and Candace Reckinger, 1987)—to cite only three possible examples that show how cinematic space ingests fictional spectators.[81] That this is possible depends on the viewers, with the aid of these proxies, experiencing the screen as a porous membrane through which they may psychically travel.[82]

On the other hand, I also know that it's really "not me" up there; I'm just enjoying a movie in a theater (in the 1930s), watching an activity staged as a performance, presented to me by someone trying to entertain me. I am in the characters' minds and bodies as Mickey, Goofy, and Donald perform for me on the clock tower, but simultaneously I know that the characters are not me. In fact, there is always the ironic possibility of my projecting myself into any story or world this way, identifying with characters in any medium.

Gunning wrote of the roots of this aspect of the cinematic experience in the first days of the medium, noting the sensation of "I know very well . . . but all the same" recorded by cinema's first observers. He concludes that since "the film image combined realistic effects with a conscious awareness of artifice," the medium played on viewers' desire for astonishment, curiosity, and wonder at the marvelous apparatus. Like the effect of a trompe l'oeil painting, in early cinema, "the realism of the image is at the service of a dramatically unfolding spectator experience, vacillating between belief and incredulity."[83] Gunning's observations are significant for our discussion of embodiment because the spaces he describes are not simply formal constructions but are experiential and co-generated by the spectator. He writes, "The first spectators' experience reveals not a childlike belief, but an undisguised awareness (and delight in) film's illusionistic capabilities."[84] Psychologically, the screen was permeable, which is a fundamental aspect of the diegetic worlds of both early cinema and the Tooniverse. As in all the arts of illusion in the nineteenth century, participants are drawn in, "absorbed," in Gunning's term (following Michael Fried), and simultaneously pushed back by their knowledge of the artifice. Erwin Feyersinger has proposed metalepsis as a narratological concept to articulate this ability to be "me . . . not me," that is, both inside and outside the fiction. He states, "A metalepsis combines the representations of contradictory concepts; two worlds that are perceived as mutually exclusive are connected at the same time. The perception of the viewers is important[,] as their knowledge of reality and common sense determines whether two worlds are understood as mutually exclusive or not."[85]

The significance of this nuance is crucial: it's not simply *either* me *or* not me, two poles of conflicting belief systems; it can be both at once. This clarifies how animated worlds are so utterly estranged from us yet are still comprehensible. We laugh at events in the Tooniverse that would be catastrophes if seen on live television. "Although the 'worlds' that animation depicts contain cultural referent, they can be represented in contexts that do not mirror our understanding or experience of the world we live in," observes Buchan.[86] Thus when we watch the cartoonist, who stands in for us in the film, being *drawn into* his cartoon (in both senses), we understand exactly what is happening without ever thinking that it's really happening to us. It is this logical paradox that operates when we accept that what we are seeing is happening spontaneously and "live" on-screen *(in),* all the while knowing that we are witnessing the unfolding process of a scarcely concealed construction *(of)*. We don't fluctuate between these impossible views but rather entertain them together, however irrational and defiant of the laws of physics that may be. That's another reason we normally don't mistake the incoherent Tooniverse for the real world. This is not as radical as it might sound. We often experience conflicts between our behaviors and beliefs, and our minds are routinely in two places at once—when we're driving the car while mentally taking care of office business, for example. Think of it as a doorway effect. We tend to organize our behavior and to compartmentalize our memories according to the physical space we occupy. We change our frames of mind when we enter the jury room, the restaurant, the classroom—or the movie theater. Similarly, we change our anticipation and belief systems when we cross the border of the cinema world, whether that world is animated or not.

Performance in animation, since it highlights "the transgression of borders: ontological borders in the case of metalepsis; imaginative, aesthetic, or ideological borders in the case of animation" (Feyersinger) may apply not only to the shifting spaces of cartoons but to acting as well. Vivian Sobchack refers to the "cinesthetic" subjects of film viewing, sort of ghostly bodies that are generated by the discrepancy between the knowledge of our everyday physical selves (lived bodies) and imagined screen characters. She claims "that it is the lived body (as both conscious subject and material object) that provides the (pre) logical premises, the foundational grounds, for the cinesthetic subject, who is constituted at the movies as ambiguously located both 'here' off-screen and 'there' on-screen."[87] Sobchack's schema helps us appreciate the immediacy of the scenes high upon the clock tower. Although Goofy is in no danger of injury if he were to fall—he's an indestructible toon—and I am in no physical danger as I watch in the movie theater, I still feel somatic anxiety, sweaty palms and all, during those scenes of giddy heights. My kinesthesia tells me that the moving cinesthetic body is in trouble. Animation partakes in what Steven Shaviro has described as the contradictory aspects of the film experience as too quick to allow for detached contemplation yet lacking the concrete presence of space and objects, either of which would defuse the experience of being there. "Film's virtual images do not correspond to anything actually present, but *as* images, or *as* sensations, they affect me in a manner that does not leave room for any suspension of my response," according to Shaviro. "I have already been touched and altered by these sensations, even before I have had the chance to become conscious of them."[88] A truly metaleptic experience, though, which I believe marks watching animated films, does not need this split-second sequencing to work; we entertain the opposites simultaneously. We live in these cartoons as we do in other films, without reflecting on the absence of blood actors or on the stacks of drawings that made the toons, precisely because the films are constructed to showcase the irony between the corporeal and the intangible in the Tooniverse.

A simplified way to describe these phenomenological states of screen consciousness is to consider embodiment as a belief system. These cinematic, cinesthetic bodies are not material, but they are real. They are beings we believe in, although the beliefs may not be enduring or strongly held. They are like imaginary playmates that we pretend are real while knowing in our heart of hearts that they are not. For some, Santa, the Tooth Fairy, Mickey Mouse, and Bugs Bunny are actual folks. This was the point of Chuck Jones's anecdote about an encounter with a child: "The six-year-old boy protested when I was introduced to him as the man who draws Bugs Bunny, 'He does not! He draws pictures *of* Bugs Bunny.'" Jones was quick to endorse the kid's articulation of the toon as a re-performed believed-in body: "He was absolutely right, and I can think of no happier career than as a man who drew pictures of such a fabulous character."[89] Most of us, though, maintain a passive knowledge base (called common sense) that's available for consultation if there's any doubt about what's real and what isn't. Thus reality has a proximity factor. Something may be very, very close to being real without absolute assurance. Real, but with a shadow of a doubt.

Embodied animation actually presumes several bodies. There is "me," the lived body watching the film off-screen. Then there are the believed-in bodies performing in the Tooniverse, that is, Betty and the others that appear on-screen, but which are really epiphenomena. They exist in my consciousness of our shared worlds. The animators have embodied them according to their vision of the characters, and I have fleshed them out to make parallel, but not necessarily identical, corresponding bodies. I believe in the toons' presence and in their liveness. I laugh at them, I fear for them, I experience their direct address to me, and I imagine their responsiveness to my desires. I understand what their actions mean, their cultural references, their humor, their interiority, and their motives. I get their jokes. These cinesthetic bodies are visible *in* animation. I understand, though, that they are absent because they are actually pictures made by the animators a while ago. We grant them *proximal liveness*. The beings come close to being real, but since my belief in their living status is not absolutely complete, they just miss the mark.

Then there is another body, the presumed "me" for whom the animation was intended. When the filmmakers visualized me watching their film, I was one of their pretend bodies. Contemporary animators are taught to practice what developed spontaneously during the studio period: to imagine the reception of their target audiences. Hooks perfectly describes how an animator embodies the future viewer when he or she "works alone, playing for the audience in his head, which becomes a surrogate for the intended audience. . . . The audience is the co-creator of the show. The animator, then, is sitting in for the audience that isn't there, the audience as he *imagines* it, and he is guessing at its response."[90] Conditional performance—one might even call it pre-performance—thus involves not only imaginatively experiencing the drawings' movement before they're projected to an audience, but it also involves the animators' ability to see the audience's reactions in their mind's eye. This is highly theatrical. As stage actors perform the same material night after night they are constantly anticipating the effect they'll produce later in the performance and planning adjustments they'll make the next time. They may be acting in the present moment, but they are also mentally preparing their performance for future audiences. "I always think of the actor as not only doing, but standing aside and watching what he is doing, so as to be able to propel himself to the next thing and the next thing and the next," one stage artist has said.[91]

This is scarcely different from the performance *of* animation, when the animators' work for future imagined viewers takes place far in advance. The animators made it that way, having previewed the flow of movement and imagery as it will appear on the screen and how I, the future consumer, will view and perhaps understand it.[92]

There also are the animators' lived bodies, which are physically absent during the screening but functionally present in my inferences. I know of them and I believe they created this work. Therefore, they're present as a material explanation of how the film came to be. I am prompted sometimes by the reflexive clues to their existence they've intentionally left for me (like "Easter eggs" in videos and games).

Although Disney aimed to be the paragon of embodied animation, as we've seen, the studio created a hybrid mode of performance that retained figurative elements. The contemporaneous films of Chuck Jones at Schlesinger's Warner Bros. studio also illustrate how embodiment could overlay primarily figurative performances. His series with the character Inki, a young cannibal, relied on formula expressions and perpetuated racist iconography based on the Sambo stereotype. However, in *The Little Lion Hunter* (Chuck Jones/Schlesinger, 1939), Inki has moments of acted-out reflective interiority and we have a fleeting glimpse of individuality. The characters of the puppies in *The Curious Puppy* (Chuck Jones/Schlesinger, 1939) and Sniffles in *The Egg Collector* (Chuck Jones/Schlesinger, 1940), although usually cited as unfortunate examples of Jones's "cute" Disney-wannabe period, are in fact good examples of his assimilation of the concept of embodied performance. His characters develop feelings through thoughtful expressions and gestures, as well as through finely observed body movements. For those of us fortunate enough to have met some animation legends, we know that Jones, when he was the lead animator of Bugs Bunny, *was* Bugs, that Friz Freleng *was* Yosemite Sam, and that Messmer *was* Felix the Cat.

The Tooniverse is a meeting place where the performances of the toons (the characters "there," on-screen, but also off-screen as my imagined beings), the animators (also "there," but off-screen and in the past), and my embodying performance (physically "here," off-screen, and cinesthetically "there," on-screen, in the present) come together to create a compelling sense that Betty, the flying mouse, Donald, and their animated compatriots are not drawn actors but films of drawn actors.[93] Walter Benjamin considered this space a "play-room," connoting an innocent, liberating space associated with childish imagination. According to Miriam Hansen, "It names an intermediary zone not yet fully determined in which things oscillate among different meanings, functions, and possible directions. As such, it harbors an open-ended, dynamic temporality, an interval for chance, imagination, and agency."[94] Stanley Cavell, writing of cinema performance in general, also expressed well the marvelous ambiguities of animated bodies in their special space: "It is an incontestable fact that in a motion picture no live human being is up there. But a human *something* is, and something unlike anything else we know."[95] The cinematic bodies of toons too are *somethings* in their world, whether or not they're human. They are strange yet familiar. This junction is neither accident nor coincidence. Although he was not writing specifically about animation, Shaviro's observation that cinema's sensorial immediacy resides in "a netherworld of simulacra and traces" describes well the realm of cartoon embodiment.[96] The filmmakers were re-performing in the cartoon world templates that invite belief and embodiment in the ecology of everyday life—or at least how it is represented in the movies.[97]

It clearly doesn't matter if the cartoon character is a cuddly mammal (Beans), a reptile (Gertie), or an amphibian (Flip, Michigan J. Frog). Embodiment may occur regardless of the character's cuteness factor, or whether it's a drawing, a photographic record of a performance, or a distorted video. Carrie Noland encountered this situation in her thoughtful consideration of Bill Viola's performance/video piece *The Quintet of the Astonished* (2000), which has visually and temporally altered images of humans. "It could be argued that what we witness when we observe Viola's videos is not a performance that actually took place and that therefore it is incorrect to designate his subjects as 'performers,' "[98] she writes. Inadvertently, she partially reiterates a situation that parallels the experience of animation characters. I say partially, because she correctly observes that the videos are not performances that took place before their presentation. However, she incorrectly concludes that consequently the subjects are not "performers." As in toon performances, which are not records of prior performances, Viola's subjects perform for the viewers/participants as they walk through the gallery installation. As paradoxical as it seems at first, each and every showing, as with animated films, is itself an original performance. Furthermore, those viewers are cocreators of the performative work. Nolan continues,

> From this perspective, the bodies we see on the screen are not real bodies but only digital photographic reproductions of real bodies manipulated by postproduction technologies to appear in guises otherwise not exposed to view. Yet, however distorted the images may seem, they have not been digitally transformed. That is, the bodies filmed did indeed execute the twitches, tremblings, and contractions that are only visible to the observer when the execution of their movements has been slowed down. In short, a trained actor's body has actually executed the movements that radical deceleration allows us to see. Furthermore, it is to those bodies and their movements that we, as spectators, kinesthetically respond. True, many of the actor's facial gesticulations and upper-body movements have not been voluntarily produced and are therefore not "performed" in the sense of constructed as part of an intention to express a particular categorical emotion. But these movements are nonetheless human movements available as potentials belonging to the human kinetic disposition. They cannot be considered skills per se, but they are the building blocks of skills. They are decidedly not products of digital remediation, pure manipulations of playback that no human body would be capable of performing.[99]

Although it is difficult to separate embodiment from nonhuman performances and "products of digital remediation," in fact, that is exactly what happens in the normal experience of animation. Although classical cartoons often simulate humanlike movements, gestures, and the body's socially accepted "techniques," often they do not. Even the movements in abstract animated films, such as *Begone Dull Care* (Evelyn Lambart and Norman McLaren/National Film Board of Canada, 1949), which consists of lines and colors applied directly to film stock, invite embodiment and perhaps sentiment. Despite "that no human body would be capable of performing" in such a film, these dynamic abstractions evoke the kinesthetic responsiveness cherished by phenomenological aesthetics. Clinging to the primacy of the physical human body in performance is understandable, but we realize too that this very attitude is an acculturated anthropocentric practice, one that animation performance undermines and routinely discredits.

The great irony of Disney's desire to achieve emotional depth and emotive power in his films is that, although his films were wildly successful commercially, beloved by generations of moviegoers, and formatively influential on the industry, aesthetically his urge was something of a noble failure when it came to remaking animation in a new image. The figurative mode still vies with and often overwhelms the embodied. He did not seem to grasp that embodiment did not take place by funneling resources into the most skilled animated acting possible, or that personality could not be created on-screen by skilled drawing alone. Whether identification and engagement took place was ultimately something that happened with the movie watcher—or not. Certainly, the finely tuned gestures of, say, Geppetto at work carving his puppet-boy or the relationships between the large and small desk lamps in *Luxo Jr.* (John Lasseter/Pixar, 1986) facilitate viewers' entries into those animated worlds. But then movie fans also humanized, befriended, and passed into the worlds of the early figurative Mickey, Betty, and, much later, the *South Park* kids and amateur Flash animations. The reason stems from the ability and propensity of humans to embody anything they want: imagine kids playing with sticks as dolls, Brer Rabbit fooling Brers Fox and Bear with a tar baby, or the Tom Hanks character in *Cast Away* (Robert Zemeckis, 2000) befriending the volleyball he named Wilson. McLaren succeeded in getting moving lines scratched onto film to "act" kinesthetically in *Begone Dull Care*. Other examples include Gumby, the TV hero of animated clay (plasticine), and Blu's animated graffiti, which is discussed in chapter 6.

Feature films utilizing the figurative approach to animation continue to thrive. *The Triplets of Belleville* (Sylvain Chomet, 2003), for example, depends on our recognition of caricatures and stereotypes (fat Americans, obsessed mamas, sports nuts) as much as on embodied characterizations. Circularity and rehearsed behaviors define the family dog's individuality, as it coordinates its barking with the train schedule. Yet no one would argue that these figural characters are lacking in personality.

Of course, the world of animated cinema, as well as cinema in general and even the actual world, were expanded and enlightened by Disney's experiment, but I am also thankful that he didn't succeed in leaving his mark more than he did. The funny thing is, his films contain many scenarios of embodiment that taught viewers that performances don't happen in screen acting but rather in the cinesthetic world shared by animators, toons, and audiences. I've mentioned Dumbo's feather as an allegory of belief. Although the story eventually explains the elephant's flight as the result of a peculiar aerodynamics (earodynamics), believing in magic feathers is still an option.

CHAPTER 2

Live and in Person: Toons!

AGENCY

Because cartoon subjects are so often allegories about the distribution of creative power, agency—the ability to cause events to occur, to control other beings, to react to events sentiently, or simply to assert autonomy—is involved in every animation performance. First there is the material agency of animation production (storyboarding, music, sound design, drawing, and manufacturing, for example). The animators are physical, creative agents. Other forms of agency include exhibition, marketing, and so on. One might speak of social agency, such as efforts to limit who sees animated films.[1] Schools and churches are social agents when they screen cartoons to illustrate a moral lesson. There is also the instrumentality of propaganda and commercials. There is legal agency, which involves the ability to certify who owns the intellectual property, the artwork, the copyright. In this chapter, however, I am mainly interested in the complicated agency that the viewers and the animators devise for the cartoon bodies. The great conundrum here is why do viewers understand these performers to be present and independent, and the performances to be as live as those in non-animated movies?

It appears at first that the animators have all the agency because everything that happens *in* the performance derives from them. Brad Bird, Don Graham, and others have insisted that everything in a cartoon is motivated, put there on purpose. As one Pixar animator expressed it,

"You can do anything in animation, performance-wise. . . . You can capture something, manufacture a performance sometimes with more control than even an actor would."[2] This means that even if the toons seem to have free agency on-screen, that perception was constructed by the cartoonists and therefore is not physical agency but a re-performance of it. Expressed another way, from Bird's point of view, the toons' agency is a figuration of the animators' control.

However, as you should suspect by now, this explanation is too simple. Agency isn't just a manufactured extension of a cultural object, nor is it an innate property. It's generated by the total experience of a performance as an ironic doubling of bodies, where the one *in* is perceived differently from the bodies *of* the performance. In Western drama, as well as in popular culture generally, performing beings such as actors traditionally have been regarded as entities separate from the beings that they perform, which are characters. Analogously, cartoon character agency plays with setting up aesthetic distances between the on-screen beings, the human animators allegedly in control, and the audience, which often is assumed to be a collection of passive spectators but isn't. The performativity of toons is comparable to that of participants in other theatrical forms, such as puppets and trained animals that exploit ambivalent agency as entertainment.

Winsor McCay, the legendary comic strip artist and animated cinema pioneer, implicitly critiqued the distribution of animator-animated agency in films when he presented his avatar as the impresario of an animal act. *Gertie* (Winsor McCay/Box Office Attractions, 1914) pairs the cartoonist with the dinosaur of the title. Do animators dominate their fractious creations just as animal trainers control their subjects? Marvin Carlson observed of bestial performance that the "public demonstration of particular skills is the important thing. These skills need not be human, as can be seen in such familiar attractions as performing dogs, elephants, horses, or bears."[3] Not only does Gertie exhibit skill in gracefully lumbering through her routine, but even Betty Boop, who might not cotton to being compared to a performing dog, shows off her "training" at the hands of the Fleischers.

Animal trainers stimulate humanlike behaviors in their subjects to facilitate audiences' anthropomorphic embodiment of the critters. Those vaudeville dogs, monkeys, tigers, and circus fleas go through their motions in a manner not unlike the way that toons enact the animators' scenarios. The trainer cracks his or her whip and the beast jumps; the animator moves the gorilla doll a bit, photographs it, repeats, and King

Kong climbs the skyscraper. In *Gertie*, McCay's whip-snapping trainer avatar puts the dinosaur through her paces. A perfectly domesticated animal would have no, or very limited, real agency as a performer. The routines are very circumscribed, usually performed with the goal of absolute regularity and repeatability from one show to the next. The situation is what Chris Wilbert has called an "asymmetrical alliance" between human and nonhuman animals, with human will replacing the agency of the animal.[4] "Accidental" and "aggressive" behavior might be rehearsed, as when the creatures roar and menace as part of the act, adding thrills and enhancing the illusion of danger to trainer and audience. In McCay's cartoon, at one point in the routine truculent Gertie snaps at him, introducing the possibility of a temperamental antediluvian running amok.

Jonathan Burt, however, argues that trained animals retain their agency and may engage or manipulate others. Animals turn viewers' expectations back on them and give the humans a behavior they want to see. An animal actor elicits "a human emotional response to its movements which now appears natural. It is in the context of these unintended effects by the animal itself that we might best understand what it means to talk about the manner in which the animal . . . does regulate its symbolic effects."[5] Similarly, toons, whether humanlike such as Betty or animallike such as Mickey and Donald, are designed to have autonomous agency through their appearance and expressive behaviors. Through embodiment, figuration, and re-performance, moviegoers attribute agency to them. In the case of animals, as long as their performances are purely figurative, and they act out the role of trained animals, all is well. Watch out, though, if they don't cooperate. The 2003 Siegfried and Roy incident, in which one of the duo's white tigers mauled Roy Horn during a show in Las Vegas, showed that complete domestication of trained animals might not occur. Animal performers may reclaim their suppressed agency and perform their own unscripted behaviors, reembodying themselves as wild things that annul the trainers' agency. Animal activists seize upon such cases to attribute thought and intelligent resistance to the beasts and to condemn their captors for upsetting natural hierarchies.[6]

But things are different when animals are filmed. Look at the case of Rin Tin Tin. Although he is largely forgotten now, in the 1920s, when he appeared in nearly two dozen films, he was considered one of Hollywood's greatest actors.[7] Rin Tin Tin executed humanlike feats of derring-do while supporting an anthropomorphized bourgeois on-screen family, consisting of his "wife" Nanette and the pups. "Watching Rin-Tin-Tin perform his wonderful stunts and find his delightful plot solutions," writes Jeanine Basinger, "it's almost impossible not to start thinking of him as a person instead of a dog. This is what makes him stand out. Lassie was an animal who helped out her human owners, but Rin-Tin-Tin was a leading man, a semihuman character in charge of most of the thinking and all of the action."[8] This effect was carefully crafted. In his films and others featuring animal actors, scenes are routinely reenacted in many takes, with the animals' "natural" but unwanted behaviors edited out. Multiple animals stand in for the star; as many as eighteen dogs played the part of Rinty.[9] Behaviors are synthesized with editing and special effects, such as split screens, matte shots, and (in more recent years) animatronics and digital compositing. As in animation, there is no single continuous performance that the camera passively records. It's only when the film is shown that the creatures' natural behaviors come together as performances.

Animals are sometimes humanized in a more literal fashion by being dressed in costumes or shown walking upright or even talking. Mediatization, then, routinely takes away animals' physical agency, only to re-perform and contain it within the humanizing templates defined by the filmmakers and expected by the viewers. Animal bodies become blank screens for the benefit of moviegoers who impute thoughts and feelings to them. The authors of Rin Tin Tin's fan mail made it clear that they regarded him as an autonomous thinking being and a human-dog hybrid: "Has he not shown that he was human—human in the real big sense of the word? . . . [I] feel that the only difference between man and beast is perhaps in the way we walk." And "Rin Tin Tin registers more range of emotion than any other dog actor known to the screen has attained. He shows in his expression and acting such deep, human, contrasting feelings as trust and distrust, sorrow and joy, jealousy and love, hatred and devotion."[10] Fans expected him to write back, and he did (via his owner, trainer, and amanuensis Lee Duncan). Viewers embody animals as performers, according to Chris Philo, by ascribing "human intentions, goals, mental states and material practices to nonhuman animals, thus seemingly erasing the 'otherness' of these animals." Such sentiments are *hylozoism*, "the imputation of intentions to nonhumans."[11] Filmed animals are therefore analogues for animation agency. Just as nonhuman actors in animal pictures play roles that figure them as humans, animated characters perform as figurations of film actors endowed with their own agency.

Take the Dogville Comedies, a series of short non-animated films produced between 1929 and 1931 that shared the bill with cartoons. In them, dogs, some trained and others evidently coerced, lampoon recent hit movies. In *The Dogway Melody* (Zion Myers and Jules White/MGM, 1930) the canines wear miniature street clothes, talk, sing, and walk on their hind legs. Sometimes strings are visible as the trainers jerk the dogs' paws and work their mouths so they appear to talk, effectively turning the animal performers into live puppets. Although the animals residing in Dogville would seem to illustrate an absence of canine identity, the dog actors nevertheless retain a modicum of agency. It comes from our recognizing them as actors performing in a film. In fact, although the films were intended as a parody, the animals' agency is the same as the humans being directed in *The Broadway Melody* (Harry Beaumont/MGM, 1929).[12]

Toons, like filmed animals, are mediatized figures that are designed and received ironically. They exploit, as Burt says, "the ambiguity that acting is both a form of agency and something done under the direction of somebody else."[13] He continues, "If one is to consider what it means for an animal [and, I claim, a cartoon character] *to act* then one has to take into account not just the mechanics of training, but the whole network of interactions between animal and humans including the general effects sought by the filmmakers and their impact on an audience."[14] Similar to animal actors, toons act and have agency because we grant it to them as part of the performance *of* animation and then we deem it to be authentic. As Cavell observed, "apparently it is natural for the animation to be of *small* animals, perhaps because they most immediately convey animatedness, quickness; perhaps because they can be given an upright posture without appearing grotesque or parodistic of the human (like chimpanzees dressed in cute clothes). The horse and the large dog (the usual principals of movies about animals) either have to be taken seriously or else they are merely comic."[15]

The characters in puppet theater operate under similar terms of agency. Marionettes and hand, shadow, glove, rod, and body puppets, like toons, may be figurative and embodied performers simultaneously. Puppets present figurative performances when they reenact a narrow range of gestures and poses that viewers will recognize. They may be stock characters, like Punch and Judy. These representations are often the result of faces, bodies, and mechanical armatures that are constructed specifically to limit their appearance and gestures. These puppets' expressivity comes largely through their body movement, which is usually anthropomorphic, and from the puppeteer's ventriloquial voice. Puppet shows often re-perform folkloric tales that rely on their audiences' familiarity with the players and the narratives, while ventriloquism acts depend on lively repartee reminiscent of vaudeville routines. There is an analogy between the mechanisms of agency in the relationships among puppeteers, puppets, and audiences and those of animators, toons, and their audiences.

Dual agency is crucial to the puppet show aesthetic. When not in use, a puppet is only a pile of materials, or a doll at best. The performance by the puppeteer resembles the conditional performance that takes place in the animation studio, except that the puppet's on-stage performance, unlike that of the toon, retains the possibility for improvisation and accident. When puppeteers operate their puppets, they and their spectators coembody the puppet actor with autonomous existence. This feeling that the puppet actor is an independent being is powerful, even when the puppeteers are plainly visible during the performance, as with "Johnny," enacted by the hand of Señor Wences,[16] or the three on-stage puppeteers who operate the human-scale figures in bunraku, the Japanese puppet theater beloved of Eisenstein. It is a testament to hylozoism and the pathetic fallacy that we easily interpret these lumps of cloth, rods, wires, and papier-mâché masks into so many intelligent animals, mindful gods, scary demons, and fellow humans.

In *Rakvickarna* (Jan Švankmajer, 1966), the setting in this non-animated film is an eighteenth-century Czech puppet theater. The puppets fight over who will feed seeds to and take possession of a guinea pig. Whether the rodent is to be a pet or a meal is not clear. The live, obliviously happy creature munches away throughout the skirmish, which proves fatal to both puppets. In the allegorical conflict over control and resources, greed leads to death. The beings with fatal agency destroy themselves, but the guinea pig keeps chewing along. Although the guinea pig apparently lacks agency, it is nevertheless the sole survivor. Does the animal represent the puppeteer's lack of control over "natural" actors, as opposed to warring marionettes that perform their own self-destruction? Is unquestioning acceptance of the status quo a survival strategy for artists in a repressive regime?

In Western puppet traditions, as in cartoons, the "illusion of life" is a powerful recurring trope. The mimetic accuracy of the characters' movements, the appropriateness of their voices, and their believability as actors are criteria for judging a successful "lifelike" show.[17] Punch kills Judy, but she'll return for a curtain call. The mysterious creation of life, its tragic fragility, and the assurance of life after death are often figured as puppet stories, as in *Pinocchio* (Hamilton Luske and Ben Sharpsteen/ Disney, 1940). Such narratives re-perform the underlying human agency. When the puppeteer stops working, the puppet loses its "animation." Profound human belief systems are mirrored and naturalized in these reassuring stories, as though we know them without having been told. These circular master narratives are parables of the shows' origins, emanating from puppet studios that remind us of animation shops.

When Bird tries to shift the agency in animated performance from the toon performers to the animators, he (presumably) is innocently reformulating a longstanding critical tradition that valorized puppets' agency over that of theatrical actors. Critics praised puppets for being devoid of sentiment, emotion, spontaneity, and grace—in short, for lacking humanity. Being capable only of figuration, critics argued, counterintuitively made them superior to human actors, who invariably introduced their own personalities, experiences, and unwanted interpretations into their roles. Embodied acting (of the kind lauded by Disney and the proponents of the Stanislavsky method) interfered with the purity of the author's intentions, the text, or the essential experience of the drama. As a result, puppet actors emerge as a radical alternative to human thespians. Because animated performers are (with rare exceptions) not blood actors, and since their agency is constrained like that of puppets, they might be even better standard-bearers for this critique of performance.

Belgian poet and playwright Maurice Maeterlinck (1862–1949) strongly opposed what I'm calling embodied performance, declaring that staging plays with actors destroyed the works' artistic essence. Accordingly, he wrote plays to be "performed" by wax effigies in Paris's Musée Grévin. Later, he advocated using puppets *(fantoches)* to deliver authors' lines dispassionately in order to replace actors with "figures who had the appearance of life without having life."[18] By coincidence, the Musée Grévin would be the place where Emile Reynaud would begin projecting his *Luminous Pantomimes* in 1892. This precinema attraction using painted figures on transparent bands to tell simple stories with animated movement might have fulfilled Maeterlinck's dreams. Reynaud's characters performed just as they were drawn and they moved according the author's whim, since Reynaud was at the helm of his apparatus as a sort of image-puppeteer. Maeterlinck's ideal just may have been achieved in animated drawings or puppets made with the figurative approach to performance. He would not have been a fan of late-1930s Disney.

English theater personage Edward Gordon Craig (1872–1966) campaigned for an actorless stage where the text would be delivered by "über-marionettes" transmitting the thoughts of the playwright-puppeteer.[19] He too was antiembodiment. "Do away with the actor," he cried, "and you do away with the means by which a debased stage-realism is produced and flourishes. No longer would there be a living figure to confuse us into connecting actuality and art; no longer a living figure in which the weakness and tremors of the flesh were perceptible. . . . The über-marionette will not compete with life—rather will it go beyond it. Its ideal will not be the flesh and blood but rather the body in trance—it will aim to clothe itself with a death-like beauty while exhaling a living spirit."[20]

Both Maeterlinck and Craig (and perhaps also Bird) were arguing that if there must be embodiment it should be the province of the author, not the actor or the observers. On-stage performers should be nothing but passive agents of the playwrights and filmmakers. Such performers would have no agency and could not "interpret" the work, or, more to the point, misinterpret it. Maeterlinck and Craig harbored a distrust of the human actor's independent agency, an attitude that percolated throughout the first part of the twentieth century. Among the partisans of this view were Eisenstein and his mentor, the Russian dramatist V.E. Meyerhold, the champion of "bio-mechanics."[21] When Eisenstein admiringly found cartoons' figurative performance to be countertheatrical, liberating, and revolutionary, he spoke from within this tradition of similar attitudes about puppets (and now, for him, toons) having no consciousness of their own. One thinks also of the snide remarks about treating actors as cattle attributed to Alfred Hitchcock.[22]

This line of reasoning is disingenuously rigged. Puppetry, like animation, is quite capable of embodied performance to express individuality and psychological complexity and to resonate emotionally without distorting the intentions of the authors or the integrity of their texts. There have been many well-developed, distinctive personae, like Edgar Bergen's poseur-playboy Charlie McCarthy and Shari Lewis's sock puppet Lamb Chop. Jim Henson's Kermit the Frog and other Muppet characters often delivered embodied performances.

Filmed and televised puppets have the same potential for becoming cinesthetic bodies as human actors. Mediatized characters such as McCarthy, Lamb Chop, and Kermit, who highlight their puppetness in movies and on TV, have more believable autonomy on-screen than in "live" performance because film separates the puppet actor's body from the puppeteer's physical presence and voice. Indeed, movies featuring these characters make a point of showing the puppet behaving on its own, without human agency in the form of hands or strings.[23] They seem self-propelled (Kermit's visible rods notwithstanding) and self-speaking (despite Bergen and Lewis's slightly moving lips). The dummies' voices are taken as emanating from their bodies on-screen, from the same place that other film actors' voices do, not from ventriloquism, as is the case on stage.

In filmed puppet shows and shadow plays, whether animated or not, the puppet bodies are images of objects that exist, or did exist, somewhere in our physical world and were filmed in action.[24] In that sense, their screen performances may be analogous to non-animated cinema. In the case of animated puppets, however, by which I mean objects that are manipulated and filmed frame by frame to create motion (say, Willis O'Brien's King Kong or George Pal's Jasper), the animators replace the puppeteers as physical agents. Film, as it does with animal actors, creates filmed puppets' second (screen performer) bodies. We recognize this, and so the puppets retain some of their residual corporeality in the imagined puppet space that corresponds to a Tooniverse.

Puppets and cartoon actors share the trait of becoming performing bodies only when they act before an audience. Richard Weihe, comparing animation in general to puppets and puppet animation, writes, "Animation employs the spectator's imagination. The craftsmanship of the animator does not produce any complete illusion of life, while it is up to the spectator to complement the visual impressions and conceive of the animated figure as a living being displaying human traits."[25] When puppetry is filmed or televised, this process of completing the illusion by the viewers is crucial. Most people encountered Bergen's films, Henson's television shows and films, and Lewis's TV appearances as mediatized enactments. The ultimate performances took place at a distance and were usually delayed because the presentation was filmed or tape-recorded. As is the case with animators, the puppeteers' actions in front of the cameras in anticipation of the show's later projection or broadcast were conditional performances. Material agency in puppetry may seem automatic because of the puppet's physical bond to the puppeteer as a doppelgänger. He lifts a string; it jumps; she thinks, it speaks. Certainly, the puppets' dialogue and movements may be figuratively conventional, with the puppet actor impersonating a known character (such as Punch). At other times, however, the working of the marionette's wires or the glove puppet's gestures are indistinguishable from the puppeteers' dexterity, vocal skills, and artistic talent, so that the puppet body seems like an extension of the master's personality and body. This situation of having two mutually performing bodies, Hillel Schwartz observes apropos of mimes, is "thespian heaven": "to take on double roles, each body moved by its own center of gravity, and yet the same sincere mind at work inside both."[26] In animation, there is a similar connection between animators and their drawings. Emile Cohl's morphing lines or the handwriting-like inscriptions of Robert Breer (in 1957's *A Man and His Dog Out for Air,* for example) become highly personal embodied expressions of the filmmakers. They are like animated doodling, as expressive and idiosyncratic as a signature.

German Romantic Heinrich von Kleist, writing in 1811, grasped the distinction between the figurative and embodied performances in puppetry, a distinction that applies to animated cartoons as well. In an essay written in the form of a dialogue with a more intelligent friend, he imagined a puppet so perfect that it could dance by itself if a machine replaced the human puppeteer:

> I replied that I had always thought this [puppetry] activity something quite mindless, rather like turning the crank on a hand organ. "By no means," he answered. "On the contrary, the relation of his finger movements to the movements of the puppets attached to them is something quite precise, rather like the relation of numbers to their logarithms or asymptotes to their hyperbola."
>
> But he believed that even this last fraction of mind, to which he had just now referred, could indeed be removed from the marionettes, their dance transposed wholly into the realm of mechanical forces, and, just as I had imagined, produced by means of a crank.
>
> I expressed my amazement that he should dignify with serious consideration this toy version of a high art, contrived for the populace. Not only did he believe it capable of higher development, he seemed indeed to be directing his own thoughts to that end.
>
> He smiled, saying he dared assert that if a mechanic would construct a marionette according to his specific requirements, he could, by means of it, present a dance such as no other accomplished dancer of the time, not even [Paris Ballet master Gaëtan] Vestris himself, was ever likely to achieve.[27]

In her book-length study of the puppet animators Stephen and Timothy Quay, Buchan applies this passage from Kleist to establish a mode of viewing and to draw an analogy between the puppet master and the animator. "But we also know that in contrast to live-action figures, puppets do not exist except as inanimate objects beyond their animation on-screen. The spectator may oscillate between this awareness and a sublimation of it that allows her to perceive animated objects as living. The animator as puppet operator not only dances; he or she is able to give the puppets a semblance of Kleist's soul via the vitalism implicit in their animation."[28]

Technology has, of course, complicated Kleist's proposal. Robotics and animatronics have reified his mechanical puppets. Animated cinema, not to mention rotoscoping and contemporary computer imaging technologies, have made it possible to achieve visually exactly the mimetic accuracy that Kleist imagined for his mechanical puppets. His metaphor of the asymptote (one that film theorist André Bazin would use to describe cinema's relation to reality as approaching but never achieving it) anticipates the concept of the uncanny valley. Proximal liveness, which describes our experience of performance without a living body, is also an asymptote: it approaches the fusion of the "live" and the "real" ever so closely, but it never quite reaches it.

Kleist embraced, and did not fear, the possibility of the perfect simulacrum. He probably would have celebrated (after recovering from being dumbstruck by) the "mechanics" of, say, *The Tale of the Fox* (Wladyslaw Starewicz and Irene Starewicz, 1930), *Peter and the Wolf* (Suzie Templeton, 2008), or modern digital-animal puppetry as in *Rise of the Planet of the Apes* (Rupert Wyatt, 2011). Such films use frame-by-frame cinematography or motion-capture to choreograph puppets (or puppetlike simulations) without wires or other visible human agency so artfully that they seem to be animals performing on their own. Although they are as "mechanical" as Kleist's automata, animated puppets defy time, space, and gravity and are therefore capable of expressing more freedom, sensitivity of movement, and embodiment than a performance by the finest marionettist. In their ability to affect audiences, these puppet figures, have their own agency.

The earliest animated films melded the traditions of puppetry and cinema. In fact, during the first decade of cinema, filmmakers were far more likely to set objects than drawings into motion.[29] Animation and puppetry intermingled freely as the pioneer animators were developing the medium.[30] Early animated puppet films took full advantage of the puppet show's tendency toward figurative performance. Cohl specifically invoked the form in his animations by referring to his drawn actors as *fantoches*, a kind of puppet.[31] His first film as a director, *Fantasmagorie* (Emile Cohl/Gaumont, 1908), consisted of a series of moving white lines on a black background depicting the strange actions of a clown character. The clown is an object as well as a drawing, revealed at the end when the filmmaker's hands come into the frame to mend its broken paper body. In *Le Tout Petit Faust* (Emile Cohl/Gaumont, 1910), one of several ambitious doll animations he made, Cohl adapted the puppet show into a puppets-without-wires cinema play.[32]

Whether the toons are puppets or drawn bodies should, in principle, have little effect on their agency. It's possible, though, that the special means of image production and the viewers' different expectations for films with animated objects may produce different animated worlds. "Puppet animation," Buchan argues, "elicits a different set of questions as it is a complex hybrid form in this respect. The sets and puppets exist, and although they may appear to have anthropomorphic proportions on screen, they are constructed on a smaller scale. Yet although the events we see on screen *did not* occur, the objects *do* exist. Puppet animation thus represents a different 'world' for the spectator, something between '*a* world', created with the animation technique, and '*the* world', in its use of real objects and not representational drawings."[33]

There are some further convergences in concepts of puppet and animated character agency. Puppets, like toons, provide the opportunity for audiences to project being and autonomy onto the actors. Such fantasies of self-willed puppets are often the stuff of horror: consider the non-animated *Puppet Master* (David Schmoeller, 1989) and its nine sequels to date. At the same time, none but naïve observers would think that puppets were real in the same way that persons are real. The displays are highly marked as performances. Like wild animals and toons, puppets can range from emblematic figures (like caricatures and stock characters) to fully embodied ones asserting their own agency. As in animation, puppet agency is a co-construction. There is a strong presence of the cinesthetic body of the animator and puppeteer at work just out of sight, outside the frame. We know that between each frame of an animated puppet film, the filmmaker's hands have entered to adjust the objects. Although we never see Cohl or the other object animators in their films, the animator's physical agency, like that of the traditionally hidden marionettist, is implicit.

The industrialization of animation beginning in the 1920s rendered the puppet cinema a minor but robust subgenre, with O'Brien, Pal, and Ray Harryhausen as landmark directors. In Europe, puppet animation has continued as a viable film tradition. Aardman Animations' Wallace and Gromit characters and the "embodied" toons of computer animation, notably the toy actors of *Toy Story* (John Lasseter/Pixar, 1995), offer a CGI re-performance of puppetry. Technologies such as motion capture produce "digital puppetry" without the benefit of preexisting filmed puppets.[34] They populate "animated" and "live-action" films alike, confounding the distinctions historically implied by those labels. These puppets are often undetectable as constructed beings. Perhaps, then, they are the quintessence of the longed for embodiment without a human body or the "appearance of life without having life" for those who saw their ideal actors in *fantoches* and über-marionettes

Agency in animation performance is closely related to body doubling, and, as Schwartz points out, "Where there be one head and two bodies, that way lies theater."[35] Both the animators and the animated actors claim autonomous agency. Often in classic cartoons, toons acknowledge the agency of the animator and then confront it. The behavior *in* the cartoon acts out agency; Betty, for example, selects and reanimates her previous movies, an action that seems to usurp the agency of the animators and viewers. This results in two Manichean conflicts in animation performances: *parthenogenesis,* the story of how animated characters come to exist—or I'd rather say, re-perform being alive; and *autophagy,* the story of how the rebellious characters annihilate themselves and their narratives by self-consumption.

Parthenogenesis, or the act of self-reproduction, is an apt metaphor for an animated film's tendency to visualize the film's origins from its own matter. This tendency, the basis of the primordial hand of the artist motif, clearly expresses nineteenth-century Romanticism and postindustrial ambivalence about technology, which was alternately seen as progressive science and as diabolical hubris. The animators picture themselves as avatars in the films that create the beings, demonstrating the animation process or some fanciful version of it. In *Spontaneous Generation* (Emile Cohl/Gaumont, 1909), for example, a medieval wizard discovers the power to transform drawings into living beings. The creations then vie for the animator's agency, sometimes rebelling and sometimes appropriating his powers, as Ko-Ko does in the 1920s Out of the Inkwell series.

Toons resisting their control-freak creators thrived as a cartoon motif. Betty, not Max, stage-manages the show in *Rise to Fame.* She decides when to dance topless and when to duck behind her dressing screen to change costumes. She is the agent controlling the performance, the one who inks the voyeuristic reporter at the end. María Lorenzo Hernández calls such situations examples of *equivocal identity*: "The narrative pretext lies on the audience's initial mistake regarding the situation, eventually mitigated by the sudden emergence of the character's authentic nature, making the animated short film an elongated gag."[36] We accept that Betty has agency, but it proves to be inauthentic when she reverts to ink. The villains nearly eradicate the animator in *A Cartoonist's Nightmare*. Porky Pig (*You Ought to Be in Pictures*, Friz Freleng/Schlesinger, 1940) and Elmer Fudd (*The Big Snooze*, Robert Clampett/Warner Bros., 1946) petulantly tear up their studio contracts. The tradition continues in modern independent animation, as when the "bookling" drawings get uppity with the animator who appears as a rotoscoped actor in *Pencil Booklings* (Kathy Rose, 1978) or as do the filmmaker's avatars in *Animator vs. Animation* (Alan Becker, 2006). The conclusions of the stories reestablish (although not quite exactly) the narrative stability of the opening, a situation that is perhaps best symbolized by Ko-Ko reentering the metonymic inkwell. This type of ending establishes the toons as equivocal identities and suggests, as Bird insists, that the animators are in command of toon agency because they are the filmmakers and are in charge of everything, thus explaining why toon rebellions are doomed to fail. Although toons may appear to rebel against their creators, they cannot. Nor can the animators grant physical agency to their toons, setting them free, as it were.[37] Perhaps it's the case that toons have agency in the world they share with the viewers, the animators have agency in the world they share with the toons, and audiences have agency in both worlds.

Moviegoers, along with animators, assign specific agencies to various characters. For example, we all recognize that Bluto's agency derives from his physical strength. Popeye, his foil, keeps his strength harnessed until he claims a moral imperative to unleash violence, symbolized by popping the totemic can of spinach. Popeye's agency might appeal to some in his audience who would value his being a nice guy over his dubious social and sexual prowess. He derives his agency from his confidence that the spinach, in spite of (or because of) its ironic ordinariness, will provide all the agency he needs to evoke his superpowers. Similar to Dumbo's talismanic feather, the spinach stands for an entire belief system, the anthropocentric empowerments we like to think that nature holds for us, and our parallel belief in the omnipotence of animation. Popeye's performance is presumably an object lesson for youngsters. Olive Oyl too initially seems to have little physical power, although her unlimited stretchiness seems to compensate. Her agency asserts itself in her ability to turn what appears to be a total lack of physical attractiveness into comically irresistible sexual stimulation for Popeye and Bluto. She becomes a sort of über-Betty for them. The irony of almost every

Popeye cartoon is that the men's testosterone-fueled hypermasculinity is nothing compared to string-bean Olive's sexual agency.

Of course, viewers too have agency. Their embodiments, interpretive skills, tastes, receptivity, fandom, and potential for continued economic support guide the work of commercial filmmaking. Agency in animation, then, is a power grid around which the various players align themselves in relation to each other *in* the animation (other characters and environmental elements) and *of* the animation (to the agencies of the animators, the viewers). Agency isn't an absolute entity possessed by anyone or anything but rather sets of flexible relationships.

As active participants in the film experience, viewers are free to create, to represent, and to perform their own meanings. For example, I find the implied agencies within the Popeye–Bluto–Olive Oyl relationship to be redolent of sadomasochism. Gratification is mingled with inflicting and receiving pain. I'm not just making this up; it's an inference I draw from the plots and behaviors of the characters. Whether the animators intended or understood the underlying sexual dynamic in their films would be interesting to determine, but it is probably not knowable, and at any rate it is irrelevant to my deduction. The point is that viewer agency is out of the filmmakers' control.

LIVENESS MACHINES

It may seem peculiar to bring a discussion of the "live" into animated cinema. But there's a difference—sometimes minuscule, to be sure—between proximal liveness and being alive. Moreover, the issue of vitalism underlies our previous discussions of performativity, figuration, embodiment, and agency. Now, it should be clear that only the childishly naïve or the delusional would perceive toons as living, flesh-and-blood, corporeal, physical, lived bodies (a fine string of euphemisms for "real beings"). Nevertheless, as works of fiction, as cinema, and as performative events, the actors of animation, as inhabitants of and agents in their cinema worlds, intersect with our living world. I encounter their bodies with my intelligence, my belief, and my experience as I watch them in real time in a real place, whether in a picture palace, in a classroom or living room, or on my handheld device. The filmmakers have exploited this over the years, inviting viewers to embrace their constructed beings and their environments just as viewers would the other actors and locales on the movie program. Steven Shaviro notes of cinema in general that "images themselves are immaterial, but their *effect* is all the more physical and corporeal."[38] Filmmaking conceits such as the one that cartoons are filmed recordings of "live" toons show the effort to draw the viewer into the Tooniverse. Such films construct the action as live, sensory, and immediate. They postulate the toons as corporeal performers.

There was a time when common sense dictated that the liveness of the stage was diametrically opposed to the self-evident non-liveness of the movies. Live performance could be defined as "a limited number of people in a specific time/place frame [who] have an experience of value which leaves no visible trace afterward."[39] This concept is satisfying, but it has been challenged on several fronts by performance theorists. Meanwhile, some argue that filmed performance might not be a performance at all. These debates are relevant for us because they underscore the peculiar liveness of animation that enables us to entertain such contradictory notions as "Betty Boop isn't a real body, yet she's a live performer." This is explainable in part as a demonstration of the embodying power of reception, and in part it is traceable to the ambiguities introduced by cinema's technology.

Philip Auslander has argued that there is no opposition between live and mediatized performance because "historically, the live is an effect of mediating technologies."[40] Mediatized performance "is performance that is circulated on television, as audio or video recordings, and in other forms based in technologies of reproduction." Irked by traditional unreflective thinking, Auslander rejects "assumptions that fail to get much further in their attempts to explicate the value of 'liveness' than invoking clichés and mystifications like 'the magic of live theatre,' the 'energy' that supposedly exists between performers and spectators in a live event, and the 'community' that live performance is often said to create among performers and spectators."[41] Similarly frustrating are rationales for animation performance that simply state that it creates an "illusion of life."[42] In making a case against the traditional criteria of physical actor-audience presence, the uniqueness of the dramatic event, and the superior instrumentality of live over recorded presentation, Auslander "[does] not consider 'the live' to be an ontological category. It is, rather, a historically and ideologically determined concept that appeared only in the modern era and whose exact meaning and cultural importance are subject to change, especially in relation to technological development."[43] He claims that designating and recognizing a performance as "live" could only occur historically when the possibility of recording, transmitting and representing it existed, that is, after mechanical reproductions of it were possible. There was no "live theater" before radio and cinema, only "theater."

It was around 1934, according to Auslander, that "the concept of the live was articulated in relation to technological change. Recording technology brought the live into being, but under conditions that permitted a clear distinction between the existing mode of performance and the new one."[44] It is misleading, however, to date this cultural shift to the 1930s. In fact, the pattern has spanned three centuries, beginning with automata that performed nightingale songs, dolls that played the harpsichord, and Kleist's hypothetical mechanical puppets. The clock that our heroes clean in the Disney cartoon is a descendant of the carillon bell towers of the late Renaissance, which were designed to publish the authoritative time, thus synchronizing the times kept by the Church, city dwellers, and laborers, and whose chimes and moving statues performed without human agency by means of a rotating drum studded with pins.[45] In the nineteenth century, photographic, phonographic, and what we might call luminous technologies (magic lanterns and photographic projections, optical toys, Reynaud's Musée Grévin spectacle) constructed mediatized acoustic, pictorial, and theatrical spaces. These applications generated being-in-the-image-ness and liveness without visible hands.

In the mid-1890s, several inventions ramped up the liveness stakes by introducing sophisticated apparatuses designed to turn visual and acoustic raw materials into live performances. The cinematograph did this with reels of still photographic images, each frame capturing a snapshot of an unfolding event. The player piano (marketed as the Pianola) did it with reels of perforated paper.[46] "By 1900," Ian Christie observes, "time had become a commodity. It might be invisible, but it could have immense value. . . . Like money, it could be saved and spent; it could be squeezed and stretched. Thanks to recent inventions, it could be collected in the form of photographs, phonograph records, piano rolls—and now moving pictures."[47] Liveness, of which time is a necessary component, also became commoditized. This canning of performances (which thus rendered the originals "live") ironically called attention to the effaced human operators who seemed to have retreated behind the scenes, back in time, leaving the apparatus apparently to operate on its own uncanny accord.

Following Auslander's schema, in the first decade of the twentieth century and the cinema it became possible and necessary to differentiate between "live" and filmed natural scenes, melodramas, dances, slapstick comedy, and stage routines such as lightning sketch acts. The nascent cinema experience capitalized on the viewers' ability to embody themselves as beings, with avatars (pedestrians, actors) that effortlessly moved into and journeyed through cinematized landscapes, city streets, and boxing arenas. Christie noted the popularity of experiencing the forme-ness of travel and actuality films: "Being there, doing it, seeing with one's own eyes—these were all attractive for men, and women, of action. But was it not equally satisfying to visit by proxy, to travel without leaving home, to range across centuries and millennia while remaining in the present?"[48] The inventors of many of these machines tried to capitalize on their ability to create liveness by suggesting that their effects were not just live, but alive. The creators of these systems evoked movement and organic life by giving their inventions vitalizing names such as *kine, bio,* and *vita.*[49]

These competing versions of liveness stemmed from the ability to produce these double bodies (the one on-screen and the one off-screen). Tom Gunning has discussed this uncanny dimension of early cinema. "For the most part," he writes, "this took the form of a contradiction between cinema's mastery of a new level of realistic representation, the capturing of motion combined with photography's visual acuity, and its lack of the other signifiers of reality: sound, colour, three-dimensionality, and an unbounded field of vision. . . . But the capture of motion held a particular fascination embodied in the word 'animation,' a sense that life was not simply captured but engendered."[50] One may add, following Gunning, that early cinema mastered the stage—not to mention the luminous industries, spiritualism, and religion—to accomplish the Romantic dream of art engendering life. Except that it was not really life but its re-performance that viewers witnessed. The sensation of mechanical devices performing life resonates with the appeal of early animated films, but also with a much more pervasive instrument, the player piano.

The 1896 Pianola soon found its way into millions of homes as well as "public spaces like restaurants, bowling alleys, railroad depots, skating rinks, ocean liners, grocery stores, brothels, movie theaters, and other commercial contexts."[51] Critics attacked the practice of listening to music performed on it in a discourse that paralleled attacks on early photography and early cinema. John Philip Sousa is said to have coined the term "canned music" to describe the effect.[52] This would qualify as an Auslanderian moment since it creates a distinction between canned performance and "uncanned"—that is, live—music.

One application for the Pianola and its modern descendants has been "live" concert presentations of player pianos performing the rolls of famous pianists, usually dead ones. These recitals have all the traits of any other piano concert, except that, like animation, they are mediatized human performances.

The Pianola is a digital computer. Its software takes the form of punched paper rolls, with one hole activating one key or pedal. Each key is "off" when there is no hole in the paper, but, when there is a perforation present, it is "on" (that is, playing), as the hole permits compressed air to operate the keyboard. The machine doesn't store an image of the original recording piano's acoustics, like microphone recordings of piano performances do, and it doesn't record any direct or ambient sounds. When the rolls play, the performance heard does not reproduce any prior "live" performance. It is an original performance, albeit one produced through technical means. From the 1900s through the 1930s, the rolls were produced either by mechanically punching the holes in scrolls of paper during hand playing, or by composing directly onto the paper and then punching holes, without any piano or human playing at all. Either way, the rolls were seldom untouched records of playing; errors were corrected, parts were added, and tunes were embellished.[53] As happens during puppet rehearsals or when animators are at work, the recording or composing of the rolls was a conditional performance. The players/composers/animators produced the elements that they expected technology to translate into performances that would occur later when auditors and audiences listened/attended. Neither the piano rolls nor the digital files created by today's Disklaviers nor animation elements are performances themselves. Nor is the piano, the animation camera, the movie projector, the DVD player, or the iPad a performer. Rather, these systems convert the static elements designed for each machine into a performance. In this sense, the cinematograph, the player piano, and animated movies are information-processing systems. They do not record or playback liveness, but they store data in order to create a new, live performance when actuated.

One might reasonably object that player pianos, DVD players, and phonographs are only playback devices that mechanically "access performances carried out by other entities (i.e., the human beings on the recordings) at an earlier time" and that these devices only play "fixed programs that unfold the same way every time."[54] In his discussion of film projectors, Noël Carroll proposes that such devices do not perform or create performances but play templates. In other words, film reels (and piano rolls) are records—he uses the term *tokens*—of prior performances by actors, or, in our case, pianists.[55] He concludes that because film actors' interpretations during filming are permanently etched in celluloid, "in one sense, motion pictures are not a performing art—i.e., they are not something whose performance itself is an art."[56] This seems legalistic and absolutely logical—as long as one ignores mediatization and the environmental and participatory components of performance. His disqualifications might apply to player pianos, cartoons, and cinema in the laboratory of theory where the machines process their data programs. In everyday life we seldom encounter such circumstances.

Susanne Langer presciently observes that screen performances need not be linked to living bodies: "The screen actor is not governed by the stage, nor by the conventions of the theater; he has his own realm and conventions; indeed, there may be no 'actor' at all." Going further, she concludes, "The cartoon does not even involve persons merely 'behaving.' "[57] Those embodied cinesthetic beings we've been discussing might be people, animals, puppets, or pixels, or they may be toons. In the realm of the movies, whether they are linked to a flesh-and-blood body is irrelevant; all have equal ontological status.

Making 'Em Move lampoons ad absurdum the idea of animation "tokens." We saw in chapter 1 how the animator characters in the film slavishly drew their posing model, etching it on celluloid. Their cartoon of the hula dancer would be an animated token because it was a recording of the toon's prior performance. But, of course, this only happens in the Tooniverse. In real animation there is no profilmic performance that the cartoon records.[58] Of course, the animators rehearsing characters' motions and expressions might have inspired some of the drawings in a cartoon. The result, however, is not a token based on photographing those actions, as might happen in a non-animated acting scene.[59] Therefore, even if we accept on trial the alleged impossibility of non-animated cinema performance, then animated performance, because its products are not tokens, is exempted on a technicality.[60]

Auslander distinguishes between the interpretive performer, "who does not merely execute the instructions contained in a text but who interprets the text and expresses something of his or her own through the act of interpretation," and the technical performer, who, like an orchestral musician, has developed skill in subjects such as reading sheet music and playing the notes accurately without variation or "interpretation." The Pianola, like Kleist's dancer, is a technical performer. It doesn't compose new material or riff on the original piece, but it does replay the notes with perfection, thereby giving a technically perfect recital analogous to the computer performances cited by Auslander.[61]

The self-playing piano concert has other elements of liveness. The acoustics of the performance are "live" and vary according to the kind of piano, how it's tuned, and where it's placed. The concert instrument is usually not the same as the one on which the piece was originally played, which was specially outfitted for punching the rolls or recording digital files in those cases where the rolls were produced by hand playing. In such concerts, as in any other performance, including cinema, the listeners experience the event in real time. They experience the music not as a recording of past liveness but as instrument-generated sounds in the present.[62]

Obviously, in the technical performance the sequence and strength of the keystrokes and the intervals between them never change, just as the single-frame photographs of the animation drawings or models in projected cartoons are permanent. The circumstances of reception, however, are highly variable and depend upon not only upon material factors, but also the auditor's belief systems. We have to take into account, for example, the listeners' readiness to entertain the "presence" of famous "absent" pianists, a contradiction that parallels Gunning's observations about the uncanniness of cinema. When artists such as George Gershwin are advertised as re-performing their works via their old piano rolls, the creepiness of the event is often a leitmotif in concert accounts. "Finally, the nine-foot Disklavier was taken to the auditorium," recalled Artis Wodehouse, "where it played Gershwin's rolls from a floppy disk for the microphone, as if Gershwin's ghost were present at the session."[63] When the instrument is playing *as though* a human pianist were playing it, it enables a firsthand experience of the composer's artistry through technology. We know there is no human at the keyboard of the player piano as we listen to it, yet we have the sensation of a pianist performing for us as though live and present, prompting the uncanny clash between the body that is absent (or deceased) and the acoustically present but invisible body that is operating the keys.

Our belief in the existence of ghosts (or, more likely, our imagining that we believe in them) provides the rational template to explain the irrational. Robert Spadoni describes this consciousness as arising from "inanimate objects that momentarily appear to be alive and, conversely, animate ones that appear not to be alive."[64] Similarly, toons too are both present and missing; they are palpably acting on the screen, yet they are absent inasmuch as they are images without physical bodies off-screen. Mediatized performances, such as carillons, automata, player pianos, radio, and, of course, cinema, fragment the body so that it exists in doubles, triples, or any number of replications and clonings. These uncanny bodies that exhibit liveness but are not alive—the dead pianist who continues to play or the being that exists as an audiovisual image—have existed imaginatively in shamanistic rituals, theater, and other performances since there have been performances.[65]

Animated films, like Pianola and computer performances, are technical performances, and live. On one hand, Betty doesn't depart from her script, although the script does have "accidents" and "improvisations" written into it, such as Betty getting caught with her hair in curlers or her dress flying up. On the other hand, she does perform in real time before a live audience with agency. As in the case of certain machines and computer-generated robots analyzed by Auslander, toons "are themselves performing entities that construct their performances at the same time as we witness them."[66] He refers to chatterbots, which are computer programs that carry on conversations with computer users, typically in online chat rooms.

Not surprisingly, the view that computer entities (and here I include player pianos) may perform is controversial, and so it may be for media entities such as toons. Herbert Blau has rejoined Auslander's claim that chatterbots are capable of performing. Since these bots "are without biological presence or corporeality, [they] are virtually immortal too." Such beings, Blau continues, would therefore "hardly have any presence at all, any sense of liveness whatever, were it not for the omnipresent shadow of the apparently vanished being, who, dead or alive, endows the notion of liveness with meaning or substance to begin with." He compares these performing bots to the "tradition, from Kleist through Gordon Craig to Roland Barthes on to the Bunraku, in which puppets were preferred to actors whose impoverished subjectivity only got in the way."[67] His insistence on a human connection actually bolsters the case for toons as live performers, because they do atavistically bear the "human" traces, or shadows, of the animators' work (as graphic drawings and as handiwork in posing puppets). And toons may have embodied characters, whereas bots often only have names and no other "personality." Blau's reference to the "omnipresent shadow of the apparently vanished being" describes the pianists' and the animators' roles as the invisible enablers of liveness and reminds us of their uncanny absent bodies in the performance *of* animation. Kevin Brown has entered the debate and observes that Auslander may have overreached in attributing too much autonomy to his bot, which "could be said to be 'performing' intelligence. Therefore, the capacity for a machine such as a chatterbot to perform 'live' may depend more on an observer's *perceptions* than any innate ability of the machine to perform."[68] The same could be said for animation and Pianola performances: determining agency liveness is one of the parts played by the film viewers and the player-piano audiences.

One difference between bots and toons might be that, in classic animation, no one was fooled into thinking that a toon was an alive body on the loose in the theater. Auslander's chatterbots, on the contrary, are meant to deceive users into thinking they are chatting with other humans. Brown concludes with an observation that is critical for understanding how animation—and non-animated cinema, for that matter—may be live: "'Liveliness' and 'presence' must be understood as qualities experienced by an audience of a performance, not just as qualities of the performer giving that performance. A performer does not necessarily need to be 'alive' in order to convince an audience member that their performance is 'live.' A performer does not necessarily need to be 'present' in order to demonstrate 'presence.' Instead, the performer *performs* presence and *performs* liveness. Therefore, presence and liveness, viewed in this way, are *beliefs* held by the audience."[69]

Of course, insisting that performativity is a belief system invites innumerable debates anchored in aesthetics, anthropology, philosophy, ideology, psychology, and religion. The pertinence for animation performance is that toons, whose on-screen bodies are unstable, and who have no off-screen living bodies, no physical being, no psychology, and no personality except that which has been constructed for them, may nonetheless perform for us in real time because the screen evidence suggests that that is what's happening, and we grant it. This is similar to the relationship we have with our computers. Michele White noted, "Computers are often spoken about as if they were animate. Phrases like 'it told me' are used to describe system error notices and other software-generated texts."[70] Similarly, animation aficionados cocreate liveness and enjoy embodying inanimate characters as alive. It's often useful to believe in, and to encourage others to believe in, the existence of something known not to be present.

Animators, indeed, have been playing this game of toon-human commutation for many years. Animated characters often have appeared on-screen with filmed humans, and humans have often performed as toons. Most of Cohl's films use hybrid or alternating scenes of human actors and animated action. Animation's early association with vaudeville also anchored the form in the framework of liveness. After McCay would put Gertie through her paces during his stage version, and he had entered the frame to have her carry him off for the finale, live McCay returned

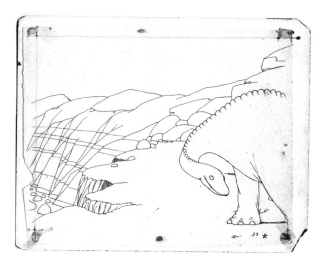

FIGURE 7. *Gertie* (1914). Curtain call sequence. Original drawing courtesy of David L. Nathan, M.D.

for his curtain call—and brought out "live" on-screen Gertie for hers. Although the sequence was not included in the 1914 film version, the stage performance (for which some of the original drawings exist) had Gertie returning for her curtain call. She bows to the audience and acknowledges their applause (Figure 7).[71] Another early example is from *Alice's Wonderland* (Ub Iwerks/Disney, 1923). An animated mouse on a drawing board pokes a "live" cat in the ear, essentially engaging it as though it were a fellow toon (Figure 8). Alice enters the animated world by camera tricks and performs toonally (for example, by graphically signaling her emotions as punctuation marks). In *Rudy Vallee Melodies* (Dave Fleischer, 1932) Betty "brings to life" the most popular crooner of her day by inviting him to join her party. She conjures Vallee's portrait from a sheet music cover into the live-action filmed singer. The "human" animator in *The Cartoonist's Nightmare* is made to experience what it's like to be a toon. (It's not pleasant.) These cartoons "work" because on film the live-animated relationship is transposable. This explains how Betty can act as a "live" character and have a conversation with "live" Eddie Valiant in *Who Framed Roger Rabbit?* Viewers are content in their belief that they're both movie actors. And, more generally, the predilection for animated films to adapt fairy tales or to make original narratives with fairytale-like stories shows a pantheistic belief in the continuity and interchangeability of living and inanimate beings.

FIGURE 8. *Alice's Wonderland* (1923). A live-cat and cartoon-mouse game.

When Disney pushed his animators to innovate embodied acting, personality animation, and toon behavior based on human emotions, he was attempting to reduce the live-real gap of proximal liveness. "Life" became one of his favorite metaphors. He repeatedly exhorted his staff to provide audiences with "a caricature of life and action."[72] In some revealing remarks on *Snow White*, he professed a Stanislavskian belief in the ability of animation to provide individuation, emotion, and personality for the characters. He dismissed figurative performance—implicitly that of passé Mickey Mouse—as "just shadows": "Our most important aim is to develop definite personalities in our cartoon characters. We don't want them to be just shadows, for merely as moving figures they would provoke no emotional response from the public. Nor do we want them to parallel or assume the aspects of human beings or human actions. We invest them with life by endowing them with human weaknesses which we exaggerate in a humorous way. Rather than a caricature of individuals, our work is a caricature of life."[73]

Disney, despite a bit of obfuscation, honed in on a crucial attribute of animation performance. In non-animated film performance, representation relies on photographic traces of human actors. Cartoon performance, however, with its manufactured bodies and environments, allows more control over the degree of liveness than does non-animated film. Disney's experiments focused on the animators, whom he charged with drawing the characters in moving and expressive ways to "invest them with life," that is, to make it easier for viewers to experience them as individualized actors and participate in world-making as they would in ordinary cinema. At the same time, he implies that an excessively mimetic style (for instance, rotoscoping) would paradoxically deprive the beings of some of their liveness if their properties as toons diminished too much.[74]

Animators from most of the studios developed a penchant for simulating the optical conditions of photography in the animation drawings.[75] Incorporating animated "accidents" into the film (breaks in projection, out-of-focus shots, hairs in the picture, peeks at Betty's bra) exploited neatly the conundrum of cartoon liveness. In *Mickey's Fire Brigade* (Ben Sharpsteen/Disney, 1935), a fire hose sprays the "lens" of the "camera" and the water sheets down, distorting the image for a second. There are layers of liveness here: first, it's implied that the scene is being acted out in front of us, as if it were a filmed movie with "live" action. (If that had really been the case, the cartoon might have been a token, not a performance.) Second, although the performance is occurring in the real time of projection for the theater audience, it's obvious that the plot is set in another time and place, and that the cartoon has been executed in the past. Furthermore, we have no expectation that the hose will get *us* wet. Then the exaggerated, vertiginous point-of-view shots exploit somatic immersion in the scene (the famous rollercoaster effect). That Mickey careening on his ladder can make us woozy suggests that the experience is as live as real life.

It may be that "liveness" is a troublesome and indistinct category because mediatization deprives a performing human being the aura of uniqueness and irreproducibility that we've come to expect in popular dramatic art. Auslander gives as an example the "live" adaptations made from Disney features that routinely emulate those cartoon properties:

> [Live performance's] traditional status as auratic and unique has been wrested from it by an ever-accelerating incursion of reproduction into the live event. Following [Walter] Benjamin, I might argue that live performance has indeed been pried from its shell and that all performance modes, live or mediatized, are now equal: none is perceived as auratic or authentic. . . . Similarly, it makes little sense to ask which of the many identical productions of *Tamara* or Disney's *Beauty and the Beast* is the "authentic" one. It does not even make sense to ask which of the many iterations of that *Beauty and the Beast*—as animated film, videocassette, CD, book, or theatrical performance—is the "authentic" iteration.[76]

Such performances highlight the commutation of human-toon bodies. The anonymous actors who figure Disney characters in theme park costumes are the necessary vehicles for the live performance, but they are uninteresting as actors in their own right. The humans are interchangeable, without uniqueness. It is the character that is the authentic performer, not the living, sweating college student in the princess outfit. She is the "animator," but her identity and the fact that she is alive are of little aesthetic consequence.

Animators and cartoon aficionados were way ahead of the theorists. The liveness of animation long ago became a joke enjoyed by filmmakers and audiences alike. The mockumentary style of *Betty Boop's Rise to Fame* and *Making 'Em Move* and the psychodrama of *The Cartoonist's Nightmare* bolster Auslander and Shaviro's claims by unmasking the ambiguity of liveness in the performing arts. They subvert—caricature, we're tempted to say—Disney's "caricature of life." The "presence" of toons further caricatures the putative liveness and uncanniness attributed to all cinematic experiences.

A STAR IS DRAWN

Stars, as Richard Dyer's book title so succinctly expressed it, are heavenly bodies.[77] But can toons like Betty, Mickey, Popeye, Porky, and the others be stars when their bodies are so far from heaven?

Performance studies and the study of film performance and stardom developed along parallel but mutually unaware tracks, both focusing on the rhetoric of the body. But when applying the study of film stars to that of toons, there's an obvious problem when we try to define stardom as a dialectic clash between the appearance and behaviors of actors on-screen and their private lives off-screen. This is because of the peculiar status of toon bodies. They are corporeal—as we've seen, through embodiment, agency, and proximal liveness—yet they have no physical body, which short-circuits the film theory. If stars must have two bodies, one an artificial construct and one "real," then we must look again at those believed-in beings, the toons.

I insist that Betty Boop was a movie star. Maybe she was no Garbo, but she held her own with the likes of, say, Ginger Rogers in the 1930s. Mickey and Popeye became hugely popular stars, but were they John Waynes? Let's begin with Betty, who was, as her theme song claimed, "the little queen of the animated screen."[78]

Since *all* performance *in* animation is constructed, the ingredients of stardom must be included in that category. Historically, animators have often assembled figurative performances by poaching traits from stars in the non-animated firmament. In the 1920s and '30s animators studied the physical movements and personae of silent clowns Chaplin and Keaton, for example, to re-perform them as Felix and Mickey. Cartoons from the 1930s and '40s are rife with animated cameos by Chaplin, Garbo, W.C. Fields, Al Jolson, and, of course, Brice and Chevalier.[79] These re-performances bask in the auras of movie stars by equating the status of the animated actors with that of the humans. Caricatures of powerful Hollywood personalities also demonstrate how toons acquire agency through parody. Drawing movie czar Will Hays as the crowned "king" of Hollywood in *Mickey's Gala Premier* (Burt Gillett/Disney, 1933), or smudging the line between human and animated existence and venturing into the uncanny valley by having toon Betty address human Chevalier too intimately as "Chevy," are animators' ways of mixing bouquets and brickbats: flattering by inclusion, while mocking or demeaning the social agency of Hays and the megastar cred of Chevalier. The filmmakers imported these non-animated movie-star trappings to re-perform the artifice of stardom.

Paul Wells's remarks on CGI animated characters are applicable to all toon stars: their existence interrogates "the boundaries of 'star' paradigms predicated on codes and conventions which do not embrace them."[80] This happens through parody and creative re-performances of "straight" stardom that foregrounds its flagrant self-construction as toon celebrity. In *Mickey's Gala Premiere,* iconic (human) Hollywood stars embrace the mouse as one of their own in the "real" Grauman's Chinese Theater—until the scene is exposed as the fantastic dream of a starstruck Mickey. Of course, being awakened by Pluto's slurps while dreaming of Greta Garbo's moist kisses implicitly acknowledges that, in 1933, Mickey and Pluto's popularity rivaled Garbo's. Mickey's stardom, in John Belton's happy phrase, lay precisely in his "imaginary form of existence."[81] So Mickey's wet dream of being bussed by a movie star ironically comes true, but it's toon star Pluto and not the Divine One who is kissing him. The animators brilliantly use the dream narrative to celebrate Mickey and Pluto's star power while effacing it behind Mickey's "aw shucks" veneer of countrified humility—precisely one of the humanizing traits that helped make him a star.

Cartoons also parodied the mediatized lives of stars as they rose to fame by creating, for instance, off-screen biographies of Bugs Bunny in *A*

Hare Grows in Manhattan (Friz Freleng/Warner Bros., 1947) and *What's Up Doc?* (Robert McKimson/Warner Bros., 1950). Through most of the twentieth century, Hollywood colluded with the popular press to convince moviegoers that screen performances were simply recordings of actors' "natural," effortless, unacted behaviors; according to this interpretation, there is no distance between screen acting and the lives portrayed.[82] *Rise to Fame* and *Making 'Em Move* depict this star-making process for us, substituting toons for human actors. Those animated actors are simply cartoon characters being themselves before the camera.

This publicity strategy of on-screen/off-screen convergence in early Hollywood practice led to typecasting, which Pamela Wojcik has described as "the assumed homology between actor and role, and role and appearance."[83] Most later theories of screen stardom rejected the identity of actor and role and emphasized instead the dissonance between the performed image of the human star on-screen and the unmediated life and activities of the actor-worker, the "real" person, the "lived" being off-screen.

The existence of animation stars triggers a reassessment of this neat somatic definition of stardom. Toons, according to the homology approach, would be perfectly typecast actors. How they appear is who they really are. Barrier, for example, observed this unity of character in *Snow White*: "In [Vlad] Tytla's animation of Grumpy, that gap between 'inner' and 'outer'—the gap that Stanislavski called upon the human actor to bridge—simply did not exist. Whatever passed through Grumpy's mind, it seemed, was simultaneously visible in his face and body, through acting of a kind that was possible only with a cartoon character."[84] Achieving stardom, however, is challenging for animated beings that don't inhabit physical bodies and therefore lack the performed body/real body umbilicus that so many acting theories insist on. Although it makes sense when critics say that a human actor has mastered or owns a particular character, in cartoons Popeye doesn't own his character; he *is* Popeye.[85]

The human stars of the classical Hollywood period were largely commercial products of invention and consumption, as were animated actors. The stars' screen personae were related to their off-screen lives, of course, but the studio system and the popular media also shaped the public's knowledge of those lives. Although actors who are stars frequently have special skills and innate talents, those who shape the image and those who adore it determine stardom too. Thus the alleged gap between screen image and human being out of which the star was supposed to emerge was itself a fallacy. When we learn about Betty's professional history and private life from her films and the visit of the fan magazine reporter, it is comparable to what the public understood about the private lives of their human stars.

Wells listed some figurations of classic toon stars: "The 'symbolic' identity of the characters was well understood—Mickey as 'John Doe', Donald as 'the average irascible American', Betty as the sexually harassed 'flapper', Bugs as a 'wise-ass-victor'—and this, in effect, was part of their currency as 'stars.'"[86] Star identities are created and function in the same way for toon and human performers because this process is a function *of* the animated performance, external to the films. Certainly, studios, animators, and commercial sponsors would like their characters to be idolized at home, at the box office, and in the toy store and supermarkets, but these volatile meanings are not something they can control.

Toon and human stars share the bond of both being highly constructed identities that develop over time, a performativity that extends beyond their acting in any particular film.[87] When we speak of a non-animated screen performance, whether it's Ginger Rogers in *Kitty Foyle* (Sam Wood/RKO, 1940) or John Wayne in *Stagecoach* (John Ford/Walter Wanger Productions, 1939), we are not referring to the separate takes and retakes, the edited-out footage, the special effects, the work of Foley artists and vocal dubbers, the ingenuity of the makeup and prosthetic artists, or the actors' stand-ins, stunt doubles, and body doubles during the filming, not to mention the director. Rather, we mean the composite finished performance that we believe to have been acted out by whole, unfragmented human actors. True, toon personages like Betty, Beans, and Mickey were completely manufactured, but so too were the on-screen characterizations created by Rogers and Wayne as their careers developed alongside classic animation. Ginger and John had off-screen identities, although it was hard to know how much was genuine and how much came from the pens of imaginative writers. The toons had off-screen lives too, also blatantly designed and fictitious. Paraphrasing the reflexively prescient Jessica Rabbit, they were just drawn that way.

There is, of course, a robust genre of "a star is born" non-animated movies. Not surprisingly, there are also cartoons that burlesque the myth. In his detailed analysis of *A Star Is Hatched* (Friz Freleng/Schlesinger, 1938), Hank Sartin shows how the parodic cartoon manipulated the myth of the girl who comes to Hollywood and becomes a star against all odds. "The cartoon thus works as parody always does, eliciting pleasure in the viewer[s] by affirming their mastery of cultural knowledge. This mastery involves both an acknowledgment of the cultural value of the object of parody, and the pleasure of mastering that object through transgression."[88] The celebrity mechanisms are supposed to be invisible, creating the impression that movie stars are anointed spontaneously by the public's affectionate (or scandalized) responses. However, everyone knows—and this is why the cartoon parodies work—that press agents, fan magazines, and star biographies developed the behind-the-scenes legends that were supposed to show the private lives of the stars.

Thus, according to their biographical legends, the young Marion Morrison and Virginia McMath were predestined to become John Wayne and Ginger Rogers. Their individual traits (they were good-looking WASPs, with an unpretentious manner, laconic speaking style, and distinctive but pleasant Midwest accents) and their talents (his "natural" acting, her singing, dancing, and wisecracking) precertified them for stardom. Screen acting, according to these discursive constructions, extends from a person's natural expression, as in Wayne's "masculine" gait. "Wayne," we learn, "though too slow to succeed at college football, was well coordinated, surprisingly graceful for a large man. He had what Howard Hawks would call 'an "I-own-the-world" way of walking.' That was the effect [director Raoul] Walsh was looking for: 'The sonuvabitch looked like a *man*.'"[89] (Note the importance of body movement as a character- and gender-defining trait, both in live-action and animated performance.) For Ginger Rogers, her not-yet-a-star performance as a chorine singing the pig Latin version of "We're in the Money" in *42nd Street* (Lloyd Bacon/Warner Bros., 1933) was evidence of her exceptional natural skills and her innate star quality.

Richard DeCordova referred to these off-screen body performances as a discourse on the *picture personality*. Graver called the offstage actor's body the *personage*. According to DeCordova, "As the actor is increasingly individualized, the name supports an expansion of the actor's identity through writing that reveals what she or he is 'really like' behind the screen. The actor is assigned a personality, a love life, and perhaps even a political persuasion."[90] We're invited to extrapolate this identity primarily through signs that build the character from the outside, through studio and journalistic narratives, and across films, as illustrated in *Betty Boop's Rise to Fame*. Graver insists that personages "have presences generated by stories outside the immediate context of the play." There is a clear parallel between picture personalities, theatrical personages, and the similarly fabricated stories of cartoon beings' off-screen lives. He continues, "The interior of this body can be composed of personal history, public gossip, or a performing career." Hence, in biopics like Betty's, the "rise to fame" narrative positions her as a celebrity body because audiences "see on stage [read: on screen] what they know (or think they know) about the life and career of the actor. . . . The exterior of the personage is composed of distinctive physical features, typical gestures or vocal tones, the marks of personal history or the ghosts of past performances."[91] Betty's clips validate her as just such a personage. The high-profile Helen Kane affair, when the songstress who first had popularized the spit-curled look and Boop-oop-a-doop song sued the Fleischers, thus challenging Betty's agency and questioning her legal right to exist, added just the right touch of off-screen scandal.

Fans may construct stars against the actors' will. Despite stage mother Lela Rogers's campaign to cast her daughter in roles that would highlight her comic and dramatic talents as well as her dancing ability, Ginger Rogers's fans, recalling her performances in *42nd Street* and *Gold Diggers of 1933* (Mervyn LeRoy/Warner Bros., 1933), tenaciously, albeit incorrectly, believed that she had begun her career as just such a chorus girl.[92] For Wayne, his figuration as an American cowboy defined his stardom, and the public insisted that he live the part off-screen. As Garry Wills opined, "He had to fill some need in his audience. He was the conduit they used to communicate with their own desired selves or their own imagined past. When he was called *the* American, it was a statement of what his fans wanted America to be."[93] We have since learned that Wayne privately hated horses, preferred suits and ties to jeans, and "had to remind himself to say 'ain't' offscreen."[94] What analogous cultural conduits were imagined for toons such as Betty?

For one thing, Betty Boop captured the ambivalent image of assertive, sexually liberated women that the media cultivated in the late 1920s, blending the Prohibition-era showgirl and burlesque queen with the songstress Kane and the film stars Colleen Moore, Joan Crawford, and Clara Bow. These movie flappers expressed contradictory traits of childishness and voluptuousness, virginity and availability. By the early 1930s, though, the flapper no longer was a viable social presence. The Depression movie heroine was more materialistic, like Barbara Stanwyck, or spunky, wholesome, domesticated, and practical, like Rogers. Betty's character transformed after 1934 as well, when animators curbed her performance of exuberant femininity under the influence of the Hays Code. Whether girls and women in the early 1930s responded against the grain to read Betty as a model for their own embodiment and cultural resistance is a subject for further research.[95] As a female who outsmarted patriarchy and rose above her sexual aggressors to achieve powerful screen agency, she may well have connected with self-realizing women of the time. Certainly today's performative appeal of Betty as a sexed female body is strong, not the least as a design archetype for the empowered girl-women of anime and as a tattooed emblem of contemporary girl culture.

For humans, the preparatory or conditional phase of acting involves learning a part, establishing ownership of the role, staying "in character," and finding the right "mask," in Naremore's terms.[96] For toons, the analogous pre-performance included the animators molding a character's type and developing a distinctive personality that was consistent from film to film (although it could evolve). Studios enforced character consistency by providing animators with specific guides (for instance, model sheets) and general education through figure-drawing classes and apprenticeships under senior artists.[97] The producers encouraged moviegoers to engage with stars by joining fan clubs and attending Saturday matinees as affinity groups (Mickey and Betty fans, for instance). Just like human actors, the leading animated stars had their own catchy theme songs, doll effigies, lunch boxes, paper cutouts, and other franchised products, such as canned spinach, carrots, and peanut butter, all of which helped to authenticate their off-screen existence. Then there are the notorious Tijuana bibles, those pornographic booklets that purport to show us the raunchy sex lives of stars such as Betty and Popeye— sometimes together.[98]

Graver has challenged Stanislavsky's embodiment model that posits twinned actors, one "living" and another being who is the character represented on stage. In fact, he claims that members of theatrical audiences scarcely attend to the actor: "We do not really see the character in a drama in addition to the actor representing that character; rather, we see the actor as a character within drama's universe of discourse."[99] For animation performance, we might rewrite this as: We don't regard toons as additions to the drawings of the characters or as the constitutive work of the animators (acting); rather, we see the animators' conditional performance and the toons' performance unified as one in the Tooniverse.

A personage has a history, that is, an on-screen series of roles and an off-screen biography. "Almost from the beginning, movie stars were regarded as aesthetic objects rather than as artists, or as personalities who had a documentary reality. Griffith and many other directors strengthened the 'organic' effect by inserting details from an actor's real life into the fiction," writes Naremore. He notes how the classical narrative worked recursively to unite these identities: "In *True Heart Susie,* for example, when Susie carries on imaginary conversations with the photograph of her dead mother, the picture she looks at shows Lillian Gish's own mother, cradling the infant Lillian in her arms."[100] The filmmakers use re-performance to prove the toons' prior existence by including movie clips from Betty's and Mickey's past films, by including earlier characters from Schlesinger cartoons (Beans, the villains), and by showing them dialoguing with "live" actors or caricatures of human stars.

It follows that, since toon stars' agency on the screen is often in question (because of their obvious artifice as graphics or puppets), audiences must constantly reauthenticate them on their own terms to sustain their belief. Graver's *performer* category of embodiment applies to them, as exemplified by Betty. The actor "displays an expressive body, a body involved in a communicative activity. If, in conventional drama, the characters and dramatic action are the message of the theatrical event, the actor's performing body is the medium of this message."[101] As in his example of a street performer, our animated performers also have to establish their authority and credentials, hence it's important for Betty to reenact and reauthenticate her rise to stardom as a movie.

TOONS AND CAMP

Dyer's classic take on stardom focuses less on the studio-constructed image of stars than on the conflict between the lived biological body of the actor and its reception. In these consumer-created off-screen bodies, he sees contingency and capriciousness wafting on the whims of popular opinion. He writes, "Logically, no one aspect [of the phenomena that define a star] is more real than another. How we appear is no less real than how we have manufactured that appearance, or than the 'we' that is doing the manufacturing. Appearances are a kind of reality, just as manufacture and individual persons are. However, manufacture and the person . . . are generally thought to be more real than appearance in this culture. Stars are obviously a case of appearance—all we know of them is what we see and hear before us."[102] In other words, he thinks that it doesn't matter that much to film audiences how closely a star's image matches the person, since most of them prefer an actor's qualities as a manufactured being to those of the underlying person.[103] That this reasoning is relevant for understanding toons as stars seems clear: although toons don't have physical bodies or lived lives, for their stardom that's immaterial from the fans' perspective.

There are some human celebrities who are stars precisely because moviegoers will not accept as real either their on- or off-screen image. When fans appropriate a star's image and construct a rogue version of it that denies the star's authenticity, the result is camp. Subcultural fans substituted their own self- or group-constructed bodies for stars of the likes of Montgomery Clift, Marilyn Monroe, and Judy Garland. Dyer points out that such viewers believe that the star's on-screen performance is "acting," that is, not authentic. They also reject, however, the off-screen story of the actors' private lives. The stars' "authentic" authenticity resides only in the group's collective construction.

We usually associate camp with gay cultural and aesthetic performativity; in animation, it is best exemplified by the king (and queen) of camp, the cross-dressing, same-sex-kissing Bugs Bunny.[104] Although there is by no means an agreed-upon definition of camp, performances exhibiting this quality generally depend on "style, taste, wit, parody or drag," notes Michael Bronski. Camp's hallmarks, exaggeration and flamboyance, are a kind of joke, yet at the same time they are serious expressions. "Camp," Bronski continues, "is the re-imagining of the material world into ways and forms which transform and comment upon the original. It changes the 'natural' and 'normal' into style and artifice."[105] For animated performance, not only is gender constructed according to these criteria, but everything about toons is a reimagining of one believed world as another. Animators unmask stardom and vogue stars and assimilate their personae into a show of what we might call *secular camp*.

It's easy to see the relation of specific animated performances to camp practice, as when Betty repossesses the bodies of known stars to "do" Brice and Chevalier or when Pluto plays Al Jolson. But, indeed, the whole enterprise of making toon stars is inherently camp in the sense that the performers are living the lives of movie actors vicariously for their fans. Steven Cohan contends, "Camp strategies for achieving ironic distance from the normative have always exploited the slippery space between a 'posture' and an 'imposture,' between 'resembling' and 'dissembling'—in one way or another, camp signaled the queer eye for a straight guise."[106] When Popeye behaves as a sailor, when Mickey performs in blackface, and when Porky Pig recites poetry though challenged by his stuttering, these animated beings are transforming and commenting on the performativity of actors with lived bodies. The animators construct their film actors to mimic bodied actors, thereby hoping establish through audiences their characters' otherwise elusive authenticity. As a critical practice, seeing animation as a form of camp not only gives us insight into Hollywood gender and sexual performance conventions, but it also emblematizes cartoons' relationship to mainstream cultural production as a secondary, marginalized production practice.

Betty's performance is camp because she *resembles* a woman, but, because she's a toon, she also *dissembles*. This is "feminist camp" of the sort Wojcik describes. Betty re-performing "womanliness" is without biological authenticity, but her performance is also without social authenticity, since it is a product solely of male manufacture. "The masquerade," Robertson Wojcik writes, "mimics a constructed identity in order to conceal that there is nothing behind the mask; it simulates femininity to dissuade the absence of a real or essential feminine identity."[107] Toon bodies, whether masculine, feminine, or androgynous, similarly act out masquerading beings, appearing to be figures or embodied actors despite their lack of a living actor's body. Paraphrasing Robertson Wojcik's comments on gender parody, this body parody in animation doesn't differ in structure from the activity of the masquerade, but it self-consciously theatricalizes masquerade's construction of toons' identities.[108] Like camp appropriations of stars' looks and bodies to produce something that is more authentically felt than what studios and fan magazines provide, toons similarly practice movie acting to create authenticity without authorization by the stars they caricature or by the film industry at large.

Authenticity usually means that fans accept actors as they "really" seem to be in private. This view assumes that fans are naïve and don't know that these images have been "spun." Authenticity, according to Dyer, "is both a quality necessary to the star phenomenon to make it work and also the quality that guarantees the authenticity of the other particular values a star embodies (such as girl-next-door-ness, etc.). It is this effect of authenticating authenticity that gives the star charisma."[109] Riffing on Dyer, we can say that Betty's "rise to fame" is a perfect example of faking authenticating authenticity. The scenes resemble those on a clip reel, which we believe to be proof of a prior existence. Her visible ability to move in the same filmic universe as humans and to possess apparent weight and mass (she responds to gravity and casts a shadow, for example) give her somatic traits that temper her distinctly not-human and unreal qualities. This is in addition to all the tools of the trade of "character animation" that went into this masquerade (movement, voice, figure design, scale, character-centered narrative). When Betty performs sexuality, she's clearly camping it up.

Mickey's Gala Premier actually provides a neat allegory for reading cartoons as camp versions of Hollywood. As the stars rollick in the aisles laughing at Disney's cartoon within the cartoon, Mickey is at the center of their attention as well as ours. And he's the center of the story. He's the star. He's the authentic masquerade. This cartoon gives us a world where human movie stars are reduced to hollow caricatures. They've become less authentic than Mickey Mouse and have been demoted to disembodied members of the real star's supporting cast.

ANIMATION PERFORMATIVITY

What we consider acting in cartoons is really no different from other acting, whether on or off the movie screen. In the age of artificial intelligence and the convergence of humans and computers in the arts, entertainment, and everyday life, it's increasingly likely that performativity will become a crucial issue.

There are many lovers of animation who prefer to see it as a radically different, implicitly subversive form that operated against Hollywood. Examining its performativity, though, shows that classic cartoons' difference from movies was a matter of emphasis, not essence. True, toons' flamboyant, campy otherness vis-à-vis humans has often marked animation. Their cartoon worlds have tended to create and celebrate strangeness. Unlike the abstract, avant-garde, and independent animated films that reject, ignore, or attack the fundamental assumptions of Hollywood cinema, the commercial studio productions we've been focusing on maintain an entente cordiale with mainstream movies. This is most apparent in cartoon acting, which, as we've seen, is subject to the same controversies and competing conceptualizations as acting in general.

Naremore introduced his foundational text on screen acting by observing, "The most interesting figures on the screen often look 'natural,' as if they were merely lending themselves to the manipulations of script, camera, and editing." It's unlikely that he had animated actors in mind, but his words are pertinent. We sense a strong performing presence, even in those toons that are simple figurations, as though they're at home in their worlds. Characters in the embodied mode are capable of poignant or comic engagement by viewers. Naremore concludes, "Clearly films depend on a form of communication whereby meanings are *acted* out; the experience of watching them involves not only a pleasure in story-telling but also a delight in bodies and expressive movement, an enjoyment of familiar performing skills, and an interest in players as 'real persons.' "[110] Cartoons give us real movement, real acting, real-time performances. They convey liveness. That the actors don't possess real bodies is irrelevant because the animators, as the mainstream filmmakers did, have provided them in the form of implied bodies and made-up biographies. What the cartoonists don't supply, the fans do.

If film performances by human screen actors are masquerades or secular camp built on simultaneously affirming as real something that obviously isn't, then animation performance is an extreme manifestation of irony. Not only may toons be constituted as personages and accepted as stars, but it is entirely possible that certain animated performers and performances will be more effective than those in mainstream movies. This might be the case, for example, with the child actors in *Grave of the Fireflies* (Isao Takahata, 1988) or the animated autobiographical protagonist of *Waltz with Bashir* (Ari Folman, 2008). As for favorite performers, assuredly there are those who will prefer Betty to Ginger, Mickey to John Wayne, or Homer Simpson to . . . well, to anyone.

PART TWO

Historical Contingencies

CHAPTER 3

The Acme of Variegated Entertainment

On January 25, 1914, the bitter cold kept most of the regular patrons of Hammerstein's Victoria Theatre at home. The show people didn't mind. New Yorkers were blasé and hard to please. On the other hand, the out-of-towners in the house, called "rubes" by the vaudevillians (most of whom themselves hailed from some flyspeck hamlet, Brooklyn, or the Lower East Side), were reliably enthusiastic. These customers delved deeply into their bellies for laughs, applauded wildly after every magic trick, and could be counted on to cry during the melancholy songs about consumptive daughters and drunken fathers.

As the weight lifter grunted through his labors, Myra killed time in the wings knitting, making a woolen hat for her boy while mentally calculating and spending the small sum they would make tonight. Joe did what he did best, talking to Myra or to himself—it was hard to say which—about improvements to the routine. The boy could wander about anywhere he liked as long as he didn't get in the way of the other performers or stand where the patrons could see him. His big eyes sucked in every sight. He attended to every sound and smell, especially the showgirls' sweet scents, but he seldom said much. Joe didn't know if he was really smart or really dumb, but he knew that he was their bread and butter. He was eighteen years old, not really a kid anymore, but thank God he still looked like one. When he came out as a pugnacious leprechaun, with his red wig and scraggly beard, green suit, and clay pipe, even the New Yorkers screamed with mirth. As Myra and Joe sang and danced their jigs, Joe batted the boy around. After many pratfalls, for the big climax, Joe would chuck him into the orchestra, where a cornetist waited to catch him.

Tonight there was a new attraction on the bill. As he did with all the acts, the kid studied this one closely. He had never heard of Winsor Mc-Cay, but he knew "Little Nemo in Slumberland" in the funny papers, and this guy drew it. To get a better view, he snuck out into the house. The cartoonist made a few charcoal drawings on a big easel. The boy had seen lots of lightning sketch acts, and this one was no better or worse, but then the cartoonist said that he would bring his drawing of a dinosaur to life. That would be something! A sheet descended from the flies and the orchestra segued into a quiet syncopated cakewalk. Damn, he did it. The cartoonist's lines flickered like they had the St. Vitas, but sure enough, the big monster was moving as though alive, did tricks, and seemed to understand the cartoonist's patter. It brought down the house. McCay returned to the stage and his pet dinosaur came along to take a bow with him. Buster did not applaud, but his big eyes stayed wide open.

Buster Keaton could not have imagined that he would be an internationally famous filmmaker himself in a few years. He succeeded in part by re-performing elements of vaudeville as movie gags and delivering them with the grace of a body hardened by a thousand falls. But the memory of these nights with the dinosaur Gertie haunted him. In his film *Three Ages*, Keaton paid homage to McCay, first in the title and plot, which were inspired by McCay's "The Seven Ages" act, and then when caveman Buster makes his appearance on the back of an animated clay dinosaur. In one scene in McCay's cartoon, a woolly mammoth swims far out into a lake before Gertie picks up a stone and flings it at the swimming target, hitting it with perfect precision. In *Our Hospitality* (1923), Buster swings out over a waterfall to snatch his girlfriend just as she goes over, his exquisite timing the equal of Gertie's. A cannon in *The General* (1926) seems destined to blast Buster's locomotive, but the instant it fires, his train hits a curve and the cannonball fires instead on the enemy's engine far up the track. In other films, though the cartoon references are not explicit, Keaton plots the timing with the exactitude of an animator.

McCay's finish was unforgettable. When the wiry little man wearing an evening jacket and snapping a trainer's whip called on Gertie to take him for a ride, she obliged by lowering her head. McCay slipped behind the sheet, reappeared in the picture as an animated version of himself, and exited triumphantly on Gertie's back. McCay adapted this vaudeville trick as the basis of the feature film *Sherlock Jr.* Projectionist Buster, just as the cartoonist did on stage, crosses the threshold of the movie frame, enters the picture, and leads a life therein that is much more romantic, heroic, and fantastic than everyday life outside the movies.[1]

THE PALACE (THEATER) OF MEMORY

In classic cartoons, a show could pop up anywhere, be it Santa's workshop, the night kitchen, the barnyard, or the bookstore. Institutions of live performance were among the venues that figured most prominently in animation plots and scenery. Nightclubs, burlesque shows, opera houses, circuses, cabaret, boxing rings, bullfight rings, and, not surprisingly, Hollywood studios and movie palaces constitute some of the privileged sites of the Tooniverse. Among the entertainments portrayed were singing, dancing, revues, follies, minstrel shows, carnival sideshows, and the ever-popular chorus lines. As a result, the performativity of cartoons became synonymous with traditions absorbed from the popular theater, many of which survive as cartoon archetypes. If Hollywood cartoons have a soul, it is vaudeville.

My thoughts turned to this intermediality while pondering *Vaudeville* (Dave Fleischer/Red Seal, 1924). Many of the Out of the Inkwell films are fragmented, bizarre, and inscrutable, but this one is among the strangest. It will launch an exploration of the debt that the Tooniverse owed to burlesque and vaudeville, once-vibrant popular entertainments. The animators also availed themselves of burlesque's body humor and risqué content. These films, like *Vaudeville,* transformed the fast-paced, heterogeneous, surreal, and race- and gender-bending elements once associated with popular theater into something uniquely cartoonish. They are memory palaces and chronotopes, that is, fictionalized times and places that we may call the *cartoon-vaudeville timescape.* All this exemplifies how animation developed historically to respond moviegoers' propensity to cocreate on-screen worlds of fiction and fantasy.

Although the era is now almost forgotten, there was a time when Americans' taste for live entertainment was satisfied by traveling shows. Itinerant celebrities did one-night stands in the local opera houses, theaters, burlesque halls, and vaudeville houses. A rich and varied institution since the 1880s, American vaudeville in its heyday was probably the second-favorite national pastime after baseball, and it peaked in popularity in the 1910s, just when Buster was watching McCay present his cartoons onstage.

Before the advent of radio and cinema, vaudeville was the cornerstone of the culture industry. Professing refinement and middle-class decorum, the colorful, energetic world of popular theater was a powerful cathartic for the new leisured middle class hoping to escape the routinized quotidian life of industrial America. In addition to astounding feats of singing, dancing, acrobatics, magic, and "science," one could experience the bizarre world of exotic "foreign" entertainers and their music. And animation, like vaudeville before it, provided audiences with a similar place to go for imaginative release.

Classic animated cartoons referenced stage acts, presentation styles, and character types so much that cartoons became a symbolic repository of past culture and the accrued knowledge of vaudeville. Especially when cartoon acting was primarily in the figurative mode, up until the mid-1930s, the approach resembled and extended vaudeville's performativity. Taken as a whole, cartoons are like the "memory palaces" described by Barbara Kirshenblatt-Gimblett, institutions that preserve artifacts of the past and construct histories, rationales, and intelligible interpretations of those objects. She observes, "The museum, particularly the natural history, science, and technology museum, is an archive of outmoded knowledge formations that have sedimented themselves in collections, catalogues, storage arrangements, particular modes of display, and the historically formed dispositions of its viewers."[2] Cartoons are not physical edifices. Rather, they became something like Malraux's concept of photography as a "museum without walls," preserving the outmoded knowledge called vaudeville, but also transforming it.[3] The memory palace is also like an archive in Foucault's sense: "By the word [archive], I do not mean the mass of texts that have been collected at a given period, or chanced to have survived oblivion from this period. I mean the set of rules that . . . a given period and . . . a definite society defined."[4] From the 1920s through the '40s, when vaudeville was dying, animation was setting the rules, preserving the knowledge of vaudeville and sculpting its meaning.

Dicing the idea of the memory palace a little finer, we can see that such institutions, whether museums or cartoon subjects, tend to be static, archiving their artifacts in ways that both preserve them and maintain their culturally approved interpretations. Many cartoons, especially those made during the era when vaudeville was still viable, provide archived traces of popular theater. "During the first few decades of the twentieth century," according to J.B. Kaufman, "a long-standing repertoire of gags and situations had become part of the basic equipment that united the brotherhood of stage and screen comedians."[5] Early animators were both contributing to vaudeville and living off it somewhat parasitically. After vaudeville was no longer a significant component of popular entertainment, it was still useful to cartoonists as an idea. It became historical fiction. The conundrum to consider now is why this declining popular entertainment remained such a fertile source of inspiration for animators.

One answer may be that vaudeville provided a readymade world, available to be shared as memory by filmmakers and their audiences. Specifically, this complex of associations is the *cartoon timescape*, an idea I am adapting from art historian Erwin Panofsky (who called it "historical time"), literary critic Mikhail Bakhtin (who called it a "chronotope," a Greek-inspired neologism literally meaning "time-place"), and sociologist Henri Lefebvre (who called it "representational space").[6] These related concepts express, with divergences, how meaning is produced for works that derive from historical phenomena. The timescape isn't a snapshot but rather a persistent fiction representing a bygone era.[7] Knowledge, imaginary significance, and symbolic functions have become attached to a certain place at a certain time in history. The term has been used, for instance, to describe how science fiction creates imagined settings that extrapolate the future from past and present environments.[8] Victor Hugo's evocation of medieval Paris in the novel *Notre-Dame de Paris* (1831)—its vivid street life, typical inhabitants, and cathedral—was based on romanticized history that had little to do with real life in the twelfth century. Later re-performances of Hugo's story, such as Disney's *The Hunchback of Notre Dame* (Gary Trousdale and Kirk Wise/Walt Disney Feature Animation, 1996), reinvoke, reinterpret, and then process the accrued meanings into something new. According to Panofsky, "When a historian says 'around 1500,' he does not mean a point in time at which, according to a conventionally determined starting point, the earth has made 1500 rotations around the sun. Rather, he means a point in time that is indicated not only by concrete events but also by specific and concrete cultural characteristics."[9]

Robert Stam notes that although Bakhtin "does not refer to the cinema, his category [the chronotope] seems ideally suited to it as a medium where 'spatial and temporal indicators are fused into one carefully thought-out concrete whole.' "[10] In fact, the notion of the timescape or chronotope seems *even better* suited to animation than to live-action cinema because animators specifically construct the spatial and temporal indicators in their films in order to achieve a predetermined effect and their audiences adapt the films to their own uses.[11]

The vaudeville-cartoon timescape mobilizes the past in the service of cartoon stories much in the way that literature and painting use history. For example, Bakhtin's treatment of the singer/author of epic songs and folktales is prescient for understanding how Out of the Inkwell and other reflexive animation narratives operate. These authorial figures write themselves into the chronotope as characters in the historical setting to show how they assisted in its construction. The author's self-performance in these epics became an expected part of the folkloric tradition, just as it did in self-figuring classic animation. Bakhtin continues, "Thus we can with relative clarity sense in the segmentation of ancient epic songs the chronotope of the singer and his audience, or the chronotope of storytelling in traditional tales. But even in the segmentation of a modern literary work we sense the chronotope of the represented world as well as the chronotope of the readers and creators of the work. That is, we get a mutual interaction between the world represented in the work and the world outside the work."[12]

In the Out of the Inkwell shorts, the distribution of performative power is layered, conforming to Bakhtin's model, but it is also circular. The person Max Fleischer is Executive Max, who is in charge of the studio and, in the organization chart, the boss of Director Dave. When he appears as an actor, though, his role is Sketcher Max, and Ko-Ko is his creation and reluctant avatar. In his capacity as head of animation, Dave is not usually seen on-screen, but he is present in the figure of Animator Dave. Animator Dave's avatars (since he directs and animates them) are Sketcher Max and Ko-Ko. It's also the case that Ko-Ko embodies Dave, both in shared clownish sensibilities and in their shared physical body. (Dave wearing a clown suit would be rotoscoped to generate Ko-Ko's lifelike action.)

In *Vaudeville*, we first see Sketcher Max as the familiar on-screen artist and Ko-Ko as his creation on the sketchpad, analogous to the subject and the song. Simultaneously, Executive Max and Animator Dave are operating outside the film (as with Bakhtin's author). These two realms are not separate but impinge upon each other in the manner of folk narration. They also correspond roughly to the concept of performance *in* and *of* animation. There are hints within the work of the structure of power outside the film (which Lefebvre and other Marxists considered to control the work invisibly). *Vaudeville* recalls the plots of antique literature, in which, Bakhtin observed, "we find the author outside the work as a human being living his own biographical life. But we also meet him as the creator of the work itself, although he is located outside the chronotopes represented in his work[.] He is as it were tangential to them."[13] This split author anticipates not only commonplace animation narratives but science fiction ones as well.[14] Accordingly, the film performances are designed to facilitate (albeit rather confusingly) the metaleptic experience of the observers, that is, their sensation of being involved in the action while watching it from the outside, which is "perceived as discrete and exclusively disjunctive."[15] Sketcher Max plays the role of artist-magician, drawing the clown and bringing it to life. Significantly, in the Out of the Inkwell narratives, Sketcher Max is not an animator and Ko-Ko is not an animation character; the former is a cartoonist making drawings and the latter is a pen-and-ink graphic on paper, the actions of which the neutral movie camera supposedly is recording. Both are performers *in* the animation. Executive Max and Animator Dave operate outside the fiction as the constructive agency behind the film, the performers *of* the animation.

A disembodied hand at a sketchpad draws a still image of Max Fleischer at his drafting table. It's difficult to read the hand as belonging to Sketcher Max because he is the subject being drawn by it. More likely it's the conventional hand of an off-screen animator-narrator who sets the film going, then withdraws from the on-screen action and remains out of sight for the duration. (Animator Dave here is reprising the "hand of the artist" motif dating back to the origins of animation.) Even at this point early in the story, the performance is nested and complex.

The hand of Animator Dave next paints over Max's sketched outline to complete the picture, which becomes a photographed image of Max. Once the photograph is complete, it springs into motion, revealing to us that it was a frozen film frame. Max, now a "normal" moving film image, enacts the role of sketch artist and applies his pen to fill in Ko-Ko's outline with black ink. Ko-Ko jerks into action, walks across the paper, and leaves the black "fill" of his drawn body behind him. This highlights his dual status as a drawn cartoon and as an animated image (composed of two elements, "ink and paint," that is, outline and fill). The segment also confirms Sketcher Max's dominance within the hierarchy *in* the story.

Max continues to antagonize the clown until it (the drawing/animated being) zips out of the white space of the paper into the studio and onto Max's shoulders. The sequence is a delightful demonstration of the existential leveling that occurs when animated and so-called live actors appear together on the screen; Sketcher Max (the animated human) and Ko-Ko (the animated clown) are equivalent products of photomechanical replication.

Max peels away the sheet of sketch paper to reveal the outline of a "set" representing a vaudeville theater. Ko-Ko starts working there as a ticket seller. A specific period, place, and mode of performance are invoked, with the obvious expectation that audiences will understand that the vaudeville setting is a memory palace and a timescape.

Vaudeville foregrounds the economic basis of the show as a cheap variety entertainment. Among the ramifications of the low cost of admission—we see that Ko-Ko's show costs thirty cents—is that the customer base is heterogeneous, which forces Ko-Ko, following a logic of free association typical of the Fleischers, into a hyperbolic joke on diversity. The clown devises a novel way of charging admission by assessing how much real estate each patron will occupy. He measures a rotund customer's ample derrière and sells her three tickets. Gags highlighting corporeality migrated freely from burlesque to vaudeville to cartoons. Trixie Friganza (fat and bawdy) and Charlotte Greenwood (skinny and limber), for example, were stage stars whose nonconforming physiques were part of their personae.[16] Cartoonists latched onto this body comedy with a vengeance. In *The Opry House* (Ub Iwerks/Disney, 1929), the customer who can't fit through the entrance to the theater is a fat pig. Mickey Mouse deflates him with a pin and in he goes. Similarly, Foxy punctures a rotund trolley passenger in *Smile, Darn Ya, Smile!* (Rudolf Ising/Schlesinger, 1931). Buxom sopranos were routinely caricatured on the stage, where they were often played by men in drag, as well as in cartoons, where they were represented by the likes of the fat soprano in *Piano Tooners* (John Foster and George Rufle/Van Beuren, 1932). The preeminent example of the cartoon soprano is Disney diva Clara Cluck, a statuesque operatic hen.

Inside his own vaudeville theater, Ko-Ko is now the master of ceremonies. He introduces each act, starting with the "Imitation of Will Rogers." (Rogers, the immensely popular former cowboy, had become a star of the Ziegfeld Follies, delivering trenchant political monologues while twirling his lariat.) Reminiscent of Keaton in *The Play House*

(1921), Ko-Ko performs all the roles, plays all the instruments in the pit, and even works as a stagehand. Naturally, each attraction is a bit of cartoon lunacy; in the trained seal act, the trainer turns out to be a seal disguised as a man.

When the Fleischers' short film appeared in 1924, its ostensible subject was in serious decline. In fact, cartoons and movies were part of vaudeville's problem. Because films were cheaper to produce than live acts, vaudeville managers ran short subjects to pad the program. Paul Terry's Aesop's Fables series, which included weekly Farmer Al Falfa cartoons, was made to be screened in the Keith-Albee-Orpheum national circuit of vaudeville houses. From 1921 to 1929, KAO was a part owner of Aesop's Fables. A program from a Keith house in 1921 shows an Aesop cartoon as the curtain raiser following intermission—probably a typical placement.[17] So the Fables, with their menagerie of anthropomorphic animals and hordes of mice running amok, were shown as interludes between live stage acts on the entertainment program. Even at picture palaces, cartoons were interspersed with live acts. Films such as *Amateur Night on the Ark* (Paul Terry/Van Beuren, 1923) or *In Vaudeville* (Harry Bailey et al./Van Beuren, 1926) would have meshed with the live novelties on the rest of the program. At Grauman's Metropolitan Theatre in Los Angeles, for example, Koko the Clown[18] shared the program with the feature film and with soprano Alice Gentle singing from "Cavalleria Rusticana," Don Phillippini conducting an orchestral interlude, and the Brown Sisters playing their accordions.[19] Viewers would have divided their attention among the short acts, the short films, and the feature. The likely result was a degree of commutability between film and vaudeville liveness.

An American Masters television program on vaudeville argues persuasively that the form incubated the comedy and the presentation style of classic cartoons.[20] Vaudeville action was fast-paced. The performances were short, similar to the length of a classic cartoon. They had to be "grabbers." The content was spectacular, over-the-top, compelling, and hypnotic—literally, in the case of popular mentalist acts. Moreover, like the *Literary Digest* or the Sunday newspaper, performances were calculated to appeal to viewers of every age and taste, from well-educated vaudeville aficionados to immigrants who did not speak English.[21] Vaudeville historian Robert M. Lewis emphasizes the urbanity and fast pace of the attractions: "By the 1890s vaudeville was perceived to be the variety show best adapted to the modern city. It was the distilled essence of the major entertainments, lowbrow, middlebrow, even high-brow. With machinelike efficiency, an assortment of brief, fast-pace acts passed in rapid succession—acrobats and animal acts, ballerinas and boxers, clowns and comedians. It was an eclectic mix, a miscellany—magic tricks and technological innovations, one-act playlets and slap-stick comedy, operatic arias and high-wire acrobatics. Almost any skill well-executed was included in the program."[22]

As Hollywood cartoons enjoyed their most prolific and commercially successful period, from the late 1920s until the early '50s, animation re-performed this cultural template, especially in the period surrounding the arrival of sound in the early 1930s. Henry Jenkins has shown that vaudeville had an immense impact on non-animated film comedy of the time.[23] The same is true for animation. For cartoons, however, the inter-action with live popular theater extended back through the 1920s and continued onward as a memory of a performing style well into the tele-vision period. The vaudeville-animation connection blossomed into a mindset, an organizing principle for moviegoers and cartoonists.

The film *Vaudeville* has so far identified that institution as a place of cheap amusement, a location where a succession of riveting acts ap-pealed to many classes of spectators. This was consistent with the origi-nal character of the institution. A 1905 paean to vaudeville validated its seemingly eternal popularity: "When one can go to the theatre and see the best of dramatic, operatic, farce comedy and comic or music farce and even grand opera, with sprinklings of science, physical culture, some of the sawdust of the circus, marvelous children, wonderful train-ing of wild animals, magic and illusion, all in one performance for the puzzlingly small price charged by the vaudeville theatre, the acme of variegated theatrical entertainment appears to have been reached."[24]

Acme indeed! A pregnant word choice, given its later use as a running joke in cartoons. *Vaudeville* reminds us of how the shows' heteroge-neous acts reflected the multiplicity of the audience members and im-plied a democratic ideal. Magnate Edward F. Albee also extolled the "wide diversity of its attractions," explicitly connecting the content of the vaudeville program with the demographics of its consumers: "We who seek to please so many different kinds of people, so many divergent preferences, can never rest from the task of maintaining an endless sup-ply of contrasted attractions, great singers and famous clowns, fine dra-matic actors and wonderful musical instrumentalists, the funniest come-dians, the best dancers, the greatest illusionists and the foremost artists in every department, no matter where we have to go to get them."[25]

PLATE 1. *One Froggy Evening* (1955). The singing frog is associated with the memory palaces of old vaudeville.

PLATE 2. *The Flying Mouse* (1934). The image conceived of as a "picture box" or shallow theatrical setting.

PLATE 3. *Little Hiawatha* (1937). The character moves through a complex setting that blends foreground and background spaces.

PLATE 4. *Mickey's Fire Brigade* (1935). Technicolor made it possible to create cinematic depth by applying classical principles of atmospheric perspective.

PLATE 5. *Popeye the Sailor Meets Sinbad the Sailor* (1936). Heavy black outlines and primary colors create a color comics look. Bluto's body is trimmed in each frame to make it appear as if he's entering a tunnel.

PLATE 6. *Elmer Elephant* (1937). Dappled transparent shadows delineate the character's round body, create atmosphere, and bind the character to his 3-D environment.

PLATE 7. *The Country Cousin* (1936). Compare to the scene instruction sheet, Figure 42. The animators used pastel colors and finely drawn outlines to integrate foreground and background spaces.

PLATE 8. *Snow White and the Seven Dwarfs* (1937). The guttering light from the candle causes the animals' shadows to flicker.

PLATE 9. *Three Orphan Kittens* (1935). Moving background drawings, animated to correctly render motion parallax, creates a dynamic space for the playful kitten to inhabit.

PLATE 9. continued

PLATE 9. continued

PLATE 10. *Pigs Is Pigs* (1937). Our hero's dream of continuous eating ends badly. Kaboom!

PLATE 11. *Eat* (2000). A persistent waiter triggers an emetic display. Courtesy of Bill Plympton.

PLATE 12. *Frog in a Blender* (2000). The viewer/player becomes a willing participant in the animal's demise. Courtesy of Joe Shields.

PLATE 13. *Flora* (1989). The goddess writhes, dehydrates, and decays. Courtesy of Athanor Ltd. Film Production Company, Jaromir Kallista, and Jan Švankmajer.

PLATE 14. *Dimensions of Dialogue* (1982). Lust and cannibalism combine in Švankmajer's ludic clay forms. Courtesy of Athanor Ltd. Film Production Company, Jaromir Kallista, and Jan Švankmajer.

PLATE 15. *The Big Upgrade* (2007). The new digital animation industry destroys one of its old inhabitants. Courtesy of James Dick.

Albee's "contrasted attractions" idea differs from Sergei Eisenstein's "montage of attractions." Eisenstein, writing on a constructivist play that incorporated circus acts, emphasized the incongruity and distress caused by the aesthetic clash of unexpected juxtapositions. These thwarted traditional empathetic reactions and instead forced audiences to respond self-consciously to the dramatic material (favoring the figurative, not the embodied, mode). Eisenstein's attraction was "calculated to produce specific emotional shocks in the spectator."[26] This is the opposite of Albee's intention.

Albee was interested in the novelty of individual acts, but he didn't wish to shock people. On the contrary, he wished to touch as many common denominators as he could in a diverse audience. "And the more widely contrasted, the more unusual, the more beautiful these novelties prove to be, the more certain they will be to win the approval and patronage of our cosmopolitan and always inquisitive vaudeville public," he wrote.[27] Unlike the Soviet filmmaker, with his shock-and-awe aesthetic, Albee emphasized the equilibrium of the total program, with the more extreme vaudevillians' exotic or outrageous tendencies offset by calming, genteel acts. "Although certain types of acts became standards on the vaudeville program," Robert C. Allen observed, "virtually every show business attraction that could fit on a stage appeared in vaudeville—with, of course, the important qualification that it had to be morally unobjectionable and satisfy middle-class notions of propriety and taste."[28]

It's easy to see animation's figurative predilection toward the Eisensteinian attraction in cartoons' in-your-face content, their fast pace (montage, as it were), and their disregard for natural and cinematic laws. In this respect the Fleischer films are exemplary. This, however, is a bit misleading, if one considers their place in the vaudevillesque aesthetic, because the films were exhibited as a counterbalance, integral to the entire entertainment bill. Toons contributed to the movie program's democratizing mission of providing something for everyone. The motto of Educational Pictures, distributors of cartoons and short subjects, said it all: "The Spice of the Program."

Vaudeville's cheap tickets brought immigrants and their cultures in contact with American "natives" throughout the nation. On one hand this fostered international awareness and promoted assimilation. On the other, vaudeville also spotlighted differences through its inevitable spreading of stereotypes and prejudices based on gender, race, and ethnicity. (The Three Keatons' "Irish" act is a good example.) Again, Albee emphasized that the material reflected its diverse viewers: "Not only are all the arts represented in vaudeville, but all of the nations and races of the civilized world are also represented by and through some characteristic form of expression. Thus, in the arrangement of the ideal modern vaudeville program, there is [sic] one or more sources of complete satisfaction for everybody present, no matter how 'mixed' the audience may be."[29]

Albee promulgated a chamber of commerce vision of a democratic America. Of course, this stated ideal would prove to be problematic if checked against reality, given the objectification, stereotyping, and minstrelsy being performed on the stage, not to mention the social and legal barriers preventing some patrons from mixing in the audience because of their race. Nevertheless, vaudeville as a self-proclaimed democratic amusement resurfaced in cartoons, usually as hyperbole and an opportunity for scandalous parody, as seen in *Vaudeville*.

Ko-Ko's vaudeville show within the cartoon has its own "mixed" audience, which exists in a strange, unreadable space in relation to the stage space depicted in Max's drawings. Ko-Ko's vaudeville viewers reside in their own cinematic subspace. Sometimes the audience, seen only during cutaway shots, is a wildly applauding crowd, and at other times the spectators are yawning. This is complicated even more by Max's seeming presence both within and outside the space of Ko-Ko's off-screen audience. He participates as an individual within the vaudeville theater, applauding and shouting at Ko-Ko, while paradoxically—that is to say, metaleptically—remaining seated alone at his desk. When the clown presents a magic act, Max yells angrily, "Get off the stage. You're nothing but a big ham." This is strangely ironic, since Ko-Ko exists, according to the fiction set forth by the film, as Sketcher Max's creation, but Max seems to have lost his agency. He becomes a disruptive spectator interfering with Ko-Ko's autonomous performance.

The audience member that behaves badly is an important component of the vaudevillesque. As in contemporary stand-up comedy, hecklers were commonplace at stage entertainments and therefore in cartoon representations as well. Some performers flourished by turning the tables on those that would disrupt the show. According to Jenkins, "The so-called Nut Comics experimented with even wilder intrusions of spectator space. Olson and Johnson hurled raw eggs, rubber snakes, and live chickens at the audience, planted confederates who heckled them from the house and ticket scalpers who romped the aisles selling passes to rival shows, attacked spectators with gusts of air from the stage, and broadcast comments and jokes through an intercom system to patrons waiting in line to buy tickets for the next show."[30] Interestingly, although one imagines that this behavior should have annoyed audience members, it had the opposite effect and elicited laughs. Rather than derailing the institution of vaudeville (and, by extension, cartoons), "no other aspect of the performance was more important than establishing and maintaining a bond between performer and patron."[31]

Disruptors were a cinematic and televisual motif from *Uncle Josh at the Moving Picture Show* (Edwin S. Porter/Edison, 1902), in which Josh tears down the screen, to the *Muppet Show* (Jim Henson/ATV, 1976–80), in which Statler and Waldorf, two cranky old men, jeer at the music hall acts. In *The Play House,* Keaton in the crowd heckled Keaton onstage. In several early films, Chaplin re-performed a character he had developed in the Fred Karno revue, an annoying fellow who interferes with the spectacle. *A Night in the Show* (Charlie Chaplin/Essanay, 1915) has drunken Charlie bedeviling the orchestra conductor, a gag that inspired many later cartoonists. Disney reprised it in *The Opry House,* in which a rowdy cat in the audience behaves badly with his soap bubbles, dumping the liquid into the horn of one of the players.

Mickey's Revue (Wilfred Jackson/Disney, 1932) is set in a rustic opera house where Mickey conducts the pit orchestra, harried by an obnoxious spectator who eats nuts and distracts everyone with his goofy laugh. (The character eventually morphed into Goofy.) Mickey and Minnie persevere through the disruptions, which are compounded when a litter of kittens converges to interfere with the organized music making (yet, serendipitously, they make their own music). The other audience members eventually take care of the disruptor (Figure 9). Similarly, *Shake Your Powder Puff* (Friz Freleng/Schlesinger, 1934) features a coarse Pluto-like dog with a drinking habit. The drunk boos the stage actors and laughs in a Goofy guffaw. He then falls onto the stage, and the audience members get their revenge by pelting him with vegetables.

Consider Donald Duck's distracting behavior when he harasses the orchestra and its leader, Mickey, in *The Band Concert* (Wilfred Jackson/Disney, 1935), or when he disrupts the prestidigitation act from a box seat in *Magician Mickey* (Dave Hand/Disney, 1937). In *Orphan's Benefit* (Burt Gillett/Disney, 1934; remade as *Orphans' Benefit* [Riley Thomson/Disney, 1941]), Donald tries to recite "Mary Had a Little Lamb" while facing a theater full of Bronx-cheering, pea-shooting, catcalling kittens. The audience is also hostile to Donald in *Mickey's Amateurs* (Pinto Colvig et al./Disney, 1937). The duck is among the acts being

FIGURE 9. *Mickey's Revue* (1932). The audience takes charge.

featured on a radio show amateur hour, but he can't recite the words to "Twinkle, Twinkle, Little Star." When he gets the gong, Donald leaves the stage, comes back, and then fires into the audience with a tommy gun (Figure 10). *Mickey's Grand Opera* (Wilfred Jackson/Disney, 1936) has Pluto playing the disrupting figure, mixing it up with the rabbit in the magician's hat and then intruding on the duet by the fat soprano Cluck and Donald. Mayhem ensues. *Long-Haired Hare* (Chuck Jones/ Warner. Bros., 1949) builds to a monumental finale in which Bugs Bunny gets revenge on an opera singer during his performance at the Hollywood Bowl, destroying that monument to high culture. Disruptive audience members continued into the TV era with Yosemite Sam and Daffy as Bugs's regular hecklers on *The Bugs Bunny Show* (Chuck Jones, Friz Freleng, et al./American Broadcasting Co., 1960–68). In *Beavis and Butt-Head* (Mike Judge et al./J.J. Sedelmaier Productions Inc., 1993– 97), the two slacker protagonists trash-talk about music videos from their couch and interrupt the show with their remote-control channel surfing.

There's a spatial dimension, too. Interrupters unmask theater's artifice by defying the expectation that the proscenium is a barrier between stage and audience, the fourth wall. The disruptive spectators in the theater are (or appear to be) spontaneous and unplanned elements of liveness. Their distractions prove that the space of stage and auditorium are shared, since the hecklers often throw objects onto the stage and the

FIGURE 10. *Mickey's Amateurs* (1937). Donald fires into the audience (in the vaudeville house and in the movie theater). Original in color.

performers respond to the taunts, sometimes by throwing things back.[32] In cartoons, heckler figures are more like the shills and Nut Comics of vaudeville. Though they re-perform vaudeville's liveness, the spontaneity must, of course, be planted, that is, planned and drawn. Heckling in cartoons, then, is reflexive. Audiences understand the show within the film to be a fragile constructed spectacle that reveals the animators' agency behind the performance.

The heckler motif in animation establishes a fictional performance situation within the narrative and then introduces a character that disrupts its flow. Although hecklers are part of the on-screen audience in these films, they're a disreputable element. These liminal characters transgress by distracting from or usurping the "normal" spectacle, becoming the show (in the pejorative sense of making a spectacle of themselves). Rather than consumers of performances, they are unauthorized performers. Their counterperformance works against the impression that the cartoon is a self-contained autonomous event, yet they're also avatars of the audience—which is why we enjoy them. Like us, they're both part of the show and kept outside the legitimate spectacle. Maybe viewers momentarily identified with the pleasures of rebellion, especially if they were outsiders themselves, alien to the genteel, decorous theater crowd.

This is what happens next in *Vaudeville*. Max is the heckler. He criticizes and interrupts the film as though he were outside the stage

FIGURE 11. *Vaudeville* (1924). Max magically transforms himself into an Orthodox Jew.

performance, and yet his heckling is scripted within it. He moves beyond verbal heckling to interfering and tries to upstage magician Ko-Ko's sleight of hand act. Using a large handkerchief as a magician's prop, he covers his face and rapidly transforms himself (through the switching of actors in stop-action substitutions) into a Native American in war paint, a woman, an African American, a tall man wearing a monocle, and an Orthodox Jew (Figure 11). In nineteenth-century theater and vaudeville, the quick-change act was a staple. According to Matthew Solomon, "They performed as part of variety programs and, in certain cases, in full-length stage shows. . . . [T]he performer rapidly assumed a series of widely different personae that varied wildly in gender, age, social class, and occupation. Much of the appeal of protean artistry hinged on the speed with which an individual performer could make costume changes that effected complete and striking transformations of character."[33] Here, in Max's ne plus ultra re-performance, he's cartoonlike as he uses the handkerchief as a shutter, changing his image—indeed, his very being— with each new exposure. Ko-Ko responds to Max's trick by exuding the ink from his body, which slides around the vaudeville stage as a formless blob. After the paint reconstitutes itself in the clown's form, Ko-Ko begins unraveling his inked outline (Figure 12).

Max raises the ante in this game of one-upmanship by drinking the bottle of ink. Sketcher Max's fluctuating powers are confirmed when he replicates the metamorphoses of the toon body as it changes with each new drawing, stretching and squashing. He instantly turns into a large ink puddle that splashes across his desk and onto Ko-Ko's stage, where it soaks up all the lines of the drawing, including the theater set and Ko-Ko. Meanwhile, as Max becomes cartoonlike, Ko-Ko becomes less so. He loses his inking, then his drawn outline, and finally his motion and

FIGURE 12. *Vaudeville* (1924). Ko-Ko reverses the process of his creation by removing his inked outline.

autonomy in an unwinding of the process of his creation that we saw at the film's beginning. In the end, the cartoon magicians annihilate each other and devolve into primordial inky ooze. The distinction between the human and the toon disappears. Both are shown to be controlled by and avatars of mischievous unseen Animator Dave. The liquefied protagonists flow off the paper and into the now turbulent inkwell.

Some vaudeville! The playhouse sequence began simply enough as a device for delivering ad hominem jokes about the audience members, then it became a performance space for parodies of typical vaudeville fare. When Ko-Ko and Max escalate their dueling movie magic, at stake is vaudeville or cinema's dominance. There also are competing systems of visual representation between "mechanical" reproduction using film and photography and pre-technological drawing by hand. The film resolves these conflicts in a circle-closing end, when again all is ink.

Vaudeville lays out the economic system of popular theater as a joke at the expense of its patrons. It challenges the vaudeville institution by putting it up against movie cartoons, re-performing the structure of the program as a series of short acts, turning them into performances within performances. The acting is quixotic and plastic, responding to the exigencies of the rapidly shifting spatial terrain. The masklike identities that Ko-Ko and Max adopt, the physical slapstick, and the actors' lack of coherent form and consistent behavior prevent us from completing them as embodied personae. These relentless shifts in the protagonist's race and gender and the fragmentation and inscrutability of the plot not only echo fast-paced vaudeville, but they also reflect (or parody) the viewers' flickering experience of cinema in general, as optical points of view, subjectivity, and identification engage them in quick changes. The film's finale shows the tools of the cartoonist's trade obliterating the stage. In a remarkable display of media autophagy, *Vaudeville* shows us animation consuming the vaudeville memory palace from whence it came, leeching off it to hasten its demise, but keeping it alive as a timescape.

RE-PERFORMING VAUDEVILLE

Vaudevillian spoor is evident in animation from the silent period onward. Witness Earl Hurd's title for his mid-1920s series, Pen and Ink Vaudeville.[34] Felix the Cat's lineage went back through Chaplin to that comedian's roots in the English music hall, while Mickey Mouse's ancestry may be traced to Chaplin, Keaton, and the vaudeville touring circuits. The animators' sense of context, subject matter, and gag timing were informed by these traditions. As a teenager in Chicago, Walt Disney, for example, was a habitué of vaudeville, taking notes at the shows he attended, and he developed a Chaplin impersonation act as well.[35] Dave Fleischer was the animator most directly involved with vaudeville. As Langer traces in detail, young Dave worked as an usher at the Palace on Broadway and learned his comic timing by observing the famous acts of the day, such as Joe Jackson and Weber and Fields. Among the influences on the later cartoons, Langer counts the structure of the "two-act" (the Max and Ko-Ko duo) and the patterns of repetition and variation seen in stock characters and routines (Popeye's spinach and rivalry with Bluto). Dave aspired to be a vaudeville clown, and, in a way, he ultimately succeeded when he performed Ko-Ko in the movies.[36]

Animators in the 1920s and early '30s assumed that their viewers had knowledge of various popular entertainments. Characters "put on a show" in such films as *The Betty Boop Limited* (Dave Fleischer/ Paramount, 1932), in which a troupe of show people (well, critters) put on an impromptu program on a train, and *Popeye the Sailor* (Dave Fleischer/ Paramount, 1933), in which the sailor man makes his first cartoon appearance dancing a hula duet with Betty Boop on a sideshow stage.

In the early Mickey Mouse films, the show often took place in a makeshift performance setting, as when we meet Minnie dancing in a cantina in *Gallopin' Gaucho* (Ub Iwerks/Disney, 1928), or when a barnyard serves as a stage in *Mickey's Follies* (Wilfred Jackson/Disney, 1929). There's *The Karnival Kid* (Ub Iwerks/Disney, 1929), in which Minnie Mouse is a hoochie-coochie dancer. Elsewhere, stories were set in theaters, as in *The Opry House*.

In *Mickey's Follies* the farm animals set up a stage, complete with a curtain on a clothesline. There is the essential ingredient of an audience within the film, in this case in the form of raucous animals that will break down the boundary between stage spectacle and observers. There is a chorus line of ducks, a fat soprano pig, and two chickens doing an "Apache" dance. The latter act, however, fails. In fact, it literally lays an egg, as the hen has to make an urgent exit to squeeze one out. The audience, however, greets this as a bonus attraction and goes wild. Next, disruptive fans interfere with the show by forcing the highbrow singing sow back into the barn. The rustic spectacles depicted in such films take the populist appeal of vaudeville to the extreme by setting the show on the farm and in small burgs.

Sophistication is mocked. *Mickey's Follies* goes out of its way to simulate stage liveness, such as by showing the film audience applauding and interacting with the performers and by displaying "accidents," as when the soprano's panties keep falling off. Most striking is Mickey's direct address to the film viewers when he croons to the "camera" and leads the theater audience in a sing-along. Like all good programs, this follies has a headliner—Mickey, naturally. He plays the piano and saxophone, dances, and sings "Minnie's Yoo Hoo." It's his new theme song, announced by a duck with a placard.

Meanwhile, at the Schlesinger studio, Harmon and Ising's Mickey wannabe, Foxy, was visiting a cantina to see his heartthrob, Roxy, sing the song with the same name as the cartoon, *Lady, Play Your Mandolin!* (Rudolf Ising/Schlesinger, 1931). The variety of this cartoon's performance spaces and the fluidity with which the action traverses them mimic the swiftly changing vaudeville program. We have the traditional stage space where Roxy sings under the glare of a spotlight. When Foxy joins her in a duet from the floor, they share a space that connects the stage and the auditorium (Figure 13). At the same time, the waiters and other audience members join in as the chorus. One man even hosts in his hat a mouse that comes out to join the music, creating its own minute performance subspace. Everyone performs, inviting the film audience to join in singing the catchy song. Foxy's horse, all the while, has been tippling

FIGURE 13. *Lady, Play Your Mandolin!* (1931). Foxy and Roxy
bring together the spaces of stage and audience.

some firewater (Prohibition notwithstanding) and interrupts the show
with his drunken behavior. Eventually this disruptive Nut Comic character takes over the spectacle and becomes the program's closer.

Rather than transforming the space of the traditional stage setting
into a cartoonlike counterpart, as in the examples above, *Stopping the
Show* (Dave Fleischer/Paramount, 1932), starring Betty Boop, goes to
great lengths to re-create the timescape of big-time vaudeville theater by
staging the performances in an authentic-looking theater, most likely the
Palace, so dear to Fleischer in his early years.[37] The show is presented
from start to finish, each act identified by a gag title card. The orchestra,
for instance, plays the "Over chewer." As in a typical vaudeville program
of 1932, this one included films, so here we have the Paramouse Noose
Reel ("The Eyes, Ears, Nose and Mouth of the World")[38] as well as a
fictitious "Koko and Bimbo" cartoon. The disruptive spectator in this
audience is a baby eating peanuts and annoying an elephant. Showgirl
Betty is the emcee as well as the headliner. She does Fanny Brice singing
"I'm an Indian" (Leo Edwards and Blanche Merrill, 1928). The Brice
number is especially pertinent for both vaudeville and cartoons, since
the lyrics are about the instability of identity, both ethnic and ontological, recalling Max's startling transformations in *Vaudeville*. In the original, Jewish Brice adds a reflexive touch when she sings in her trademark
over-the-top Yiddish dialect about a Jewish girl marrying a Native
American ("And now oi oi my people/How can I tell them how/Their

little Rosie Rosenstein/Is a terrible Indian now?").[39] When Betty performs the song, she "becomes" Brice, metamorphosing from ethnically ambiguous to Jewish and from a toon to humanoid. The same oxymoronic tension that exists when Brice declares she's a hybrid "Yiddishe squaw" manifests itself when Betty morphs into Indian-Jewish Brice. This toon-human confusion also underlies Betty's discreet charm as a cartoon character. Before she mimics Maurice Chevalier, we see her nonchalantly tossing her dress, bra, and panties over the onstage dressing screen. She's all surface, but, paradoxically, there is a nude woman under her ink-and-paint exterior. Betty Boop is thus a superb example of the self-contradictory "horrible prettiness" that characterized the burlesque queens of an earlier time. These stars that lived off men gazing at their bodies "evoked both the threat of gender revolution and the fear of working-class contamination."[40] Betty also does both.

The seasoned vaudevillian Betty takes curtain calls, telling her appreciative audience-in-the-theater-in-the-film, "You're so sweet to me." At a time when American legitimate theater was moving toward a unified aesthetic effect, necessarily foregrounding the director, vaudeville continued to emphasize individuals who were capable of "stopping the show."[41] It is felicitous Betty, of course, not the humans she imitates, who is the star and who elicits the applause.

Although drag acts and race masquerades were commonplace in vaudeville, cartoons trump the stage because the characters are not simply imitating others in the way that Brice imitates an Indian. Instead, toons perform a figuration, extracting the celebrities' looks, idiosyncrasies, ethnicity, sex, charisma, and personhood—in short, their stardom.

Cartoon Minstrelsy

Albee and others claimed that the variegated vaudeville program, more so than legitimate theater, was an inclusive and accurate reflection of America. Indeed, vaudeville has come to symbolize the turn-of-the-twentieth-century melting-pot social order. It remains an open question how the actual members of this "mixed" audience—say, Jewish, German, Polish, or Irish—received these songs, skits, jokes, and caricatures at their expense (even when the performers were of those groups). More specifically, vaudeville routinely billed performances derived from that enshrined institution of race musical, the minstrel show. Early animation avidly populated the vaudeville timescape with the same characterizations and stereotypes. Christopher Lehman, while noting the paradoxical paucity of blacks in the cartoon business, is nevertheless able to claim, "American animation owes its existence to African Americans."[42]

The racist depiction of minorities in early cartoons is becoming increasingly apparent as uncut versions of classic animation from major studios become available on DVD and online, bringing potentially offensive stereotypes onto the laptop, into the living room, and into the classroom. It can't be ignored. Arthur Knight writes, "Crucial foundations for the U.S. economy, society, and culture were set with the appropriation of black African bodies and labor, and most strands of white U.S. culture have sustained themselves by further appropriating elements from black cultures. Blackface performance stands as a particularly stark and obvious marker of such appropriations, and cultural critics and analysts need to recognize the obviousness."[43] The racialized depictions in classic cartoons should be addressed for these reasons, but also they need to be viewed in the historical context as re-performing vaudeville.

In popular graphic humor there was a tradition of sketching African Americans according to a formula: make a circle, fill it with black ink except for the white eyes and mouth, and you have the face of Sambo.[44] Add the appropriate hair, ears, and big eyes and you have the faces of Nemo's cannibal sidekick Impy, Felix, Beans, Oswald, Mickey, Bosko, Honey, Foxy, Flip, Inki, and others, including an actual series of Little Black Sambo cartoons by Ub Iwerks in the 1930s. Add recorded sound and you have the opportunity to exploit clichés about the alleged innate talent and natural rhythm of blacks as they sing, dance, and re-perform minstrelsy and dialect.

Cartoons depicting actual minstrel acts were rare. One exception was *Wot a Night* (John Foster and George Stallings/Van Beuren, 1931), in which all the singers are images of the minstrel personage Mr. Bones—literally, they're skeletons with black bones. The earliest Bosko films, such as *Sinkin' in the Bathtub* (Hugh Harman and Rudolf Ising/Schlesinger, 1930), figure the humanoid protagonists Bosko and Honey as minstrels, with exaggerated Sambo features, curly hair, plantation costumes, and a penchant for spontaneous singing and dancing. Bosko's mannerisms are typical for Zip Coon, down to his drawl. This was the minstrel show's ignorant or naïve southern black who is out of place in the "sophisticated" North.[45] In *Plane Dumb* (John Foster and George Rufle/Van Beuren, 1932), Tom and Jerry (humans) blacken up and speak in "Negro" dialect on their way to Africa.

One film uniquely documents cartoon vaudeville as a "mixed" institution, both onstage and in the represented audience. *Making Stars* (Dave Fleischer/Paramount, 1935) opens with crowds pouring out of the subway to see Betty Boop headlining in a revue in which she introduces baby acts, the "stars of the future: on screen and on stage, they'll all be the rage." The babies, whose graphic design (like Betty's) echoes the popular Kewpie dolls, do their infantilized vaudeville turns. Then she introduces the "Colorful Three," drawn in the usual Sambo style. The black babies stand before a painted backdrop of a cotton field and sing a song that riffs on Cab Calloway's "Hi Dee Ho" refrain. They are part of a program that reflects vaudeville's variegated aesthetic and culturally diverse performances, but the performance ghettoizes the Colorful Three's act by identifying it with "race" music.[46] The difference between the Colorful Three and the other babies (who are cartoonlike, but not as grossly exaggerated) is brought home at the finale. Being babies, all the performers start bawling. Bottles and candy lure the white babies offstage, but it takes a giant watermelon slice, a perennial signifier of blacks' association with southern agrarian culture and slavery, to entice the Colorful Three.

Now the film makes a somewhat startling leap to the audience. A black baby watching the show from her (his?) mother's lap begins to cry. Both are rendered in the same coarse caricature style as the Colorful Three, and she is dressed as a mammy. The baby, taking a lesson from the stage act, also sings "Hi Dee Ho" and disturbs the fellow attendees. Mammy reaches into a bag and pacifies the child with her own watermelon slice. After devouring it, the baby spits out the seeds, targeting the bald head of the man in front of her (Figure 14). The vaudeville audience is represented as integrated, but these are the only two visible black members, and they are graphically and behaviorally segregated.

A Language All My Own (Dave Fleischer/Paramount, 1935) inflects minstrelsy differently, although it still emphasizes the manipulability of body and language performance in vaudeville. Seen from the wings, showgirl Betty is finishing her act onstage. She finishes the show, flies to Japan, and lands her plane atop a Tokyo theater.[47] Crowds pour in to hear Betty sing the title song—in Japanese! Apparently she can alter her linguistic performance to suit any nationality. Onstage, Betty transforms herself into Chinese and Italian women.

The toon version of vaudeville's democratic ideal translates into animals taking on specific racial identities. Having nonhuman toons appear in blackface further complicates the performance. In a sense, it's superfluous, since all these cartoon beasts are masquerading as humans

FIGURE 14. *Making Stars* (1935). Watermelon pacifies the baby in the audience, but its unruly behavior irritates the white spectators.

anyway—in humanface, if you will. The animators felt the need to make their performances not just anthropomorphic but human-centric. The practice destabilized the identities of these nonhumans. Take Mickey Mouse in *Blue Rhythm* (Burt Gillett/Disney, 1931), a cartoon set in a jazz revue. He begins by playing pretentious classical music, but he quickly switches to a blues style reminiscent of Eubie Blake or Art Tatum. At one point the lights go out and Mickey channels Jolson in blackface, crying out, "Mammy,"[48] making us wonder why animal characters that are already black would need to appear in blackface. Minnie's performance is less ambiguous. She appears as a female from a southern plantation outfitted with a large parasol and rustic clothes (Figure 15). When her skirt flies up, we see patches on her panties, a recurring element in her design denoting her low socioeconomic status. She is playing the stock minstrel character, Miss Lucy Long, a flirtatious mulatto.[49] Her appearance might have been patterned on Ethel Waters in *On with the Show!* (Alan Crosland/Warner Bros., 1929; Figure 16). There Waters portrayed a plantation type wearing a bright bandana and polka-dotted dress. Minnie is singing "St. Louis Blues" (W.C. Handy, 1914) in the style of Memphis Minnie.[50] In patterning Minnie Mouse on Waters, Bessie Smith, Lizzie Miles, or Memphis Minnie, the animators gave her a sort of horrible prettiness, identifying her with attractive but intimidating sexuality

FIGURE 15. *Blue Rhythm* (1931). Minnie as a minstrel stock type, Miss Lucy Long.

FIGURE 16. Ethel Waters in *On with the Show!* (1929). George Eastman House Motion Picture Department Collection.

and racial otherness while also powerfully imbuing her with countercultural expression. The animator-animated power distribution evokes that of master and slave. "St. Louis Blues," Lehman notes, conveys "musically the despondency of the slaves. For this reason [the] choice of a blues song by an African American composer especially underscores the black identity of the [animated] animal slaves."[51] Minnie's performance has the same effect; though comically exaggerated, it conveys abjection. When Mickey conducts the band, the music shifts to a hot jazz cover of Cab Calloway and the Missourians' version of "St. Louis Blues," a recording released in July 1930. Mickey's racial identify oscillates between blackface (Jolson) and authentic black (Calloway).

Mickey's Mellerdrammer (Wilfred Jackson/Disney, 1933) begins with Mickey and Clarabelle Cow applying burnt cork for their stage production of *Uncle Tom's Cabin* (Figure 17). Mickey predictably shouts "Mammy" to the "camera." While one might think blacking up to play an African American character would confirm whiteness, since we see the application of makeup on-screen, this isn't necessarily so. Bert Williams was one of several black vaudevillians who performed in blackface for both white and African American audiences. In films, including *Mickey's Mellerdrammer,* the application of cork is performative. Knight considers the process as "both spectacularizing and 'narrativizing' blackface performance, [and] it altered the frames in which blackface had been ordinarily placed and understood. With some notable exceptions ... blackface performers appeared in most films both with and without their makeup, foregrounding a diegetic shift from 'natural' character to

FIGURE 17. *Mickey's Mellerdrammer* (1933). Using an exploding firecracker, Mickey "blacks up" to play Topsy.

'made-up' performer."[52] It's important, then, for us to see Mickey applying the cork as confirming that his blackened self is performative, different from his "natural" ethnicity—whatever that may be.

Bright Lights (Ub Iwerks/Disney, 1928) finds Oswald the Lucky Rabbit trying to get lucky with Mlle Zulu the Shimmy Queen, headliner at the local "Vodvil" show where all the actors are black. Most of the story involves Oswald crashing the stage door because he doesn't have fifty cents for admission. For him, the vaudeville theater is a space (and a space that's a consumer commodity) dedicated to erotic display and "African" spectacle. Oswald's lust makes him a particularly destructive fan.

The Shimmy Queen might have been a caricature of Josephine Baker costumed for her famous "banana dance." Although she was flourishing in Paris at the time, Baker was relatively unknown in the States in 1928, so perhaps Disney and Iwerks were depicting Mlle Zulu as a generic cooch dancer, an act popular since the days of Little Egypt on the Midway. Oswald's infatuation with the black dancer suggests that he also is an African American. This was already clear in his first appearances, when he was costumed in homespun single-suspender coveralls of the type worn by workers picking cotton. Oswald is also a version of Zip Coon. Further emblematizing his African American association, he's "lucky" because his rabbit feet, in racist depictions of black behaviors in Americana, would bring good luck to crapshooters. Besides, if Oswald were not "black," his desire for Mlle Zulu would imply the prospect of miscegenation.

Minnie plays another version of Mlle Zulu in *The Karnival Kid.* She's a sexy shimmy dancer and a kind of black anticipation of showgirl Betty. Her design, like Mickey's, was also based on Sambo. It is her re-performance of the erotic ethnicity of the sideshow/cabaret/vaudeville milieu that confirms Minnie's black roots. We may assume that Mickey's attraction to her was not an interracial romance.

When animator Ub Iwerks left the Disney studio to start his own Flip the Frog series, his reliance on inspirational vaudeville continued. *Fiddlesticks* (Ub Iwerks/MGM, 1930) is set in a woodland community with a stump for a vaudeville stage. Most of the film consists of Flip's languorous dancing and jazzy piano playing. His costume, a cutaway with a bow tie and big shoes . . . er, flippers . . . costumes him as a black or blackface minstrel, probably based on Mr. Bones (compare Figures 18 and 19).

Cartoons thrived on an aesthetic of metamorphosis and fusion, so the form could easily re-perform the hybrid bodies of minstrelsy and race acts with which audiences were familiar. Cartoons' figurative performance tendencies were ideal for reducing body type, sexual orientation, color, ethnicity, national origin, religion, and any urban or rural trait to a malleable two-dimensional caricature. Lewis's description of vaudeville also fits cartoons: "It was comedy stripped down to instant identification of stock types and quick-fire repartee. As well as the traditional blackface, 'Irish,' and 'Dutch' (German) acts, it depicted recent arrivals to the city."[53]

These cartoon re-performances of racial and ethnic stereotypes are the cornerstone of the vaudeville memory palace. Take, for instance, *Clean Pastures* (Friz Freleng/Schlesinger, 1937). Loosely a parody of the non-animated feature *The Green Pastures* (Marc Connelly, William Keighley/Warner Bros., 1936), one toon is an Al Jolson caricature. But Jolson isn't just blacked up, he *is* an African American (confirmed when the Stepin Fetchit caricature warns him against trying to enter the Kotton Klub, saying, "Yuh-yuh-y'all cain't go in there"). By usurping blackness, toon Jolson gives up the white Jewish American identity that would have admitted him to real Cotton Club–like establishments where blacks performed blackness for whites. Cartoons, evidently even more than vaudeville, encourage viewers to play "me . . . not me." These swift on-screen changes offered viewers a fleeting identification with

FIGURE 18. Minstrel Lew Dockstader in blackface on a vaudeville stage (1902). Prints and Photographs Division, Library of Congress.

FIGURE 19. *Fiddlesticks* (1930). Flip the Frog's early minstrel appearance. Original in color.

other cultures and races. Daniel Goldmark wrote of the representations of blackness, "The cartoons that simultaneously presented the ideas of jazz and primitivism also (in a tone mixing envy and condemnation) emphasized the stereotyped notion that blacks live their lives with careless freedom."[54] Thanks to animation's absorption of the vaudevillesque ideal of diversity—within bounds—his remark applies as well to the myriad other spoofs and caricatures in cartoons. Today, DVD program hosts disclaim and apologize for these gauche displays of racism and insensitivity. These historic animation performances, however, constitute one of America's most persistent memory palaces. At the time of their distribution these cartoons reflected America's casual objectification of nonassimilated others, whether blacks, Jews, Asians, East Europeans, Latinos, homosexuals, or those with differing body types. For many original viewers the films may have embodied their own anxieties about retaining one's cultural heritage and identity in the face of the implacable melting pot.

Animating Liveness

The liveness of the Tooniverse is one more vestige of animation's cartoon-vaudeville timescape. Vaudeville capitalized on the traditional allure of theater's intimacy, spontaneity, and improvisation. Pleasure was derived especially from the physical copresence of spectacle and spectator. For Albee, this meant that his show people were unique original entertainers, not ringers, imitations, or recordings on film. Vaudeville, he wrote, "does not offer the smaller cities and towns any 'substitutes' for its metropolitan list of attractions. It offers no 'just as good' imitations of anything. The same great singer, comedian, dancer, tragedienne, magician or other headliner that has delighted Broadway, is presented in person and without substitution all over the circuit."[55] Cultivating an inimitable aura for the live entertainer and the one-of-a-kind performance ("in person and without substitution") was an essential strategy for the vaudeville star system.

Although he wrote in 1923, during the "golden age" of the silent cinema and the era when the popularity of radio was expanding, Albee never mentions these media, either as competitors or, in the case of film, as a component of most of his stage programs. The broadcasts of headliner acts, phonograph recordings, and, soon, the talkies, would turn vaudeville into a mediatized performance. Jolson and Eddie Cantor, for example, both told tales of having to compete with themselves on the screen during runs of their stage shows. At the same time, when stars appeared onstage they were expected to look and sound like their screen and radio personalities. As Auslander might express it, mediatization was provoking a crisis of the auratic value of the body as a unique entertainment commodity.

To create worlds with proximal liveness, animators based their designs on the vaudeville world's essential being-there-ness. The challenge was constructing common physical spaces that seem to link performer and viewer. The effort shows in the Popeye film *Puttin on the Act* (Dave Fleischer/Paramount, 1940). Olive Oyl runs in with a newspaper to show Popeye a headline, "Vaudeville is coming back!" We're supposed to assume that it refers to the "revivals" of live shows that were being advertised at the time when *Puttin on the Act* was in theaters. The Paramount in Times Square, for instance, was again programming variety shows along with films. As a result, big bands were sharing the stage with Popeye. In the cartoon, Olive's euphoria motivates Popeye to reconstruct their vaudeville past. As the characters do this, the film posits that the characters have had an existence outside their screen world; it asks us to believe that they lived lives before their film careers began. In the attic of the house where Popeye and Olive live together, Popeye dusts off his old magician's costume from the couple's tours on the "Short Circuit." The top hat still has an aged rabbit living in it. The decrepit prop and Popeye's old-fashioned morning coat, silk hat, and cane connote a past lodged in the archives of entertainment memory. The rest of the film shows their futile effort to reanimate this past on a makeshift proscenium stage in their living room, where they recall—literally, reperform—their old headline acts. The film calls into question the fundamental conflict between "live" entertainment and "canned."

The creation of a vaudeville past for Popeye and Olive embodies the toon actors as living stars. Movie stars, in DeCordova's famous formulation, have attention paid to their existence outside their film work, with stardom lying somewhere on a continuum between their screen characterizations and their private lives.[56] Many other cartoons assume that the audience will engage with toons as they would with "live" actors, however irrational that might seem. *A Hare Grows in Manhattan* begins with a gossip columnist interviewing movie star Bugs at home by his pool. His story of youthful dancing in the streets of the Lower East Side is a star-worthy biographical legend. The next installment of Bugs's formation as a star was recounted in *What's Up Doc?* As in the Popeye film (and in the famous flashback in *Singin' in the Rain* [Stanley Donen, Gene Kelly, 1952]), the trip to stardom began during the vaudeville days. Elmer Fudd, big-time star, takes on Bugs as part of his act. During one show Bugs resists having to play second banana and serendipitously invents his tagline, "Eh, what's up, Doc?" Success brings him to Hollywood. He makes a screen test with Warner Bros. and the rest is cartoon history. Well, the cartoon version of cartoon history. The significance of vaudeville in this self-aggrandizing yarn can't be underestimated. The stage is shown as having nurtured other great stars of the past. (When Bugs is down and out, he sits with other unemployed vaudevillians, including Jolson, Cantor, Jack Benny, and Bing Crosby.) Unlike them, Bugs survives and thrives. He is from vaudeville, but he has outlived it in cartoons.

The commonplace re-performance of live stardom in classic animation has become part of its vaudevillesque world-making. "Viewers have come to expect that animated character performances portray the illusion of a living being," writes Leslie Bishko. "As a determining factor for believability in animation, authenticity functions on two levels.

First, we suspend our disbelief and engage with the character; there is no question of the character's aliveness. Second, through characterization, we experience an authentic being whose inner intent is communicated outwardly, and made unmistakably clear."[57] The processes of engagement, characterization, and authentication that she cites are typical of the embodied acting approach. In *Puttin on the Act,* Popeye and Olive's roles are believable precisely because they are "authentic beings" shown in their everyday habitat in the private sphere, but additionally they are theatrical entertainers. They perform their characters as stage personalities, which may authenticate them as cartoon stars but discredits them as live entertainers because they perform so badly due to lack of practice. Shockingly, they have aged.

Puttin on the Act generates authenticity by reviving Popeye and Olive's old shtick, affirming that they've led earlier pre-stardom lives. Infant Swee'Pea, who is mute because he's a baby, "announces" each performance by changing the between-the-acts placards. The succession of acts simulates the quick change of attractions in the standard vaudeville program. "The Body Beautiful" shows Popeye inhaling to make his chest tattoo swell into a B-52 bomber; Olive's terpsichorean demonstration takes stretch and squash to an extreme as she twists herself into a pretzel knot. "Impersonations" are next, wherein Popeye does Jimmy Durante, Stan Laurel, and Groucho. Characteristically, he doesn't simply imitate the others, he *becomes* them. In "The Adagio" he uses Olive as various props in a violent slam dance that culminates with the unanticipated (for them, if not for us) act of Popeye hurling Olive out the window.

Although vaudeville was distinguished by its liveness, it was also constrained by it. Animators, however, can do better. Their characters perform surprising, even dangerous, feats of metamorphosis that would be impossible for human actors. Their performances carry a high risk of accident, disfigurement, and death. Of course, since toon bodies' liveness is mediatized, death has no sting. Rather, it's part of the act. The wizened bunny in Popeye's hat has not died and never will. The animators explicitly devalue vaudeville by showing the permanency—indeed, the immortality—of animation. Take that, vaudeville! Swee'Pea throws water on the show when he spots the date of Olive's newspaper. The "rebirth" of vaudeville was in 1898. Popeye laments, "Olive, we're too late!"

The cartoon's punning title conveys the ambiguity between live shows and animated liveness. Literally, the subject is putting on—that is, mounting—a show. However, the film itself is a put-on, a send-up, and a teasing deception about performance. We are promised a vaudeville show, but we get it through the mediation of a cartoon.

Perhaps the ultimate parody of liveness in the cartoon-vaudeville timescape is in *Magical Maestro* (Tex Avery/MGM, 1952). During the baritone's recital, a hair apparently catches in the film gate of the movie projector. Once a familiar sight to moviegoers, along with dust and splices, the unwanted artifact bounces around in the lower left of the frame. (Its realistic motion was supposedly achieved by rotoscoping a strand of hair from a found strip of film.) The ephemeral event would be an unwelcome injection of liveness into a film screening, reminding audiences that they're watching a movie in the real time of its projection. Suddenly, the cartoon's singer plucks out the animated hair with a loud "poing" and flicks it out of the frame. Lasting perhaps four seconds, this event punctures the vaunted liveness of stage performance by showing us that even the so-called mechanically reproduced cinema has elements of liveness when experienced in a movie theater. This produces a baffling question: How can the toon that is performing as an actor on the vaudeville stage in the film see the film of himself and know it is being projected with a hair in the gate? This could happen only if he were performing in live time, and if the edge of the frame were a physical proscenium in the space shared by him and the audience. Along with the hair, he can't be performing in the past; he's in the audience's present. He is responding to the animator's mischief that was drawn in the past, and yet he, the toon, senses the immediate audience's distraction, now in the present. It's metalepsis. It boggles the mind.

Magic Acts and Hyp-Nut-Tists

When Max and Ko-Ko present their competing sleight of hand in *Vaudeville,* they are re-performing one of the time-honored turns in popular theater. Solomon observes, "Up-to-date magic was an integral part of variety theater programs because its rapid appearances, disappearances, and transformations were uniquely in tune with the quick rhythms and abrupt transitions of the multiple-act bill." Unlike the late-nineteenth-century style of magic show performance, which cultivated the personality of the presenters—an embodied method, we would say—vaudeville magic was figurative: "Instead of creating distinct onstage personas, many up-to-date conjurers . . . made their very identities mystifying through masquerade and quick-change, shrouding their identities in Orientalist guises or rapidly metamorphosing between different impersonations."[58] Magic was a tradition that bled into cinema via stage prestidigitators like Georges Méliès and James S. Blackton, and into animation by way of the trick film genre. It's a particular kind of performance in the cartoon-vaudeville timescape. The crux of the problem is what does it mean when toons perform stage magic?

Disorderly Donald Duck interrupts the mouse's vaudeville act in *Magician Mickey*. Seated in a box by the stage and therefore getting a privileged view of the show from the side, he doubts the legitimacy of Mickey's tricks. Mickey puts various spells on Donald, who steals Mickey's wand to retaliate against him. The magic stage is a dangerous place for Donald; at one point Mickey wads him up into a bullet and fires him from a pistol.

According to the fiction of the film, Mickey's actions are not "illusions." They are not proximal. They're "real" in the sense that the film purports to be a token (in Carroll's sense), a straight recording of a feat of magic transformation. This is quite different from stage prestidigitation, of course, where we know that, however convincing the illusion appears, it must be a trick. The lady isn't really sawed in half—"true lies," as Solomon oxymoronically puts it. In animation, by contrast, every aspect of the film is a believed-in trick, beginning with the fundamental illusion of animated beings, so nothing can be singled out as a trickier trick. In 1934 Lewis Mumford wrote a determinist elegy for magic that redeemed it as the crucible of science: "But magic was the bridge that united fantasy with technology: the dream of power with the engines of fulfillment. The subjective confidence of the magicians, seeking to inflate their private egos with boundless wealth and mysterious energies, surmounted even their practical failures: their fiery hopes, their crazy dreams, their cracked homunculi continued to gleam in the ashes: to have dreamed so riotously was to make the technics that followed less incredible and hence less impossible."[59]

Much of the pleasure of watching magic performances is in matching wits with the magician and trying to divine the mechanics. Modern magic, reflected Tom Gunning, was symptomatic of a general decline in the belief system of "the marvelous." The art of the trick, then, replaced the status of the spectacle as a supernatural belief system built on miracles with one based on secular pseudo-scientific illusion. One can easily imagine the joy of early magicians and their kindred spirits discovering the cinema. The new "engine" had the potential for reviving their powers. "The seeming transcendence of the laws of the material universe by the magical theatre defines the dialectical nature of its illusions," noted Gunning, who continues:

> The craft of late nineteenth-century stage illusions consisted of making visible something which could not exist, of managing the play of appearances in order to confound the expectations of logic and experience. . . . The magic theatre labored to make visual that which it was impossible to believe. Its visual power consisted of a trompe l'oeil play of give-and-take, an obsessive desire to test the limits of an intellectual disavowal—I know, but yet I see.
> . . . [T]he illusionistic arts of the nineteenth century cannily exploited their unbelievable nature, keeping a conscious focus on the fact that they were only illusions.[60]

The vacillation between credulous and incredulous participation in the magic show anticipates the metaleptical "me . . . not me" of animation, except that such oscillation need not occur; the conflicting beliefs may be held together, which produces the distinctive effect described by Gunning as both attractive and disquieting.

Magic performances on film produce no enigma for the spectator to resolve; there are no tricks beyond those inherent in the reproducing apparatus, that is, how trick films and cartoons are manufactured. Méliès, for example, re-performed his theatrical illusions as cinema by innovating the stop-action substitution technique, using invisible editing, highly restricted staging, precision framing. The cinema mechanism was very different from the mechanics underlying the stage experience. Cinematography constructed an equivalent world that replaced the physical being-there as magic occurred onstage with a sensational spectacle of an even more impossible happening.[61] As with cartoons, the magical happening of the recorded trick occurs not on film but in the audience.

Cartoon magic is real, that is, it's a mediatized version of a world in which enchantment, shape shifting, and transmutation really happen. In *Magician Mickey,* Donald actually does become a bullet, the handkerchief becomes a bird, and so on. The animators' trick was in creating the illusion that the illusion of magic is not an illusion. We even see the lines of "magic" force emanating from Mickey's eyes. He *is* a magician!

As Chuck Jones said, "You must give the absolute illusion of reality to something no one has ever seen before. You are dealing with the utterly impossible."[62] Animators developed conventions that would be perceived as wondrous sorcery on a vaudeville stage, say, the ability to stretch one's hand to accomplish a trick, or to levitate beings with a magic wand, as does Mickey. These shorthand signs that magic is occurring, though, are barely perceived in a cartoon because they are from the animators' everyday arsenal, such as the stretch-and-squash style and the "force lines" derived from comic strips that denote invisible energy.

Many cartoons that re-perform magic highlight the role of the audience. The films' internal witnesses of the magic acts are the avatars of us, the external watchers of the movies. On the vaudeville stage, the magic act was interactive, with bystanders joining in the spectacle as unwitting volunteers or as paid accomplices. The films capture some of the stage's dangerous fascination for the moviegoer. The "Hyp-Nut-Tist" (Dave Fleischer/Paramount, 1935) depicts Popeye and Olive as spectators in box seats at the vaudeville show watching hypnotist Bluto. Bluto's magic is not a trick. The enchanted cane walks on its own; the drum beats itself. When Popeye disrupts the show he ticks off Bluto. Reversing the spectator-cinema relationship in which the viewer watches the movie screen, in this vaudeville act Bluto's stare is directed outward from the stage toward Olive Oyl. His lightning-bolt gaze enthralls her and she "volunteers" to be hypnotized. Soon Bluto has her performing a chicken, clucking and pecking—not *like* a chicken, but *being* a chicken. Her poultrified body even lays an egg. When Popeye can no longer stand to see his girl humiliated, he engages Bluto in battle. Now it is Olive and Popeye who have become the stage spectacle, she as a chicken-woman and he as a fighter.

Besides the risk to one's life, limb, and self-determination, there is also an implied threat to the spiritual body. Bluto's is an "Eastern" magic, a fact that is reflected in his faux-Arabian costume topped with a turban bearing the Islamic crescent. Popeye's victory is hence the triumph of Christian (or Jewish?) might over infidel magic. Popeye unwinds Bluto's turban like the string of a top. When the sailor puts the trophy on his head, the crescent magically falls back into place (Figure 20). Like the wizard's hat in "The Sorcerer's Apprentice" from *Fantasia* (James Algar et al. /Disney, 1940) and Bugs's headdress in *Show Biz Bugs* (Friz Freleng/Warner Bros., 1957), the crescented headgear identifies the magic as oriental. The masquerade is a kind of minstrelsy, too, ascribing a preternatural talent to a race or culture. Foreign sorcery, however, can never threaten the strength of Western ingenuity or the native power that vaudeville's assimilationist ideology heralded. Meanwhile, Olive is still clucking and pecking for worms. Though Popeye

FIGURE 20. *The "Hyp-Nut-Tist"* (1935). Popeye uses his muscles to overpower "Eastern" magic and rescue Olive Oyl.

now possesses Bluto's magical crescent talisman and could apply its magic powers to break the spell, he instead opts to use force to release her, and he socks Olive with his fist to jolt her out of the hex.

Of course, animators delighted in imagining everything that could go wrong on the vaudeville stage. When Poochini, the "world's greatest baritone" in *Magical Maestro,* rebuffs Mysto the magician and throws him out of the theater for audaciously proposing to open the headliner's vaudeville act, the conjuror spitefully bewitches the singer. Mysto levitates the conductor out of the orchestra, dons his wig and tails, and conducts Poochini with his magic wand. The rapid-fire succession of transformation gags (reminiscent of the transformation scene in *Vaudeville*) takes the unflappable Poochini through a couple dozen changes of costume, character, gender, race, and species, all while he is persevering, unfazed, through an aria from "The Barber of Seville" (Gioachino Rossini, 1816). In the end, Poochini wrests the wand from Mysto and turns the magician's powers against him to get revenge. The closure suggests that the power of magic rests in the apparatus, that is, the wand, perhaps a symbolic re-performance of animation's competing agencies. Mysto, the pesky toon magician in the performance, then, is an avatar of the controlling animator.

Competing for top billing on the program also motivates Daffy when he feuds with Bugs in *Show Biz Bugs.* The manager tells Daffy that the acts are billed according to their drawing power (which was historically accurate and not trivial; the headliners' salaries could be many times those of the other performers). Using a triple entendre that anticipates Bugs's role as animator in *Duck Amuck* (Chuck Jones/Warner Bros., 1953), Daffy shouts, "That rabbit couldn't draw flies if he was covered in syrup" (readers to add their own lisp).[63] No matter what classic vaudeville routines the characters perform—whether it's Bugs performing a soft-shoe dance or Daffy Duck showing his trained pigeons (they immediately fly out of the theater)—the audience thunderously cheers for Bugs but not for Daffy, whose performance is followed only by the chirping of crickets. For his big finish, Bugs—in the turban with the crescent—does his sawing-in-half routine, with the duck substituting for the customary lady. Despite Daffy's protests, "It's fake, it's a fake," his body separates in half when he jumps up and down. He really has been sawed in two! When he realizes his predicament, he goes out of character to reveal his alternate life as a worker in the cartoon industry and muses about his health insurance coverage: "Hmm. Good thing I've got Blue Cross." Daffy, true to the vaudeville aesthetic of the wow finish, invents the ultimate topper using his last available tool, the integrity of his own body. "Closure was of little importance to the vaudeville performer but climax was," observes Jenkins.[64] After admonishing the audience ("I must warn those with weak constitutions to leave the theater for this performance"), Daffy finally succeeds in outdoing Bugs and gets deafening applause—by blowing himself to smithereens. Ironically, Daffy has surpassed Bugs in drawing power, but he won't be around to savor his triumph.

Cartoonists share with magicians the pleasure of manipulating bodies and, as Solomon wrote about magicians, making visible the impossible. "Human bodies," he continues, "were the fulcrum on which many of these illusions hinged: Magicians made bodies appear and disappear at the wave of a wand, transported bodies through physical barriers, and exchanged them for one another instantaneously. Magicians penetrated, severed, and otherwise violently traumatized the body (before restoring it unharmed) or else dematerialized it entirely into spectral form."[65] Magic and cinema, he continues, "were in fact overlapping sets of practices that renewed, incorporated, and responded to each other historically."[66] These toon magician figures are troubling nevertheless because, like the disruptive spectator, they hypothesize a space outside the story that dangerously undercuts vaudeville and entertainment culture in general. They exhibit what Feyersinger has called "bidirectional transgression," suggesting that there is a danger that the spectacle may not remain on the screen and that the moviegoer might somehow become implicated in and endangered by it.[67] One might say that these outsider characters in the films relate to vaudeville in the way that the animators did to the craft of animation and to Hollywood. They were inside the institution, to be sure, but they also undermined it, like termites.

FROM MEMORY PALACE TO VAUDEVILLE-CARTOON TIMESCAPE

Stage variety shows made something of a comeback during and after World War II, but they often took the form of sporadic items sandwiched between double-feature movie shows. It was the time of big bands, Frank Sinatra, and USO stars such as vaudevillian Bob Hope. With big-time vaudeville dead, though, its representations in cartoons changed from a lost part of the American memory palace to a reconstructed cartoon world.

The Nifty Nineties (Riley Thomson/Disney, 1941) begins with a nostalgic look through an old photo album. We see Mickey Mouse in a black-and-white pose, followed by a flashback to the 1890s, exactly the timescape that Disney would realize a few years later in the Main Street USA section of Disneyland. Mickey and Minnie go to a vaudeville theater (admission is ten, twenty, or thirty cents). The asbestos curtain is decorated with advertisements for typical trades of the time, with in-jokes playing on the names of the animation staff.[68] Illustrated song slides, a turn-of-the century vaudeville attraction, recount a melodramatic story of "Father, Dear Father," accompanied by a barbershop quartet. The sentiment brings Minnie to tears, but Mickey reassures her with the self-referential, "Don't take it so hard, Minnie. It's only a show." In this remarkable moment, the film displays many of the appeals of the world of melodrama: the theme of the threatened family unit, music that evokes bathos, the empathy of spectators as they immerse themselves in the story, and the tagging of emotion as a feminine trait and rationality and stoicism as masculine. Mickey is dismissive of the show and its tear jerking. The nineties were not as nifty as they might have seemed at first glance, the film suggests. The content of the slide show suggests fissures in the ideal family unit. Then, Mickey's utopian faith in technology is challenged when, upon leaving the theater, he crashes his new horseless carriage.

The Dover Boys at Pimento University or The Rivals Of Roquefort Hall (Chuck Jones/Schlesinger, 1942) is the celebrated parody of boys' adventure books and famous as an experiment in stylized graphics and so-called limited animation. It also was set at the turn of the twentieth century. It doesn't explicitly represent a vaudeville show, but it does incorporate stage melodrama into its plot and adopts farcical theatricality. *The Dover Boys,* like the Disney film, marshals precinematic lantern slides to present its gaslight "meller." The self-conscious modernism of the graphic style contrasts with the clichéd story from the days before D.W. Griffith and introduces self-parody (anticipating *The Rocky and Bullwinkle Show*). Such animated trips to yesteryear were the counterparts of trends in mainstream cinema, the most notable of which is probably *Meet Me in St. Louis* (Vincente Minnelli/MGM, 1944), which revolves around the World's Fair of forty years prior.

Michael Chanan, writing on how documentary films produce their figures of symbolic locales, observes, "Representational spaces thus tend towards a more or less coherent system of nonverbal symbols and signs. The products of representational spaces (to follow Lefebvre) are symbolic works, in this case, films, either fiction or documentary, or some admixture of the two." He then wonders if specific film practices produce different screen worlds: "Does this also mean we can distinguish different types of representational space which correspond to different modes of filmic utterance? Is documentary perhaps a different screen world from fiction? (And what about animation, and new technologies and media of image (re)presentation?)."[69] This describes how vaudeville imagery functions in the screen world of the Tooniverse, so the answer seems to be yes. The animators seized upon the defunct institution and re-performed it to create new knowledge of the past and fake nostalgia. Fake, because most of the consumers of cartoons in the 1940s and later had little if any actual experience of live vaudeville except when mediated through the memory palaces of radio, film and television.[70] Simultaneously, by ironically representing it as an "outmoded knowledge formation," animators were tearing down the contradictory tendencies in the vaudeville edifice.

Behind the Stage Door

Piano Tooners exemplified those films that stole from the vaudeville timescape opportunities for cartooning strangeness, bodily danger, and erotic excess. Much of that film involves the opera house stage as a setting for bizarre and sensuous happenings. For example, when the plump orchestra members strike up a song, we see they are incongruously playing toy instruments. We voyeuristically glimpse the heavyset soprano in her dressing room as she changes her costume behind a translucent screen and steps out to adjust (and display to us) her underwear. Onstage, the curtain rises unexpectedly to show her still fidgeting with the garments. At the film's end, her body expands to hit the highest notes, eventually breaking through the theater's roof. She takes the protagonists, Tom and Jerry, to her ample bosom (Figure 21). All this seems rather Freudian.[71]

It is *Stage Door Cartoon* (Friz Freleng/Warner Bros., 1944) that plays the keys of the vaudeville-cartoon timescape like a fine-tuned instrument. Elmer Fudd chases Bugs Bunny into a vaudeville theater that advertises "12 Great Acts."[72] The stage is a place where the spectacles are diverse and voyeuristic. The potential for violent interaction between audience and actors is high. Just seeing dancing cancan girls onstage turns Elmer literally into a wolf. One dancer, though, is Bugs in female disguise, and when Elmer realizes that he has been tricked, his lust turns into rage and a hail of shotgun fire. He learns that although the theatrical spectacle is designed for erotic gazing, its horrible prettiness is duplicitous.

Bugs and Elmer have contrasting relations to the stage. As a vaudevillian, Bugs is at ease there; as a member of the voyeuristic clientele, Elmer is out of his element. Bugs, when the rising curtain catches him by surprise, shows his familiarity by improvising an agile tap-dance number. Elmer, however, freezes in stage fright. His hilarious disguise as a piano that stalks onto the stage prompts Bugs to launch into his next number, another vaudeville staple, a trick piano solo. Fudd is befuddled by the string hammers and is mercifully ejected into the stage wings. When the curtain rises again, a frightened Elmer meekly complies when Bugs directs him up the high-diving platform, from which he dives into a glass of water. Next, Bugs tricks Elmer into appearing as Romeo. Petrified and behaving as if mesmerized, Elmer follows Bugs's directions from the prompter's booth. As happened with Olive Oyl in *The "Hyp-Nut-Tist,"* the ordinary person surrenders his or her will upon entering the stage. Elmer gets through some Shakespeare but degenerates quickly into making faces at the audience. One more curtain and we see Bugs behind Elmer using his arms to lead Elmer through a striptease, working him like a puppeteer. When he gets down to his shorts, a southern sheriff (a character that would evolve into Yosemite Sam the following year) marches in from the wings and arrests Elmer, presumably for his foray into burlesque. The sheriff is marching the indecently exposed Elmer out of the theater when a cartoon ("Warner Bros. presents Bugs Bunny") appears on the screen above the stage. The sheriff shouts, "Hold your

FIGURE 21. *Piano Tooners* (1932). Fat soprano Mlle Pflop with Tom and Jerry.

hosses, it's one of them Bugs Bunny cartoonies comin' on!" We see an anachronistic black-and-white film of Bugs reciting, "Eh, what's up, Doc?" Now things get weird.

The cartoon within the cartoon shows us Bugs backstage when he was dressing up as the sheriff, alerting Elmer, who is still in the sheriff's clutches in the audience, to the charade. Yet when Elmer yanks the clothes off the "twickster" sheriff, it's not the rabbit but a human. Indeed, it's the real sheriff (Figure 22), who, though now clad only in his skivvies, escorts the nearly naked Elmer out of the theater. This echoes the earlier scene of Elmer's impromptu striptease. As the audience's avatar in this film, Elmer's repeated near nakedness suggests that vaudeville is like a recurring bad dream. Back on the movie screen, the final bar of the Looney Tunes exit music plays and we see a conductor leading the orchestra under the "That's All Folks!" closing title card. The conductor removes his Leopold Stokowski wig and—surprise—it's actually Bugs in yet another masquerade. Trickster to the end, he impersonates Jimmy Durante and delivers the famous line, "I got a million of 'em!"

Stage Door Cartoon, with explicit figurations of vaudeville as a place of danger, surrealism, and the uncanny, exhibits a film noir sensibility. The empty streets of the nondescript town outside the theater suggest the morbid vacuum of the wartime home-front city. Oddly, this contrasts

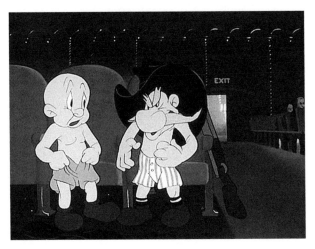

FIGURE 22. *Stage Door Cartoon* (1944). Law and disorder prevail as the sheriff (or is it Bugs Bunny?) arrests Elmer Fudd in a vaudeville theater. Original in color.

with the packed theater interior, where the audience ogles the cancan dancers. The stage door is a demarcation between the outdoors, constituted as a deserted urban landscape devoid of life, and the theater interior, a realm of irrational magic. The door, like Mickey's looking glass, is also a cartoon film frame; pass through it and leave your dry, sterile world for a land of nightmares. Vaudeville is a place where gender, identity, and the social order are not as they seem. Customers and performers, for instance, fire guns with impunity (recall Donald in *Mickey's Amateurs*). Spectators risk bidirectional transgression in being tricked into becoming part of the program, its most dangerous part. It's a performance of madness.

Although *Stage Door Cartoon* at first appears to chronicle that time when movies were integral to vaudeville programs, in fact the image that emerges doesn't make sense historically. The Bugs Bunny "cartoony" is not in Technicolor (as they all were after 1941), and a live orchestra provides the cartoon's music, as if the film were a silent. (Yet we do hear Bugs speak his tagline in the film. Odd.) If this is a memory palace, then Bugs is the phantom of vaudeville. Although he is not represented as a magician, he behaves as one, controlling the artifice, the misdirection, and the assaults on identity. For example, although we had seen Bugs disguising himself as the sheriff in the dressing room, a scene that was repeated in the projected cartoon, we were fooled as much as Elmer was when the sheriff enters because we could see Bugs standing on stage with Elmer. Bugs seems to be in two places at once. His final masquerade as the conductor shows that he has been in charge all along, both acting within the incoherent narrative and controlling it as an outside agent. In other words, he is the figure of the animator.

Lunatic Tunes

One of the masterpieces of American animation simultaneously preserves and debases the popular theater of days past. The interpretations of Chuck Jones's *One Froggy Evening* (Chuck Jones/Warner Bros., 1955) are superficially straightforward, but the film stays devilishly enigmatic. The filmmakers planted temporal and geographic clues to suggest that the cartoon is concerned fundamentally with critiquing the timescape of vaudeville.

An employee of the Acme Building and Wrecking Company is tearing down the fictional J.C. Wilber Building when he finds a time capsule. It contains a document giving the precise date on which the cornerstone was laid: April 16, 1892. Although this date might have had some special significance to the animators or producers (it is as yet unknown),[73] it definitely sets the building's construction at the height of vaudeville's popularity and in the year just before the movies began (with Edison's Kinetoscope in 1893). It is from this era that the inhabitant of the capsule, a singing frog, has survived with no ill effects.[74] He brings with him a repertoire of songs from old Tin Pan Alley.[75] The worker who finds the frog with the marvelous talent immediately dreams of exploiting it in vaudeville, and we see his mental images of the Palace with placards announcing the singing, talking, dancing wonder (Plate 1). However, one New York City impresario after another, including the head of the Acme Theatrical Agency, refuses to take an interest because the frog will not sing in the presence of another human except for the worker who found him. The despondent man's sighting of the boarded-up Hippodrome theater inspires him to invest his savings into fixing it up to showcase his unique attraction. The rendering of the auditorium in the cartoon doesn't resemble the historic New York Hippodrome, which shuttered in 1939. The image serves only as a sign of that emblematic theater.[76] Its run-down status indicates that the story takes place at vaudeville's nadir.

The frog's singing continues to be heard only by the man, which drives him into the lunatic asylum. Clues tell us that he was incarcerated in late 1954. The newspaper on the park bench that he shares with the frog contains the obituary for Lionel Barrymore, who died on November 15 of that year.[77] This temporal trace connects *One Froggy Evening* to the memory of America's "royal family" of stage and screen. It also exemplifies Bakhtin's notion of how the present tends to intrude into the timescape of the past.

In the story, then, less than a year passes between the asylum scene and the present time, 1955, marked by the date on the foundation stone of the "Tregoweth Brown Building" under construction.[78] By this time the man, who has become a beaten-down homeless person, places the still-mellifluous frog in the time capsule for the next generation. Fast-forward to 2056, when the Brown Building is being wrecked by the Acme Building Disintegrators. Another worker finds the frog in the cornerstone, still high-stepping and singing his old-time songs. Like vampires, Popeye's rabbit, and Peter Pan, the frog never dies.[79]

Despite the Da Vinci Code–like time markers the filmmakers left for us, the chronology of the plot is indeterminate. The crucial date we do not know is when the story begins, that is, when the Wilber Building was razed. The scenes in which the man takes the frog to auditions and tries to launch it in vaudeville seem to take place in the late 1920s or early 1930s. The old-fashioned equipment of the switchboard operators and their costumes suggest a pre–World War II period. On the promoters' walls we see signed pictures of their star clients from the 1920s, including one who looks like Greta Garbo, as well as a prominent portrait of a flapper signed "Lena," possibly a reference to the Lina Lamont character in *Singin' in the Rain* (1952), which was set in the first years of the talkies. Regardless, the temporality of the plot coincides with the rise and fall of vaudeville.

A simple but ambiguous fable, the film invites us to deduce easy morals from the story: It's wrong to steal stuff. Greed is destructive. You can't profit from others' talent. Art is a cruel mistress. Art and commerce don't mix. However, these interpretations don't adequately explain the film's assertive foregrounding of vaudeville's demise.

One Froggy Evening is not so much a tribute to vaudeville as it is an elegy. Many of the components of the memory palace are glossed in the film: There are visions of the great vaudeville theaters of the early twentieth century. The heterogeneous audiences of vaudeville are caricatured as a beer-swilling crowd. The entertainment comes in short, incisive bursts. We see the audiences' appetite for public displays of great talent, for oddity, for the unnatural and the irrational, for the countercultural and liminal. Animals act like humans. The live stage is characterized by social and ethnic diversity, but also by madness.

Although ostensibly about vaudeville, the film perhaps mirrors the animation industry's apprehension in 1955. It had been in artistic and economic decline since 1948, following the end of block booking, the distribution practice ensuring that shorts would be marketed with features. *One Froggy Evening,* in fact, had been a victim of the malaise, its production having been delayed since 1953.[80] The biggest cause of anxiety for the film business was television, which must have appeared to animators as both a blessing and a curse, much like the frog in the box. Jones, in fact, was prescient. The allegorical progression from the wrecking ball to what seems to be a nuclear disintegrator reflects technology's incessant advance. Like the coming of sound in the early 1930s and the transition to computer animation in the early 2000s, the rise of network television in the mid-1950s must have rocked the animators' world.

In the end, *One Froggy Evening* transforms vaudeville into something far more fantastic and outlandish than any show at the Palace or the Hippodrome. Coming at the end of the studio cartoon period, the film, with its elegiac sentiment for a culture on the edge of oblivion, suggests that the filmmakers were looking not only at their past but into their own future.

CHAPTER 4

Shadow of a Mouse

Animation Performance Spaces

> Surface, volume, density and weight are not optical phenom-
> ena. Man first learned about them between his finger and the
> hollow of his palm. He does not measure space with his eyes
> but with his hands and feet. The sense of touch fills nature
> with mysterious forces. Without it, nature is like the pleasant
> landscapes of the magic lantern, slight, flat and chimerical.
> —Henri Focillon (1934)

> [In] the painting that came to us through the Italian Renais-
> sance, we are much more preoccupied with volume and much
> less with space; and of course volume being more defined,
> having a true outline—which space has not—we are much
> more constructive. We deal with weights, with outlines, with
> things that the Chinese or Japanese are not preoccupied with.
> —Jean Charlot, speaking to Disney animators (1938)

Performers, even toons, must have time and space in which to exist, an
environment in which to move, a place that surrounds and restrains
their behavior. This is why the unseen animator in *Duck Amuck* (Chuck
Jones/Warner Bros., 1953) is so diabolical when he torments poor Daffy.
He changes the backgrounds without rhyme or reason and forces the
duck actor to reprogram his performance on the spot in order to keep
up with the unpredictable environment. "Buster," Daffy objects, speaking to the off-screen, silent, unknown animator/narrator, "it may come
as a complete surprise to you to find that this is an animated cartoon,
and in animated cartoons they have scenery, and in all the years that

I—." Whereupon the cartoonist asserts his superior agency and erases the luckless duck completely.

From our view in the audience, we see that one of the most fundamental expectations about classic cartoons, the character's autonomy and existence in a dedicated spatial environment, is being yanked abruptly from under Daffy. The gag is hilarious, but it also reveals what we often conveniently ignore about cartoons: that there are two levels of spatial construction, the figures drawn on cels and the "scenery" before which they strut in their constructed worlds. Toons, as embodied characters to which we attribute personality, independence, and volition, need to be anchored in an on-screen environment, need to be masters of their Tooniverse. At the same time, that world appears to be governed by a Hobbesian deity that vacillates between whimsical and sadistic.

Chuck Jones's joke is a throwback to McCay's *Little Nemo* and Cohl's animated abstractions, in which moving graphics frolicked and metamorphosed against blank white or black backgrounds and drifted in an inchoate space of the imagination. Animation from the studio period, however, would have none of this environmental indeterminacy (although there were some exceptions). We are made to think about cartoon space as a place that is not only inhabited by toons but also fancied by viewers. Indeed, one of the things we like about animation is the alternate world that it conjures, a world in which the rules are suspended and viewers allow themselves to be mesmerized by alien screen beings, and their sounds, sights, and sites.

In non-animated cinema, the mise-en-scène is a photographic given. Audiences are used to naïvely conflating "location" with the real world, although filmmakers routinely have to go to great lengths and expense to place their actors in an appropriate environment. Eisenstein wrote of his jealousy of animators, "In live-action cinema, what is difficult is teasing out the line of the composition from the real material. However, we were only able by chance to film the right cloud we needed. We tried forty times before that, but it was always wrong. . . . But Disney is lucky. He can just draw the outline he wants."[1] Disney art teacher Don Graham expressed the idea similarly. Unlike in non-animated films, in which physical attributes are "fixed," in animation, time and space are limitless and obey arbitrary laws. He described live action as "earthbound."[2] Natural laws don't affect animation, though. If the artist can visualize it in time he can animate it. Sometimes directors of non-animated films have to extract their actors from or place them into the surrounding scene, by using mattes or digital editing, for example. In either case, live-action film environments are selected, constructed, and manipulated as much as cartoon environments, but the techniques for doing so are disguised, creating natural believability, a cinematic trompe l'oeil that passes for reality. In traditional animation, on the contrary, the characters inhabit a space that is ostentatiously constructed. It isn't fixed, but responsive, accommodating any of the signature animation actions, eye-popping effects, and zany characterizations.

Creating cartoon space is partly, but not simply, a mechanical operation. Because of our expectation that cartoons are movies, albeit different from noncartoon films, the rules of narrative and the conventions of audience engagement enter the picture. Context matters. Thus, when see Ko-Ko the Clown hopping about against a white background in an Out of the Inkwell film, it isn't a figure on a blank screen that we see, but rather a character who is acting out a story on a blank sheet of paper on Max's sketchpad. The blankness is quickly rationalized because of our inferences and expectations. When Ko-Ko (or Porky in You Ought to Be in Pictures, or Jessica and Roger Rabbit, or Homer Simpson in Homer[3]) journey from the flat space of the screen into the volumetric world, the characters' metaleptic changes of spatial zones define their scale, their dimensionality, and their bodies' limits. Their environment is integral to their personality and psychology and is usually a correlative of their psyches. One reason the off-screen meddler's actions in Duck Amuck are so disruptive is that the animator is stripping the character of its expected integration into a consistent, though cartoonal, world.

The most intense period of transformation of the performance spaces and the mechanics for producing them in animation took place in the 1930s. The rapidity of the transformation was extraordinary. Think of how a typical cartoon from the beginning of the decade—say The Merry Dwarfs (Ub Iwerks/Disney, 1929), Barnacle Bill (Dave Fleischer/ Paramount, 1930), or Bosko the Doughboy (Hugh Harman/Schlesinger, 1931)—looked. Then compare these to the features Snow White and the Seven Dwarfs (David Hand/Disney, 1937) or Gulliver's Travels (Dave Fleischer/Paramount, 1939) or the short subject Peace on Earth (Hugh Harman/MGM, 1939). Everything has been taken to a new level: length, color, sound, movement, characterization, and acting as well as narrative, spatial, and graphic complexity. In ten years, animation changed forever. The question is how and why did this happen?

Pictorial design in 1920s cartoons had achieved a happy medium because the dominant style of comic strip art, with its high-contrast black-

and-white palette, simplified forms, rounded characters, and inconspicuous backgrounds, contributed to an overall impression of flatness, the so-called New York style.[3] It is a misnomer, however, to call silent-era animation "flat"; it merely represented a different attitude toward the screen. The animators understood this space as unified with and emanating from the character's body. Paul Crowther has aptly called this *proxy space*. It expanded and contracted, becoming sparse or rich as needed. "Here, a familiar frontally presented shape allows the two-dimensional forms to be seen as three-dimensional by virtue of the way in which the frontal aspects' shape forms a crude surface plane defined against an immediate rather than gradually emergent background plane,"[4] he writes. This concept of space as contingent differs from the alternate one of arraying bodies within a preordained picture governed by the rules of classical perspective.

Other systems of representation that created the illusion of coherent environmental depth were not the opposite of flat or proxy space; they simply were other options. The historical trend was to move away from graphic or comic strip space toward camera space. Two examples show typical 1920s strategies. *Felix All Puzzled* (Otto Messmer/Pat Sullivan Cartoons, 1925) uses slanting lines to create simple foreshortening that may be read as two-dimensional and as receding in space (Figure 23). A different approach is seen in *Tall Timber* (Ub Iwerks/Disney, 1928), where the softened lines and smaller scale in the clearly separated background contrast with the sharp lines and larger scale in the foreground (Figure 24). The spaces in both films create a necessary backdrop for the toons' performances, but they show little depth, since the characters don't move back and forth in space, only to the left and to the right. The association of this cartoon style with comic strip graphics that were already familiar to viewers made for a highly legible spatial system, comprehensible at a glance. Such background treatments were uniform from film to film, and therefore relatively cheap to produce.

Furthermore, animators loved to offset this nearly exclusive two-dimensional shallowness against plunging thrusts created by characters running back and forth, in and out of depth, and dynamic point-of-view shots in which the background cycled up to or away from the screen surface. It was a very touchy-feely cinema, dwelling on sensory effects and the celebration of the toon body flying through its roller-coaster world.

During the 1930s, however, all the producers to some extent moved away from these graphic recipes to grapple with specific aesthetic

FIGURE 23. *Felix All Puzzled* (1925). Simple foreshortening suggests distance while preserving the flatness and linearity of the composition.

FIGURE 24. *Tall Timber* (1928). Depth is suggested by scalar differences between foreground and background and by the background's lower contrast.

problems in spatial representation. Walt Disney, unfazed by this more labor-intensive mode of production, and taking advantage of abundant cheap labor during the Depression, gambled on research and development, thus raising the bar for everyone else. Some studios tried to compete, while others intentionally kept their distance.

Writers disagree about whether these aesthetic transformations of the 1930s were beneficial, leading to progress in cartoon art, or a detriment, causing producers and consumers to lose sight of the essence of the animated art form. The discourse centers on Disney. The former camp sees the changes as a demonstration of increased sophistication. Barrier writes, "In effect, Disney asked [Jack] King and his other animators to recapitulate overnight the transition from the art of the Middle Ages to the art of the Renaissance—a transition marked in part by a shift from hard, precise, formulaic drawing to loose, exploratory sketching."[5] John Canemaker observed of the early 1930s Disney studio, "One can see the animators struggling painfully to transcend the woefully inadequate formula structures of the characters and the old rules of animation technique in order to simulate actions seen in nature."[6] The Disney studio art classes often held up their own earlier work as inadequate examples of characterization, storytelling, and spatial practice. Speaking in 1937, *Snow White* animator Tytla dismissed the studio's short films and predicted that in five years the animators would no longer be drawing Donald Duck: "The type of stuff we have been doing here the last few years has been a change from what preceded it, and will be different from what is about to follow." In the early days—by which he meant only a few years prior—differentiating characters that were physically different (as in *The Three Little Pigs*) was a challenge. "Today," however, "we are really on the verge of something that is new," he said.[7]

Disney always preached the importance of technological innovation, saying, "How very fortunate we are, as artists, to have a medium whose potential limits are still far off in the future; a medium of *entertainment* where, theoretically at least, the only limit is the imagination of the artist.... [T]he unseen future will take care of itself if one just keeps growing up a little every day."[8] This utopian vision leads inexorably to the received opinion that there was a golden age of Hollywood cartoons.

The contrary opinion is that Disney's philosophical transformations were steps in the wrong direction and that the modifications of cartoon space introduced in the 1930s caused something of early animation's verve, jazzy spontaneity, and ludic surrealism to be lost. Many fans of 1920s cartoons loved the fantasmagorical, kinetic vibrancy of Felix the Cat, Inkwell Imps, Oswald, the earliest Mickeys, and Silly Symphonies— the boundless world of cartoons that Eisenstein called "plasmatic." As the 1930s marched on and most of the animation industry became economically dependent on the Hollywood distribution system, this vivacity gave way to a less imaginative, less rubbery, more realistically inclined cartooning concept, according to some. Wells sums it up: "Disney's concentration on innovations in the apparatus to facilitate the animated film ultimately had the consequence ... of undermining the distinctive aspects of animation itself.... With each technical development ... Disney moved further away from the plasmatic flexibility of many of the early Silly Symphonies, and coerced the animated form into a neo-realist practice."[9] This feeling that something was sacrificed in the rapid development is a minority view among fans, but it's the opinion that many academics hold.

As polemics go, these are useful. They help us grasp the big-picture issues. (Such is the intent of my figurative performance–embodied performance contrast.) Not surprisingly, the two different categories become less distinct when they are examined closely. For one thing, as Mark Langer has pointed out, a hegemonic vision did not emerge from the Disney studio in the 1930s.[10] There were disagreements among the artists about the collective artistic direction of the studio, as evidenced in the hybridized, fragmented mindsets of *Fantasia*. Also, the meaning of terms such as *flat, rounded,* and *realist* and the concept of Renaissance space were not at all settled. The differing positions are also often ahistorical and immaterial, assuming a "natural" evolution (or devolution) without adequately accounting for the cultural milieu of cinema in the 1930s, the prevailing aesthetics, or the mechanical nature of the animation process. The biggest problem is that dichotomies may distract from the significant underlying issue, which is what was the motivation for the changes in the first place?

I contend that the desire to redesign cartoon space occurred in lockstep with and was seamlessly integrated into the studios' new attitude about animation performance. In a nutshell, the transformations of the 1930s were driven pragmatically by the studios, which were retooling the simplified space of the 1920s Tooniverse to better accommodate the increasingly complex characterizations of toons. Put another way, space construction followed the evolving concept of animation acting from figurative to embodied. The Disney studio was emphatic about linking pictorial space and personality. According to Graham, in the early films, the animators could not reproduce such natural forces as gravity and motion in a convincing three-dimensional space. Therefore, acting too was nearly impossible to animate. He pointed out that Mickey, although he exemplified a stock (figurative) character, survived because of his compensating loveable personality.[11]

The constructive elements of cartoon space, consonant with animation aesthetics generally, are profoundly entangled with technology. Machinists coaxed their equipment, which was designed to render linear graphic space efficiently, to enhance deep-space scenes on the two-dimensional screen instead. The markedly different visual representational system that became popular in the 1930s eventually replaced the comic strip style, which had often verged on modernism with its dynamic compositions. The new style emulated anachronistic illustration styles that were borrowed from popular bourgeois children's books and from literary classics of the Victorian canon.

As a hands-on mode of performance, animation in the studio era required deploying many workers in well-defined hierarchies of labor. Production was also predicated on specialized equipment, engineering support, and specific cinematographic techniques. In only about twenty years the tools of the trade had gone from filmed ink, paper, chalk, and clay to high-tech equipment that sped up the labor of image rendering (notably the refinement of the cel process) and the replication of drawings (through the use of assembly lines and sophisticated aids to drawing and by streamlining the drawing-to-film photographic processes). These new tools enabled work to be completed according to a tight schedule and on a restricted budget, but the practices also imposed technological constraints on how cartoonal space and motion could be created.

PERFORMANCE SPACE: MAKING ROOM FOR BODIES

Studio archivist David R. Smith relates that Walt Disney's interest in achieving a more convincing illusion of depth in the animation of pictorial space began around 1935, when his plans for a feature-length animated film began to take shape in earnest.[12] In fact, however, an examination of the films shows that the animators were exploring alternate spatial concepts much earlier. Furthermore, the innovators in the Disney shop were not working in a vacuum. Rivals were exploring alternatives to 1920s performance space and introducing their own technologies for simulating three-dimensionality.

In the early 1930s, the performance style of toon characters was mostly figurative. The budding interest in pictorial space at Disney and other cartoon shops crept in at exactly the same time Hollywood was considering embodied concepts of character, personality, and "the Method" approach to acting. Perhaps this evidences Disney's drive for perfection, but the developments were also a competitive reaction to changes in space emerging from Iwerks's new studio and from Van Beuren and the Fleischers. Disney was passionate about product differentiation.[13]

A case that strikingly demonstrates the Disney studio's interest in altering traditional space is *Egyptian Melodies* (Wilfred Jackson / Walt Disney Productions, 1931). It begins with a friendly spider spinning a web near the Great Sphinx. A secret door opens and the spider beckons us to follow it inside. We pass through a winding labyrinth until we reach an interior chamber deep underneath the Sphinx. This sequence animated by Dave Hand contains an astounding visual effect.[14] The spider progresses through four dynamic spaces. The shading of the stone walls creates a checkerboard pattern with receding lines of one-point perspective. As we descend the stairs behind the spider, sharing its point of view, we move forward into the illusionistic depth of the stairwell. We round a corner and enter a new space, a long hall. We keep moving, turn onto another stair, and the process repeats (Figure 25). The effect gives the impression of walking down four halls connected by flights of

FIGURE 25. *Egyptian Melodies* (1931). The inquisitive spider descends the scary staircase as the perspective lines shift constantly.

stairs. It also is highly kinetic, generating a strong sense of liveness and being-there, thanks to the constantly readjusting perspective lines. Players of "first-person shooter" video games will recognize the spatial effect immediately. Instead of being rendered on the fly by a fast computer, however, the effect in *Egyptian Melodies* was handcrafted. The scene is striking in its sensuality and how it swallows up viewers in a kind of alimentary opening, an unexpectedly deep orifice in the flat screen.

The spider (and the viewer) then observe the murals of the chamber come to life as figures drawn in an "Egyptian" style compete in a horse race, wage a battle, and finish with a grand chase. One gag is that they are bound to their two-dimensionality and can't escape the wall upon which they're drawn. A commander, however, fails to follow his troops marching around a corner and inadvertently strides out of the frieze and into the space of the room, thereby violating the spatial conceit of flatness—until he realizes his mistake, retreats to the two-dimensional surface, and runs to catch up with his soldiers (Figure 26). One attacking soldier is pursuing another around a column. The assailant chucks his spear, but it misses its target, goes full circle around the back of the column, and emerges to stick into the thrower's rear.[15] Next, the spider witnesses a long-shot scene of enormous complexity. The friezes show hallucinatory moving images twisting in serpentine strings and interminable chases in frantically conflicting directions. These chaotic visions

FIGURE 26. *Egyptian Melodies* (1931). The hieroglyphic
commander marches off the two-dimensional frieze into
volumetric space and then retreats back to his flat world.

are all too much for the spider. It retraces its route through the labyrinth, reversing the deep perspective descent, exits the Sphinx (in a manner suggesting regurgitation), and runs screaming over the horizon.

The moving linear perspective sequence of the labyrinthine descent
was constructed with lavish care and detail. (Some of the background
drawings were used again in *The Mad Doctor* [David Hand/Disney,
1933].) The enveloping space of the film is interactive. It responds to
the spider's entry, to its movements and its vision. What is the meaning
of the frieze scene at the climax of the cartoon? This film, in which bold
applications of preclassical and perspectival treatments of space clash,
may echo the then-current debates among the animators about pictorial
space, conversations to be expected during the introductory period of a
new concept. We'll return to *Egyptian Melodies* later.

After chief animator Iwerks left in 1930, Disney recruited new talent
with original ideas and diverse artistic backgrounds. The reorganization
of the animation department led to changes in the pictorial concepts that
Iwerks and Disney had established. Crucially, a new 1931 contract with
United Artists gave the studio the ability to budget its own productions
and set its own release schedule, thus affording the time and capital for
ambitious experiments.

Some of the animators began organizing group life drawing lessons
on their own, and some attended classes at the Chouinard Art Institute,

the predecessor of the California Institute of the Arts. Disney began sponsoring these sessions informally in 1931. In 1932, Disney invited Don Graham to give regular classes to the staff on the studio premises; in 1934, he set Graham up as director of new expanded studio classrooms.[16] It was during this period that the fundamental concepts of pictorial space, the color palette, and performance philosophy as well as the films in general began to change into what Langer calls the West Coast style of animation.[17] In a lengthy 1935 memo to Graham, Disney said he was convinced that "there is a scientific approach to this business, and I think we shouldn't give up until we have found out all we can about how to teach these young fellows the business."[18] His language urging scientific solutions and inventions is reminiscent of Lewis Mumford's in his just-published *Technics and Civilization*. In that work Mumford saluted Disney, along with Chaplin and René Clair, as masters of pure comedy, lauding "their interpretation of the inner realm of fantasy." Mumford's progressive humanistic vision of science might have resonated with Disney's:

> The translation of the scientific knowledge into practical instruments was a mere incident in the process of invention. . . .
> Out of this habit grew a new phenomenon: deliberate and systematic invention. Here was a new material: problem—find a new use for it. . . .
> In a whole series of characteristic neotechnic inventions, the thought was father to the wish.[19]

Graham taught Disney's artisans the building blocks for this new approach. Under his tutelage and that of his Chouinard colleagues, the artists began rendering pictorial space by taking into account observation, classical conventions for pictorial space, standardized procedure, and trial and error—in a word, science. These lessons were learned in "sweatbox" conversations between Walt and his directors, and increasingly in the studio classes, where the crew listened to lectures illustrated with clips from older cartoons and roughs of new work in progress. The nominally "scientific" approach was easily assimilated within the standard art school practice, the "crit," to form its own creative pedagogy. Under this new system ideas were debated, sometimes heatedly, and criticism of the studio's own work was direct, even harsh. Through this procedure the animators (some more than others) imbibed the viewpoints and specific practices of illustration and painting that Graham and his cohorts were expounding at Chouinard.

Graham's particular interests were in color, line drawing, and the construction of classical space. The two courses he taught at Disney were on action analysis and perspective. He insisted that an animator must be proficient in pictorial space in order to create a believable fantasy world. As artists had done for centuries, the animators learned how to render the illusion of depth on two-dimensional surfaces by imagining the drawing or canvas as a glass window. This picture plane is the base of a visual pyramid, or, as Graham called it, the cone of vision. Parallel lines (think of railroad tracks) seem to come together at a vanishing point on the horizon line. These receding lines are orthogonals (or, as Graham called them, vanishing lines). The lines parallel to the picture plane and the horizon are called transversals, or horizon lines. Artists used these lines as well as color and shading—highlights and shadows—to express volume (characterized by "great density") and to create space ("a mass of lesser density"). Graham's writing suggests that he conceived of screen space as a prerequisite for performance: "Animation deals with photographs of drawings and paintings projected in time. . . . But we should remember that no matter how the illusion of action is achieved, the images we see occur on the screen, a surface. The motion picture and the still picture have one thing in common, each is an image on a surface."[20]

Graham also opined that the viewers' first impression of movement begins in the drawings themselves when the artists deliberately unbalanced the space in the composition. The best compositions, he claimed, establish a tension between perspective and variations in color that make "space seem real" and, at the same time, they suggest action and movement by "generating a sense of disturbance in those who view [the artist's] work." There is a clear expectation that the animator (like the Method actor) would require viewers to participate in the psychology of this performance space. For example, we find it physically disturbing to look at a picture painted with the shapes off-balance. When artists intentionally introduce such compositions, viewers respond actively, trying to mentally balance the scene, resulting in a sensation of movement and vitality, even in still pictures. Especially when the pictures show physical work, they symbolize dynamic gesture and expression.[21] The use of dynamic oblique compositional "movement" is clearly visible, for example, in *Pluto's Judgement Day* (David Hand/Disney, 1935) (Figure 27).

Using a sixteenth-century painting as a model, Graham described its pictorial space as "like a little stage, which is referred to as the picture box. As we shall see the picture box takes many forms and its use is constantly changing. In its classic form it represents a small stage usually viewed from normal standing eye level and easily encompassed by the eye. The distance separating objects on this stage can easily be suggested graphically." One may envision the animators arraying their toon figures in such an imaginary vaudeville setting. He urged his animators to estimate with great accuracy the volume of "floor space" that each object and action would require. "The only limit we must impose," he wrote, "is that the little stage be confined to shallow depth and a reasonable dimension from side to side or top to bottom."[22] This shallow "picture box" built around acting figures was precisely the space that Graham was trying to get the animators to master. We see this "little stage" concept both in interiors, as in *Pluto's Judgement Day* (Figure 27 again), and in exteriors, as in *The Flying Mouse,* where the scene is conceived as a shallow theatrical setting (Plate 2).

The influence of this technical training at the 1930s Disney studio is easily discernible in the Mickey Mouse and Silly Symphony films. The figures become anatomically solid and less "cartoony," while their movements become smooth and more natural, thanks to being imagined as fanciful bodies with accurate skeletons upon which gravity pulls. Graham articulated this concept of animation performance space in a section of his 1970 textbook tellingly entitled "Space as a Medium for Action." He wrote, "It seems reasonable to conclude that as long as action is possible a spacious condition exists. This space may or may not be visible."[23] This new comprehensive notion that space and motion were a continuum—not to mention the provocative idea of invisible space—flew in the face of the traditional relationship of figures to background that had defined animation's look up until the early 1930s. The extent of Graham's influence on the animation staff is evident in the transcripts of studio training sessions, such as one that Ken Anderson conducted in 1936 in which he emphasized the relationship between story and screen space. Under the heading "Perspective," he noted that the animators were not stressing perspective enough and how important the device was to "put across depth." He explicitly stated that space and acting interacted: "Wherever it is possible and good from our story angle, try to get the character to show the depth of the field he is working in. Get him to go back in the room or come up in the room. Make a perspective chart of the figure in your layouts—you don't have to finish up the character, just indicate where the head is and where the body would be in correct proportion in the field." Anderson advised

FIGURE 27. *Pluto's Judgement Day* (1935). The diagonal composition was claimed to generate instability and therefore an impression of potential motion. Original in color.

the layout crew to study the scene in *Pluto's Judgement Day* in which the judge's face seemingly bursts through the picture plane, a scene for which the layout artist had made optically precise schematics. "You should make a perspective chart for the animator showing the various extremes in the action."[24]

Disney and Graham were in agreement, and the boss acknowledged that the artist's teaching had transformed the studio from a hierarchy, in which the animators with seniority passed down their techniques to apprentices, to something like a meritocracy. Disney also realized that this art school structure contributed to his goal of embodied acting. Speaking in 1940, he said, "In fact, our studio had become more like a school than a business. As a result, our characters were beginning to act and behave in general like real persons. Because of this we could begin to put real feeling and charm in our characterization. After all, you can't expect charm from animated sticks, and that's about what Mickey Mouse was in his first pictures. We were growing as craftsmen, through study, self-criticism, and experiment. In this way, the inherent possibilities in our medium were dug into and brought to light."[25]

The emerging West Coast style was more consistent with the codes of classical Hollywood cinema. Under the Disney influence this style became dominant, but it never completely eradicated New York style manifestations in Hollywood cartoons. The geographical distinction also had probable origins in the artistic ideologies from Chouinard that had been inspiring the Disney studio. Plus, there was an infusion of European artistic sensibility, not just aesthetically, but also personally in the form of hires such as Albert Hurter, Vlad (a.k.a. Bill) Tytla, and others. Robin Allan observes that the Disney artists "had a cultural background and an understanding of European influences which [Disney] utilized and made anew in the popular American form of cinema."[26] This new artistic vision was readily assimilated at the studio because it was compatible with a major influence of local origin, the California watercolor movement.

Reviewing the 1929 art scene, a *Los Angeles Times* writer noted, "The Chouinard school of water colorists are very much in evidence. They are having a little Renaissance of the medium all their own, and, as a group, make a fine impression through their close study of luminous values, good design and habit of seeing simply."[27] It so happened that at the same time that Disney was striving to use animation to tell beguiling moral tales with sympathetic entertainers and embodied actors, Southern California was abuzz with interest in reviving traditional painting techniques, a movement variously called the California Watercolor style, the California Scene, the California School, and "The Wave." Graham's professional circle at Chouinard was at the center of the California Water Color Society (CWCS), a professional organization that fourteen artists had founded in 1921 to "restore dignity" to watercolor.[28] A remarkable number of them had in common their association with Chouinard and their connection to the animation industry.

The leading lights of the CWCS group were Pruett Carter (1891–1955), Millard Sheets (1907–89), and Phil Dike (1906–90). Although their work was representational, depicted local landscapes and cities, and (with the exception of Sheets's work) showed little influence of post-Cubist European modernism, these regional artists were by no means backward-looking nativists. In *Migratory Camp near Nipomo* (1936), for instance, Sheets arranged objects by diminishing size and receding color values to create depth.[29] They practiced an alternative modernism that emphasized light, color, and spatial volume created by classical means, including perspective and shadowing—exactly the virtues extolled by Graham and the other visitors to the Disney classes. These artists took advantage of the properties of the watercolor medium, avoiding outlined forms and emphasizing transparency, low contrast, a palette that tended toward pastels, and the quality of light (especially backlight). Their influence in the backgrounds of Disney's color films becomes apparent beginning in the mid-1930s. The palettes become brighter, with more white space, and more "naturalistic," as in *Little Hiawatha* (David Hand/Disney, 1937). Furthermore, Graham brought to the studio his Chouinard colleagues' color sensitivity, classicism, and knowledge of anatomy, as well as his own disciplined attitude that fit in with the Disney ethos of embodiment, in contradistinction to, say, Terry, Van Beuren, or the Fleischers' cartoony New York style.

Phil Dike, an artist "best known for city views," taught at Chouinard beginning in 1932.[30] He aided Graham in setting up the initial classes at Disney and taught color theory and life drawing there. In 1934, according to Graham, "Dike was put in charge of the color coordination of all production work which went through Technicolor."[31] He had the responsibility of verifying the accuracy of the photography of all the artwork. His *Grape Harvest* shows Dike's command of light, transparent shadows, and atmospheric perspective.[32] When Disney charged Graham with recruiting workers for *Snow White,* Dike was hired as a background artist.[33] In 1938 he also became president of the CWCS.

Other prominent Chouinard watercolorists included Preston Blair (1908–95), who studied with Sheets in the 1930s. He was a key figure in the California Scene movement and president of the CWCS in 1935, all the while working at Universal, then at Disney. He began as an animator on a Donald Duck short, *Sea Scouts* (Dick Lundy/Disney, 1939), and then joined the animation crews of *Pinocchio, Fantasia,* and *Bambi.* Later he worked for Tex Avery at MGM, where he became the legendary animator of *Red Hot Riding Hood* in the 1940s.[34] His younger brother and another Sheets pupil, Lee Blair (1911–93), worked as a background artist in the studios of Iwerks and Harman-Ising, then he began at Disney in 1938 at the same time that his national reputation as a painter was growing.[35] By far the most influential artistic presence at Disney who also was an active member of the CWCS was Mary Robinson Blair (1911–79), who was married to Lee. She had studied with Pruett Carter at Chouinard and was a lifelong watercolorist. She was a veteran of the Iwerks and Harman-Ising studios before working for Disney as a color stylist and designer.[36] Her early credits at Disney include *Saludos Amigos* (Wilfred Jackson et al./Disney, 1942; art supervisor), *The Three Caballeros* (Norman Ferguson/Disney, 1944; art supervisor), *Make Mine Music* (Robert Cormack/Disney, 1946; art supervisor), and *Song of the South* (Harve Foster and Wilfred Jackson/Disney, 1946; background and color stylist).[37]

The CWCS circle directly influenced the look of Disney films when its members became studio artists in the late 1930s and '40s. It's also likely that their teaching, collegiality, and mentorship had been relayed to the Disney animators indirectly much earlier via Graham's classes. In addition to the specific contributions that they made, their general attitude and conceptualization of the land-, sea- and cityscapes of California as mythopoeic nature studies provided fitting atmospheres for Disney's new animated worlds.[38]

ACME PERFORMANCES

Kristin Thompson was among the first scholars to ruminate on the relationship between animation's technologically driven production requirements and film style. One of her points is especially pertinent here. The widespread adoption of the patented Bray-Hurd cel process during the 1920s streamlined cartoon manufacturing and affected the aesthetics of the animated image. "The crucial aspect of cel animation," she wrote, "is its separation of the different foreground and background layers."[39] It is precisely this spatial rift between segregated cels and backgrounds that many animators were coping with in the 1930s. By decade's end at the major studios there was a new kind of cartoon space that was more accommodating for the characters, more engaging for the viewers, and closer to live-action mise-en-scène. The characters themselves were more fully rounded, graphically and psychologically, and needed spaces that, as art historian Focillon might have said, were less "slight, flat, and chimerical."

The formal properties that Thompson describes were interleaved with the economics of commercial distribution and production, and they were engineered into the equipment used in making animation. Anne Friedberg's thoughts on the camera obscura of the seventeenth century as a device that "helped the artist to transform the three-dimensional space of vision to the two-dimensional *virtual* plane of representation" apply as well to the animation apparatus of the twentieth century.[40] Although the animators could draw anything in any way, their tools circumscribed the ways they could construct space.

There were three spatial systems in play: the biplanar systems of cel and background and a third, virtual one that was created at the time of projection. *Cel space* was the surface plane where the moving figures resided, depicted as bodies in the dynamic constitutive poses that would move when projected. *Background space* was normally a static plane that the artists handled much as they would with any picture—using casual or strict perspective with one or multiple vanishing points, or using aerial perspective, for example. Additionally, it had its special function of providing a space for the characters to inhabit. The cel and background planes were not arbitrary; they mimicked the figure/ground relationships of normal depth and motion perception. Then there was the cinematic *camera space* that resulted when the combined spatial systems were viewed. The animation apparatus allowed these spaces to be executed separately, usually by different people, and then blended during photography to cinematize the static artwork. When projected, this became the space of the performance.

All the elements, including dialogue, music, and sound effects, were scrupulously coordinated on exposure sheets (a.k.a. bar sheets or dope sheets) so that all would come together during photography, editing, and projection. As in a non-animated film of the period, editing and continuity were crucial for achieving a holistic, unified effect. Disney animators were advised that each scene "should carry an underlined feeling that will move smoothly along with the scenes which precede and follow it." As in classical Hollywood's invisible editing approach to continuity, "an audience must not be made conscious of the separate parts of the picture—the audience should only be conscious of the continuous flow and movement of the story or sequence from start to finish. As in music, when one false note strikes a discord, it disturbs the whole rendition—distracts or breaks the mood."[41] The final result was a machine-made model of visuality akin in theory to the optical apparatus described by Friedberg, one that similarly invited viewers to participate in a cinesthetic engagement with the created world.

Production methods and equipment had been slowly standardized during the 1920s. Some studios, such as Pat Sullivan's and the Fleischers', had resisted taking out licenses for the Bray-Hurd process and continued to use anachronistic techniques such as the slash system for image composition.[42] The Disney studio had gradually begun using cels during the silent days and had kept abreast of the latest technology ever since. This state of affairs grew from Disney's special relationship with Adolph Furer's Acme Tool and Manufacturing Company in Los Angeles.[43] In 1930, Acme began modifying Bell & Howell cameras for Disney and making custom animation equipment for the studio. Soon they started their own line of products, which they sold on the open market.

The animation camera was their leader, but they also supplied all the accessories and tools of the trade. The Acme brand, the future coyote's product of choice in his pursuit of the toothsome Road Runner, was the standard for all studio animators in the 1930s.[44] Because of the high degree of standardization in the industry, the studios worked on a remarkably level technological playing field. Therefore, if one wanted to innovate in the domain of performance—as Disney obviously did—then, following Mumford's recommendations, one would have to adapt existing technologies and renovate methods to modify form and content.

Based on existing Acme-type systems, animators tackled cel and background spaces (which are always in a dialectic relationship because they're physically distinct), and they improvised camera space (which deploys such devices as shadows and graphically simulated cinema effects). Let's examine each separately.

Cel Space

The cel was where the action was.[45] The figures on the cel, even when separated from any background, were not bereft of space. The simplest stick figures, recalling Crowther, implicitly carry with them their own proxy space.[46] The rounder the figures, he adds, the more proxy space they posit. When these characters had to move through planar space, that is, when they had to leave shallow foreground space to retreat from the picture plane, the relationship between the foreground cel and the background art with its own spatial system became problematic. Animators adapted conventional solutions for generating the impression of three-dimensional space on a two-dimensional drawing and added a few of their own.

Normally, any part of the picture that was supposed to move was drawn on paper with motions subdivided into discrete phases of action. The work began with the animators (a collective workforce that included the assistants, cleanup staff, and in-betweeners, for example) drawing the figures using the Acme animation board, which was also called the animation disk (Figure 28). Perforated drawing paper fit snugly over the pegs on the top or bottom, maintaining registration while allowing the artist to roll or flip the drawings to check the animation.[47] The outlines of the finished drawings were then traced onto the cels during the ink-and-paint phase of production. These disks were mounted in a drafting workstation and could rotate 360 degrees to facilitate drawing with minimum fatigue. The place where the hand hits

FIGURE 28. Acme animation board. Acme Equipment Catalogue.
Courtesy of Photo-Sonics, Inc.

the paper might be thought of as the part of a machine that unites the
animator's graphic rendering and his or her imagination.

Fields

Acme animation paper and cels were 12 inches wide by 9.5 inches high.
Animators referred to their drawings by how much of the sheet it used,
or its *field size*. A *12-field* meant a drawing that covered the entire surface of the cel, although in practice the largest part of the cel photographed was 10.5 inches by 8 inches.[48] The animators normally did not
use the full drawing for every scene. Instead, they would direct the
camera technician to move the camera closer to the cel in order to
frame selected areas. I use the term *refielding* to refer to the creation of
performance space by repositioning the camera during frame-by-frame
photography, moving up or down, perhaps in combination with cel and
background motion, to reveal a bit more or less of the drawn image.
Refielding was indicated with penciled red lines as in Figure 29, a layout artist's drawing from *The Mail Pilot* (David Hand/Disney, 1933).[49]
To maximize the potential for refielding movements in each scene, the
animators worked in field sizes that were quite small, as tight as 5- and
4-fields. Smaller fields were controversial, however, because less of the
background art was photographed (and therefore effort was wasted),
and yet the level of detail in the background had to be very high in order

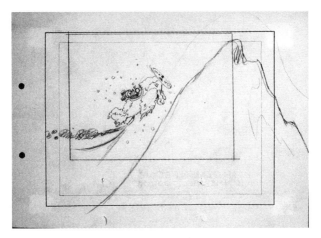

FIGURE 29. Animation layout showing fields for a scene in
The Mail Pilot (1933). Courtesy of Bob Cowan.

for it to look good in close-up. These minuscule compositions required
the camera to move in very close, with the result that the paper grain,
pigment particles, lens defects, and microscopic glitches in the ink and
paint would become visible. According to background artist Nelson,
"The subject of small fields is dynamite."[50]

A seventy-five-watt bulb under the glass surface enabled artists to
compare the current drawing with those preceding it to achieve the desired motion effect. They constantly flipped the sheets back and forth to
verify the animation. The bulb also allowed a rough sketch of the future
background composition or a field size grid to shine through. This scored
clear sheet, called a *graticule,* helped to register refielding notations.[51] The
cartoonists' and technicians' everyday terminology reflected their atavis-
tic 2-D conception of screen space. They used the cardinal compass
points to describe the space: "north" and "south" were used for up and
down, "east" and "west" for right and left. The vocabulary for depth was
limited because it was usually expressed as field size—that is, the distance
from the camera—within these coordinates. For cartoon analysts, the
layperson's descriptive terms for camera space after the mid-1930s are
inadequate for accurately describing the performance action. We may resort to three-dimensional annotations derived from theatrical movement.
For instance, "upstage–center stage" indicates a movement from the back
of the virtual stage toward the audience. Sometimes methods borrowed

from choreography would also be appropriate to describe camera space (tracing a floor path, for example).[52]

Overlay and Underlay Cels

Overlay and underlay cels (also called top cels, bottom cels, and slip cels) were extra layers used for special effects and to suggest multiple-depth planes. Because the transparent sheets of cellulose nitrate had a yellow tinge that photographed on black-and-white film as gray, typically no more than three layers were used. "This leads to innumerable complications," wrote Robert Feild. "Since the celluloid is not completely transparent, each additional level modifies the tone of the colors underneath. The Painting Department takes this into consideration wherever practicable, but situations may arise when changes of tone are unavoidable."[53] The nitrate darkening is apparent in the stairway sequence of *Egyptian Melodies*. Filming in color made the use of nitrate cels unacceptable. After the studios converted to clear acetate cels, they routinely made setups that contained four layers, and sometimes setups contained as many as eight layers. Studio tests showed that there was a 25 percent difference in illumination between the top and bottom cels in a four-layer stack.[54]

In the simplest situations, top cels would be used only to add rain, snow, or cloud effects, for example, as in *Winter* (Burt Gillett/Disney, 1930), which begins with streaks of falling snow. The sequence of cels was repeated—cycled—to make the streaks dance in rhythmic ziggurats synchronized with the music beat. These applications complicate the scenes, but they don't add much depth. In *Springtime* (Ub Iwerks/Disney, 1929), a row of cattails moves in front of a stalking stork during the "tracking" shots, but the foreground moves at the same rate as the background sheet. As a result, there are three planes of motion (background, figure, front) but little impression of depth.

In *Summer* (Ub Iwerks/Disney, 1930), however, a variation on the top cel technique makes the pictorial space much deeper. A second cel is applied over the animated figure drawings and moved laterally along with the action, but its movement is slightly faster than that of the background, which produces an effect Thompson calls *temporal parallax*.[55] Though the effect still uniplanar—that is, the movement is only east-west—the method creates a more complex space by sandwiching the character's action cel between the static background and the moving

FIGURE 30. *Spooks* (1931). At least four layers of cels add to the thrill and visual excitement of the storm.

top cel, thus establishing a middle ground and some resemblance to a live-action panning shot. Fleischer Studios often used top cels in this way, as in the foreground jungle trees in some shots in *Wild Elephinks* (Dave Fleischer/Paramount, 1933). There's an especially effective temporal parallax scene in *Shoein' Hosses* (Dave Fleischer/Paramount, 1934), in which two slip cels move laterally at different rates, one behind Popeye (a fence, mailboxes) and one in front of him (trees). Layered cels are used similarly in *Milk and Money* (Tex Avery/Schlesinger, 1936) to provide spatial complexity to scenes of travel. The action in all these samples, though, remains very close to the picture plane and doesn't create deep space.

Top cel depth effects became quite elaborate. *Spooks* (Ub Iwerks/MGM, 1931) has Flip the Frog and his horse (one cel) traversing the screen east into the teeth of a storm. His horse's hooves become mired in mud as he walks (a separate cel, which also contains the mountainous landscape moving behind them). Coming from behind and in front, on separate cels, leaves and rain pelt them (top cels). Strokes of lightning flash across the background (another top cel). They encounter a shack trembling in the wind (another top cel). They spy an old house and, as they approach, they pass behind its fence (yet another top cel) (Figure 30). *Simple Simon* (Ub Iwerks/Celebrity Productions, 1935) has a surprising scene showing Simon in what seems to be a room. A lion

FIGURE 31. *Mickey's Fire Brigade* (1935). Goofy and Clarabelle in deep-focus mise-en-scène. Original in color.

appears and the "camera" refields out while, simultaneously, jail bars (each on slip cels) move in from the east and west revealing that the "camera" has "tracked" from inside a lion's cage outward.

Mickey's Fire Brigade (Ben Sharpsteen/Disney, 1935) shows us Clarabelle the Cow taking a bath as seen through a transom window. In the foreground, Goofy's big head pops up on a top cel (Figure 31). The composition is analogous to deep-focus framings in live-action cinema, as in Gregg Toland's camerawork in *Mad Love* (Karl Freund, 1935). Unquestionably, the animators looked to Hollywood for graphic inspiration as well as for stories and characterization. *The Thirty-Nine Steps* (Alfred Hitchcock, 1935), *Les Misérables* (Richard Boleslawski, 1935), and *The Garden of Allah* (Richard Boleslawski, 1936) were among the films discussed in studio training sessions. Ken Anderson advised his neophytes that the layout man must study cinematography: "By understanding the camera, I mean going to the [movie] theatre, noticing what kind of camera angles are taken, and why; what kind of moves are made, and why. There is a lot we can learn from the use of the movie camera in the regular industry that would enable us to surpass that use in the future." Of course, he was quick to reserve a special distinction for the animator: "We draw everything—we don't have to build sets; we visualize everything, and what we can conceive of in our imaginations we can do. There are no limitations, really . . . it is all up to us."[56]

In *Little Hiawatha,* the complex opening shot shows the title character paddling his canoe in the distance while a waterfall flows in the foreground. As Hiawatha approaches the picture plane, he makes a turn and passes west, *behind* the waterfall (Plate 3). Although the shot does not utilize the multiplane camera system, the animators were laying out the scene with the sort of spatial complexity that that device was supposed to activate. The character traverses the space of his environment, moving closer to the picture plane to establish facial recognition and familiarity with the viewers. At the same, viewers may find themselves gradually advancing into Hiawatha's intimate world.

Walks and Runs

As early as the 1910s, animators had established conventions for showing walks and runs, a skill that was important in developing action-oriented narratives as well as maintaining visual interest in the film. Having characters move toward the edge of the frame expands the performance space by suggesting that the Tooniverse may extend beyond what is shown on the screen. The figures always maintained the possibility of metalepsis, the ability to leave the visible space of the screen and to enter the cinesthetic space of the viewers (though only Ko-Ko regularly did so). Creating walks and runs in cartoons was completely unlike following the action in a "live" film, where the camera has to move to keep a laterally moving actor framed. In the basic animation setup, neither the character nor the camera is locomotive; it is the background that moves. As codified in how-to manuals such as Lutz's *Animated Cartoons* (1920), the phases of a run could be reduced to four or eight drawings, photographed in sequence, and the sequence repeated for as long as desired.[57] The character normally remains more or less centered in the frame with his or her legs moving. So, when a scene is filmed with the background moving east, it creates the impression that the "camera" is following the toon as it travels west. Disney's distaste for the system he had routinely used in the past is audible in a statement he recorded: "The old action was limited to limber legs and trick runs. In *Snow White* we had to have this stuff believable. You couldn't pull a tear out of anybody with a clown run. So I went to Graham on *Snow White* and we worked like the dickens to get that over, you know."[58]

Uniplanar and Cross-Planar Movement

The action set in 1920s compositions adheres closely to the picture plane. The cel system made the compositions naturally uniplanar, since the animators typically focused only on the parts that moved, such as the feet. So the action tends to take the form of a frontal display, as though on a shallow theater stage such as a vaudeville chorus line. The mummies' dance in *Egyptian Melodies,* the skeletons in *Skeleton Dance,* and the chickens in *Confidence* (Walter Lantz/Universal, 1933; Figure 32) are typical frontal displays. They retain the stagey presentation format of a vaudeville routine, even when the setting is a tomb or graveyard. Characters perform for the "camera" that represents the point of view of an idealized spectator in a theater, and they often acknowledge the viewer's presence through a direct gaze, mimed gestures, or speech, as when the spider shouts an Al Jolson–like "Mummy!" at us. Creating these impressive visual displays with multiple characters moving in unison was easier than it looks. The secret is that once a figure has been sketched out in its component motions, an assistant simply retraces the drawings to make another identical character to position next to the original. Repeat as needed to make more clones. If the drawings are flipped left to right before tracing, then mirror-image figures dance with each other in the same steps, but they move in the opposite direction.[59] They may face each other and slap hands, for instance (Figure 32 again). By retracing and cycling the drawings, a complicated dance sequence with several characters could be done, all based on a single original sketch series.

The frieze was one of the uniplane devices most commonly used by animators in the early 1930s. *Mother Goose Melodies* (Burt Gillett/ Disney, 1931) tells the story of Old King Cole, who marches west across the screen in a "pan" until he reaches his throne. Then the "camera" "pans" back east to encounter various Mother Goose characters in their storybook settings. Here the Disney animators framed their characters full figure or from the knees up, as was typical of animators in the late 1920s and early 1930s. Later in the '30s, the artists began showing more half figures and more facial close-ups, consistent with the more character-oriented comedy and the individuation of personalities. The gradual disappearance of the frieze composition coincided with a more spatially complex world for the performers at Disney. At other studios, the frieze remained a viable method of stringing together visual gags, as in *Porky in Wackyland* (Robert Clampett/Schlesinger, 1938) and the various

FIGURE 32. *Confidence* (1933). Dancing chickens perform in a typical frontal display. The central dancers are in unison, achieved by flipping the original drawing to create the second dancer.

"revue" format cartoons, such as *Have You Got Any Castles?* (Frank Tashlin/Schlesinger, 1938).

Uniplanar movement could be animated efficiently because after the artist had sketched the beginning and end points of an action, called the "keys" or "extremes," assistants would then draw the phases in between. This system militated against defining very deep spaces, since the distance the character traversed was kept rather short. Repeating cels for characters' limbs and cycling backgrounds contributed to the match of visual and musical rhythm in early sound animation, so-called mickey-mousing. An eight-cel sequence repeated three times lasts one second and provides a throbbing visual tempo that syncs up perfectly with a musical score composed in 4/4 time.

Cross-planar movement was more difficult to animate than uniplanar movement because each drawing had to be completely rescaled. If a character was to recede into the distance (that is, move downstage–upstage) in a perspective run, the figure would need to become progressively smaller in each drawing. *Plane Crazy* (Ub Iwerks/Disney, 1928), one of the most spatially innovative of Disney's early films, is a showcase of most of the comic strip spatial compositions typical of the New York style. In the sequence in which Minnie is chasing Mickey in the runaway plane, the aircraft zigzags all around the barnyard, flying per-

FIGURE 33. *Smile, Darn Ya, Smile!* (1931). The wild cross-planar trolley ride oscillates between fore- and background, creating a dynamic camera space for the passengers and the moviegoers.

pendicular to the picture plane (that is, directly toward and then away from us) and executing diagonal flights (approaching the viewer while also flying east or west, or, in theatrical blocking, moving downstage left and upstage right).[60] Frequently in *Plane Crazy*, characters move to or from the "lens" in wide-angle distortion while the background also rapidly recedes or approaches (made by cycled background drawings). A particularly brilliant example is in *Smile, Darn Ya, Smile!* (Rudolf Ising/Schlesinger, 1931; Figure 33). Inspired by such films as *Mickey's Choo-Choo* (Ub Iwerks/Disney, 1929), the film shows a trolley breaking loose and taking Foxy and Roxy on a wild roller coaster ride over hills and through tunnels.

As the 1930s progressed, oblique movements became commonplace. In *Ali Baba* (Ub Iwerks/Celebrity Productions, 1935), when the forty thieves run past us, they do so in repeating waves into and out of deep space, their forms distorted by simulated wide-angle refraction (Figure 34). Entrances and exits in *Porky and Teabiscuit* (Cal Dalton and Ben Hardaway/Schlesinger, 1939) are all made diagonally. One peculiar feature of cross-planar movement is that frequently a character will streak to the left or right before turning on a dime and racing toward the horizon. In other words, when a character changes direction, it is usually an abrupt right-angle turn from a chorus line movement to a depth

FIGURE 34. *Ali Baba* (1935). The bandits streak obliquely from the distance to near space and mimic camera blur and wide-angle lens distortion to re-perform cinematic effects. Original in color.

movement, or vice versa. This is "free" animation, since no artists' effort was required; the same drawings were simply photographed again in reverse order.

The cross-planar effect is narrativized in the Popeye cartoon *Seasin's Greetinks!* (Dave Fleischer/Paramount, 1933). When Bluto punches the sailor he flies into the distance and rebounds four times. The back-and-forth action extends the screen time by cycling the same drawings, but it also connotes the repetitive, machinelike world that Popeye inhabits and proves that he seriously needs a spinach pick-me-up.

Elmer Elephant (Wilfred Jackson/Disney, 1936), *Little Hiawatha*, and other cartoons from the late 1930s self-consciously highlight movement on the diagonal. Because the camera "pans" to follow the figures, there are two perspective vanishing points in the background, one at the left horizon and one at the right. *Woodland Café* (Wilfred Jackson/Disney, 1937) is a good example. Two bugs enter the dining room from the west and the maître d' escorts them toward their table back and to the east (upstage–stage left). The apparent size of their bodies correctly increases and diminishes with each step—a remarkable animation tour de force.

A cross-planar movement that produces a striking depth effect is the aggressive wide-angle charge. Again, the changes in the use of this effect chart the studios' adoption of embodied performance. In the silent and early sound films, a figure will suddenly loom into the "lens" of the implied camera, simulating a fisheye lens and producing a decidedly in-your-face gesture. Disney's many spiders that swing into the "camera," grimace, and then swing back are typical. When Minnie flies into a cow in *Plane Crazy,* the animal's udder and teats soar toward us in a screen-filling close-up. As the airplane continues to zigzag down the road, telephone poles loom into view until they render the screen completely black for a couple of frames and then recede. Pilots Mickey and Minnie collide with assorted pedestrians and vehicles as they fly down the road. (They crash head-on into a car that, when the film is examined in slow motion, seems to be driven by Felix the Cat.) A point-of-view shot shows us Mickey's sight of the up-rushing earth as he plummets from the plane. Such effects seem to be an attempt to create a somatic experience for the audience by generating vertigo and the "roller-coaster illusion" that makes the viewers feel as if they're moving in space.

Minnie's mouth opens wide and swallows the "camera." The effect discloses a new space, now inside the toon body (Figure 35). Animators of the early 1930s relished such occasions to show us the uvula, as well as the teats of cows and pigs flying into our faces. Not daring to name these shots the *uvula and udder motif,* I'll instead opt for Crowther's term, *relational foreshortening,* a dynamic device that carries "enough relevant visual cues to establish the idea of representing a single recessional space within the limits of the individual work."[61] It is also evident that using the wide-angle charge energized the film with fly-through ingestion imagery that creates an organic vortex where the space opens and sucks the protagonist and viewer's avatar inside.

Other examples of the wide-angle charge are in *The Plowboy* (Ub Iwerks/Disney, 1929), in which the horse does a perspective run into the backward-tracking "camera" until it almost presses its nose into the "lens." Startling bats fly into the "camera" in *The Haunted House* (Walt Disney/Celebrity Pictures, 1929). Another excellent use of a "wide angle" to evoke depth is the beast in *The Gorilla Mystery* (Burt Gillett/Disney, 1930), whose growling fisheye-distorted mouth fills the whole screen. When the gorilla carries Minnie toward the "camera," he grows larger as he approaches. Later, he walks past the "camera" on a diagonal, presumably into the space of the movie theater. There's also the wild buzz saw blade in *The Dognapper* (David Hand/Disney, 1934), which chases Peg Leg Pete, Mickey, and Donald in exaggerated depth. In *Pluto's*

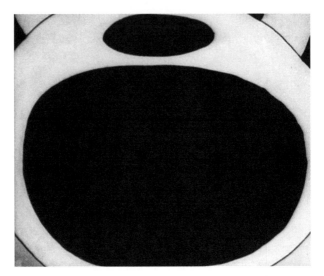

FIGURE 35. *Plane Crazy* (1928). Minnie's gaping mouth swallows the "camera."

Judgement Day, as the pup comes tearing out of the distance in hot pursuit of a cat, his head is shown in extreme wide angle as he rounds the curve (a near-right-angle turn) and races west. Another excellent example is the extreme wide-angle shot that occurs in *Mickey's Kangaroo* (David Hand/Disney, 1935). Pluto leans his face toward the "camera" and addresses the viewer in an aside. We hear Pluto's thoughts ("That's the last straw . . .") as a voice-over. The three asides are rendered in fisheye-lens fashion. The wide angle can deepen the space of the action, but, as in this case, it can also bring the action into the implied space of the spectator in the theater. These glimpses inside characters' bodies, often with highlighted uvulas, and bodies charging through space renounce the measured worlds of perspective. Instead we plunge—and, often, we vertiginously hurtle—into "soft" organic space.

The aggressive wide-angle distortion effect seems to have been associated with evil beings and objects and with threatening creatures, such as the arachno-villains in *Springtime, Mother Goose Melodies,* and *Woodland Café.* The cat judge in *Pluto's Judgement Day* bends closer and closer to the camera until only his demonic eyes fill the screen. Similarly, the bats in *The Old Mill* (Wilfred Jackson and Graham Heid/Disney, 1937) glide toward us, their scary fangs becoming brief abstract filigrees. The visual shock created by this intrusive disruption caused by shattering the picture plane is a correlative for these figures' physical threat. The unpleasant creatures could leave their performance space, invade the theater, and engulf or gobble up the viewers. These shockers are linked with the spatial disruptiveness of the wide-angle charge as it breaks out of the little box of the mise-en-scène. The lead skeleton in *Skeleton Dance* hops toward the camera until he engulfs it, an act that is indicated by black frames. Then the "camera" and the viewer pass through the skeletal pelvic opening in what might have been intended as a scatological joke. It's as though the space of the movie suddenly irrupts into the theater and threatens to devour the moviegoers. The result is always an eye-popping attention getter that conveys viewers into the space, or propels them out of it.

Later, as close-ups were used to develop character intimacy and psychological interest that were appropriate for the developing embodied acting style, animators tamed the wide-angle charge. "Since the chattering skull in *The Skeleton Dance* zoomed into the very faces of the audience," wrote Graham, "the close-up had been used primarily as a shock device. Slowly the idea of using the close-up as a means of creating a sense of *intimacy* became apparent." He cited *Mickey's Pal Pluto* (Burt Gillett, 1933), with its celebrated scene of a little angel and a devil arguing on Pluto's shoulders, as an early instance of the close-up to show emotion. He noted that the effects had to be brief to remain surprising and thus effective. In fact, the shorter the shot, the more the audience seemed to feel its emotion.[62] This is exemplified by an impressive shot in *The Gorilla Mystery* in which Mickey, who is in the backyard, is seen from the interior of Minnie's house. He approaches the house, growing in size, enters through the door, and continues east in the same shot. In the upstairs hallway, he and the gorilla increase and decrease in scale as they move up and down the hall, toward and away from the "lens." Pursued by the gorilla, Mickey backs downstage–center, toward the "camera," until only the backs of his ears fill the screen (Figure 36).

Although establishing depth at the level of the cel was challenging, the graphic conventions described above routinely allowed animators to do so, primarily by having characters and objects change in scale according to their implied distance from the picture plane, mimicking the effects of natural vision, and by using movement to create proxy space. To be fully illusionistic, though, these drawings had to be placed within an environment. This was the function of the backgrounds.

FIGURE 36. *The Gorilla Mystery* (1930). Beppo the Gorilla pursues Mickey through oblique planes of camera space.

Background Space

The other element of the binary pictorial space of classic cartoons is the background or layout, also called the scenery, setting, or set.[63] The ability to compose the action drawings by themselves on transparent cels without having to redraw the static parts of the picture for every exposure was one of the great breakthroughs in animation technology that enabled commercial mass production.

Acme furnished the industry with blank backgrounds, which were sheets of heavy Bristol paper slightly larger than the cels; a 12-field background was 12.5 by 10.5 inches. The animation hardware of the 1930s made it possible to have backgrounds that could be moved independently of the cels on "compound tables" and were usually much wider than cels. These oversize sheets were called 1½ pans, double pans, and so on. A 12-field 3-pan background, for instance, was 37.5 by 10.5 inches.[64] When the scene called a character to run over a distance the background was planned so that the extreme right and left sides would match, say, by having a horizon line begin and end in the same position. The camera operator would simply begin the background anew from the right when the paper ran out on the left. It could be cycled over and over because the end would "overtake" the beginning seamlessly. Although called "pans" or "panoramas," following the language of live-

FIGURE 37. *The Dognapper* (1934). Mickey and Donald run past this background six times.

action filming, the effect really creates a "traveling" or "trucking" shot because of the lack of parallax.

Although the system of cycling backgrounds to extend a run produces the desired effect of giving the impression that a character is moving a long distance in a lateral direction, upon close consideration the cycled background is spatially irrational. One of innumerable examples of this is in *The Dognapper* (Figure 37). During the chase in the sawmill we see Mickey and Donald run past the same three saw blades hanging on the back wall six times! This is a significant spatial anomaly. Logically, because characters keep passing the same repeating background markers, they must be running in a circle. Cycled backgrounds thus construct a cylindrical space for the characters. The more they walk, the closer they seem to get to the point where they began. Here the binary split between cel and background becomes most interesting topographically.

The world of the classic animated background, therefore, is curvilinear, as characters circumnavigate their little globe every few strides. The strides themselves, however, are in a straight line (since, through cycling, it's the same stride over and over on the flat cel). If this fact is carried to its logical—or illogical—extreme, the characters, who can only go straight, should eventually walk right off their round world! The jokes in *Egyptian Melodies* self-consciously reference this anomaly when the spear hits its thrower in the behind and the commander walks off the column. Such is the incoherent topology of the Tooniverse.[65]

Performance Clearings

Layout artists had many pictorial devices at their disposal to construct their spaces. One was creating *performance clearings* for the characters. The artist reserves a conspicuous blank space in the center of the picture. Sometimes floor planks and foreground landscape will just stop, keeping a white zone in the center of the frame for the figures' actions. This convention originated in the studios of the 1910s that animated on paper using the "slash" system rather than cels. The Disney staff had practiced a variant of this in the silent Alice cartoons. Following the example of the Fleischers, who double-exposed Ko-Ko onto Max's white sketch pad, Iwerks and Disney left a "white" area in the center of the animation background onto which the live actor portraying Alice was superimposed. Even after these double-exposure systems were obsolete and there was no longer a technical reason to compose the background with an open space in the center, the practice lingered on, perhaps because it preserved the clear separation between foreground and background. At Fleischer Studios in the 1930s, *I Eats My Spinach* (Dave Fleischer/Paramount, 1933) and other films still used performance clearings as a compositional device.

When later films used performance clearings, the plot rationalized them. In *Three Orphan Kittens* (David Hand/Disney, 1935), for example, a sequence on a table was designed with a plain center, but the background is a white tablecloth. Instead of serving as a work-around to overcome the separateness of foreground and background, as in the older films, here we see the kittens on the clear white center of the tablecloth cavorting in their believable environment.[66] The device survived as a vestigial "look" for cartoon composition, transitioning from obsolete technique to visual style.

Atmospheric Perspective

The painting technique of atmospheric perspective (also known as aerial perspective) mimics natural vision to create the illusion of distance without foreshortening. Owing to the scattering and refraction of light by particles in the air, things in the distance are hazier and bluer than things seen close-up. The Disney artists employed the technique early on, for example, as shown in *Tall Timber*. During the close-ups of Mickey and Minnie in the plane in *Plane Crazy*, the background is rendered in smudged pencil or charcoal to simulate the atmospheric effect, while the foreground cels are drawn with the usual hard-edged outlines. In *Building a Building* (David Hand/Disney, 1933), a skyscraper provides the opportunity to combine linear and aerial perspective effects. When the characters are seen from above, the distant ground is drawn with soft and hazy strokes. After the adoption of color, the arrival of formally trained staff artists, and the increasing influence of the California watercolorists, the look of the films began to change. These painterly treatments of layouts became the new standard. Of course, the studio had a huge advantage over the others because from 1932 through 1935 they had exclusive rights to three-color Technicolor and its subtle palette. In color films such as *Mickey's Fire Brigade* (Plate 4), distant scenes are rendered in violet shades, an effect also visible in Renaissance and impressionist paintings and the works of the Chouinard artists.

Oil and Water

The divide between background and cel space in classic cartoons stems from differences in the graphic medium itself. Typically, backgrounds were done in light watercolor washes. This could suggest aerial perspective, but it also contrasted with the figures that were inked on the cels in solid lines and in-painted with opaque gouache or tempera. The paint was applied verso—that is, on the back of the cels—so when the cels were photographed from the front, or recto, the color was confined within and delineated by the inked line. This made the character stand out from the background, creating a poster effect without using perspective, as in *Blow Me Down* (Dave Fleischer/Paramount, 1933), in which Olive dances in front of a pale backdrop of static figures suggestive of a smoke-filled cabaret. The Fleischer color film *Popeye the Sailor Meets Sinbad the Sailor* (Dave Fleischer/Paramount, 1936) preserves the look of the Sunday comics. The characters painted with primary colors stand out from their soft watercolor backgrounds (Plate 5). This aesthetic is the antithesis of a Disney color film like *The Country Cousin* (Wilfred Jackson/Disney, 1936), in which the backgrounds are in watercolor and the figures are painted with opaque pigments but the inked outlines are no longer heavy black lines. Softened cel drawing style and the nuances of pastel coloring blend the figures into the background to mitigate the foreground/background separation (Plate 6).

Camera Space

This third space is the composite one created when the cel space and background space are combined and projected to activate the animation performance. The person in charge of coordinating the melding of foreground action and background treatment as the scene design progressed was known as the layout man. These crewmembers were jacks-of-all-trades, adept at all phases of the animation process, from the start to the finished "setup," as the combination of cels and backgrounds is called. "The layout man," said Ken Anderson from experience, "must not only have a good sense of humor; he must also have a fine-arts background—a good knowledge of composition—so that he can go beyond just planning a composition for still pictures." Much of the work of layout artists was conceptual; they visualized how the film would "play" in the virtual camera space of projection. "Our work requires that we constantly plan our compositions for action," Anderson noted.[67]

The Acme animation stand was engineered specifically to combine graphic elements to create cinematic space (Figure 38).[68] The apparatus held the camera aloft at a suitable distance over the platen (a steel-and-glass frame that held the background and cels in precise alignment) for photographing the setup. This was the site where cel space and background space came together. The camera and its lens of fixed focal length moved up and down through a limited range above the platen on a calibrated support shaft (called the *mast* or *pole* by animators). The shaft was marked with field position markers, so the highest camera position was (originally) a 12-field. By following the animators' field size instructions, the operator would move the camera up or down a tiny bit between exposures to create a zoom-in or -out effect when the film was projected. The stands were engineered to routinize the chore of photographing thousands of frames individually. The animatographer would sit at the platen assembling foregrounds and backgrounds, implementing the animators' field and cycle instructions, and photographing one sheet after another. A visitor to a studio might have had the impression of one of Mumford's megamachines engulfing the human drone that served its needs.

FIGURE 38. Acme animation stand, ca. 1940, outfitted with a special effects projector for combining non-animated and drawn images, an Acme animation camera, an Acme sliding cel board, and lights and accessories. Courtesy of Academy of Motion Picture Arts and Sciences.

The original Acme animation stand enabled the camera to rotate horizontally above the drawing setup, making angles and combined pans relatively easy to accomplish, as when Bosko and Honey are chased down the vertical mountain in *Sinkin' in the Bathtub*. The bulky Technicolor camera, however, only moved up and down on the shaft and couldn't pivot. Any oblique movement therefore had to be simulated in the background drawings or the whole setup had to be rotated. Charles Philippi explained that animators' notations still indicated that the camera would be rotated at a certain angle for a scene, but, "what really happens is that the circular table [the platen] is turned to fit the action if you call for a tilted field."[69]

In refielding shots, the picture widens or narrows, but it remains resolutely uniplanar unless there are other pictorial clues. Scrutinizing these reframings reveals them to be what they are: the camera moving closer to or farther from flat drawings. The animators designated the area of the cel to be photographed by indicating its field setting on the exposure sheet. These instructions guided the camera operator, who translated them into motion sequences on film. Moving-camera shots that corresponded to trucking, traveling, and dolly live-action shots (where the "camera" moves along the ground) could be simulated simply by providing the calibrations to the cinematographer. (Usually the animators referred to all simulated movements as "trucking.") This could be done graphically by indicating the start field and end field of drawings on a layout. In the *Mail Pilot* layout (see Figure 29 again), the animator's rectangles indicate the fields of view that will pull in (or back) during filming. Or it could be done numerically. If the camera focuses tightly over one area of the cel (let's say a 4.5-field centered in the northwest quadrant) and pulls back to a 10-field height while the setup moves to the center straight under the camera, the whole operation taking forty frames of film, this will replicate a diagonal trucking shot out from the scene from upstage left to center stage. The notation to the camera crew would be something like "Start: 4½ F, N2W4, End: 10 F 0:0, 40 frames."[70] Nowadays, this rostrum-generated space is sometimes called the Ken Burns effect, named after the documentarian's predilection for that treatment of photographic sources.

Refielding did not create the illusion of depth, but it added mobility to the image and served the crucial function of segmenting the drawing to imply off-screen space (perhaps what Graham was calling invisible space). This could also be reinforced on the soundtrack or suggested within the frame. For instance, off-screen space could be created through standard editing (cutting between two spaces). A character may gaze at something off-screen or interact with an off-screen character, as when Bluto throws something at unseen Popeye. Refielding provided yet another very convincing illusion that the cartoon story is occurring not on some strange puppet stage but in a world not completely bound by the frame.

From the 1930s onward, refielding was used routinely. In the early years it provided a kinetic change of scale that fit the hyperactivity of the action, as in *The Mail Pilot*. It was a kind of special effect. Later, refielding used increasingly gradual movements to follow the action and keep the figures appropriately framed. Rather than making a point, it adjusted pictorial space to accommodate characters' actions and psychology. This space tool—and this applies to most of the space-generating devices discussed—called attention to itself at the beginning of the 1930s and became less assertive toward the end of the decade. Watching a Disney animated feature, we may not even be aware of the many changes in field size. In *Snow White*, a layout artist explained, "we are trucking down usually when Snow White's action is slowing down in a large field, that is, we are moving down as the action slows up. If Snow White goes across the room and we want to be in a closeup shot at the end of her move, we start trucking down as she starts to slow up to go into her step." Sometimes these refields were quite subtle. "In one action of Snow White in which she just walks across the room, we start with a 4½ field and stop in the same size field. To get variety just out of a field movement, we drop from the 4½ down to a 4 field, then go back to the 4½ field."[71] The technique provided variety, to be sure, but it also made the scene play more like one in a typical Hollywood feature.

Shadows

There is no better way to chart how mechanics, form, and content aligned to reconceptualize performance space in the 1930s than by observing the changing treatment of shadows. Because they connect cel and background space within the totality of camera space, they are essential for generating the illusion of unified depth. In a medium that is fundamentally projected shadows, creating shadows within cinema posed special problems for animators. For most of the 1920s and early 1930s, the studios treated them as an expressive element, not as a way to generate space. Similar, perhaps, to the way that filmmakers used sound and color in early films, animators regarded shadows as surplus value, something to turn off or on according to the requirements of the plot. Take *Sure-Locked Homes* (Otto Messmer/Pat Sullivan, 1927). In almost every shot, grotesque shadows on floors and walls frighten poor

Felix the Cat. As he walks past a moonlit window, his shadow dramatically stretches across the floor and fills the frame in an anamorphic perspective rendering.[72] Films like *The Gorilla Mystery* typically did not give characters shadows during the "ordinary" scenes, or when their feet were grounded. In scenes of high drama, though, they would have dark foreshortened shadows, as when the gorilla holds Minnie captive in the attic.

These shadows were drawn on the same cels or sheets of paper as the figures (if the shadows moved) or on the background (if they didn't). Of course there were the usual fiscal considerations; this extra drafting task slowed down the production schedule. Additionally, however, the practice was an artistic legacy of comic strip style. Since the cartoonists were not aiming to create a realistic effect in their drawings anyway, there was no need for shadows. Some films mocked the convention by calling attention to the shadow's existence on a plane separate from the figure's. We assume that a gyrating shadow in *Karnival Kid* is the advertised Minnie the Shimmy Dancer. It turns out to belong to a string puppet operated by the barker. *Winter* (Burt Gillett/Disney, 1930), for example, pokes fun at the shadowless world of early cartoons. The groundhog emerges from his lair to predict the end of winter. When he doesn't see his shadow, the neighbors rejoice at the prospect of an early spring. Then the sun returns from behind the clouds and the groundhog's shadow appears. The rodent runs back into his den, slamming the door. The left-behind shadow bangs on the door to gain entry. In *Porky's Double Trouble* (Frank Tashlin/Schlesinger, 1937), bullets miss the fleeing character but riddle his shadow with holes. It dies. The implicit message is that shadows in the Tooniverse are separable from their bodies and are expendable.

In the Fleischers' Popeye cartoons the characters were drawn with strong black shadows, but the outlines did not precisely match the characters' bodies; rather, the small squiggles and black blobs underneath the characters merely suggested a shadow. I call these *noonday shadows* because the light source, although ill defined, comes from straight overhead. The noonday shadow doesn't create much of an impression of depth, although it does imply that the vertical body has proxy space, density, and contact with the horizontal floor. These were vestigial reperformances of the treatment of shadows in comics, in which characters such as Popeye in Elzie Segar's *Thimble Theatre* strip cast negligible floor shadows, executed with sketchy crosshatching, which would have been laborious to duplicate in moving cel animation. In the mid-1930s,

FIGURE 39. *Vim, Vigor and Vitaliky* (1936). Bluto and Olive Oyl
cast opaque black "noonday shadows" painted on the cel, unlike
the props, which have low-contrast shadows painted on the
background.

the shadows in the Popeye cartoons became very bold, inked onto the
cels along with the characters (Figure 39). The shadows would expand
when a character left the floor or ground, suggesting their altitude as
they approached an off-screen overhead light source. The outlines were
not a strict fit but instead intuitive. Even when there was a light source
in the picture that would have cast shadows, as in *Poor Cinderella*
(Dave Fleischer/Paramount, 1934), the shadows remained vaguely non-
directional. The Fleischers avoided transparent shadows, even in big
color productions such as *Poor Cinderella* and their ambitious feature
Gulliver's Travels, in which the characters' shadows are muted but still
opaque.[73]

Not surprisingly, the films made by former Disney animators utilized
the same shadow strategy. The Bosko films (for example, *Sinkin' in the
Bathtub*) have inconsistently drawn noonday shadows in light gray. In
Iwerks's cartoons, like *Ali Baba* (Ub Iwerks/Celebrity Productions,
1935), we also see shadows rendered in the standard style. Films from
Burt Gillett's studio at Van Beuren, such as *Parottville Post Office,* follow the same formula. In *The Merry Kittens* (Shamus Culhane and Burt
Gillett/Van Beuren, 1935) the kittens sport noonday shadows in spite of
the contradictory leftward shadows cast by the props in the background. Most of the black-and-white Schlesinger cartoons of the 1930s

FIGURE 40. *A Car-Tune Portrait* (1937). The lion's shadow specifies the space between his body and the curtain behind it. Original in color.

also used these gray shadow schemes (when they used shadows at all), while the color films tended to use few if any shadows. Paul Terry and Walter Lantz's approach was straightforward: they usually avoided shadows altogether.

Two 1936 films from the Schlesinger Studio show how inconsistent shadowing was. In *Alpine Antics* (George King/Schlesinger, 1936) there are no figure shadows, although trees and props have shadows painted on the background. In *Milk and Money*, by contrast, shadows are hit or miss. Porky's milk wagon throws a shadow, but the horse pulling it does not. When the landlord comes to foreclose, before we see his body (in a top cel), we see his ominous shadow on the scene (in another top cel). Porky and Poppa Pig, however, have none.

Animators at all the studios used shadows for special effects. One convention was to generate stage space by using a spotlight to emphasize the three-dimensionality of the performer to situate the action within the proscenium space surrounding it. As the lion master of ceremonies in *A Car-Tune Portrait* (Dave Fleischer/Paramount, 1937) addresses the movie audience, he is shadowless until the spotlight hits him. Then he throws a correctly drawn silhouette onto the stage and curtain (Figure 40). In *Toy Time* (Harry Bailey and John Foster/Van Beuren, 1932), a mouse puts on an impromptu show when he finds a flashlight (Figure 41). In the generally shadow-free *Katnip Kollege* (Cal Howard and Cal

FIGURE 41. *Toy Time* (1932). A flashlight beam turns the mousehole into an impromptu stage.

Dalton/Schlesinger, 1938), the exception is a shot where some syncopated alley cats jive with their shadows on a fence.

The spotlight's shadow, like all shadows, makes the space between figures and their background measurable. It re-performs a familiar space—the vaudeville stage—while adding a hint of naturalism, since the light beams obey the laws of physics. The spotlight is usually "behind" the audience—that is, both the audience in the film and, by implication, the audience watching the cartoon in the movie theater—so it implies that the viewers and characters are sharing the same performance space.

In pre-1935 Disney films, shadows were rendered in this standard noonday style, as in *Mickey's Steam Roller* (David Hand/Disney, 1934) and *Playful Pluto* (Burt Gillett/Disney, 1934). Disney's practice diverged from that of his competitors, though, as his approach to characterization began to change. Shadows were important agents in the studio's shift from figurative to embodied performance. The opaque shadows painted on the cels in light gray in the early color films had the disadvantage of sometimes appearing more like a rubber floor mat or puddle than a shadow. Even more disconcerting, in shady scenes, characters' shadows appeared lighter than the shadows cast by objects in the scene. In *The Flying Mouse*, for example, the mouse's shadow appears gray against the darker shadows of the foliage on the ground.[74]

The Disney studio implemented an alternative method. Animators had used multiple exposures to create special effects for years, as they did in the double-exposed friezes in *Egyptian Melodies*. Rather than painting the shadows in gray on the cels along with the figures, under the new system the shadows were painted in solid black on a separate top cel and then photographed as a double exposure. The transparency could be controlled with mathematic precision. The cel and background would be shot once at, say, 90 percent exposure, without the shadow top cel. Then the shadow cel would be placed over the setup and the scene would be shot again at 10 percent exposure, producing a fully exposed scene with translucent shadows. Of course, since each frame of each setup had to be photographed twice, this doubled the labor for shadowed sequences. In *Who Killed Cock Robin?* (David Hand/Disney, 1935) the mystery assailant who shoots his arrow is shown only as a transparent shadow cast upon the trees in the background. *Mickey's Garden* (Wilfred Jackson/Disney, 1935) uses double exposures for all its character shadows. Since, unlike in comics, shadows in nature are not opaque, this produced a more photorealistic effect that obviously fit into the studio's ongoing conversion to a less cartoony performance program.[75] Soon the technique became the standard one at the studio; indeed, the revised scene instruction sheet that the layout department delivered to the camera department had provisions for noting shadow density and the angle of the light source (Figure 42). By the late 1930s, Disney had added a dedicated shadow department to the animation assembly line.[76]

The task of keeping these perspectively shifting characters and their shadows anchored to the ground and their environment fell to the animation assistants. "Attention Assistants," the boss reminded them in a memo, "see that your characters fit the planes that they are working on. Check on perspective and see that the action fits the background."[77] At Disney there was an organizational workflow developed (probably by Dave Hand) to keep track of all these complicated effects. Looking at one of the scene instruction sheets for *The Country Cousin,* we see how this information was managed. In addition to the identifying data on the scene (animator, footage budgeted, brief synopsis, characters, props, and matching information to show how the scene relates to others), the sheet has preprinted blocks for information on mechanics, effects, color, paint and ink, and general. Scene thirty-five, in which Abner Mouse shushes Monte (a.k.a. Monty), is a simple one, with no pan movements (Plate 6 again). The instructions call for an underlay cel (the toast that

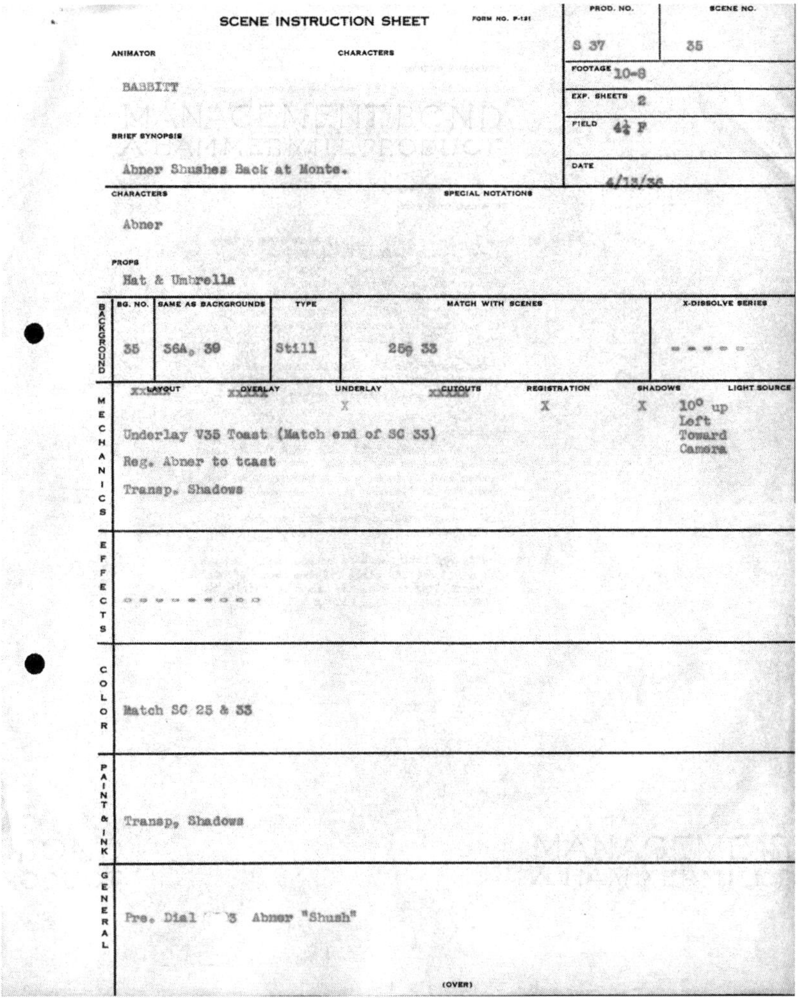

FIGURE 42. Scene instruction sheet for *The Country Cousin* (1936). Art Babbitt Papers. Courtesy of Bob Cowan.

Abner chews through) and for "Transp. Shadows" in both the mechanics and paint and ink sections. For this scene, the implied "light" that determined the size, density, and angle of the transparent shadow was indicated as "10° up/Left/Toward Camera."[78]

The double-exposed shadow was also occasionally used at other studios. At Schlesinger, for example, the landlord's shadow mentioned above is transparent, as is the town crier's detailed shadow in *Have You Got*

FIGURE 43. *Have You Got Any Castles?* (1938). Transparent shadows created by double exposure. Original in color.

Any Castles? (Figure 43). For the rest of that film the characters were shadowless. Whether because of economics or because it was not considered necessary to the studio's aesthetic program, the Schlesinger animators, who clearly knew how to apply the technique, used it infrequently.

Disney's double-exposed shadows, unlike the indefinite outlines and formulaic light sources earlier in the decade, subtly articulated a believable performance space by better defining characters' volume and their place in that environment. In *Elmer Elephant,* for example, the figure twice walks under patches of jungle foliage that dapple the body with shadows as the elephant passes through the scene (Plate 7). Elmer's rounded volume defines his pachyderm mass and its relation to the atmosphere and the earth around and below him. Increasingly, films like *Little Hiawatha, Pluto's Quin-puplets* (Ben Sharpsteen/Disney), *Woodland Café,* and *The Old Mill,* all from 1937, relied on shadows to anchor the characters in a mensurate space.

Convincing shadows could be rendered intuitively with relative ease when they fell on the floor or ground of the background. If the shadow fell on a curved or oblique surface, however, the task became enormously more complicated. To facilitate rendering these sorts of shadows, the Disney studio developed a device they called the Shadowgraph, and in September 1936 they applied for a patent for it.[79] To use the Shadowgraph, first the background art would be photographed. It would then be used to construct a miniature stage with three-dimensional cardboard objects, such as tables or rocks, placed in their proper location on the floor plan. Next, the transparent cel with the character that was supposed to cast the shadow would be set up in front of the set and a strong light would be shone through it. The character's opaque outline would then cast a real shadow upon the set and the props. As Bob Martsch of the special effects department described it, "The shadow necessarily follows the animated cells, is made by them, and distorts and changes over the three dimensional background which has been built to register with the layout of the scene. The shadow may be made long or short, to move over curved, flat or angular surfaces in true relationship to the character casting the shadow."[80] A camera above the set photographed each cel's shadow. This operation was repeated for every cel in the sequence. Using these photographs, specialized layout artists would ink the shadows on top cels in their proper place to be included in the scene setup. As an example, Martsch projected a scene from *Snow White*. Throughout that film, not only does the transparency of the shadows vary according to the strength of the ambient lighting, but the shadows are also true to their sources. When Snow White ascends the cottage staircase, for example, the candlelight throws shadows onto the stairs and floor in perfect perspective. Furthermore, when the candle flame flickers, so do the woodland animals' shadows (Plate 8). Accurate as a sundial, these custom shadows have replaced the generic noonday kind. So when our heroine sees the dwarfs off to work, we see the slanted violet-tinged shadows of dawn. When the witch comes calling and her engulfing shadow heralds her, it's an effect borrowed from German expressionist cinema, as when the vampire's shadow moves across the heroine in *Nosferatu* (F. W. Murnau, 1922).[81]

These shadows were a very important component of the studio's performance project because they break down the division between foreground and background. As in a photograph, the animated shadows, as well as light beams and water ripples, situate them in a unified visual world. The cel-drawn figure of Hiawatha in Plate 3 inhabits a rapturous space that outspreads in all directions. In this closing shot, he floats on shadowed rippling water (cel under- and overlays) into the distance in a glow of sublime light reminiscent of early American landscape painting as well as the work of the contemporaneous California watercolorists.[82]

In these Disney films from 1937 and in the features that followed, it is no longer meaningful to speak of the shot's foreground and background, since now the entire scene is camera space, a common, modulated performance environment that incorporates the actor. Rather than calling attention to the biplanar nature of animation, this staging exists to facilitate an embodied performance. With his usual poetic flourish, Feild enthused about the organic symbolism of this phase in the development of performance space for Disney's cartoon actors: "From the moment they were conceived as embryonic beings drifting around in undefined space, they have been inseparable from their environment. Yet when the Studio comes specifically to define this transcendental realm, it has no better name for it than 'background'!"[83]

Parallax

Refielding is a simulated zoom and not a true trucking shot (as with a moving camera in a natural setting) because there is no parallax displacement.[84] Parallax is a crucial concept for defining camera space. It is the difference in apparent size of objects when seen at varying distances from multiple sightlines, measured as the "angle of inclination."[85] In natural vision, the slight distance between our two eyes, called binocular disparity, produces a parallax view that allows us to see in depth. When we view an object in nature or photograph it with a movie camera lens, it appears to grow larger or smaller as we approach or back away from it, and overlapping objects seem to slide past each other. Moving across the scene laterally makes objects that are farther away appear to move more slowly than nearer objects, an effect called *motion parallax*.[86] All movies shot and projected through a single lens produce a monocular view on the screen. But when this camera moves, motion parallax gives the impression that we are seeing in depth.

Walt Disney claimed that neglecting to animate parallax was a serious flaw: "Besides being merely unrealistic, the old-fashioned flat background could also create a false effect." Using an animated clip showing a refielding shot moving into a moonlit scene, he pointed out that everything in the picture grew larger, including the moon, which was unnatural. "The problem was how to take a painting and make it behave like a real piece of scenery under the camera. The trouble was, we were photographing a flat, two-dimensional background."[87] During this simulated trucking movement, the performance space expands or contracts, with the edges appearing to slide out of the frame in all directions, but all at the same rate, thus producing no parallax and thus no depth perception.

FIGURE 44. *Mickey Cuts Up* (1931). A bench displays unexpected solidity as it foreshortens during a scene of motion parallax.

Graphically Simulated Space

That perspective and three-dimensionality were topics in the air is apparent simply from watching the films. In *The Jazz Fool* (Ub Iwerks/ Disney, 1929) there is a brief shot of a piano keyboard that shows the keys in moving perspective as the "camera" trucks past. Two films released close to *Egyptian Melodies,* which appeared in August 1931, show parallax experimentation. In *Mickey Steps Out* (Burt Gillett/ Disney, July 1931), as the "camera" "travels" west and the mouse traipses down a sidewalk, playing its boards like xylophone keys. As he does so, the boards constantly shift perspective. *Mickey Cuts Up* (Burt Gillett/ Disney, November 1931) embeds its spatial gag within the performance space. Pluto is dragging Mickey and his lawn mower west. As the "camera" "pans" left, we approach a bench. Its receding orthogonal lines change with each frame as though it were a solid object (Figure 44). The effect is quite jarring, especially because a tree on a top cel is not similarly foreshortened. The two-dimensionality of the figures, which have no roundness or depth and cast no shadows, contrasts markedly with this three-dimensional invasion in their world.

It is likely that the animators' interest in academic drawing and Graham's class on perspective were manifesting themselves in this sequence and the ones in *Egyptian Melodies*. Animator Shamus Culhane, a pupil in Graham's art classes, recalled some provocative lectures by guest artist Jean Charlot:

> The lectures were a delightful combination of Gallic wit and erudition. He talked a great deal about composition, and the conscious use of geometry by Renaissance painters.
>
> During one talk he pointed out that it was normal to show several views of the same object in a painting. When this was challenged by one of the more conservative artists in the audience, he answered by saying that we naturally saw everything from two points of view, since we had two eyes. What was unnatural was our acceptance of Italian perspective, since it was based on the theory that the viewer had only one eye!
>
> Charlot's lecture argued for a wider acceptance of the aims of modern art, and he must have been successful because there were many heated discussions in the parking lot after the meetings ended.[88]

Charlot seems to have alluded to this incident when he chides "laymen" artists:

> [The artist], seeing Nature as a spectacle outside himself, wishes consciously to capture and assimilate her as a desirable thing that his job will make available to others. Just like the scientist, he wishes to make a census of the world in a most objective way. But his gathering of facts though optics instead of logic results in an unorthodox version, a shuffling of facts as methodical but as unexpected in its implications as the neighboring of words in a dictionary. It may be the effort needed for this new reading, the jolt to the established habit, which so irks the layman that he prefers to deny the validity of such research.[89]

Richard Neupert writes that Graham too "liked to quip that the great weakness of Italian perspective was its limitation of the single eye's vantage point. The artist should instead modify and adjust drawings by imagining how objects look not just from two eyes, but from four or more."[90] It is evident that the animators were grappling with a wide range of somewhat contradictory advice in their classes, which ranged from lessons on how better to copy appearances (as in the intensive lessons on how to draw drapery folds to reveal the body beneath) to doses of contemporary modernism. Graham himself insisted that his students master classical one-point perspective, but he also gave them alternatives for suggesting solidity on the flat canvas or screen, such as by showing objects occluding one another to suggest three-dimensional space. Neupert observes, "Graham may not have been much help on the temporal dimensions of storytelling, but he excelled at creating striking representations of objects in a variety of spatial contexts, and of exceeding what he saw as the limitations of two dimensions."[91]

This interest, however, was hardly limited to Disney's crew. Perspective experiments were frequent in the Fleischer cartoons of the early 1930s. In *Popeye the Sailor* (Dave Fleischer/Paramount, 1933), as the hero runs across a rope bridge and the "camera" "pans," the planks shift in perspective. In *Axe Me Another* (Dave Fleischer/Paramount, 1934), as Popeye manipulates his runaway rowboat, it twists and spins through space gimbal-like in correct foreshortening. When Bluto and Popeye duke it out on floating logs in the same movie, the lines recede toward consistent vanishing points. The beams of a skyscraper under construction challenged the animators in *Sock-a-Bye Baby* (Dave Fleischer/Paramount, 1934), in which a "pan" creates a carefully calculated synthetic motion parallax effect with the angle of view constantly changing. Compared to *Building a Building* (David Hand/Disney, 1933), in which Mickey's steam shovel rotates in limited perspective and there is a brief shot—about two seconds—of the building's girders moving in perspective when it collapses at the end, the Fleischer film's use of moving perspective is more mathematically planned and better executed.

The Fleischers produced the most celebrated showcase of pre-1935 moving perspective, *A Dream Walking* (Dave Fleischer/Paramount, 1934). Olive goes for a stroll in her sleep and heads straight for a nearby construction site. Even before she gets out of bed, there are signs of the animators' interest in exaggerated depth. Olive's feet, in a Caravaggio-worthy performance of fisheye lens space, are hugely magnified, as is the rest of her body when she arises and approaches the "camera." On the way to a skyscraper, there's a spatial trick when it appears that she's about to walk off the edge of one building's cornice but makes a sudden right turn. When she turns again, she steps onto the neighboring building that had appeared much closer to the foreground but is now revealed to be farther back and close enough for her to step onto it safely. It recalls the gag with the commander who marches off the wall in *Egyptian Melodies*. On the skyscraper, Olive follows the girders suspended in the air as they glide in and out of deep space. There are several very labor-intensive renderings of perspectively accurate beams that move into position to catch Olive's footfalls with split-second timing (Figure 45).[92] Whether it was coincidence or a case of one studio's animators imitating the others, there was a noticeable uptick in interest in creating cartoon parallax at Disney following these Fleischer forays into deeper space.

FIGURE 45. *A Dream Walking* (1934). The foreshortened girders
appear just in time to catch Olive's footsteps in her nocturnal stroll.

Graham, picking up on Charlot, compared ancient art to modern
animation: "Through the painting of long friezes, large mural decora-
tions, designs encircling vases, and scroll paintings they [early artists]
attempted to depict continuity of action. The comic strip of today is
merely a new application of a timeworn principle. Ingenious though
these devices were, they scarcely anticipated the graphic revolution of
the moving picture."[93] He specifically singled out the "Egyptian" way of
representing space symbolically, and he illustrated his remarks with
pictures of hieroglyphic stelae (Figure 46). The Egyptian design, he observed, avoided depicting depth by painting a "shut-off plane to limit
the depth of his painted picture."[94] The uniplanar spaces of 1920s cartoons are analogous to these shut-off planes.

Although Disney has been credited with the innovative exploration
of performance space, it seems clear that the idea originated in discussions instigated by Graham, the teachers from Chouinard, and, of
course, the art student–animators themselves. It is likely that Disney's
awareness and excitement about dimensionality flowed upward from
his employees. Significantly, in the eight pages of the 1935 memo to
Graham in which Disney elaborates his "scientific" approach to caricature, rhythm, gesture, and character, he never mentions the ability to
add depth to scenes as desirable. His concern is with creating movement and "caricaturing life" to create performances. However, Graham

FIGURE 46. In *Composing Pictures: Still and Moving* (p. 151),
Donald Graham used this bas-relief Stele of Chaywet to illustrate
Egyptian art's flattened space concepts. Courtesy of Seattle Art
Museum, Thomas D. Stimson Memorial Collection and partial
gift of Hagop Kevorkian.

and the animators knew that this could not happen in a spatial vacuum;
the same principles that drove the push to embody performances were
behind the need to create encompassing acting spaces.

Graham brought a definite philosophy of art to the job of designing
the Tooniverse.[95] He wanted his students to understand the basics of creating space on a flat surface, but he was also aware that he was working
in the film medium. He drew a sharp line between how space should be
conceived in painting and in animation. Painting is always framed in
some way. In cartooning, however, the physical experience of watching
the work in an inhabited theatrical space changes the viewer's relation to
the image. Anticipating theories of theatrical absorption, the animator, he
counseled, must not let the audience become aware of the frame:

> In painting, the consciousness of the picture surface is preserved; in anima-
> tion the consciousness of the rectangular screen in the theatre must at all
> times be avoided. The following principles are fundamental: If an action
> starts in one direction and is continued indefinitely, the audience soon be-
> comes conscious of the theatre screen, and the principle of variety of direc-
> tion of action is broken. The action of objects in the distance must be held
> down in relation to close foreground action, or their respective positions in
> space will be destroyed. This is the principle of relative action in space.[96]

Here he is defining ideas that are diametrically opposed to the performances of Disney and others in the early 1930s in which planes ostentatiously called attention to their two dimensions, asserted their madeness, and reveled in their cartoon-ness in almost every scene. Graham also advises not having actions in the foreground and background at the same time (apparently a reference to the carnivalesque opening shots discussed below). These biplanar compositions distract the viewers by revealing the artifice of the constructed space.

Three Orphan Kittens, a film that explores several of the principles under discussion in the art classes, contains the most astonishing spatial experiment in constructing synthetic motion parallax. It reflects an intensification of efforts to impart moving perspective depth based on the synthetic parallax demonstrated in *Egyptian Melodies*. Disney, according to archivist Smith, asked animator Anderson, a former architect, to "animate the complete scene, the background as well as the characters."[97] Although the multiplane camera was under development elsewhere in the studio, the experiment here was using the background drawings as a means to create an illusion of three-dimensional mise-en-scène.

In three sequences of *Three Orphan Kittens,* the "camera" "trucks" laterally. Instead of moving the background east or west behind the cels, according to the usual method, Anderson made individual perspective drawings for each frame of moving background. The first shot using the technique shows us the kittens on a highly polished tile floor. Because the viewpoint is at the same level as the kittens' bodies, the tiles' edges are rendered as extremely foreshortened lines. When the "trucking" shot begins, the floor lines shift very precisely, just as they would if they had they been filmed action (Plates 9 a–f). A kitchen counter's edge foreshortens as the "lens" moves past it, creating a convincing illusion of depth and motion parallax. There are other amazing moving shots following a kitten from one room to another as we accurately view the dividing wall first from its right and then from its left side, and a vertical shift in point of view as the kitten goes up a stair. Another shot uses a top cel to show a kitten passing *behind* a perspectively shifting kitchen table, not unlike the effect in *Mickey Cuts Up*. Though Anderson later described the experiment as disappointing ("it seemed to jitter, stutter"),[98] these shots remind modern viewers of video game imagery or computer graphics. Obviously, though, this approach to linear perspective was labor- and time-intensive, as it required vastly more finished drawings than standard animated spatial movement. Nevertheless, for a few seconds it powerfully creates an embodied space, that is, a 3-D environment that we experience through the kittens' moving eyes and bodies.

Anderson's statement suggests another reason for the technique's lack of success in his estimation. The moving sequences in the rest of the film that had been rendered traditionally contrast strikingly with the space depicted in the parallax scenes. The 3-D effects stood out and called attention to themselves as virtuoso performances at a time when the artists were trying to integrate spectacle and narrative into a self-effacing classical whole. This was not the solution that Disney or Graham was seeking. Using synthetic parallax to simulate three-dimensionality was unsatisfactory; in the new Disney cartoon 3-D had to blend into the style of the film unobtrusively. We saw this in *Clock Cleaners*. The animators orchestrated their deep spaces to allow Donald, Goofy, and Mickey to develop their unique personalities while interacting freely in a believable high-risk environment atop the clock tower. The scenes of Mickey falling off the tower and Goofy dangling over the edge are convincing enough to trigger a somatic response from us. The cartoon emulates the dizzying anxiety evoked in such films as Harold Lloyd's *Safety Last!* (Fred Newmeyer and Sam Taylor, 1923), when Lloyd dangles from clock hands over a street, and Laurel and Hardy's *Liberty* (Leo McCarey, 1929), when the lads act up on swinging aerial girders.

Synthetic parallax continued to pop up in Disney films, as in the housecleaning sequence in *Snow White*, when the "camera" "trucks" along a countertop and back, and the background perspective shifts as in *Three Orphan Kittens*. The shots are so well integrated into the overarching action, though, that a viewer may not be consciously aware of their existence. According to Disney's new conception of performance space: perfect.

Multiplane Cinematography

The tendency toward increasing classicism in pictorial space (what Wells calls neorealism) led to the invention of various multiplanar camera devices. For the Disney studio, the idea of filming more than one plane of images was partly a competitive response. Iwerks had invented a prototype he called the multiple animation stand in the studio he formed after leaving Disney. Its effects were featured prominently in *The Headless Horseman* (Ub Iwerks/MGM, 1934). At Van Beuren, in *Spinning Mice* and *The Picnic Panic* (both Burt Gillett and Tom Palmer/Van Beuren, 1935), Gillett took the simple expedient of placing cel animation over still photographs of modeled sets. This created depth to the extent that there was perspective in the photos, but it also created a sort of dollhouse impression of space. The Fleischers released several cartoons utilizing the "setback" (also known as "turntable") process that Max Fleischer had patented (he used it, for example, in *Betty Boop and Grampy*, in 1935, and notably in *Popeye the Sailor Meets Sinbad the Sailor*, in 1936).

The Stereoptical Process, the trademarked name for the invention, used a horizontal turntable on which miniature sets were constructed.[99] It could rotate through a limited arc. The animation camera filmed it through a vertical platen supporting the cels. When photographed, the figures seemed to move across the relief background, which was turned a little with each exposure. In several complicated scenes, as when Bluto passes through a tunnel (Plate 5 again), the space is multiplanar. Bluto, on cels, walks into the opening. Although the front edge of the tunnel would be downstage of Bluto as he entered in a "real" world, because the cels are in front of the setback background, the appearance of his going inside had to be simulated in the drawings. Thus the cels incrementally slice off Bluto's body as it aligns with the front edge of the tunnel to make it look like he's walking into it. Additionally, an out-of-focus top cel of some moving foliage in the foreground adds to the depth effect. The result was flat toon figures in cel space that had their own spatial systems, moving past sculpted 3-D backgrounds that moved with true motion parallax. Rather than integrating figure and ground, however, the effect highlights the discrepancy. The impression of a cylindrical world was even more noticeable than it was with traditional paper backgrounds because the space really was spherical.[100]

The Disney machine for multiplanar effects was patented by his engineer, William Garity, and constructed by Acme. Although it was called a multiplane camera, the term *camera* is a misnomer since the apparatus integrated superstructure, lighting, and camera systems.[101] It consisted of a camera modified for Technicolor filming mounted atop an eleven-foot-tall animation stand. It contained up to six platens that supported glass sheets eighteen inches apart. They could accommodate cels, painted glass (opaque or translucent), and moving and static backgrounds. Using the example of moving scenes and the moon, Disney explained to his TV audience how the multiplane camera solved the problem of a lack of parallax. He noted,

> The different elements in the scene were separated according to their varying distances from the viewer. This put the moon on a plane farthest away from the camera. With our original picture broken down in this manner, it is pos-

sible to control the relative speed with which each individual part of it moves to or away from the camera. But the moon remains absolutely still, and so it will always remain the same, neither growing nor shrinking in size. . . . This trick of obtaining a real feeling of depth and dimension in our painted backgrounds was used extensively in the feature cartoons.[102]

As the camera moved vertically to and fro above the drawings, the viewer experienced the illusion of depth in two ways. The camera was fitted with a long lens that produced a shallow depth of field, meaning that the planes gradually went in and out of sharp focus as the camera moved, realizing relational foreshortening. And the spacing between the glass plates meant that when the setup moved laterally, the angular velocity of the near cels was greater than that of the far cels. This produced natural motion parallax, which the camera duly recorded.

The Old Mill was planned as a road test for the multiplane system. First we see the mill in the distance, framed through a close-up of a spider tending its web. As we enter the scene the "camera" passes through the cobweb. Unlike the depth effects of top cel simulated parallax, this movement really produced an impression of spectators traveling into the distance. The web goes out of focus as the camera and viewer seem to pass through it. We approach a lateral procession of cows behind the mill and a duck family swimming in the rippling pond in the foreground. Nearing the base of the mill, the camera seems to pass through a chink in the wall and discloses a bluebird sitting on her nest. The point of view shifts vertically to show the other inhabitants of the mill's interior: doves, a colony of scary bats, and a grumpy owl who resents the viewer's intrusion (mirroring our own disembodied presence inside this unprecedented cartoonal space). The setting sun and a brewing storm show through a crack in the boards. This sequence is at least three separate multiplane shots subtly laced together by dissolves into a single smooth motion. Although the studio planned 41 of the film's 102 shots as multiplane,[103] the parallax effect is visible in far fewer shots in the finished work. Most of the midsection of *The Old Mill* appears to use conventional refielding and top cels to simulate spatial movement. Reverse-tracking multiplane footage returns at the end of the film after the storm has passed, concluding as it had begun with the spider repairing its now-broken web.

The spatial extravagance and nonnarrative presentation in Disney's not-very-silly symphony invites various interpretations. *The Old Mill* establishes a multifaceted performance space for the animal inhabitants. It also launches a drama of mechanical performance when turning gears threaten to kill the mothering bluebird, not unlike the hazards of some falling rocks in *Egyptian Melodies*. The wind is an invisible performer in the film. We see its effects but not the instrument, symbolic, perhaps, of the off-screen vital force of the animators making cartoons. The narrative symmetry (which also reprises the 1931 cartoon) suggests an implicit moral concerning capricious nature and rejuvenation. The circle of life finds its correlative also in the circular windmill gears and rotating blades and grindstones. The motifs of repetition and circularity also suggest the repetitive nature of the behind-the-scenes making of animation on an assembly line, re-performing the cycled cels, reused backgrounds, and endless labor of cartoon manufacture. If *The Old Mill* has an instrumental message, it surely has something to do with believing in eternal nature and having faith that time will restore everything—an aptly hopeful response to the seemingly never-ending Great Depression. It was also suitably ironic that Disney premiered the latest word in animation technology in a film that reanimates an ancient technology.

The unveiling of the multiplane system marked a sea change in animation spatialization at the end of the 1930s. Using technology to create compositions in deep space was demonstrably more "scientific." It relied on complex mathematical computations, high-tech optics, and imposing apparatuses. This transformation of space seemingly replaced the hand of the artist with a machine. The innovation coincided with developing multifaceted characters and navigating the transition to animated feature production. Always the utopian, Disney felt that the multiplane system was only the beginning of full dimensionality. "There is no knowing how far steady growth will take the medium," he wrote in 1940, "if only the technicians continue to give us new and better tools. For the near future, I can practically promise a third-dimensional effect in our moving characters."[104] As in the live-action studios of the time, the idea was to have a completely systematic production design, coherent and organized at every level.

RE-PERFORMING PICTORIAL SPACE

The cartoon industry, like the Hollywood film industry generally, developed patterns, conventions, and genres as well as technical innovations with the aim of deriving profit from creative work. Along the way, this hybrid of factory and atelier established the potential for a new kind of mass-culture art. A studio system in microcosm, the staff of the animation shops developed patterns of representation and aesthetic principles that they used, reused, modified, loaned out, and stole back until they became motifs. Re-performances of various spatial systems codified conventional patterns that led to the impression—rightly or not—that cartoons are a cinema genre.

Carnivalesque Opening Shots

As one illustration of how the space-generating effects discussed above became a particular stylistic trait through re-performance, consider the carnivalesque opening shot. I'm giving these opening shots this name because they present a Bakhtinian topsy-turvy version of the ordinary world with the potential for social allegory, because they offer several centers of visual interest (such as the decentered three-ring circus), and because they generate the air of the surreal, the grotesque, and the outré with their strange characters.

Alpine Antics (Jack King/Schlesinger, 1936) opens on a landscape of lively winter sports, which is followed by an ice-skating cow diva who skates from the distant edge of a pond into an ultra-close-up at the "camera" and then back in a series of pirouettes. The extra time and labor required to produce this over-the-top initial sequence is evident and part of the cartoon's allure. When the opening shot ends, the camera refields in, "trucking" into the scene, and the story begins.

At Disney, the Mickey Mouse and Silly Symphony series often began with an outrageous view of some sort, either a perplexing black-and-white pattern or a very complicated scene with multiple simultaneous performances. In a typical fashion, *Plane Crazy* begins with a barely comprehensible opening shot. The black shapes become a cow and a duck that amble through a performance clearing. Other animals are hard at work assembling Mickey's plane. A worm is popping in and out of its hole in the ground. The duck grabs it, is drawn into the worm's subterranean lair, and then pops out of another hole. The duck charges the camera, and its distorted wide-angle bill fills the screen as he blows a raspberry.

The Disney animators referred to this type of opening as the *plant,* suggesting that this was when the concept of the upcoming film was planted. They called the effects that telegraph the story elements to the audience *banners. The Karnival Kid* (Ub Iwerks/Disney, 1929) is a fine example of these carnivalesque effects because the abundantly grotesque opening setting actually is a carnival. The first frames of the film are black with abstract white patches. Gradually there coalesces the outline of a black cow, with a prominent udder, as seen from the rear. She wafts away from the "lens," borne aloft by balloons, drifts into the distance, and then drifts back (through cel cycling). This time she fills the screen with her face (using an aggressive wide-angle effect), blows a raspberry at a peanut vendor, and blows a noisemaker at the viewer. All the while this motion is unfolding, we see the carnival in an encompassing establishing shot—tents and performers' trailers in the middle ground, carnival rides in the distance. The landscape is populated with dozens of tiny figures going about their carnie work, filing into tents, chasing balloons, and so on, all animated by cycled cels (Figure 47). The overall visual effect is of great excitement and commotion. Such scenes demanded complex cycled motions on at least two top cels. The payoff, though, is obvious. The opening immediately rivets the viewer's attention on the scene and announces the film's surreal cartoon world: we are now in the Tooniverse. For the viewer trying to make out all the minute actions within the scene, it's rather like studying a "Where's Waldo" drawing—in motion. (Minnie the Shimmy Dancer's trailer is one of the items discernible amid the clutter.) These inscrutable opening frames pique our curiosity about what kind of performance will take place in such a movie.

Other examples of complex carnivalesque openings are in *Springtime,* with its swaying trees and flowers in long shot, one of which opens its petals and transforms into a stage; in *Night,* which shows dancing cattails on top cels; in *Pioneer Days* (Burt Gillett/Disney, 1930), in which viewers see a curving deep perspective shot of a wagon train that cites the opening of *The Big Trail* (Raoul Walsh, 1930); in *Just Dogs* (Burt Gillett/Disney, 1932), in which multiple mutts raise a ruckus in a dog pound; and, finally, in *Bugs in Love* (Burt Gillett/Disney, 1932) and *Woodland Café,* both of which open with swarms of cycled insects. The Disney studio created a particularly impressive carnivalesque opening in *The Spider and the Fly* (Wilfred Jackson/Disney, 1931). It begins with a close-up of a fly putting on ice skates. The shot refields out to a wider view showing lots of flies skating on what appears to be a strange ice rink. The entire picture then rotates 180 degrees, revealing that the "rink" is the ceiling of a country kitchen that we had been viewing upside down from our point of view, but right side up from the flies'. The "camera" then refields onto a jam pot and a rather conventional film ensues, with the rest of the action mostly in frontal displays.[105]

A distant view of a burning apartment house opens *Mickey's Fire Brigade.* The many intricate movements engage the viewer's close atten-

FIGURE 47. *The Karnival Kid* (1929). The carnivalesque opening shot provides much to see in a busy decentered composition.

tion as we watch occupants jump from windows, firemen climb ladders, and so on, all animated with cycled cels. Then we see Mickey speeding toward the camera in a wide-angle run while the road whizzes behind him. He makes a quick right-angle turn and the action continues laterally (east). Cycled top cels add patches of smoke in the foreground. The clangorous soundtrack gives credence to the hectic images.

The carnivalesque opening shot functions as a way to reset the viewers' expectations for cartoon watching: action, toe-tapping music, hyperkinetic toons, and general zaniness. These introductions are sometimes like non-animated cinema's establishing shots. They set the stage and ease us into the plot. Just as often, however, they define a performance space in which things are not clear, predictable, or even right side up, which makes them unlike the openings of most feature films.

The carnivalesque shot diminished in frequency in the mid-1930s as animation's focus shifted from introducing groups of characters to individual protagonists, and the function of the opening changed from setting up gags to establishing a believable location for the narrative. The Disney animators came to speak with disdain of the older practice of placing "plants" and "banners" in the first scene. In an action analysis session, they praised the new improved approach that was exemplified by the opening of *Elmer Elephant*. We see the main character enter the scene through a distant gate in the west, amble toward the "camera," and then move off to the east. Graham observed approvingly that Elmer's early action forecasts what would happen later. We see that he's familiar with his trunk and swings it naturally. Later, however, he's awkwardly embarrassed by it. The business with the trunk wasn't a short-lived gag but a plant that prepared the audience for its important function later in the story. The viewers sense this and so suspense builds up.[106] Clearly, the opening shot is no longer carnivalesque. It has been subsumed into a classically integrated performance. The visual scheme is no longer frantic but rather catches the eye with a subtle, multifaceted composition. The motion, perspectival depth, and shifting shadows are suitable for the individualized character in its personal setting. Such a beginning with its stately pace opposes the early 1930s ideal of loony, merry, silly openings.

'Egyptian Melodies': A Rosetta Stone?

At the trend-setting Disney studio, the changes in space construction were neither random nor organic developments but instead were a specific praxis based on prevailing discussions about the performativity of animation. Inspired (or cajoled) by Graham and the other Chouinard teachers and lecturers, and under the influence of the California watercolorists and the Europeans that Disney had hired, the filmmakers looked outside cartooning for inspiration. According to Graham, "A drawing principle is a drawing principle. If it works in a Rubens it must work in Donald Duck. If it works in the Duck it must work in Snow White."[107] Looking back at *Egyptian Melodies*, we can now see hints of the origins of this sensibility and place it in its larger historical framework.

Antonia Lant has chronicled the waves of "Egyptomania" that gripped American popular culture in the nineteenth and early twentieth centuries.[108] Disney's film predates Universal's *The Mummy* (Karl Freund, 1932) by just a year, and it came nine years after Howard Carter's breach and descent into the burial chamber of Tutankhamen in 1922. The beginning of *Egyptian Melodies*, in which the spider-protagonist accidentally discovers the opening at the base of the Sphinx, re-performs the famous discovery of King Tut's treasure-strewn crypt. Inside, it is not the dancing mummies that intrigue the modern viewer but the journey into the sphinx through the perspective-perfect moving stairs as well as the animated hieroglyphic texts and murals in the tomb. Let's try a speculative reading.

Why a spider? Unlike the gruesome eight-legged villains that appear in several Disney cartoons, this androgynous sneaker-clad character (who appeared in two other films) is friendly and personable. Its beckoning gesture foreshadows the spider in *The Old Mill.* The spiders' web work requires infinite patience and many "hands," which also describes the work of animators. That suggests that the performing spider is a self-figuration, an avatar of the animator-performer, much as Arachne personified artists in mythology. As the eight-legged actor descends into the dark alimentary passage on its way into the tomb, it enters a zone of three-dimensionality hitherto unprecedented in any Disney film. It's a threatening space; the spider narrowly avoids pitfalls and crashing masonry. Then, after surviving the mummies' assault, the spider witnesses the astonishing moving friezes of the murals, the space of which calls to mind the lateral processions of characters populating the shallow picture boxes of so many cartoons of the 1920s and early 1930s. When the figures march around a corner and must be redrawn in perspective, their aversion to diagonal walking recalls the cartoon characters that shunned oblique movements. The hieroglyphic characters trapped in the pictorial space of the columns spend their existence running in a circular world, not unlike the cartoon characters that, thanks to cycled traveling backgrounds, run in never-ending circles (Figure 48).

Why do the streaming friezes of animated figures make the spider's brain spin (indicated by the rotating point-of-view shot) and provoke it to flee the crypt? Reading the toon mind—always a risky proposition— suggests that the irreconcilable binary of these clashing visual extremes, the enveloping moving perspective of the stairs and the relentless two-dimensional marching of the friezes, has triggered a crisis of pictorial space. Overwhelmed and trapped between two competing representational systems, the "Egyptian" space of old-style cartooning and the newer representational paradigm preached by Graham, the spider-animator goes planes crazy!

Egyptian Melodies is a good illustration of the prevailing distinction between tactile (or haptic) and optical modes of spatial representation as originally articulated by the early twentieth-century art historian and connoisseur Aloïs Reigl. By the 1930s, this dualism had been absorbed into the "standard story" taught in art schools.[109] It influenced, for instance, Focillon, who opined, "Knowledge of the world demands a kind of tactile flair. Sight slips over the surface of the universe."[110] Charlot's guest lectures to the Disney animators were infused with this felt/seen dichotomy. In his 1938 talk he suggested that they should compare carpenters and painters. The former works in volumes and solidity, while the latter (exemplified by abstractionist Paul Klee) deals with space and optical designs. "We have to get out of that idea of the craftsman as

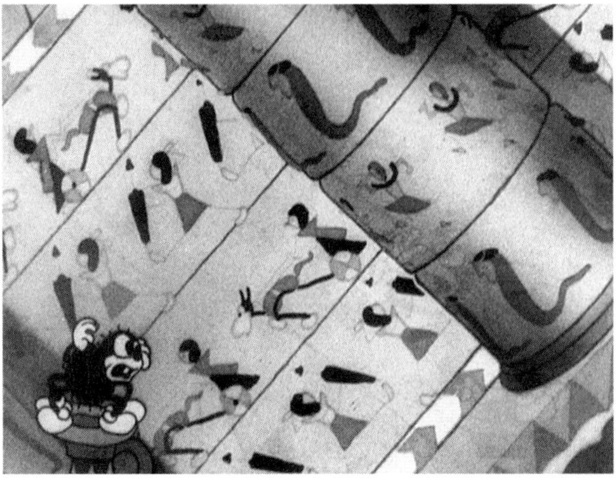

FIGURE 48. *Egyptian Melodies* (1931). Moving friezes surrounding the columns mimic the spherical space of animation lateral motion.

building up the art object; we have to make a difference between a table, which is entirely physical, and the picture." He observed that a table in the dark is still a table and useful, but a picture in the dark is not. "The picture is physical in a certain sense, its existence is not so much within the wood and canvas that constitute a picture, but the optical image within our eyes. The picture is, if you want to call it that, an accumulator of vision, but what counts is not so that your picture exists only optically. That may sound a little Chinese—the difference between physical things and physical things whose use is not entirely physical—yet it is important to know that it is so in a picture."[111]

Charlot tried to awaken the animators to the possibilities of unconventional constructions of pictorial depth by promoting, for example, Picasso's Cubist works. Although they were framed pictures, they retained the physicality of objects:

> Unlike the Impressionist who tried to push you away from his picture so as to make you forego the physical reality of the canvas, because he wanted you to believe that the canvas was an open window, Picasso is a man who brings you to his canvas by all sorts of tricks—I would say microscopic tricks. You have to actually put your nose on the canvas and look at little pieces of newspaper that are stuck in there, and look at parts of the picture that are painted with sand—and not only [do] you have to look at the thing but you have to put your fingers over it; you have to be absolutely conscious of the physical reality of a Picasso to appreciate it.[112]

Charlot urged the animators to make spaces that gave the sensation that they could be touched. Graham's vision, however, seems to have aligned more with the "open window" optical construction of space.

Graham's course of instruction included the study of photographs of Egyptian art, which were presented as a contrast to paintings from the Renaissance. Borrowing from Riegl's theory, unacknowledged and filtered through decades of art school discourse to be sure, Graham taught that the Egyptians understood and expressed space by touching and moving around solid objects. He wrote, "Two extremes are possible: a picture dominated by volumes [corresponding to haptic], or a picture dominated by space [optical]. How we equate these factors determines the character of our picture."[113] These haptic art cultures produced fetishes, effigies, body ornament, pyramids, and other objects based on the hand and movement. This mode of spatial construction is also visible in the graphic space of cartoons in the 1920s, where spatial relationships are mainly expressed by the relative scale of characters and objects and by opaque figures that occlude the background and each other. Space is intuitive rather than plotted by rulers. It is the pre-perspective world.

The optical mode, by contrast, developed fully in the Renaissance with linear perspective, the mathematical system for representing solid objects and 3-D space on flat surfaces. This was said to mimic vision, not touch, and, as Focillon pointed out, led to picturing sculptural objects on canvas as imaginary (chimerical) surfaces. The optic expression creates the illusion of objects' physical presence by tricking the eye with mathematical vanishing points. Lenses are purposely crafted to reproduce these perspectival effects. David Hockney has suggested that artists since the Renaissance commonly used pinhole cameras, curved mirrors, and proto-photographic devices to translate their viewing into perspective forms.[114] Graham and the European staff artists agitated for the Disney animators to jettison the sparse graphic, haptic mode of space construction and to replace it with richer illusionistic camera spaces more suitable for habitation by the characters of the late 1930s who were more rounded, both physically and psychologically.

Among the corollaries of this approach was that the animated body lost its traditional tendency to fragment, distort itself, and animorphose during movement. "In cartoons of the thirties and forties," Norman Klein observes, "there are no Disney gags where characters who slam into a wall turn into metal coins and twirl noisily as they land. . . . According to the Disney rule, once a character's body was shown— rubbery, watery, humanlike—its substance was irreducible. Walt was convinced that revealing the drawing behind the flesh could wreck the atmospheric effects that he prized so highly."[115] Embracing a primarily optical world entails a lack of tolerance for anything that undermines its visual laws.

Given this motion-friendly conception of pictorial space, it should not be surprising that Charlot and Graham—along with Eisenstein and many others—felt that the animated cinema had instigated a historical redefinition of space. Graham insisted that animators exploit this exceptional space differently from traditional visual artists or photographers. What he called cinematic space was light-based and defined by highlights and shadows. Graphic and pictorial devices, however, generate a unique "animation space," which involves the passage of time. Whereas the space of normal cinema is bounded, the unlimited space of animation was something new and exceptional.[116] Flat drawings on paper that created pictorial space through illusionist depth suddenly acquired a new dimension and the impression of real parallax when the image was seen on the big screen and in motion. This was no gratuitous "special effect" but rather a space generator that set the stories and the characters in a world as believable as anything in a play or a movie.

Egyptian Melodies is not a treatise on art history. It is nevertheless a film that re-performs the inquiry and debate about the nature of space and vision that was occurring in the student-animators' after-hours classes and during their on-the-job training. Reflecting the currents of change, the studio was effectively concocting a tongue-in-cheek parable about the ontogeny of cartoon space.

As winsome as the utopian critical thesis is—that the animators were imbibing the whole history of Western art in a few years, and that the old techniques were being replaced because they were inadequate—it is a little misleading. The argument implies that the artists drew flat pictorial spaces because they didn't know how to draw better and had to be educated. Clearly, though, the animators, most of whom had had at least basic training in perspective drafting in art school or through self-teaching, knew how to create depth. Said one artist, "A stream, road, fence, wall, or row of trees or bushes progressing across the landscape toward the horizon may be an old gag, but it is a sure fire distance getter."[117] Common sense suggests an axiom: If you can draw Clarabelle the Cow, you can probably draw perspective lines on a floor. The dystopian thesis that the new realism not only destroyed the verve and inventiveness of silent cartoons but also tainted post-Disney animation with literalness and sentiment needs to be rethought as well. It's reminiscent of Rudolf Arnheim's similar claims about the films of the 1930s, when he argued that technological "advancements" such as sound and color destroyed essential cinema.[118]

Neither the utopian nor the dystopian position can stand alone because the transformations I've charted are neither progressive nor regressive. Although it is natural to assume that what comes later and is more complicated and represents "progress," in fact, it may only be different.[119] Or, it may be that expectations have changed. Multiple forces appear to have sparked the evolution of space in 1930s cartoons. It wasn't caused by an innate urge toward three-dimensionality or the will of one person. The increasing narrative complexity and character psychology in animation required more complex mise-en-scènes to envelop such performances. To enhance this, the main studios began reengineering the Acme-based technology of animation in order to render convincing depth with machinelike precision.

The shift to the new style in studio animation was consistent with parallel trends in American art in the 1930s, a time of collisions between European and American visions, pan-Americanism and regionalism, and realist versus Cubist space strategies—all accompanied by debates about the instrumental role of art and the involvement of the masses. In its small way, what was happening in animation reflected strains in American art. We see this trajectory in the teaching at Chouinard, which steadily deemphasized fine-art watercolor in favor of commercial design and architecture. The Disney classes were rife with these tensions. Former Disney animator John Hubley claimed, "The marvelous training [by Graham and his associates] developed your imagination and ideas, which were then inhibited by the need to conform to a tepid standardized style."[120]

Commenting on the how the technology of the telescope changed pictorial space after Galileo, Friedberg noted, "Here, in the most material sense, the technologies of glass and transparency—aided by developments in lens-grinding and glass-making technique—played a determinant role in the scientific transformation of the modern world."[121] Compared to Galileo's big splash, the animators' reorchestrations of opacity and transparency, of bodies and shadows using Acme's steel and glass, are a tiny ripple. However, it's still too early to know where computer-assisted animation will take us.

Kinesiophile filmmakers and their audiences have never stopped reveling in the illusion of objects and beings moving on their own, seemingly in touchable and sharable spaces, or in imagining moving inside those fantastic spaces. Walt Disney, despite having campaigned for developing optical space in his major films, must have been one who continued to savor that kinetic experience. In fact, he seems to have had a closet obsession with the haptic. Look at his hobbies: charging down the polo field on the fastest Argentinean ponies and piloting his model train over the hills and dales and through the tunnels of his estate. Many of the original Disneyland rides swallowed up visitors and transported them through dark Sphinx-like caverns. As for the ultimate expression of Disney's kinetic art, it's not a far cry from the runaway train of *Mickey's Choo-Choo* to Big Thunder Mountain Railroad and the other thrilling rides that would deliver superabundant haptic thrills as they careened through the twisting "imagineered" spaces in the theme parks of the future.

PART THREE

Instrumental Animation

CHAPTER 5

Infectious Laughter

A man laughs, and another man feels merry; he weeps, and
the man who hears this weeping feels sad; a man is excited,
annoyed, and another looking at him gets into the same state.
With his movements, the sounds of his voice, a man displays
cheerfulness, determination, or, on the contrary, dejection,
calm—and this mood is communicated to others.

—Leo Tolstoy (1899)

The principal effect of any of the fine arts is to arouse
a purely emotional reaction in the beholder.

—Walt Disney (1957)

It is axiomatic that cartoons from the studio period were made to make
us laugh. Big belly laughs. Speaking as someone who attended the local
show almost weekly for most of the 1950s—after the big producers had
been forced to divest themselves of their theaters, but before economic
pressures, changes in the audience, and competing entertainments put
the Hollywood cartoon industry in its downward spiral—I can attest to
the producers' and exhibitors' success in the jocularity department. We
kids laughed like crazy at the cartoons. So did the grownups. Movie
audiences seem to have been more extroverted then. If it was funny,
we laughed. We cried when appropriate, too. I recall my parents snif-
fling along with the kids when it dawned on us that Wendy could not fly
back to Neverland with Peter Pan just because she was growing up.
Was this the origin of our 1960s rage against injustice? Did the models
of parenting so strongly presented (and so Victorian) in Disney films
affect our behavior as parents when we grew up?

Both young and old moviegoers laughed en masse at cartoons, but I have no way of proving it except to note that one finds a few corroborating comments by theater managers in trade journals. When audiences are represented in cartoons, they are always pictured in an uproarious state. Many cartoons seemed to aim for crazy laughter, provocative gags, and low comedy. Certainly the short subjects in film programming, a carryover from vaudeville, tended toward comedy. It is also likely that for very dense and interconnected reasons audiences and filmmakers were delighted by cartoon content that went beyond the merely funny to the hilarious. The irresistible laughter that these films generated entertained and distracted viewers, but the films were also capable of having a deeper significance for their audiences. Can we mine those lost meanings now?

When one watches the cartoons of the 1930s, it is obvious that there was more to them than just some sort of tickle. The filmmakers used the performative signature of infectious laughter to excite their audiences. This is not surprising. After all, the rise of Hollywood studio animation played against the backdrop of the worldwide Great Depression of the 1930s. It stands to reason that the producers and consumers of mass culture would reflect and engage the profound socioeconomic circumstances of that era. Indeed, scholars in many disciplines have stipulated this. Steven Watts devotes a chapter of *The Magic Kingdom* to these aspects of Disney's Mickey Mouse and Silly Symphony cartoons of the 1930s, maintaining that they articulated an ideology of "sentimental populism."[1] Not only did Disney's optimistic presentation of the inevitable triumph of the little guy over insurmountable societal forces become the ur-plot of many cartoons, but it was also a leitmotif of much of Disney's adoring contemporary appreciation. "Many critics not only discerned a populist message in Disney's films," Watts observed, "but praised them as an effective political and social assault on the Great Depression."[2]

Deep thinkers since Plato's era have argued about the social good or evil of artistic production and reception, as well as the value of comedy and laughter in society and in one's life. Frankly, it is doubtful that satisfactory answers will ever be determined for these questions of aesthetics and ethics. Nevertheless, I will venture into one tiny crevice, armed with the hypothesis that cartoons, which since the 1910s were usually designed to provoke laughter and often were reasonably successful at it, were performances requiring some sort of social engagement. Were these benign performances, eliciting mirth and nothing else? Or did animation have an agenda, hidden or overt, that affected moviegoers? And if animation performance can cause changes in individual or cultural behavior, is that good or bad?

Going for the guffaw was the animators' stock-in-trade, but many cartoons of the 1930s also casually elaborated an underlying ideology that validated laughter and sentiment as beneficial to society. But here is the conundrum. On the one hand, filmmakers publicly clung to their position that animated performances were nothing but entertainment and if the laughs they elicited did some good, well so much the better. On the other hand, because the films depend on structures and narratives that traditionally have been vehicles for allegory and moral instruction, they invite—or demand—ideological interpretations. Although this situation may always prevail in the popular arts, during the uniquely stressed times of the 1930s, this performative ambivalence is overwhelming. In the cartoons there were connections to timely issues and there were stories that prescribed or demonstrated the behaviors of individuals within the state and within the national economy. In what has become a memory palace dedicated to cartoon social effectiveness, *The Three Little Pigs* (Burt Gillett/Disney, 1933), we have a film that has been universally accepted "as a Depression-era fable."[3] Furthermore, it was one of the most-watched films of its time. J.B. Kaufman has declared, "It has become, by any commercial standard, the most successful one-reel cartoon in history."[4] The audience members for such a film must have found something in it that was especially entertaining, valuable for their lives, or even for curing the national blues. But the conundrum remains.

BENIGN LAUGHTER: FORGETTING THE DEPRESSION

There are so many books on the nature and function of laughter, it makes you want to cry.[5] The connection between laughter and audience behavior has established credentials. "Laughter must answer to certain requirements of life in common," Henri Bergson wrote in 1904. "It must have a *social* signification." Bergson also recorded something that is obvious to anyone who has attended a spectacle, sporting event, or stand-up comedy performance: "Our laughter is always the laughter of a group. . . . How often has it been said that the fuller the theatre, the more uncontrollable the laughter of the audience!"[6] Sigmund Freud writing on humor claimed that it takes at least three people for a joke to work. For him, humor was always about symbolism and power. He noted how often jokes favored the weaker (think of the three pigs) over the stronger (think wolf) and how seemingly harmless laughter could be a weapon to make someone "contemptible and rob him of any claim on dignity or authority" (think of the Big Bad Wolf's scalded butt).[7] This use of laughter to redeem suffering also informed Freud's "analysis" of Charlie Chaplin:

> He is undoubtedly a great artist—although he always plays one and the same part, the weak, poor, helpless clumsy boy for whom life turns out all right in the end. Now do you think he has to forget his own self in order to play this part? On the contrary, he invariably plays only himself as he was in his grim youth. He cannot get away from these impressions and even today he tries to compensate himself for the humiliation and deprivation of that time. He is of course an especially simple, transparent case.[8]

Thus Freud saw in Chaplin's tramp character a re-performance of the actor's impoverished and emotionally devastated childhood. His power as a great artist was an aggressive redirection of repressed anger against the establishment, expressed by making audiences laugh.

So laughter as performance seems to have a built-in proclivity toward group expressivity. It appears to be mere entertainment, but it may also be a disguised social weapon. How appropriate for Hollywood cartoons! If our initial response to comic film performances is harmless, it may be because the industry has always promoted its product as "pure entertainment" and possibly a means for bettering lives. The moguls and mass-market journalists have always agreed that cartoons were foremost a business and designed to please the most people while offending the fewest. One reason for animation's success, wrote an arts columnist in 1933,

> is the fact that it is pure entertainment, objective in character; another that it rescues the mind and emotions from the humdrum world by projecting them into an imaginary realm. Like other forms of radical art, it repudiates representation, but it aims to provoke the poignant reality of the unreal. It, too, goes back to the study of the primitive and the child in its basic realization that to both a fairy tale is more real than actual experience. The adult of today, harassed by trying realities and a work life of monotony, is keenly susceptible to the same magic.[9]

This prescient analysis touches upon some of the claims that I, too, have been making for animation performance: it establishes an imaginary world, the Tooniverse; its representational system tends toward abstraction (observant, since this was written when cartoon style was still primarily figurative); and it involves the metaleptic paradoxes of "me ... not me," trusting yet incredulous, live but not alive ("the poignant reality of the unreal"). These alternate worlds, like those in fairy tales, may promote belief systems that are magically more powerful than our "realities." Ironically, although the author was making the case for cartoons as escapism, she also unintentionally bolstered the possibility that animation's performativity could rally to the cause that cartoons could be instrumental performances.

Associating cartoons with psychic regression, childhood, and preindustrial leisure insulated them, in the minds of some, from any taint of the instrumental. Richard Maltby has commented on the entrenched conservative political and social stances in the production companies of Hollywood. "The entertainment ethic," he wrote, "proscribed an area of human activity, going to the movies, as being detached from political significance. Movies were, according to the accepted wisdom of their manufacturers, mere 'harmless entertainment,' at most influencing only fashion and shirts."[10] Disney was exhibit number one, always denying the existence of social messages in his films. It should be added, though, that producers were willing to take credit for progressive content when it suited their purpose—as Jack Warner did for the social problem and crime films produced by Warner Bros.

Moviegoing in the 1920s and '30s had become such an everyday occurrence for many Americans that, as has often been noted, it acquired many aspects of rituals, which are invocative and always instrumental. Schechner's observations may also apply to classic studio animation: "Performing rituals helps people get through difficult periods of transition. Ritual is also a way for people to connect to a collective, even mythic past, to build social solidarity, to form a community. Some rituals are liminal, existing between or outside daily social life. Because of their liminality, ritual performances can produce communitas, a feeling among participants of something greater than or outside of their individual selves."[11] The idea that the movies, and cartoons in particular, might be able to do something about the Depression was easy to promote. Although laughing individually might lighten one's disposition, an audience laughing together as a community could generate, the moguls and apologists for mass entertainment implied, tangible improvements in morale and, by extension, the economy.

Some writers support the possibility that comedy may be just what it appears to be—benign. Peter Berger, for instance, distinguishes between dark Dionysian humor and neutral forms that "offer no threat to the social order or to the paramount reality of ordinary life. They provide a vacation from the latter's worries, a harmless diversion from which one can return refreshed to the business of living."[12] Unlike wit, he goes on, laughter "does not make excessive intellectual demands. Unlike irony and satire, it is not designed to attack. Unlike the extravagant creations of folly, it does not present a counterworld. Rather, it is harmless, even innocent. It is intended to evoke pleasure, relaxation, and good will. It enhances rather than disrupts the flow of everyday life." By contrast, humor that has passed down from "Dionysian ecstasies" is always exposing weakness and attacking it. Berger continues, "One might perhaps argue that this darker side is always there, under the surface of the most innocuous jokes, but it is almost completely hidden, present if at all as a mere *soupçon*."[13] It is precisely this shadow, the darker side of humor that ushers in the instrumentality of laughter in art.

INSTRUMENTAL LAUGHTER: CURING THE DEPRESSION

Benign laughter, in Berger's terms, may exist, say in the giggles of very young children watching *The Three Little Pigs*. However, since even kids laughing on the playground may be displaying meanness, jealousy, or other "Dionysian" intent, truly benign laughter may be rare. Similarly, children's laughter in the movie theater may mask their concern for the piggies' well-being or even cover up their own anxiety about being eaten. More than one jolly cartoon has provoked nightmares in young viewers.

Comedy performance that influences opinion or behavior or provokes a thoughtful reaction is instrumental performance. Although there are numerous hypothetical models for how film may affect its audiences, it turns out to be appropriate to resurrect an artifact of early twentieth-century aesthetics found in the writing of Russian novelist and philosopher of art, Leo Tolstoy. He did not write much about film, which is understandable since it wasn't introduced to his homeland until 1896, but he had a definite opinion that art was instrumental and, furthermore, that it spread from artist to receiver as a metaphoric infection. His ideas, which we'll get to later, have an unexpected connection to animation, and so they are doubly appropriate for our brief investigation.

A non-animated 1934 film that explicitly embraced the power of movies and popular entertainment as a curative is *Stand Up and Cheer!* (Hamilton MacFadden/Fox Film Corp., 1934). The president of the United States summons Broadway showman Lawrence Cromwell (Warner Baxter) to his office and tells him that the nation is in the red, but the people's faith is not: "Any people, blessed with a sense of humor, can achieve such a victory. We are endeavoring to pilot the ship past the most treacherous of all rocks—fear. The government now proposes to dissolve that rock in a gale of laughter." Roosevelt has accordingly created a position for a new cabinet member, the secretary of amusement, whose duty will be to "amuse and entertain the people, to make them forget their troubles."[14]

A sympathetic parody of Franklin D. Roosevelt, the film picks up on a passage in the president's inaugural address that promoted the arts for attaining intangible happiness: "Happiness lies not in the mere possession of money; it lies in the joy of achievement, in the thrill of creative effort."[15] Cromwell succeeds in bringing the Depression to an end and throws a massive victory parade. Jenkins observes in his astute analysis of *Stand Up and Cheer!*, "The film's narrative offers an elaborate apologia for Hollywood's own role as a central national institution during a national crisis, arguing for the social importance of entertainment and the need to 'stand up and cheer' in the face of adversity."[16]

The film industry's self-promotion as being benignly optimistic and patriotic is apparent in the many films that include music associated with the New Deal and FDR. The widely heard "Happy Days Are Here Again" (Milton Ager and Jack Yellen, 1929) was already a film and radio favorite, but it became permanently associated with Roosevelt after he adopted it as his 1932 campaign song.[17] The song creates a fantasy consensus that music will restore communitas. In *Stand Up and Cheer!* the song "I'm Laughin'" (Lew Brown and Jay Gorney, 1933) specifically asserts the need to cultivate infectious laughter: "I'm laughing./And I got nothin' to laugh about,/so if I can laugh, sing, dance and shout,/brother, so can you." This refrain unites an astonishing cross-section of down-and-out and marginalized Americans: an Irish mother with kids, some rural hayseeds, a Jewish seamstress in a sweatshop, cops, construction workers, chorines, showgirls, sanitation workers, blacksmiths, a train engineer, and even Aunt Jemima. The crowd then sings "Stand Up and Cheer!" (Harry Akst and Lew Brown, 1933) to celebrate the Depression's end. "Sing hallelujah, sing it loud," they proclaim, "because the big, bad wolf is gone." Could animation similarly rout the Depression wolf?

THE THIRD PIG

The *Three Little Pigs*'s guileless, familiar narrative and its classic status belie its complexity as a performance. Like most fairy tales, one of which it re-performs, it uses anthropomorphism and figuration to establish multiple layers of meaning for children (for whom the story exemplifies moral behavior and good choices) and for adults (often suggesting strategies for parenting and achieving the good life vicariously through children). It acts out (hopefully exorcising) primal anxieties and fears specific to one's environment (like the possibility of animal attacks or cannibalism or just going to hell). Surprisingly, then, for a work seemingly so simple, *The Three Little Pigs*, from its release in 1933 until the present, has had a contested reception history. The film's message, like that of many movies in the 1930s, is both crystal clear and laden with ambivalence. Furthermore, as a performance, is it really so benign, or is it instrumental? And if it's instrumental, are its effects ameliorating or negative? The film is its own nine-minute conundrum.

It opens with the three unnamed heroes going about their distinctive occupations: one toots his flute and doesn't give a hoot, the second plays on his fiddle and dances jigs, and the third is hard at work on his masonry and has no chance to sing and dance.[18] One day the big bad wolf comes to eat them all. He easily blows down the houses of the first two pigs, which are made of straw and twigs, but they escape to the third pig's sanctuary made of wolf-proof bricks. Its hominess is conveyed in part by framed pictures of Mother (with the suckling piglets) and Father (although he is a ham and some sausages). The wolf tries to trick his way in, but the pigs aren't fooled. The third pig taunts him by playing "Who's Afraid of the Big Bad Wolf?" on the piano, which he has self-reliantly constructed out of bricks. When the wolf comes down the chimney, the pig is ready with a vat of boiling water and turpentine. The wolf rockets out of the chimney and runs over the horizon dragging his parboiled posterior. The pigs reprise their song.

One approach to *The Three Little Pigs*' performativity has addressed it as a metaphor of the plight of its figured subjects, individuals, laborers, and their society. Thus, as an allegory, the pigs and the wolf have been read as figures of Americans' responses to the Depression. Another approach promotes the pigs' characterization as milestones in embodied performance in cartoons. Animators and historians, as we saw in chapter 1, have singled out the film as a breakthrough in creating toon individuality and character. Disney is said to have reacted to its preview screening by saying, "At last we have achieved true personality in a whole picture."[19] Although these two interpretative strategies at first seem to be at odds, they are complementary. There is a tension in the film's historical reception as a social allegory and as an individualized acting event.

No doubt about it, *The Three Little Pigs* was a landmark in animation storytelling, graphic style, and characterization, and although film historians have praised it as an early instance of embodied acting, many people and critics in general interpreted it as a figurative performance, that is, as an easily read allegory with stock characters. According to Watts, professional writers commenting on film "almost universally decoded the movie's symbolism as the Big, Bad Wolf representing the Depression and the Three Little Pigs representing average citizens desperately fighting for survival against its attempts to devour them." Other commentators praised the film in more general terms for just giving the wolf "hell."[20] Studying the critical reception of the film, though, reveals that there have been other divergent interpretations.

To begin with, the wolf, an integral component of the Little Red Riding Hood fairy tale, although often taken to represent economic hard times, has been a figure with highly unstable identifications.[21] "As a metaphor for human behavior, traits, and beliefs, " Debra Mitts-Smith observes, "the wolf is ubiquitous. It is present not only in fables and folk and fairy tales." The symbol's lack of specificity is its virtue as a cultural signifier: "The myriad uses to which we put the term *wolf* exemplify our tendency to use aspects of nature to create and convey meaning."[22] For pioneering political cartoonist Thomas Nast, the wolf meant something completely different than "hard times." In his 1876 drawing, the wolf is breaking down a door to get at some cowering children. It unsympathetically symbolized Catholic bishops who had allied with Democrats to fight a Republican-sponsored bill that would prohibit the government from subsidizing public schools.[23] In 1926, George Bernard Shaw invoked the wolf to personify the poverty that a socialist-proposed living-wage policy would keep away.[24]

Even in cartoons the lupine villain did not always symbolize the Depression. In *Grandma's Pet* (Walter Lantz and William Nolan/Universal, 1932), for instance, there are no obvious references to current events outside the Red Riding Hood source (Figure 49). Similarly, the Depression is absent from Disney's *Pigs* sequel, *The Big Bad Wolf* (Burt Gillett/Disney, 1934). There the moral is not that hard work and no play will banish the Depression. Instead, there is only a homily about choosing the longer, safer road instead of taking riskier shortcuts.

Many of those who originally attended *The Three Little Pigs* evidently experienced nothing more than uplifting entertainment. *Fortune*, the conservative business magazine, praised the cartoon, claiming that the films in the Silly Symphonies series possessed more artistic dignity

FIGURE 49. Another "wolf at the door" in *Grandma's Pet* (1932).

than other products of the "Hollywood inferno." According to the magazine, the series "is simple, at a time when all other entertainment in America's theatres is designed for a disillusioned and sophisticated audience. . . . And finally, the Silly Symphony is an avenue of escape from the world's confusion."[25] We have only a few records indicating how many interpreted the wolf as economic duress or saw the third pig as a figure for the new president. Perhaps those who saw no further significance in the film did not feel inclined to write about it. The bland notice in the *New York Times* did not exactly encourage further contemplation: "*The Three Little Pigs* . . . is another example of the blending of rhythm and imagination."[26]

Some published reactions to the film, however, did connect it with FDR and the economic crisis. Widely syndicated columnist Mayme Ober Peak wrote that Disney's short film "did more to restore America's old-time cocky confidence than all the eloquent flood of N.R.A. press agentry directed from Washington. Three Little Pigs climbed up alongside President Roosevelt's Blue Eagle [the NRA's logo]. And the whole country was going around chuckling and chanting to the new national anthem, 'Who's Afraid of the Big, Bad Wolf.' "[27] Bloomingdale's department store was graphically explicit. In a full-page ad, captions under three drawings in the style of the Disney film explained how the *Pigs* story supported the NRA. "We discovered something. Folks out of work couldn't buy things . . . Things unbought did not have to be replaced . . . No need for replacement, no need for manufacturing more. Now the worker and the

FIGURE 50. "Who's Afraid of the Big Bad Wolf?" A Bloomingdale's department store newspaper ad from 1933 associated the third pig's house of brick with the goals of the NRA.

boss found that the wolf was actually at the door." Under a picture of the third pig's brick house (Figure 50), the caption lauded the Blue Eagle. "It convinced employers to agree—*to stop over-production—to stop unfair competition—to shorten hours—to hire more people. It is con-*vincing consumers that the only way to keep the wheels turning is *to buy.*" Thanks to FDR and the NRA, "No wonder the whole country is singing, 'Who's afraid of the big bad wolf.' "[28]

An editorial in the *Saturday Review* cited *Pigs* as an example of a transition in America's spirit from the avaricious past to the more ethical present. "The clear shift of emphasis in the U.S.A., from making a living regardless of the life lived, to the values of living as an end in themselves, which is as much a part of the N.R.A. program as the recovery of profits, may be a first step toward more than the enriching of fairy tales. In the meantime, if you wish to see the folk tale of its age in the cradle, go to the nearest movie theatre."[29]

Did any contemporary responders see the film as an allegory, not of Roosevelt, but of former president Herbert Hoover? Richard Schickel, writing in the 1960s and well past the heyday of unquestioning Disney-philia, made the case for this interpretation. He saw in the third, practical pig an idealized figure of Hoover, and he even perceived a caricatured likeness of the porky president.[30] I have not uncovered any historical evidence that audiences perceived that, but that doesn't mean that no one saw the film that way. Some writers in the 1930s understand *Pigs* as an exposition of Hooverian virtues. The columnist Nelson B. Bell, for example, didn't mention the past president by name, but he lauded the film for "the whole timely story of the provident versus the improvident, the thoughtful versus the scatterbrained, the planner versus the opportunist, in times of crisis."[31] This echoes Hoover's refrain throughout his administration, as memorialized in his second state of the union address, in which he pledged to resist any federal intervention to boost the economy. "Economic depression can not be cured by legislative action or executive pronouncement. Economic wounds must be healed by the action of the cells of the economic body—the producers and consumers themselves." His advice to the nation is reminiscent of the pigs' redeeming strategy: "Recovery can be expedited and its effects mitigated by cooperative action. That cooperation requires that every individual should sustain faith and courage; that each should maintain his self-reliance; that each and every one should search for methods of improving his business or service;"[32] and so on. Hoover listed a litany of vague counsels that the third pig would later put into action.

If it were the case, as Schickel argued, that the values promoted in the narrative are as much Hoover's as Roosevelt's, then it's curious that so few leftist journalists or Republican-leaning organs perceived anything in the cartoon as an allegory either in favor of or against FDR or the NRA. Looking back, although there were a few such intimations, it is not at all clear that the pro-Roosevelt reading we so readily take for granted today was anything like a consensus in the 1930s.

Roosevelt's landslide victory in November 1932 sparked the "First Hundred Days" of reform and good feeling. David Kyvig, however, has pointed out that the film played against growing resistance to Roosevelt and a backlash against the NRA. An event of the era that seems most apposite was the "slaughter of the pigs." The controversial Agricultural Adjustment Act (AAA) was attempting to help farmers by paying them to destroy their cotton, corn, and hog crops, which would raise wholesale prices in the long run. To receive their subsidy payments, in the summer of 1933, at a time when many families were underfed (as Republicans were quick to point out), farmers destroyed six million pregnant sows and piglets. Kyvig agrees that the cartoon's message was ambiguous, but many viewers "equated the New Deal with the 'Big Bad Wolf' who destroyed helpless creatures. . . . In any interpretation of Disney's cartoon or popular understanding of the AAA . . . little pigs remained a central theme."[33] One would think that the timing of this event would have inspired contemporaneous remarks connecting the AAA and the movie, but apparently this did not happen.

Then there is the question of whether there was cross-fertilization between FDR's public addresses and the production of Disney's film. According to Marc Eliot, "So pervasive was the message [in *Pigs*] of the refusal to surrender to fear, many believed it was the inspiration for one of Franklin Delano Roosevelt's most memorable Depression-age rallying cries—'The only thing we have to fear is fear itself.' "[34] But were the election, the sense of recovery, and the film so directly linked?

Roosevelt's first inaugural address, which featured the "nothing to fear but fear itself" message, was delivered on March 3, 1933, when the film's animation was already underway. The movie would not be released until May 27. It is extraordinarily unlikely, then, that the film could have inspired FDR when it had not been finished. Furthermore, the film's enormous popularity developed over several months following its release, not immediately, providing even more evidence that it was not the inspiration for Roosevelt's message.

It's equally unlikely that FDR's speech affected the filmmakers. The cartoon had been in production since December 1932.[35] Although this date was soon after the election, none of the anecdotes about the film's origins suggest that there was any push to produce either a Hoover requiem or a Roosevelt hallelujah. As for Disney's politics in the early 1930s, he is said to have been somewhat pro-Roosevelt, but basically apolitical until he began to capitalize on the pundits' progressive interpretations of his film.[36]

Disney always claimed to have been surprised both by the cartoon's popularity and by its interpretation as Depression-themed. Based on her interview with Disney, Peak concluded, "Now, in Hollywood, practically every studio is filming and contributing 'shorts' to help get across the meaning of N.R.A. The truth about *The Three Little Pigs*, however, is that Walt Disney—creator of Mickey Mouse and Silly Symphonies, had no such idea in mind. Timeliness of the release and that fickle dame Luck are responsible." Disney maintained that he was perplexed by the film's success and presented this homespun explanation, replete with eating imagery: "For five years we've cooked up many a charming, hilarious little masterpiece which the public has gobbled up with enthusiasm. Why this was the first animated cartoon to achieve sensational success is as difficult to answer as why the public clasped 'Abie's Irish Rose' to its bosom while many a better bit of entertainment climbed over the hill to the warehouse."[37] Elsewhere he said, "It was just another story to us and we were in there gagging it just like any other picture."[38] When asked, "What do [animated cartoons] give you?" he denied they had any deep meaning: "Wholesome entertainment? A clean laugh? A chance to spread the tattered wings of your imagination and soar to a realm where trees dance and you forget to shout, 'Aw, neurts!'? It's not our job to teach, implant morals or improve anything except our pictures." Sounding like the third pig channeling Hoover, he concluded, "If Mickey has a bit of practical philosophy to offer the younger generation, it is to keep on trying."[39]

Prior to the release of *The Three Little Pigs,* Disney cartoonists had made films that could be interpreted as ideological statements. In *Father Noah's Ark* (Wilfred Jackson/Disney), released on April 8, 1933, we see collective labor and the commonweal exalted as the animals pull together under a divinely inspired leader (Noah *qua* FDR). No one seemed to pick up on that film's blatant New Dealism. Released on June 13, 1933, *The Mail Pilot,* which followed *Pigs,* hailed Mickey's Lindbergh-like individual heroism as he flew solo into a hostile environment. No one pointed out that he was also a self-sufficient Hooverite. If there was an ideology emerging from the studio in the early 1930s, it certainly was an incoherent one. Robert Sklar recognized the existence of these conflicting messages in the film: "*The Three Little Pigs* was the last of Disney's cartoons open to multiple interpretation. Thereafter there was no mistaking the films' moral messages."[40]

Intuitively, if the cartoon had been universally understood as a New Deal allegory, one would have expected the Democrats and left-leaning commentators at the time to have applauded its pro-Roosevelt appeal. In fact, these writers tended either to ignore *The Three Little Pigs* or to criticize it. Film director King Vidor, writing in the leftist *New Theater,* disregarded *Pigs* and gave the Silly Symphonies only a backhanded compliment. Although he praised them as evidence of Disney's talent for making fantasies for the masses, he also scoffed at their alleged populist politics.[41] A Scottish writer who had set out to find "the communalistic art of Walt Disney" did so easily. Not even Soviet Russia, which he admired, could produce "artistic activity comparable to that in the Disney studio, in which such heterogeneity of effort achieves so successfully homogeneity in its accomplishment."[42] However, he did not highlight *Pigs* as a communalistic exemplum. Eisenstein, writing on the film when he saw it in the Soviet Union, was still enamored of Disney animation's plastic stretching and squashing, but he was suspicious of the *Pigs'* "cry of optimism" and especially the song "Who's Afraid of the Big Bad Wolf." He concluded, "For there is no such slant on truthfully shot capitalist reality which, without lying, could possibly sound like optimistic reassurance!"[43] The *New Republic*'s Otis Ferguson unsympathetically claimed, "Practically everything the studio touched turned to lollypops for the kiddies." He actively disliked the film, calling it a "rather pretentious dead-end alley." Still, he did not call readers' attention to any political agenda or New Deal propaganda in its story. On the contrary, he found Disney to be "not suppressed or sponsored or anything. Just Disney, making another to go into the big gaudy houses and the little tank-town houses all over the country, under Extra Added Attractions."[44]

Rather than see the film as a populist rallying cry, these left-leaning intellectuals seem to have categorized it as yet another oppressive tool of the culture industry personified by Hollywood and Disney—if they considered the film at all. More recently, Jack Zipes has remarked on the emphasis in all three of Disney's Big Bad Wolf films on the powerful figure of the third pig as big brother, a powerful fixer who, like the prince in *Snow White,* provides narrative closure and tidies "up the mess that apparently is caused by greed and voracity." He continues, "The spectacular image of the strong rational leader as rescuer concealed, of course, the real causes of antagonism and unhappiness in both the films and the social situation of the audiences of those times, for one must always ask why the wolf is impoverished and hungry and must resort to violence to survive, and why and how the pigs got their money and live comfortably in their own homes that the wolf cannot afford. One must also ask why little people are silly, stupid, and weak and cannot fend for themselves."[45]

Perhaps the primary reason for the popularity of *The Three Little Pigs* was its infectious signature song. Music was crucial to the popularity of all studio cartoons in the 1930s. Even an undistinguished film could initiate a toe-tapping, singing, and humming contagion in the listeners. The song in this film took on an extraordinary extrafilmic life of its own. A columnist of the time referred to "that song, 'Who's Afraid of the Big Bad Wolf?' which swept its composer Frank Churchill of Walt Disney comedy cartoon film staff off his feet with its unanticipated popularity just as it bowled over all the rest of Hollywood."[46] The *Literary Digest* declared that *Pigs'* charm lay in the "haunting quality" of its theme song.[47] Mollie Merrick joked about the irrepressible tune: "You'll be so enchanted by 'Who's Afraid of the Big Bad Wolf?' that you won't be able to stop singing it and such members of your family as have or have not seen it will be driven crazy. I speak now from personal experience, for it has almost lost me a couple of nervous friends."[48] The ditty moved countless moviegoers, record buyers, and fans to purchase the sheet music, records and piano rolls of the song.

Moviegoers who returned to re-view the film and who sang the theme song both during and after watching it were relishing a newfound opportunity to merge this melody infused Tooniverse with the real-life communitas created primarily in the social cohesion pictured in the cartoon and secondarily in the massive popularity for the song among its listeners and consumers. Here ordinary folks in the figures of pigs could act out the end of the Depression, not with a parade, but with a decisive act of cathartic violence against a despised animal, by the shared ritual of watching *Pigs* together in the movie theater, and by singing, playing and buying the theme song. By such immersion into Disney's world, perhaps their homes could be more like that brick sanctuary on the screen.

Whether or not *The Three Little Pigs* was intended to be a political allegory, and whether audiences received it that way, may never be known. At any rate, the film's potential as an instrumental performance may not be limited only to politics. It is also a self-aggrandizing story that re-performs Disney's rise to fame in show business. While his brother pigs (Fleischer, Lantz, Schlesinger, Van Beuren, and Terry) cavorted in the cartoon business, the practical pig (Walt and business manager Roy Disney) worked incessantly to compete. First, Walt put the fifes and flutes to good use by innovating sound, then Technicolor. He also put up the first purpose-built Hollywood animation studio.[49] Sure, the Big Bad Wolf (early failures, swindlers, tight bankers, the Depression) came calling many times, but through perspicacity and sacrifice (Mother? Father?), the third pig survived and the stone and brick house of Disney would prosper. Although the puzzle of *The Three Little Pigs* resists solving, one thing is certain. Disney demonstrated masterfully that adorable characters with distinctive personalities, simple stories from recognizable templates, and catchy tunes could cure the studio's budget blues.

INFECTIOUS ANIMATION

The aggregate crazy laughter produced by all the bizarre plot twists, mindless gags, goofy characters, peppy music, and unbridled optimism in the movies of this era must have seemed manic as well as poignant considering the unemployment, race riots, strikes, hunger, and general misery outside the theater doors. It is intuitive that the exuberant content and the presumed infectious laughter that comedies elicited from moviegoers were purely escapist, a desirable distraction to facilitate social forgetfulness, and that such a goal was sufficient. Many cartoons of the 1930s, however, steal merriment's innocent veil.

Confidence (Walter Lantz/Universal, 1933) clearly tries to rouse its moviegoers to song. Oswald the Rabbit is a contented chicken farmer until the specter of Depression rises from the dump and invades his henhouse. A country doctor tells him that to cure his chickens' malaise he needs confidence, and he points to a poster of President Roosevelt on the wall. Since the film was released four months after the first inaugural address, it is highly likely that it was inspired by the address's message and positive reception. Arriving in Washington, D.C. (curiously shown as a drawing of the U.S. House of Representatives, not the White House, where one might expect to find the president), Oswald greets FDR in his office. "Mr. President," Oswald asks, "what will cure a depression?" Roosevelt springs from behind his desk (few knew then that he was usually in a wheelchair) and answers with a peppy song that advises that having confidence will lick the Depression (Figure 51). Now Roosevelt begins to dance. "Confidence! Hey, hey, it's our salvation." He tells Americans to "Teach it, preach it, count it, shout it. / Confidence! Just have fun with it." Oswald takes a syringe full of the presidential supply of confidence. Back home, the banker responds to his injection by reopening the bank's front door and the depositors flock in. The hens and other farm critters respond with as much vigor, and soon their music making and egg laying resume at pre-Depression levels. A chorus sings "New Day Dawnin'" accompanied by a multicultural band (well, various species, including a "Chinese" monkey) while the music continues: "A new day [is] dawnin' for Kelly and Cohen." Oswald sings the final bars, "No more bummin', we'll all get to work."

When the cartoon FDR sings in *Confidence,* he exhorts moviegoers to join in the effort to teach, preach, count, and shout confidence. This is a reference to the first inaugural address, when Roosevelt stated, "Small wonder that confidence languishes, for it thrives only on honesty, on honor, on the sacredness of obligations, on faithful protection, on unselfish performance; without them it cannot live." The dancing and playing animals come together again in the end, presumably transmitting confidence to the audience members, as when Oswald juiced the workers, bankers, and clerks mentioned in "New Day Dawnin'." *Confidence* suggests that being mirthful is a patriotic duty. And what better way to have fun than attending movies and enjoying cartoons?

Playful Pluto (Burt Gillett/Disney, 1934) is a domestic comedy showing brief vignettes of business between Mickey Mouse and his pet, Pluto. The pup is in a playful mood, but head-of-household Mickey is

FIGURE 51. *Confidence* (1933). President Franklin D. Roosevelt springs into action.

intent on raking leaves. Mickey throws a stick to distract the dog, but in retrieving it Pluto ends up spilling Mickey's basket of leaves. Stern Mickey, like the third pig, resents the frivolity. He forgives the dog, though, and offers to shake hands/paw. Mickey tricks Pluto by playing the schoolyard gag "Shake-Spear" on him, that is, by snatching his hand away and pointing his thumb over his shoulder (Figure 52). The good-natured battle escalates until Pluto rips the garden hose and faucet off the house. Mickey and Pluto go to the cellar to fix the broken pipe, with Pluto acting as the plumber's helper. A mishap hilariously sends the flashlight into Pluto's innards, and he runs around yowling crazily, the light giving us an X-ray of his skeleton with every hiccup, until he crashes through the kitchen's screen door. All the flies in the neighborhood invade the kitchen, so Mickey retaliates with sheets of flypaper. Pluto, in one of the most celebrated sequences of character animation in the Disney canon, becomes hopelessly entangled in a sheet of "Tanglefoot." Animator Norm Ferguson portrays the dog's fleeting emotions as the paper migrates from his limb to his ear and, inevitably, to his rump. Between panting efforts to free himself, Pluto pauses to "think," and we see each hopeful scheme and each defeat register in slow-motion cognition on the dog's benighted face. Finally, when he is entangled in the window shade (Figure 53), Mickey comes to rescue him, only to become stuck on the flypaper himself. Now Pluto removes it from his master and offers to shake. When Mickey extends his hand,

FIGURE 52. *Playful Pluto* (1934). Mickey plays the "Shake-Spear" trick on his pet.

Pluto gives *him* the Shake-Spear. Mickey realizes that turnabout is fair play, and they laugh together.

As a parable that teaches the virtues of civility and cooperation, *Playful Pluto* connects with other Disney fables, such as *The Grasshopper and the Ants* (Wilfred Jackson/Disney, 1934) and *The Flying Mouse*. The audience's sympathies lie with Pluto and not with Mickey, since Mickey has teased him and negligently caused pain and suffering. (The cocky Max Hare gets his similar comeuppance after giving the Shake-Spear to sympathetic Toby the Tortoise in *The Tortoise and the Hare* [Wilfred Jackson/Disney, 1935]). The film is not overtly about the Depression, however, its upbeat message is instrumental and encourages viewers to adopt virtues consistent with Roosevelt's calls for courteous citizenship.

Moments of infectious laughter arrive early in *When My Ship Comes In* (Dave Fleischer/Paramount, 1934). Betty Boop's racehorse wins the sweepstakes, so she celebrates by liberating her pets. In a nice gag, it appears that she is cruelly chucking her goldfish out the window. A cut to the outside of her house reveals, however, that a brook babbles by where we had expected a sidewalk. Betty breaks into the title song (Jack Scholl and Sammy Timberg, 1934), explaining how she will use her newfound wealth: she will buy, buy, buy until she has spent it all. "We won't need relief or unemployment; we'll have work and everything. / I'll be spending like a sailor 'cause my ship came in." A fantasy sequence

FIGURE 53. *Playful Pluto* (1934). Pluto ends up trapped in the window shade of Mickey's dilapidated house.

then shows Betty addressing some food-themed Depression-specific issues. Police officers treat two hoboes in a park to a fine multicourse meal. Her milk wagon uses silenced horses' hooves and balloons to make its deliveries to ensure that predawn deliveries won't awaken sleeping workers. Continuing the motif, some kids play on an ice cream mountain. All these vignettes are accompanied by the background tune of "We're In the Money" (Harry Warren and Al Dubin), from *Gold Diggers of 1933* (Mervyn LeRoy/Warner Bros., *1933*). When the scene shifts to Betty Boop's farm, the music switches to the anthemic "Happy Days Are Here Again." The barnyard folk are understandably very happy, with the squirrels getting free nuts from vending machines, the pigs enjoying a mud spa with a diving board, and so on. In her victory parade, we see Betty handing out cash to cheering throngs and witness the immediate results. Next to the old maids' home, a bachelor hall is built, to the delight of the cheering women. Workingmen and -women file into department stores with money and exit wearing evening clothes and carrying loads of dry goods. A decrepit factory comes to life, fills with workers, and then dissolves into a symbolic tableau showing hands of mixed race and gender exchanging money across a map of the United States (Figure 54). As Betty reprises her upbeat theme song, a village grows into a great metropolis before our eyes, complete with its own Chrysler Building.

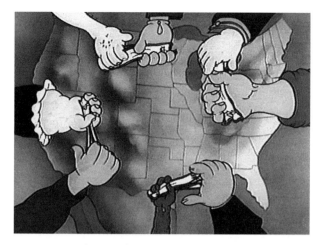

FIGURE 54. *When My Ship Comes In* (1934). Commerce unites multicultural North Americans.

Betty Boop's fantasies are humorous because they are so wildly improbable. We laugh not only at her hyperbolic solutions, but also at their incongruity in this alternate world. Charles Darwin, in his own take on laughter, opined, "Something incongruous or unaccountable, exciting surprise and some sense of superiority in the laugher, who must be in a happy frame of mind, seems to be the commonest cause [of laughter]. The circumstances must not be of a momentous nature: no poor man would laugh or smile on suddenly hearing that a large fortune had been bequeathed to him."[50] Besides the bizarreness of the gags—the mechanical dog scratcher might be the best example—we may also be laughing at, and feeling superior to, Betty, whose solution is witty and original but unworkable. She looks magnanimous, but also kind of stupid.

Warner Bros. cartoons also used humor to introduce Depression themes. *Honeymoon Hotel* (Jack King/Schlesinger, 1934) was based on the bawdy "Honeymoon Hotel" (Dubin and Warren) number in *Footlight Parade* (Lloyd Bacon/Warner Bros., 1933). The cartoon alters the song lyrics. In the apparent utopia of Bugville, the village is an analog of the world outside: "Goodbye to Depression, business here is fine," sings the chorus. The protagonists are a ladybug and a tumblebug on their honeymoon. They reprise some of the erotic jokes in the Busby Berkeley production number. Eventually, the bugs' lovemaking becomes so hot that it sets the hotel on fire. Although rubble crashes down

FIGURE 55. *Honeymoon Hotel* (1934). A crash interrupts the bugs' bliss. Original in color.

around their room, they just hang the "Do Not Disturb" sign and carry on (Figure 55). In this film, laughter comes from the sexy antics of the anthropomorphized insects and the consummation-delaying mishaps that they encounter.

In *The Shanty Where Santa Claus Lives* (Hugh Harman and Rudolf Ising/Schlesinger, 1933) a starving little boy trudging in the snow finds no shelter at church or an upper-class home. This scene flies in the face of Roosevelt's call for public and private charity. The ragamuffin finds his way to an abandoned shack, where the story's deus ex machina, Santa Claus, finds him and takes the orphan to his workshop, where the lad plays with the toys of his dreams.

Those Beautiful Dames (Friz Freleng/Schlesinger, 1934) didn't refer to the Depression explicitly, but the iconography of deprivation, the loss of family, and the effects of hard times on children make the connection unmistakable. A ragged girl treks in the snow and pauses to look in the window of a toy store. She presses on as the storm rages. Inside her cabin, where apparently she lives alone, there is no fire in the stove. Even a mouse is starving. As she sleeps, the toys come to redecorate her room and perform the rather incongruous title song, "Those Beautiful Dames" (Herbert W. Spencer), for her. The curtains then part to reveal a sumptuous banquet. She joins the toys to feast on cake and ice cream (Figure 56).

No question, all these films encourage positive, uplifting fantasies. They show utopian worlds of forgiveness, compassion, charity, and

FIGURE 56. *Those Beautiful Dames* (1934). Abundant food contrasts with Depression hunger. Original in color.

goodwill. This positive attitude was part of an industry-wide campaign designed to show that film companies were doing their bit to fight the "Depression bogey," as one executive called it. Like much of the country, the movie moguls ascribed the troubles to mass psychology. The trade journal *Film Daily* summed it in an editorial: "'Bad times' often are nothing more than bad mental conditions, gloomy exaggerations of natural cycles in affairs. Putting the public mind in a healthy state by filling it with cheer and assurance is one of the surest methods of promoting 'good times.'"[51] Accordingly, there are plenty of cartoons that are "pointless," that is, apparently designed only to amuse. But all is not candy and ice cream.

It's immediately clear that these performances reveal crises of agency. Who has the authority, the power, and the will to intervene? Upon whom do these cartoons place the onus for change? Society? The government? The movies? Moviegoers? Cartoonists?

As 1930s moviegoers, perhaps we are supposed to respond to the cartoon FDR character's call to action in *Confidence* to "just have fun with it," suggesting that benign laughter is sufficient. Since having confidence is a frame of mind and not an action, we haven't been presented with other instrumental options. This contrasts with the argument for making a commitment to the industrious life that *Pigs* seems to espouse. It isn't clear how believing in the syringe of confidence will chase the Depression away, since its message is cloaked in a somewhat obscure metaphor. When Oswald sings into the "camera" in the last scene and pleads with us to stop bummin' around, did Lantz really think that Americans were not working because they preferred unemployment? This also was the moral of *The Three Little Pigs* when the third pig declared, "Work and play don't mix." The animators don't acknowledge the obvious cause of the failure of belief, which was worsening chronic unemployment and repeated crop failures.

That *Playful Pluto* was made with the intention of discouraging bad behavior and reinforcing good seems obvious. Following the narrative form of fables, the film suggests at the end an implicit moral, in this case a version of the Golden Rule. However, even this film is not purely benign. Although these Mickey Mouse films were not really fairy tales, they "were complex symbolic social acts intended to reflect upon mores, norms, and habits organized for the purpose of reinforcing a hierarchically arranged civilizing process in a particular society." This is Zipes's description of precinema literary fairy tales. Disney's films, like these fairy tales, "appropriated oral folk tales and created new ones to reflect upon rituals, customs, habits and ethics and simultaneously to serve as a civilizing agent."[52] In *Playful Pluto*, laughter is instrumental in the sense that the film is a new story designed to impart old normative behaviors, to be inspirational, and to set an example. Although the film does not reference the Depression directly, we infer it as a structuring absence in the film's setting and decor, a Barthesian "reality effect."[53] Think of the little dust devil funnel cloud that whisks up the carefully piled leaves. There is no better symbol of capricious nature during the Dust Bowl era.

The timescapes in these films also indirectly reference the Depression or a time just before it. Mickey's home seems to be located on the edge of a small village, somewhere between town and country. According to Maltby, "Rural simplicity . . . emerged again in the Depression as the cultural, if not the economic, bastion of American virtues. The populist mythos of the agrarian community or the small town pervaded the idealized solutions to the Depression."[54] Mickey seems comfortable enough, but his residence is getting dilapidated, with torn screens, cracked plaster, patched window shades, and broken panes (see Figure 53 again). The kitchen stove is an old wood-burning model. Mickey's reliance on old-fashioned "Tanglefoot" flypaper to catch insects, rather than more effective and up-to-date insecticides, also stamps the time of the story as earlier.[55] Furthermore, Pluto's embodied performance seems designed to elicit empathy from Depression audiences. The dog, like the unemployed, had done nothing to deserve entrapment. The film may be warning, "Don't allow yourself to be caught like Pluto" while also suggesting that his condition is predestined and inescapable.

Betty Boop's solution for the Depression, and that implied in the other cartoons as well, was based on a widespread belief that the trouble was caused by unwillingness to work and spend, which damaged the retail sectors, decreased demand for goods, and led to shuttered factories.[56] Among those trades laying off workers and slashing wages was the motion picture industry. Beginning in 1933, the New Deal aimed to stimulate consumer spending through the agency of the National Recovery Administration (NRA). Giuliana Muscio, however, has asserted that "the relationship between the New Deal and Hollywood appears to be ambivalent."[57]

John Maynard Keynes did not have Betty's "boop-oop-a-doop," but the British economist did share her theory of redistributing wealth as a cure for a depression. Her performance and her song lyrics acted out a Keynesian solution. She invents ingenious jobs for workers so they might make and spend money, which will create more jobs, which will put money into the system and start a cycle of improvement.[58] Betty's plan is funny because, on its face, it embraces the Keynesian/NRA fix. But because *When My Ship Comes In* is also a parody that casts Betty a New Dealer, its meanings are ambivalent. The benign message is that workers and (implicitly) unions will be part of the recovery plan if they cooperate with management according to NRA terms. But then there is also the undermining instrumental performance: the proposed plan, like Oswald's syringe of confidence, is an unworkable pipedream.

The humor spotlights fundamental flaws inherent in the quick-fix solutions of the NRA. Where is the seed money coming from? Unlike borrowing by the government to fund its projects (a Keynesian policy that earned the president the nickname Franklin Deficit Roosevelt),[59] Betty's wonderful windfall does not increase the national debt and does not have to be paid back. Her welfare scheme, then, is exposed as a gambling long shot. The film clearly shows that Betty herself has not been doing her part. Rather than using her disposable cash to buy durable goods to boost the economy, she has been gambling on the horse races. This is consistent with critiques of Keynesian strategies, which pointed out that workers tend to use stimulus cash to pay back loans, catch up on overdue rent, and pay for similar personal expenses rather than spending it on big-ticket manufactured goods. The film also lampoons Roosevelt's appeal to the rich to help the poor through charitable giving. It wasn't happening, which underscored the need for government assistance. Furthermore, Betty's plan ignores one of the acknowledged causes of the Depression, the collapse of the agricultural economy. The urbanistic Fleischer brothers give none of Betty's largesse to distressed farmers, doling out money only to city folk.

When My Ship Comes In was produced as confidence in the New Deal had begun to wane. "Six months after the NRA's inception"—that is, by the fall of 1933—according to Meg Jacobs, "the euphoria that had surrounded it in its early days was gone. Employment and purchasing power had increased, but not enough."[60] In addition, employers had countered the rapid growth of organized trade unions with their own company unions, and the summer of 1934 saw many bitter strikes. Workers were beginning to call the NRA the National Run Around. It is quite appropriate to see in this seemingly cheerful cartoon mounting anxiety about the government's optimistic remedies.[61]

The Fleischers use the Swiftian technique of hyperbole to exaggerate the ambitiousness of Betty's programs, making them ridiculous, and therefore laughable, figures of the government's cures. Another rhetorical technique, inversion, reverses the roles of humans and animals, as well as the real and imagined worlds of the animation. There is perhaps a reflexive hint, too, that the animators were slyly criticizing the policies of the Fleischer Studio, since complaints about working conditions and the management's bias against unions were legion. The animation camera operators had formed a union in 1934 and the animators had begun organizing in 1935, an action that would lead to a strike in 1937.[62]

Confidence treats us to the spectacle of FDR in an uplifting patriotic song-and-dance number. *When My Ship Comes In,* on the contrary, is not an endorsement of the government's or the Fleischer Studio's ability to cure the Depression. The infectious laughter that Betty generates spotlights the gap between policy and reality that is hidden by the rousing patriotism in other films of the time. The music that accompanies the climax of *When My Ship Comes In* is "The Stars and Stripes Forever" (John Philip Sousa, 1896). The ending might be taken as patriotism, but more likely it's a joke laden with jingoistic irony, since the march is paired with patently absurd activities like spending money on nut-vending machines and the like. If anyone recalled the strains of

Betty's ditty about "buying, buying" and the laughter it generated, they may also have been haunted by the underlying policy weakness that the humor forces to the surface. Possibly more troubling, the film again shifts blame from the government, business management, and natural causes to the workers who constituted some part of the cartoon's original audience. Instead of feeling inspired, these viewers might have been stung by the accusatory cynicism in the laughter.

In *Honeymoon Hotel, The Shanty Where Santa Claus Lives,* and *Those Beautiful Dames,* the laughter is double-edged. If we see the movies as simply showing us how to survive adversity by laughing and copulating, like the bugs, or by dreaming of dancing toys and feasts, as in the boy's and girl's fantasies, then the laughter is benign. However, if the stories make us think about what is not shown—unspeakable alternative scenarios about social collapse and starvation—then the laughter is instrumental, but its call to action remains unspoken.

In *Honeymoon Hotel,* the bugs' honeymoon begins as an idyll, but the film quickly begins a dark slide as it re-performs the market crash of 1929. Although the final image of the bugs happy in bed as their world crumbles around them is funny, it is not an altogether salutary message. The film seems to say that you'll pay the price for your fun and laughs if you get so absorbed in your emotions that you lose touch with what's going on outside. The bugtopian Tooniverse, proclaimed in the opening shots of the cartoon to have no problems, now has plenty, just like small towns in the non-animated world.

After Santa befriends the boy in *Shanty,* he promptly disappears from the story. Left to party on his own with the toys, the revelry is threatened when a Christmas tree catches on fire. Although ostensibly the boy becomes a hero when he puts out the blaze, the fantastically happy ending isn't strong enough to offset the misery depicted in the cartoon's first few minutes. Similarly, the lack of narrative closure in *Those Beautiful Dames* leaves open the possibility that the girl does not awaken at the end of the story. Some viewers might associate these open structures, especially that of *Those Beautiful Dames,* with that of "The Little Match Girl," Hans Christian Andersen's "very disturbing tale." That story depicts the girl enjoying beautiful visions of a warm stove, an abundant feast, and a loving grandmother but ends with the girl freezing in the snow.[63] These films weave tales of fantasy and escapism, but then they show that the benign stories are unconvincing, ambiguous, and failures as solutions to the problem at hand. Likewise, in *Confidence* we never see the opening scene's Depression specter return to the dump from whence it came; presumably, in the timescape of the 1930s, it continued its haunting. These films facilitate escapism, but they also disclose its dangers.

THE CINEMA OF INFECTION

Laughter is the thing people want—not social studies.
—Review of *Sullivan's Travels*, *Hollywood Reporter*,
    December 5, 1941

The Hollywood film that best dramatizes the ideology of the prophylactic power of humor is *Sullivan's Travels* (Preston Sturges/Paramount, 1942). Though the movie is set in the "present," its timescape is the mid-1930s, not the era of World War II. In the course of a story that veers from broad comedy to averted tragedy, the protagonist's views on the nature of film art change when he realizes how movie laughter can create a community. Sturges, who wrote as well as directed the film, said that he took the conceit of infectious laughter from philosophy: "Art, Tolstoy said, is a medium for the transmission of emotions."[64] This is a rare instance of a Hollywood filmmaker giving us a clue to the intellectual basis of his film. However off the cuff Sturges's remark might have been, we shouldn't pass over it, because the erudite filmmaker was correct in his application of Tolstoy.

The hero of the movie is John L. Sullivan (Joel McCrae), a Hollywood director who is inspired to make the ultimate social realist genre movie, which is adapted from a fictitious book with the portentous title *O Brother, Where Art Thou?* One of his studio heads, LeBrand,[65] suggests that the book would make a nice musical, to which Sullivan responds, "How can you talk about a musical at a time like this, with the world committing suicide, with the corpses piled up in the street, with grim death gargling at you from every corner, with people slaughtered like sheep?" The boss replies, "Maybe they'd like to forget that." Sturges here parodies the stance Hollywood producers had taken in the early 1930s, when they parroted the line that the Depression was caused by their customers' lack of confidence and that cheering them up would cure their ills and the nation's troubles.

The hero's nickname, Sully, is perhaps an homage to the author of an influential turn-of-the-century book on the psychology of laughter, James Sully, who concluded that satire is a socially tolerable form of derision and ridicule.[66] Through a series of increasingly dark mishaps,

Sullivan ends up serving time on a southern work farm. The epiphanic plot point occurs when he, now on a chain gang, has been taken to a nearby African American church, where the preacher puts up a sheet and shows a Mickey Mouse cartoon. It's *Playful Pluto*. The congregation convulses with laughter when the dog steps on the sticky flypaper. As the men and women, blacks and white, prisoners and guards become immersed in Pluto's torment, their differences dissolve in the shared hilarity of the cartoon. Seeing and hearing the races and classes brought together by unifying laughter convinces Sullivan to abandon his "social" pretensions as a director of films that would be instrumental performances and to embrace again the restorative potential of his trademark uproarious sex comedies. That this scene is an epiphany is made clear by the preacher's prophetic remarks shortly before the prisoners arrive: "For we is all equal in the sight of God, and He said, 'and the chains shall be struck from them, and the lame shall leap, and the blind shall see and glory in the coming of the Lord.'" And so it was that Sullivan's social and artistic blindness was lifted by his redeemer, Pluto the Pup.[67] Sturges's film makes a strong case for cartoons as a vehicle for redemption, that is, as a way to save society from a seemingly irreversible decline and to restore value to one's abject life. The Disney sequence highlights animation as social and ethical practice. Pluto's subjugated existence resonated with the incarcerated audience depicted in *Sullivan's Travels*.[68] Sturges shows the cartoon's instrumentality by its power to relieve the prisoners from the misery of their surroundings.

The laughing scene actually is a good illustration of the aesthetic theory that Tolstoy developed in *What Is Art?* According to Gary R. Jahn, "Feeling (in Russian, *chuvstvo*) is the central term of Tolstoy's aesthetic theory."[69] Tolstoy's 1897 book seized on the metaphor of infection, as in infectious laughter or crying, to rationalize works of art as vessels carrying the artist's emotions to the audience. His guiding metaphor was possibly inspired by Russian advances in contagious diseases research, such as the first isolation of viruses by Dmitri Ivanovski in 1892.

Tolstoy defined art according to these premises: artistic activities arise from natural expressions of feeling on the part of artists; they unite men in their humanity; and they are communicated as though by aesthetic infection.[70] Crucially for him, Tolstoy also insisted on a fourth, ethical, dimension to this communication process. Good art conveyed positive spiritual values (as seen in his rather idiosyncratic Christianity), but "decadent" art either did not "infect" its consumers (as in the case of

Wagner's music) or it instilled immoral thoughts in them (as did impressionist painting and the various fin-de-siècle art movements). This was Tolstoy's Achilles heel because it led him to some famously strange conclusions, such as rejecting all of Shakespeare's work while glorifying Harriet Beecher Stowe's famous antislavery novel, *Uncle Tom's Cabin*. Reductive though Tolstoy's thinking might be, Sturges borrowed his "infection aesthetics" to describe the instrumentality of good films.

By pressing Disney's cartoon into service as the turning point in his drama, Sturges posits animation as an exemplary infectious art form. The scene succeeds twice, once as a "cure" for Sullivan's and the country's metonymical depressions, and again as a lesson to artists (and filmmakers) about bringing about social change. The medium—animation— is part of the message because it redeems individual isolation and existential despair through the unifying power of laughter. Tolstoy's argument is of more than passing interest for, just as it was utilitarian for Sturges's plot and his conception of the instrumental nature of laughter, it provides a model for inferring audiences' conception of animation as an instrumental performance in the 1930s and '40s. Tolstoy may seem recondite now, but he was in vogue in Sturges's times. His centenary had been celebrated in 1928, and *What Is Art?* had been reissued in English in 1932. His popular aesthetics were widely circulated and taught in schools, and there were five Hollywood adaptations of his novels in the early 1930s.[71]

Tolstoy's fundamental premise is that art must be an authentic vernacular expression. We may retroactively place cartoons in that category. Art, the novelist stated, could range "from cradle-song, jest, mimicry, the ornamentation of houses, dress, and utensils, up to church services, buildings, monuments, and triumphal processions. It is all artistic activity. So that by art, in the limited sense of the word, we do not mean all human activity transmitting feelings, but only that part which we for some reason select from it and to which we attach special importance."[72]

Animated cartoons, had they existed in Tolstoy's time, would have easily qualified for his expansive category of the vernacular. The cartoon producers, of course, designed their films explicitly to generate infectious laughter in the audience. For this to happen, according to the Tolstoyan theory, the animators' feelings (that is, their emotions, ideas, attitudes, opinions, and the things that made them laugh in the studio) must be expressed in ways that would infect the consumers with laughter. He did not use the terms "performance theory" or "viral aesthetics," but Tolstoy's philosophy shares elements of these modern-day aspects of instrumental performance. The former emphasizes the role of the interactivity of performer and audience, and how performances are cocreated between the two. The latter focuses on how reception communities constantly negotiate and distribute the interpretation of a work and transmit their own useful versions of it. Sturges seems to have been attracted to these performative concepts of art in Tolstoy's theory.[73]

For Tolstoy's model to work, the audience's feelings must closely match those of the artist, but, of course, the outcome of the infection is not guaranteed. The infectees of the artist's message are free to react in unexpected ways, or to experience inappropriate emotions. This is demonstrated in the *Sullivan's Travels* laughing scene. We may assume that other members of the audience are laughing at Pluto as an unthinking benign response—just as most of us might. Sullivan's response, however, is nonconforming. Although he laughs along with the crowd (and us) at first, he separates himself from them when he has his revelatory insight. He seems to be immune to infectious laughter, which enables him to see that slapstick can be positively instrumental.

In this scene Sturges might have had this passage from *What Is Art?* in mind:

> The profoundest works of art communicate by building feverish excitement: The simplest example: a man laughs, and another man feels merry; he weeps, and the man who hears this weeping feels sad; a man is excited, annoyed, and another looking at him gets into the same state. With his movements, the sounds of his voice, a man displays cheerfulness, determination, or, on the contrary, dejection, calm—and this mood is communicated to others. A man suffers, expressing his suffering in moans and convulsions—and this suffering is communicated to others; a man displays his feeling of admiration, awe, fear, respect for certain objects, persons, phenomena—and other people become infected, experience the same feelings of admiration, awe, fear, respect for the same objects, persons or phenomena.
>
> On this capacity of people to be infected by the feelings of other people, the activity of art is based.[74]

In his 1930 inaugural address, Herbert Hoover had characterized the national economy as a sick body. Did these 1930s cartoons do what Sturges implied they were doing, that is, did they spread infectious emotions to create a cure for the Depression? As for Disney, although he never acknowledged Tolstoy, his idea that animation communicated "a purely emotional reaction in the beholder" also embraced the infectious model artistic performance. Certainly, the viral reception of *The Three Little Pigs* and its song should have cemented that understanding for him.

"LAUGHTER BETRAYED"

A school of thought typified by the critic and film theorist Siegfried Kracauer saw the dark side of infectious laughter. He was not at all swayed by Sturges's rhetorical use of hilarity as a means for social re-demption, arguing that the laughter in *Sullivan's Travels* was not pro-gressive but downright dangerous. He gave his review the caustic title "Laughter Betrayed." Kracauer argued that infectious laughter could become a tool for unconscious oppression, hidden persuasion, and so-cial control. Singling out the Disney cartoon sequence, he observed that the antics of Pluto and Mickey presented "a paradise where wrongs right themselves automatically." For him, the degree to which the audi-ence in the film instantly succumbs to the cartoon's allure is ominous. Their contagious laughter paints them as a mob. He goes on to distin-guish between farce and satire. Farce produces an easy but pointless laugh, while satire has an ideological function. Sturges's "farce in the disguise of satire" (humor that appears benign but is actually instru-mental, like so many 1930s cartoons) is risky for audiences. Such works leave them vulnerable to psychological manipulation as they "cope with fear by defecting to the forces they fear."[75] Indeed, this seems to be what is happening with the prisoners in *Sullivan's Travels*, Betty the Keynes-ian, the bugs, and the starving children: they disengage viewers by showing that the horrible is bearable, even funny. This, however, is only half the story.

One might say that farce is the infectious laughter that occurs *in* the performance, while satire is part of the performance *of* animation. If we extend Kracauer's thinking to the films I've examined, superficially, they seem to promote infectious laughter for its own "pointless" sake, but there is also satirical or ideological content just below the surface.[76] In one of his most famous early essays on film, Kracauer observed that the movie palaces of Berlin were designed to lull their bourgeois patrons by distracting them from their social condition and by creating an amoeba-like entity, "the masses." The business elite created the illusion of collec-tive identity in order to exploit it. In 1926 Kracauer wrote about the intelligentsia, "They are being absorbed by the masses and this gives rise to the homogeneous cosmopolitan audience in which everyone has the same responses, from the bank director to the sales clerk, from the diva to the stenographer."[77] The cinema's infectious laughter is always instrumental, but, according to this view, it is stage-managed behind the scenes by the culture industry.

The Frankfurt School theorists, with which Kracauer had affinities, disputed the value of laughter in animation. Indeed, the first version of the most widely read essay from the period, Walter Benjamin's "The Work of Art in the Age of Technical Reproducibility," begun in 1935, also used Disney cartoons to probe the joys and dangers of communal laughter.[78] The essay included a section titled "Micky-Maus."[79] In his early thinking, Benjamin, much as the fictional Sullivan did, understood explosive film laughter as cathartic. He saw Mickey Mouse as a figure of a collective dream (or nightmare) symptomatic of the repression of individuals by the military and technology. All these cartoons were instrumental, he claimed, since, in Esther Leslie's paraphrase, "All Mickey Mouse films, in essence, teach audiences about the workings of fear; they do this, as does the Grimm fairy-tale, by making them leave home."[80] Benjamin presages the redemption by cinema that we witness in the episodic progression of scenes in Sturges's film: "Our taverns and city streets, our offices and furnished rooms, our train stations and factories appeared to have us locked up beyond hope. Then came film and exploded this prison-world with the dynamite of one-tenth seconds, so that now, in the midst of its far-flung ruins and debris, we calmly embark on adventurous travels."[81] The tenth of seconds reference suggests the staccato frames of movie projection, or Benjamin might have been thinking of the single-frame cinematography of the animation process.

Perhaps (unconsciously) referencing the infection theory, Benjamin claimed that exposure to such films and cartoons was a "psychic inoculation" against the state's dominance. Moreover, films were a safety valve and a tonic for audiences and served the establishment too because they diverted the moviegoers' desire for more assertive (instrumental) action. According to Benjamin, "The collective laughter signifies a premature and therapeutic eruption of such mass psychoses," and cartoons and slapstick disarm the destructive effects of technology "through technologically mediated laughter."[82]

Benjamin's friend and critical antagonist Theodor Adorno, however, dismissed this as romantic wishful thinking. "The laughter of the cinema audience is . . . anything but good and revolutionary; instead, it is full of the worst bourgeois sadism."[83] This is also the essence of Kracauer's criticism of *Sullivan's Travels*. Instead of considering collective laughter a safety valve, Adorno saw it as a sadomasochistic mirroring of the culture industry, famously writing, "Donald Duck in the cartoons, like the unfortunate in real life, gets his beating so that the viewers may get used to the same treatment."[84] Years later Adorno had an unsettling social experience that confirmed for him the instrumental power of humor. Oh, to be a fly on this wall, when Adorno encountered Charlie Chaplin and Harold Russell, the double amputee from *The Best Years of Our Lives* (William Wyler, 1946). Adorno recalled,

> Together with many others we were invited to a villa in Malibu, on the coast outside of Los Angeles. While Chaplin stood next to me, one of the guests was taking his leave early. Unlike Chaplin, I extended my hand to him a bit absent-mindedly, and, almost instantly, started violently back. The man was one of the lead actors from *The Best Years of Our Lives*, a film famous shortly after the war; he lost a hand during the war, and in its place bore practicable claws made of iron. When I shook his right hand and felt it return the pressure, I was extremely startled, but sensed immediately that I could not reveal my shock to the injured man at any price. In a split second I transformed my frightened expression into an obliging grimace that must have been far ghastlier.

Adorno was experiencing the effect of the "uncanny valley," caused by a simulacrum being too authentic, when he touched the prosthetic device that Russell used so dexterously. Chaplin then stepped in to "save" Adorno from his embarrassment by re-performing the faux pas: "The actor had hardly moved away when Chaplin was already playing the scene back. All the laughter he brings about is so near to cruelty; solely in such proximity to cruelty does it find its legitimation and its element of the salvational."[85] The experience brought home for Adorno the conclusion that Freud had arrived at by watching Chaplin's films. His sadistic humor was a reminder of Freud's dictum that a joke took three people and was a re-performance of pathos and cruelty. Although Adorno had been the butt of Chaplin's seemingly nasty and derogatory imitation, it triggered for him the same sort of epiphanic transformation that John Sullivan had undergone. Adorno generalized from his experience the essence of Chaplin's humor, which was funny because it was sadistic.

The social theories that the Frankfurt School writers formulated differed from Tolstoy's. The destruction of mass culture in the twentieth century could not have been dreamed of in Tolstoy's day; the Germans were not promoting religion, as was the Russian. However, there were some similarities in the critical theorists' views on laughter and infection. The art object is itself devoid of ethical content. It's a product of popular expression, with varying levels of authenticity. In the presence of art, a kind of osmosis takes place between the artist and the receiver, and neither party is in full control of the process. Therefore the meaning of art will always be disputed. It is partly rational, but mostly emotional, and therefore its effects may be subconscious. The transmission of artistic emotion is subject to outside interference and corruption. Whereas Tolstoy and early Benjamin thought that the results of the laughing infection tended to be regenerative, Adorno and Kracauer tended to see the effects as mixed at best but usually malignantly contagious like an epidemic.

Sturges (following Tolstoy) and Kracauer (following Benjamin and Adorno) define competing ways of understanding the social function of Hollywood cartoons as performances. Did the form exist as diversionary escapism, stimulating belly laughs to distract audiences from their plight as social victims? Or, following Hansen, did the films' "stimulation of involuntary and collective laughter . . . affect their viewers in a manner at once physiological and cognitive"?[86] To express the dynamic another way, did classic Hollywood animation dupe audiences into perceiving the violent, alienated farce of everyday life as normalcy, something to be adapted to? Or were the effects making them aware of their alienation through parody and satire, like pigs saved from the wolf but still destined for the butcher? Or a dog stuck in the flypaper of a pernicious culture industry that turns the tables on his master?

GETTING HAPPY

Tolstoy's fourth premise explicitly identified shared religion as the channel by which the art infection was transmitted from sender to receiver: "Art must be, and indeed has always been, understandable to everyone, because each man's relation to God is always the same. And therefore temples, and the images and singing in them, have always been understandable to everyone."[87] Even in the secular texts of twentieth-century theory, the discourse of religion permeates discussions of laughter. Eisenstein called "Who's Afraid of the Big Bad Wolf" a "hymn" and celebrated the "ecstasy" of animation's nonlogical forms.[88] Adorno found redemptive humor "salvational." According to Hansen, "The motif of redemption runs through Kracauer's entire work and becomes eponymic in the subtitle of [his English-language treatise] *Theory of Film: The Redemption of Physical Reality*."[89] Kracauer saw in *Playful Pluto*, for example, a duplicitous "paradise." Recall that in *Confidence*, FDR called on Americans to preach confidence for salvation. Sullivan's transformation took place in a house of worship, as though Sturges saw the kinship between humor and the spark of conversion. Tolstoy's aesthetic was theologically based on his belief in an afterlife, whereas the Frankfurt School saw redemption as another alienating tactic.

From 1931 to 1933, the Merrie Melodies theme song was "Get Happy" (Ted Koehler and Harold Arlen), a hit from 1930 that would have been instantly recognized by hip moviegoers. The song affirms the influence of African American performance on American popular culture.[90] This is especially true of Hollywood animation.[91] The lyrics are not used, but they are relevant because they derive from African American religious traditions: "Pack up your troubles and just get happy. . . . Sing hallelujah, c'mon get happy." The reason for the euphoria is that judgment day is at hand. Thus the manic merriment of the cartoons is associated with psychic escape, rapture, and the Apocalypse. Though filtered through layers of race appropriation and Cotton Club–ized, the song still captures the euphoria of the original meaning of "getting happy."

Ethnomusicologists have traced this ecstatic experience of transcendence to African rituals that hybridized with American Christian worship. James Standifer observes, "Religious expression and black musical behavior almost from the start was one and the same thing. Both manifested themselves in the experience of singing . . . and a behavior resulting from this singing called 'getting happy.' This behavior of being 'hit by the spirit' consisted of behaviors including shouting, dancing, armwaving, screaming or hollering, swaying back and forth, moaning, singing, fainting, and the like. It is highly individualistic behavior but extremely infectious to other participants."[92] Peter Berger also has noticed the similarities between paroxysms of laughter and religious experience: "At least certain manifestations of the comic suggest that this other reality has redeeming qualities that are not temporary at all, but rather that point to that other world that has always been the object of the religious attitude. In ordinary parlance one speaks of 'redeeming laughter.' Any joke can provoke such laughter, and it can be redeeming in the sense of making life easier to bear, at least briefly."[93]

It is not coincidental then, that John Sullivan's deliverance takes place in a church where the congregants "get happy" in the salvational world of animation. In the church–*cum*–movie house, the cartoon gets its viewers very happy indeed, transporting them by laughter as well as by prayer to paradise. Sturges thus links animation to true religion, much as the producers of the Merrie Melodies invited their viewers to think of the films as ecstatic interludes in the "service" that was the movie program. The infectious laughter induced by cartoons that has been dismissed as laughter for laughter's sake or mere escapism can alternatively be seen as offering to moviegoers a quasi-religious redemption.

Recognizing cartoons' potential to inspire out-of-body experiences suggests that animators and viewers sought out these parallel worlds and alternative somatic forms, the "me . . . not me" where toons behave like human actors yet retain their graphic identity, and where the forever-resilient bodies could not be hurt. Through vicarious identification with toons, one might catch a glimpse of heaven (or, sometimes, hell). The cartoon would have afforded moviegoers an imaginative retreat for a few minutes, not so that they could anesthetically forget (the reason for Kracauer's "paradise"), but so that they could redeem their difficult lives, experience cartoon liveness, have a catharsis, and get happy.

We don't know much about what historical audiences of the 1930s thought of these cartoons, but producing infectious laughter ("gagging it," in Disney's words) was the cartoonists' enterprise. No doubt there were many viewers who experienced theatrical cartoons as mindless distractions, perhaps setting themselves up for exploitation, or at least unthinking reception. Others might have found seven minutes of salvation in these visions of alternate universes where there was hurt without pain, animal actors behaving as human, pulsating spaces and brilliant colors instead of drabness, uncomplicated stories instead of life's complexities, and happily contagious tunes. Since parents and older siblings watched these films alongside their children, the cartoons might have provided a guilty pleasure in momentary regression. The opportunity for unrestrained laughing out loud in a dark public place was itself worth the price of admission.

Because the cartoons were capable of—and usually invited—multiple readings, it's reasonable to think that this multivalence was also part of what audiences anticipated. This humor is not without social history, nor is it always benign. Rather, the works are deeply imbued with what Maltby called "the invisible politics of style."[94] Cartoons might tuck their meaning behind catchy songs, hilarious slapstick, funny toon characters, and wacky worlds of entertainment, but they really are, using Kracauer's terms, satires, not farces. Vittorio Hösle observes, "In times of ideological uncertainty comedy may share the task of questioning, together with the philosophers, the basic conventions of the age."[95] Comedy as subversive ideology became a central feature of animation decades later in societies where artistic expression was rigidly constrained. Themes of resistance, stoicism, and revolution, such as in films by Jan Švankmajer, conflate infectious laughter and death. In 1930s Hollywood, however, the existence of such alternative interpretations was not obvious.

Considering animated films as a viral medium sheds light not only on the filmmakers' intent to transfer sentiment to their audience but also on consumers' sudden passionate embrace of Mickey Mouse, their embodiment of the three little pig characters, and their enchantment by the theme song. The resonance between film and viewing experience, between animator and moviegoer, was a mediated form of conversion. It was not solely that cartoons instrumentally affected viewers, either consciously or unconsciously, but rather that there was something that kept happening as audiences left the theaters. It is here that seeing infectious laughter as a type of collective performance, a ritual, reconciles the opposites of benign/Dionysian, escapist/instrumental, farce/satire, live/canned, and rapturous/apocalyptic.

CHAPTER 6

Animation and Autophagy

Art that Consumes Itself

Animation seems to have been born under the sign of the Ouroboros, the hermetic symbol of the serpent that consumes its own tail. Beginning with Emile Cohl's clown, animators have told tales of the coming-into-being of toon bodies, of characters vying for agency but ultimately losing their autonomy. Although these homunculi have taken the form of geometric shapes, barely recognizable abstractions (humanlike only in their anthropomorphic movements), funny or frightening caricatures, and (more recently) lifelike electronic simulations of beasts and humans that do not fear the uncanny valley, they remain locked within the limits of their photomechanical or digital media. Proximally live though they may be, there's no alchemy that will give them real life. In compensation, toons can't die. Their stories and their fans' retelling can always restore them.

The physiologies of parthenogenesis and autophagy are appropriate heuristics for describing these cyclical performances. Although the first of these two historical tendencies in animation performance—the one creating bodies in cinematic space, the "hand of the artist" motif—has already been noted, the other one weaving narratives about killing, eating, starving, or tormenting these screen bodies has yet to be explored in depth. In cellular biology, autophagy occurs when some of an organism's cells consume others. Often this is a restorative process of cleansing. Sometimes, however, the cells become too aggressive, leading to the death of the organism. In biology, the process usually isn't reversible; in cartoons, however, it usually is. The conundrum here is basic: Are these images of events that re-perform biology also performances that confront the inevitable?

This chapter explores the interests of animators and audiences in cartoons that dwell on digestion, biology, reproduction, evolution, dying, and regeneration. First I return to the 1930s, when the instrumental stories often exposed the effects of hunger and privation. I'll discuss some specific instances of performative eating in the films and some of the digestion motifs produced. The next section shows the persistence of cannibalism themes in animation. This discussion ranges freely through historical periods, genres, and nationalities. Finally, I come to terms with the self-birthing and -destroying narratives that have been constructed by animators and their audiences. These structures have given cartooning its distinctive circularity and its intimation of never-ending lives.

One might legitimately look at such expressions of distasteful or taboo topics as reactions to societal strictures. Bakhtin considered these folk obsessions with the "lower bodily stratum"—that is, sex, eating, vomiting, and excreting—as always instrumental, structuring inversions of religious ritual, mores, and power alignments.[1] We could debate whether using such imagery can also be benign, meant simply to provide sophomoric shocks or passing amusement. I propose, however, that we consider these cartoon performances of the "lower" realms as reflexive meditations, shared by animators and their audiences, on the possibilities and limits of human behavior. These films by constructing fantastic bodies challenge our smug belief in our inviolate bodies. Moreover, the alternate worlds these scenes establish take us to places that lure and repel at the same time. The Tooniverse is not always a pleasurable alternative to everyday life.

Put simply, in times of relative plenty—say, in the 1910s and '20s— why would animator Winsor McCay place himself in the jaws of a dinosaur? By what logic does Ko-Ko the Clown, when Max Fleischer is harassing him in *Invisible Ink,* evade his attacker by jumping into Max's mouth? Why do the animated organisms in Jan Švankmajer's films from the end of the twentieth century continuously chew themselves into an ever-finer paste, throw up, re-form, and do it all over again? In short, why are there so many images of and suggestions of eating, being eaten, eating others, or even eating oneself in animated films from the beginning to the present?[2]

PERFORMATIVE STARVING AND FEASTING
IN DEPRESSION-ERA CARTOONS

Some of the most compelling stories and most sensual imagery produced by Hollywood studios in the 1930s were associated with food—whether its lack or abundance—and eating. It's not surprising that filmmakers of the Great Depression should have worked into their cartoons allusions or explicit references to the nutritional insecurity gripping the nation. Hollywood cartoons, however benign their producers' intentions, nevertheless re-performed anxieties signaling a lack of confidence in the economy and doubts about the sustainability of physical integrity. The studios released films that delivered the expected distraction and optimism through infectious laughter, of course, but all was not Technicolor rosiness. The discrepancies between performances *in* the films and *of* the films presented opportunities for animators and consumers to author inconsistent and perhaps conflicting animated tales of want and plenty.

Historically, hard times have produced works that respond to the trauma of mass starvation by converting it into what now we would call instrumental performance pieces about extreme eating. Historian Piero Camporesi focuses on *I Dialoghi* by Angelo Beolco (1502–42), also known as Ruzante. Writing about the dialogues from 1528, a year of famine in southern Europe, Camporesi says, "The comic stamp of the dialogue (*facetissimo*, 'most facetious,' used ironically) also serves to dispel the terrible adversary, hunger, by exorcizing it with laughter."[3] In those times, Camporesi observes, peasants and noblemen alike laughed at jokes and plays about starving villagers who would confuse men with pigs and eat the former by mistake, about people who ate their own body parts, and about the desperate stratagem of plugging "the hole beneath" to forestall hunger. Benjamin could have used some of these anecdotes to support the case for art being a safety valve and an inoculation for surviving in a mad world. Our Hollywood cartoons did not go that far, although times were unquestionably tough. In the mid-1930s 40 percent of the U.S. population was underfed, and some two hundred thousand vagrant children of the type often depicted in films of the 1930s survived on subsistence diets.[4] For filmmakers of the time, the constraints of censorship, the theater managers' desire to uphold middlebrow decorum, and the need to appeal to audience tastes—in short, the culture industry—restricted Hollywood's use of drastic famine imagery. Nevertheless, food-related subjects persisted.

If we look at one of the most sumptuous of the gustatory celebrations, *Funny Little Bunnies* (Wilfred Jackson/Disney, 1934), the first impression is of audiovisual plenitude. Cuddly worker rabbits in a utopian society paint Easter eggs and bounce to bright music. Such films were offered up for the edification of implied spectators who, although not likely to be literally famished, would have been aware of encircling hunger. The film takes them to a carnivalesque Tooniverse of unrestrained eating. The Easter bunnies decorate their eggs surrounded by fountains of colorful syrups and vats of bubbling chocolate with free refills.

The Fleischer animators in *Somewhere in Dreamland* (Dave Fleischer/Paramount, 1936) at first withhold food from their protagonists and then provide it aplenty. Two starving children go to bed hungry. As they slumber, they cavort in the smorgasbord of sweets that is Dreamland (Figure 57). Upon awakening they learn that the local merchants (German, Jewish, and Italian) have taken pity upon them and provided a real meal. Again, such films dazzled with superabundant feasts, but their plenteous lands also acknowledge by omission what's left out: dark lands of want. The donation from the private sector to these children is probably a one-time gift. Who knows what morbid after-stories ensue?

Flip the Frog and his new charge, a baby mouse left by an errant stork, fight over a meal in *Little Orphan Willie* (Ub Iwerks/MGM, 1930). It's a remarkable parable showing that overpopulation increases the competition for sustenance. In Iwerks's *Jack and the Beanstalk* (Ub Iwerks/Celebrity Productions, 1933), after selling the emaciated family cow for beans and climbing up to the giant's lair, Jack barely escapes becoming the filling in a sandwich that the giant's wife is making. The giant then gives chase with a mind to eat Jack as an hors d'oeuvre. In the end, Jack, now the giant killer, treats his mother to a fine feast. In the Fleischers' version of the story (*Jack and the Beanstalk*, Dave Fleischer/Paramount, 1931), Bimbo is almost eaten alive when he is entangled in the giant's plate of spaghetti and again when he falls into a huge cup of soup. In one bizarre moment, as Betty Boop and Bimbo take flight aboard the magic hen, the bird's head separates from its torso, only to be hauled back together by two strands of intestines. *Holiday Land* (Art Davis/Charles Mintz, 1934), which was released the same week as *Those Beautiful Dames* (discussed in chapter 5), shows our hero Scrappy visiting the various holidays to get food, culminating with a Thanksgiving Day feast. That these films starring hungry children or childlike toons were released to coincide with the Thanksgiving holiday is especially poignant. The satiety displayed in their tacked-on happy

FIGURE 57. *Somewhere in Dreamland* (1936). The starving children dream of a land of plenty. Original in color.

endings, however, doesn't mitigate the dread of starving that permeates most of the films' running time.

Disney produced a food-themed animated segment called "The Hot Choc-Late Soldiers" (Ben Sharpsteen), an insert in the non-animated feature *Hollywood Party* (Richard Boleslawski/MGM, 1934). In the segment, the soldiers' pitched battle against the gingerbread army ends with a pyrrhic victory. The chocolate soldiers' triumphant return to their edible city is spoiled by the hot sun, which melts them and the city's inhabitants into a pool of ganache. Though it's not shown, the enemy gingerbread men would have been the survivors, since, with war's irony, they are impervious to the heat. *The Cookie Carnival* (Ben Sharpsteen/ Disney, 1935) stars a ragged cookie girl. A gingerbread boy transforms her into a tasty treat and they end up as king and queen of the carnival. As in *Three Little Pigs,* the film closes before the implied final chapter, leaving viewers to reflect that these adorable performers were made to be eaten.

These stories have in common their emphasis on agency as defined by having proper nutrition. Hunger is performative in the sense that the animators may provide food for their characters or withhold it to suit the needs of the plot, or just on a whim. Eating, or, as we'll see, being eaten, is about fighting for power—on the social level in the stories, and on the aesthetic level as well.

The Disney crew was aware of the unsettling implications about eating in *The Three Little Pigs* and so deemphasized the incipient horror of young animals being devoured by a vicious, cunning beast. In the 1892 Andrew Lang version of the tale, the one said to have inspired Disney, the antagonist fox (not a wolf) captures the first two pigs, planning to eat them later. When the fox descends the third pig's brick chimney, "with a yelp of pain, the fox fell into the boiling water, and before he could escape, Blacky [the pig] had popped the lid on, and the fox was scalded to death."[5] Other versions of the story, such as the 1890 Joseph Jacobs retelling, had the wolf eating the brick-dwelling pig's siblings. When the wolf came down the chimney, the pig "boiled him up, and ate him for supper, and lived happily ever afterwards."[6]

Some viewers discerned that lurking behind the tuneful Disney version of the tale was vorephobia, the fear of being swallowed and eaten. This primal anxiety runs through many folk tales and finds its classic expression in Little Red Riding Hood, where analysts see swallowing the girl as an act "symbolizing the uncontrollable appetite or chaos of nature."[7] *The Three Little Pigs* explicates for children and parents the risk of annihilation by a community outsider—a barbarian, as it were—as punishment for the sins of indolence, disrespect for authority, and general silliness. The story has the potential to instill terror in viewers who might be sympathetic to the piggies—and who wouldn't be? As Russell Merritt observes of the characters, "Visually, they are the quintessential Disney infants, graphically little more than smooth, rounded cheeks and buttocks: edible babies."[8] The essential expression of this image is at the end of the sequel *The Big Bad Wolf* (Burt Gillett/Disney, 1934) when we see the two little pigs looking out from their cottage doorway. Their sensuous pink bottoms amount to four succulent hams. But no one eats anyone in Disney cartoons.[9] The wolf in *Pigs* gets his comeuppance instead by having his tail end scalded. At least he was spared the humiliation of being eaten by his intended prey. In the sequel, the third pig loads hot coals and popping corn into the wolf's breeches. The exploding kernels must have elicited peals of laughter in particular from audience members who happened to be munching on the same snack during the show.[10]

The third pig has hung framed pictures of the family's deceased (but tasty) paternity on the wall; links of sausages and a ham are both labeled "Father." They are funny gags but also unnerving reminders of the pigs' destiny to be eaten either by wolf or by human.

One moviegoer who recognized the fatalistic rapaciousness of *The Three Little Pigs* was the humorist poet and columnist Don Marquis. In "the big bad wolf," published in 1935, the narrator, archy the cockroach (who, being an insect, can type only by jumping on the lowercase keys), muses on the moral of Disney's cartoon. After a ride to the movies in a friend's trouser cuff, archy describes his "edification" upon seeing the film. Marquis/archy seizes on the performance of cruelty, observing, with tongue in cheek, that men must be superior to wolves because the animals eat the pigs alive. A "superior" man, though, would have "lovingly" butchered them and made them into spare ribs.

> he would tenderly have roasted them
> fried them and boiled them
> cooked them feelingly with charity
> towards all and malice towards none
> and piously eaten them served with sauerkraut
> and other trimmings.[11]

Marquis looks beyond the surface merriment to see the betrayal of natural order; the pigs do to the wolf what it should be doing to them, but also what humans will soon do to the pigs. The allegory for Marquis, then, is not about vanquishing the wolf but about the futility of the pigs' salvation, since they're almost charcuterie anyway.[12] In archy's reading, this was not a story of the weak triumphing over the Depression, but rather of the pigs' solipsism as they celebrate on the eve of their trip to the abattoir to join Father.

Marquis next wrenches archy's tale into a Swiftian analogy. If the pigs were happier to be eaten by humans than by wolves, then African Americans ought to prefer being lynched in America rather than Europe or the Soviet Union. Again dripping with facetiousness, the text suggests that the black man should be grateful that he's being lynched

> in a land of freedom and liberty
> and not in any of the old world countries
> of darkness and oppression
> where men are still the victims
> of kings iniquity and constipation.[13]

For Marquis, Disney's fable re-performed vorephobic revulsion as class struggle. His prose poem puts a sharp point on the crucial debate over the social effects of humor, particularly in cartoons, that was presented in the previous chapter. Writing at the same time as Benjamin, the humorist seems likewise to regard Disney as unintentionally instrumental and the pigs' obliviousness as an exposé of their unknowing victimization by society. Marquis's "the big bad wolf" also suggests that cartoons may inoculate their audiences against evil, feeding them the pabulum that faith in hard work and a good attitude are all that's necessary to bring about a just, egalitarian, and prosperous society. The film's "benign" comic relief and duplicitous happy ending neutralize its revolutionary potential, turning it into a safety valve for the establishment. archy's facetious conclusion mocks the infectious optimism in the frenzy surrounding Disney's film: "it is a cheering thought to think/that god is on the side of the best digestion."[14]

The battle between the hungry wolf and the victimized pigs reverberated with the public in 1933. In addition to appearing around the time of the Agricultural Adjustment Act's controversial "slaughter of the pigs" (see chapter 5), the Disney cartoon also coincided with a nearly successful national campaign to exterminate wolves, which were represented as livestock predators, according to Mitts-Smith. She and others argue that there was slippage from publicly vilifying the animal to turning it into a stereotype of hated racial, sexual, and cultural otherness.[15] In the version of *The Three Little Pigs* seen by Marquis and others (before it was altered in 1948), there was no ambivalence about performing stereotypes; the wolf comes to the third pig's door disguised as an orthodox Jew.[16] The animators might have thrown in the peddler with his Yiddish-accented spiel as just another typical ethnic gag. Or it might have been more calculated. The trickster wolf's strategy was a cagey way to fool the pigs because a Jewish salesman could be trusted not to eat the distinctly nonkosher animals. The drawing of the wolf, which emphasized his scruffy blackness, his sharp fangs and claws, and his long, drooling snout, epitomized the insatiable appetite of a ravenous carnivore. Such images in 1930s popular culture made the wolf a figure of sexual and racial predation, according to Mitts-Smith: "Defined by his greedy mouth, his voracious hunger and the threat that he poses to humans and domesticated animals, the wolf is a one-sided beast seeking to fill his belly. In 'Little Red Riding Hood,' 'The Three Little Pigs,' and 'The Wolf and the Seven Kids,' as well as numerous fables and saints' legends, the wolf's desire to eat motivates his actions while shaping his interactions with the other characters. As such, his predatory nature not only keeps him hungry but also renders him treacherous and immoral."[17]

In our terms, and in the historical context, the Disney wolf gives a thoroughly figurative performance of "wolfness." At the same time, the wolf is something of a caricature of Darwinian survival of the fittest, inverting the idea while simultaneously affirming it. In the wild, of course, a wolf could easily finish off a passel of porkers, but in the film the third piglet's intelligence compensates for his weaker body, giving him evolutionary superiority. The mismatch of biological relations confirms that the story is a fable of social power, not ecology.

Merritt observes that when the filmmakers purged the fairy tale of its horrific scenes of the wolf eating the sibling pigs and then the third pig eating the wolf, "Disney . . . makes the movie less frightful (avoiding the prospect of watching a pig eat the creature that ate his brothers and thereby finessing the thorny issue of whether Practical Pig is a cannibal once removed)."[18] The Lantz studio was not as protective of tender sensibilities. The wolf's threat to eat children in *Grandma's Pet* (Walter Lantz and William Nolan/Universal, 1932) is explicitly horrifying.[19] After putting Grandma into the icebox for snacking on later, the wolf almost gets his main course, Little Red Riding Hood (Figure 58). Oswald the Rabbit makes a last-minute rescue just as she is slipping into his gullet.[20]

According to Zipes, the wolf's association with voracity was prevalent in medieval European "warning stories" circulated when the countryside was beset by attacks on children. Although these assaults were attributed to wild beasts and monsters, hungry villagers driven to cannibalism probably perpetrated some of them. Stories of the Little Red Riding Hood type were object lessons for children: "Either an ogre, ogress, man-eater, wild person, werewolf, or wolf was portrayed as attacking a child in the forest or at home. The social function of the story was to show how dangerous it could be for children to talk to strangers in the woods or to let strangers enter the house."[21] Some Švankmajer films, like *Down to the Basement* (*Do pivnice*, 1983), which shows a girl entering a spooky cellar full of potential evildoers and strange auguries, such the threatening potatoes whose "eyes" are living eyes, have the look and feel of these folkloric warning stories. What is being counseled against, however, is vague. The viewers may summon up their own appropriate nightmares and anxieties.

Animation, which by the 1930s had developed into a medium open to various readings by deft audiences, was well prepared to deliver these performances of eating that were simultaneously advisory, funny and frightening. The representations in the cartoons of contested food, starvation, gorging, and voracity are further instances of Hollywood's overt platform of instrumental humor. Filmmakers defanged the everyday

FIGURE 58. *Grandma's Pet* (1932). Could this be the end of Little Red Riding Hood?

hardships of viewers by constructing imaginative analogues and moral object lessons, and they encouraged viewers to confront their bogeys by laughing at them. However, there was no way to predict or control counterinterpretations such as that of Marquis or fan retellings. Nevertheless, it also seems that the stories surrounding food in the 1930s are one chapter in a larger work. In designing their heterotopias, animators before and since the Depression have couched their humor in cruelty, the grotesque, the profane, and the taboo. Of course, to present these explicitly was neither desirable nor possible in the studio period. That capability would have to wait until filmmaking outside the commercial constraints of the mass market was viable, leading to the gross-out indie animation, cable shows, and online cartoons of the present day.

SOME DIGESTION MOTIFS
Big Swallows

Animators in the 1930s worked against the backdrop of nutritional deprivation, but filmmakers in the early days of the medium were apparently more intrigued by the body's tactility, plasticity, and dimensionality than they were by starvation. They regarded the alternate world inside the body as a distinctive performance opportunity. These enveloping spaces anticipate those moments throughout the history of the medium in which moving point-of-view shots suck viewers into deep-space vortices. These swallowing-up scenes might be architectonic, like the staircase in *Egyptian Melodies,* or organic, like the penetrations of mouths in those uvula shots.

Scenes in which cartoon characters scream or rush toward the "camera" with uvula-flapping mouths destabilize screen spaces. They're further unsettling since they suggest vorephobia and perhaps vorephilia at work.[22] The uvula device obviously uses the grotesque to repulse us while (supposedly) making us laugh, somewhat in the manner of a Freudian dirty joke. The open mouth is the only large body orifice that may be displayed in polite society. Not only does it provide a private or clinical view inside someone's body, but it also reveals the mysterious fleshy and seemingly useless protuberance normally concealed within. In the early days of studio animation, the uvula shot was a graphic eyepopper, as when Bosko and Honey open up to engulf the "camera" with such relish in *Sinkin' in the Bathtub* (Figure 59). The parade of wide-open wide-angle mouths in *Lady, Play Your Mandolin!* is symptomatic of a fetishistic affection for the image (see Figure 13 again). As happened with other figurative performances, this graphic element became narrativized later in the 1930s, as animators introduced gigantic characters to rationalize putting the protagonist in another's mouth. For example, in *Giantland* (Burt Gillett/Disney, 1933) and *The Brave Little Tailor* (Bill Roberts/Disney, 1938), as the big men drink, Mickey, who is inside their mouths, must save himself from the torrent by clinging to a log-sized uvula. Such scenes re-perform the discrepancies in power between the small but clever Mickey and the villainous but stupid cannibalistic giants.

The eponymous hero of *Tom Thumb* (Ub Iwerks/Celebrity Pictures, 1936) has one bout of life-threatening orality after another. He's baked in a pie before being consumed by several fish, but the main adventure is when a goat swallows him whole. He hangs onto the uvula but eventually lands in the stomach. Tom's father rescues him by reaching inside with his entire arm and extracting the boy (Figure 60). Entering whales' mouths has been another movie figure for well over a century, since a friendly one (or is it a big fish?) rescued the protagonists of *Fairyland: A Kingdom of Fairies* (*Le Royaume des fées,* Georges Méliès/Star-Film, 1903).[23] Goofy and Donald are engulfed by an enraged monster in *The Whalers* (David Hand and Dick Huemer/Disney, 1938). In retrospect, the scene is a study for Pinocchio and Geppetto's sojourn in the mouth and gut of Monstro in *Pinocchio* (Hamilton Luske and Ben Sharpsteen/Disney, 1940).[24] In these instances of animals swallowing protagonists,

FIGURE 59. *Sinkin' in the Bathtub* (1930). As Bosko flies toward the "camera," his wide-angle mouth fills the screen.

the stories resolve by finding some ingenious way to disgorge the heroes (or aid the heroes, in the case of *Fairyland*), thus correcting the "asymmetrical alliance," the disturbed balance of power between human and beast.[25]

From the beginning of cinema, folks were being gobbled up. In *The Astronomer's Dream* (*La Lune à un mètre,* Georges Méliès/Star Film, 1898) the moon vomits forth a couple of dancing moonlings into the astronomer's lab, then swallows the stargazer and a few props. It spits out his masticated remains—his head, limbs, and ribcage—accompanied by a devil. A fairy queen throws the bits back into the moon's mouth and the restored astronomer returns whole. *The Big Swallow* (James Williamson, 1901) is another grand cannibalistic encounter. The subject is a well-dressed man who warns an unseen photographer not to take his picture. At this point the view of the film camera is the same as that of the fictional still camera. The man approaching gesticulates into the still/movie camera. Finally, he opens his mouth wide and engulfs the lens. Thanks to the "stretch and squash" of wide-angle lens distortion, the prim Englishman's mouth swells into a gigantic cavity capable of swallowing a man whole—which it does. As the photographer and his gear tumble inside the swallower, his throat represented by a simple velvet backdrop, the unseen movie camera continues to record the scene. As the Williamson catalogue put it, "First the camera, then the operator disappear inside. He [the gentleman] retires munching him up and expressing his

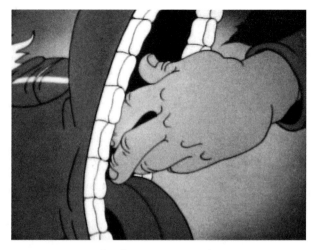

FIGURE 60. *Tom Thumb* (1936). Papa reaches into a goat's stomach to extract Tom. Original in color.

great satisfaction."[26] This display of man-eating gusto and the photographer's humorously hideous punishment contrasts with the gentleman's genteel insistence on decorum.[27] Though both are non-animated trick films, *Astronomer's Dream* and *Big Swallow* introduced concepts that animators would later adopt. The "real" body may be dependably whole, but the performed cinematic body is malleable—and edible. Body parts (such as Felix's and Ko-Ko's in a later era) come and go without apparent harm. The camera, the implied spectator, and the narrator travel freely into the body and out again. Gunning has observed that *The Big Swallow* establishes a fictitious interior of the human body, seemingly in an effort to turn natural curiosity about these "invisible" spaces of the body into fantastic screen spaces.[28] Another way to put it is that cinema, especially animated cinema, turns our mysterious innards into performative sites where any number of dreams, fantasies, and horrors may be enacted.

This fascination is consistent with the Augustinian "lust for the eyes" that Gunning hypothesized as underlying original cinema spectatorship, that is, the looking that compels us irresistibly toward unaccustomed and possibly forbidden sights. "*Curiositas* draws the viewer towards unbeautiful sights, such as a mangled corpse, and"—now Gunning is quoting Augustine, who links performance with this unhealthy urge—"'because of this disease of curiosity monsters and anything out of the ordinary are put on show in our theatres.' "[29] This is an early articulation of an "infection" theory, since the act of looking may contaminate the viewer unless the sexual or horrible sights are re-performed as socially acceptable spectacles. This way of thinking per-meated the carnival, the sideshow, and eventually vaudeville. The best example may be the sensational Le Pétomane, although arguably he appealed more to the ear than they eye. He translated the biological necessity to pass gas into a headline act at the Moulin Rouge and other belle époque music halls. By taking in large quantities of air and then releasing it through his rectum with sufficient control, he could whis-tle catchy, if a bit high-pitched, tunes.[30] Cinema tolerates—in fact, it facilitates—"lower" performances of this type by providing spaces within the safety and socially acceptable (if perhaps slightly marginal-ized) milieu of entertainment, thereby giving audiences unique points of access to bodies as fantasies and institutionalized curiosities (in Augus-tine's sense). Accordingly, early animators capitalized on the ability and expectation to make this attractive dread humorous.

Winsor McCay imagined the body as a fantastic eating organism. Perhaps the cartoonist's early work designing posters for circus side-show attractions exposed him to the world of aberrant consumption as spectacle. Extreme eating, drinking, and regurgitating were popular acts on the circus and vaudeville stage. The most famous of these per-formers was Hadji Ali, "The Egyptian Enigma," whose showstopping act consisted of swallowing water mixed with kerosene, spewing forth fire from his mouth, and extinguishing it with the swallowed liquid.[31] Then there was Harry Morton, "The Human Hydrant," who chugged "300 small mugs of beer on stage and regurgitat[ed] them before he became intoxicated," and The Great Waldo, "The Regurgitating Geek," who swallowed, then unswallowed, live animals.[32] The morbid fascina-tion with such performances lay in the unexpected, disgusting, and downright dangerous modification of the body and its functions. These individuals metamorphosed into something elastic and liminal, defying expectations of ordinary anatomy. Their live performances therefore performed the plasticity expected of cartoon bodies but not of humans. They also anticipated several short films by Švankmajer as well as the "new vaudevillians" of contemporary body performance art.

The premise of McCay's 1904–13 *Dreams of the Rarebit Fiend* comic strip was overindulgent eating.[33] The non-animated film version, *Dream of a Rarebit Fiend* (Wallace McCutcheon and Edwin S. Porter/Edison, 1906) delighted in showing the "fiend" eating massive amounts of the cheesy treat and imbibing much ale. The dozens of strips in the series featured characters eating, being eaten, or in various throes of vorephobic hallucinations. His 1905 *Hungry Henrietta* strip presented the life of a child who grows from infancy to girlhood; and, as the subtitle tells us, "all she wanted to do was eat." McCay implied that Henrietta's misguided parents overfeeding her caused her eating syndrome. Was it bulimia or pica ("a disorder in which one constantly feels the need to eat things that are not commonly considered food")?[34] Their chubby girl, though she ate everything, remained starved for what she really needed, the love of her family. Fiendishly obsessive eating is the danger portrayed in his film *The Pet* (McCay, 1921) as well. In its first appearance, the animal is corgi-like, cute, and cuddly. The creature responds to its adoptive humans' nurturing by eating them out of house and home. Completely. The pet swallows stone walls and anything else in its way. Eventually gargantuan, it devours everything until aircraft bombard it, it explodes, and its flesh rains down on the city. The couple's childless marriage is a suspected rationale for the fantasy, and there is an insinuation that the man's coldness and the woman's excessive mothering created the psychic monster.

McCay (and his cartoonist descendants) loved to blow up bodies. Exploding them is perhaps the ultimate subversion of the conception of the organism as a whole, inviolate Cartesian entity. Bursting characters would become a classic bit in Hollywood cartoons and Japanese anime, but as a performance of body-busting overeating, *The Story of a Mosquito* (Winsor McCay/Vitagraph, 1912) is hard to top. Steve the mosquito, who suffers from a compulsive eating disorder, consumes so much blood that he can no longer fly. Even after failing to achieve liftoff, he is compelled to have one more taste, bringing about his explosive end. McCay's film presents a disturbing view of the body as out of an individual's control and is a warning story about hedonism and gluttony.

McCay toys with the viewer's approach/avoidance fascination in the scenes of the grotesque swelling of the mosquito's thorax. He revels in showing the depth of the beak's insertions into the man's neck, head, and face, eliciting the revulsion of being probed and penetrated against one's will—the mosquito playing the role of succubus—as well the disgust of having another creature (such as a vampire) drink one's blood. In addition to extreme gourmandizing, Steve also summons up the scourge of malaria. Just ten years before McCay's film, Sir Ronald Ross had received the Nobel Prize in Medicine for proving that mosquitoes transmit the blood-borne disease.

Steve's is not a pretty death. Nor is that of Piggy, the protagonist of *Pigs Is Pigs* (Friz Freleng/Schlesinger, 1937). True to his porcine nature,

he thinks of nothing but eating. His dreamland adventure is nightmarish. Force-fed by a mad scientist, Piggy could have escaped, but, like
McCay's insect, he can't resist one more bite—which is one too many
(Plates 10a and 10b). Piggy's explosive fate anticipates the demise of
Mr. Creosote in the non-animated *The Meaning of Life* (Terry Jones
and Terry Gilliam/Celandine Films, 1983). The superobese epicure ac-
cepts just one more "wafer thin mint" and goes the way of his cartoon
predecessors. Bucketsful of erupted puke inundate the restaurant.[35] The
disputatious diner in *Eat* (Bill Plympton, 2000) loses his meal too. The
server reaches into his stomach, shown in a graphic view of the man's
insides, to retrieve it when he doesn't pay the bill. All of the contents
eventually return in a projectile flow of remarkable volume (Plate 11).
These characters' fluid finishes provide orgasmic finales to the horrible
engorgement and also bring closure to the films' narratives.

Filmmakers and their audiences, through their cinesthetic engagement, merge off-screen space with the oozing paste that churns within.
When the body blows up and reveals its contents, despite the repulsion,
it's nevertheless another dimension for moviegoers and animators to
cohabit. Writing on the spatial reconceptualization that the many frag-
menting bodies generate in anime, Christian McCrea observes that these
explosions posit a complicated space outside the textual space of ordinary cinema.[36] An even more implicating cinesthetic performance
would be one in which the viewer becomes an active participant.

That would be "Frog in a Blender" (Joe Cartoon, 2000). This interactive Flash animation—a hybrid of cartoon and video game—incriminates
the viewer in a violent catharsis.[37] An arrogant frog swims inside the
kitchen appliance while insulting the viewers/players and daring them to
turn up the speed (Plate 12). As participants advance through the buttons
on the blender, clicking each of them with their mouse, the blender spins
faster and the frog becomes less cocky. By the final stages, he is pleading
pathetically for mercy. I doubt that anyone has ever shown mercy. Invariably we yield to the morbid temptation, curious even though we
already know that the amphibian will soon be a smoothie. We press button number ten. The swirling frog hits the blades and explodes into a
bloody consommé of eyeball, bone, and guts.

"Frog in a Blender" invites the viewers/players to join the performance. The exploding animal performs in the extratextual space that
McCrae wrote of, and the effect is even more riveting because we're
accomplices, having physically pressed the buttons. Our participation is
instrumental and we have agency, not only in the aesthetic senses, but

physically. An apologist might point out that "no animals were injured in the making of this cartoon." Nevertheless, when we execute the frog we are more ethically accountable than in "normal" cinema. Unlike when we watch *The Story of a Mosquito* or a film with scenes of human execution, we cannot change the narrative by intervening on behalf of the victim. When we watch "Frog" we are responsible for killing the animal for the purpose of entertainment.

The ethical conundrum of "Frog in a Blender" isn't easily resolved. Pressing the final button is irresistible because a narrative-driven curiosity to see the outcome grips the participant. The potential guilt arising from perpetrating this little death without fear of retribution is offset by the event's mediatized distance and the satisfaction of inflicting deserved vengeance on a sassy nonhuman. Does our act sanction the cruelty to animals (and humans) so routinely displayed for our animated enjoyment? Not exactly. We know that this action does not actually determine the fate of the cartoon character. Cartoonist Joe has already killed the frog. His final button is patiently waiting for the viewers' push. There are no alternate endings available, no button that, if pressed, would liberate the creature from its death blender. But are we really exonerated by blaming the artist? A gallery performance piece along similar lines was organized in 2000 by Marco Evaristti, who placed live fish in a blender and swirled them up for the assembled participants to drink.[38] As was "Frog in a Blender," these were open-ended performances that gave participants the option of not partaking in the disgusting concoction, but if they abstained they would not be participating in the "art" fully. Participants' free will was limited or even illusory. Their only real choices were to kill/drink or walk away.

The ethical stakes are higher in Joe Cartoon's later works with human victims, such as "Octomom in a Blender" (2009). Although performing violent animated vivisection causes unease, re-performing capital punishment for fun is even less guiltless, since it inevitably raises the question of whether what amounts to a vigilante lynching (here, for the infraction of having multiple pregnancies) is justifiable. While the "Blender" cartoons add a new twist, in fact the series continues one of the major themes of the Hollywood studio era and all those comic chases that animated the zoological food chain. One party (say, Sylvester, Tom the cat, or Wile E. Coyote) would devour the other (Tweety, Jerry the mouse, or the Road Runner), only to have the victim disgorged and the pursuit started anew. With their fandom and their ticket purchases, moviegoers supported the ethos that turned natural animal behavior into a cruel but funny spectacle. Whether they reflected upon this is another matter. Did the viewers of these films think about the animal basis of human food consumption? On TV, *The Itchy & Scratchy Show,* the cartoon series within the cartoon *The Simpsons,* is a hyperbolic parody of these sadistic comedies of interspecies ingestion, often featuring hilarious disembowelments.

Prague filmmaker Jan Švankmajer has made many films that expose and exploit the animated alimentary. A Czech surrealist painter and puppeteer as well as film director, he uses black humor to create wonder and disgust. His films perform genesis (plant and animal production), metamorphosis (mastication and digestion), and expulsion (defecation and the filmmaker's apparent favorite, regurgitation). For example, *Historia Naturae* (1967) offers animated photomontages of plants and animals from antique prints, each series ending in a close-up of a filmed human mouth eating a bite of meat. All the world's phyla are reduced to trivial mouthfuls, the last appearing on a munching skull. The two amorous raw steaks in *Meat Love* (1989) have a lusty tryst, but it lasts less than a minute before it's off to the barbecue. Švankmajer's *Flora* (1989), only half a minute long, is disturbing. We see a female form with a hyperrealistic face modeled in animated clay. Her full-scale body is an arrangement of real flowers and edible fruits.[39] *Flora,* though, gives the Renaissance ideal a kinky twist. A backward trucking camera movement reveals that allegorical Summer is straining for a drinking glass but is unable to reach it because she's tied to a bed (Plate 13). The "animation" of the scene results from the camera's stop-motion cinematography and from the movement of the filmed subject itself as the "body" rots over the course of filming and maggots writhe within it. Flora, the traditional figure for Nature's beauty and abundance, and perhaps a metaphor of the politically repressed artist, is dehydrating to death.[40]

Such films activate the curiosity and scariness of devourment and decay to bring about the viewers' immersion, repulsion, and disavowal in the narrative. The same could be said of all these films that highlight food as performative, the mouth as a portal to otherness, the sexually charged views of the engulfing throat, which portend the individual's destruction or the disconcerting awareness that humans are part of the food chain. Being eaten or swallowed whole by another organism means giving up one's identity and acknowledging the relativity of one's position in the circle of life. Showing the engulfment on-screen, whether it is depicted as repellant, attractive, or just a novelty, is a surefire way to facilitate the "me . . . not me" of animated performances.

Cartoons Can the Cannibals

Many animated films seize our attention by alluding to the taboo act of cannibalism.[41] Emphasizing the processes of consuming other humans, cartoonists have merrily blended graphic bodies. This was violently so, for instance, in the case of *Fantasmagorie* (Emile Cohl/Gaumont, 1908). In one brief shot the protagonist clown's body swells until it is large enough to consume a film spectator. Though the scene is almost too fleeting to be processed on first viewing, it plays out the idea that the drawn animated figure has the potential to transgress the theater space and eat the moviegoer. Cohl again played with explicit cannibalism in *The Tenacious Salesman* (*Le placier est tenace*, Emile Cohl/Gaumont, 1910). In the non-animated introduction, a traveling salesman shrinks himself to pursue a similarly shrunken client into the mouth of a cannibalistic Native American chief. We follow their animated chase down the esophagus, which leads to a fantastic scene in the stomach. Cohl's paper cutout figures grapple inside the gut, which was tinted red in the original version. Cutting back to the exterior and live action, the cannibal mimes extreme gastrointestinal distress, goes behind a bush, and "relieves" himself of the salesman and his quarry, who reappear as full size actors by means of a stop-action substitution edit.[42] Cohl's darkly humorous cannibalism returned in *The Newlyweds: He Poses for His Portrait* (Emile Cohl/American Eclair, 1913), in which a grotesque sequence shows a man eating a baby.[43]

In the studio period, the depiction of cannibalistic situations was rampant, but scenes of eating were implied rather than shown or simply avoided altogether. The easiest way for filmmakers to depict cannibalism was to dredge up convenient racist stereotypes, especially of Oceanians or Africans. In *Alice Cans the Cannibals* (Ub Iwerks/Disney, 1925), when a hungry black horde is pursuing her, Alice saves the day by throwing a harpoon line through the cannibals' nose rings to send them over a cliff. Of the many other examples of cannibalism in the movies, among the best (or worst) is *Jungle Jitters* (Friz Freleng/Schlesinger, 1938). A "white" door-to-door salesman (he's a white dog) ventures into the jungle, where the black humanoid villagers collectively visualize him as a savory trussed bird. The villagers, indulging in the universal tendency of movie cannibals to launch into a ritual performance, dance in a circle around a big pot of boiling water before they start cooking him up for dinner. Humor (?) ensues. The animators call upon the racial outsiders to act out a warning tale by showing their ultimate civilization-threatening savagery. Not only is the unpleasantness of being eaten powering the archetype, but there is also the ignominy of being sacrificed in someone else's religious ritual. There is possibly, however, irony as well. The natives are caricaturing imperialism when they "colonize" and resist the white invaders' domination by eating their bodies. Hollywood couldn't address cannibalism without distancing it as a cartoon, a slapstick comedy, or a horror film.[44]

Blu is the pseudonym of an Italian muralist who specializes in graffiti on a monumental scale.[45] In his short animation *Child* (Blu, 2005), he depicts digestion with hints of cannibalism. The film begins with a tiny circle on a blank white background. The circle splits into two embryos, and one of them becomes encased in an eggshell. A female shopper buys the egg at the store and takes it away. Inside the shopping bag the egg/embryo jostles with a grenade, a car, a computer monitor, a bottle of household cleaner, a crucifix, and a skull. The egg is juxtaposed with and perhaps threatened by these allegorical trappings of modern life. The woman swallows the egg, her head transforms into a skull, and we see the yolk descend down the alimentary canal. Inside the impregnated stomach, after the yolk/fetus has developed into a miniature child, it is joined by a swallowed medicine capsule, possibly a "morning after" contraceptive or some other medication. It breaks open and pellets flood the stomach/womb. As the child drowns in a sea of pellets, the image fills with circles. The bubbles evaporate, leaving only one tiny "cell," the exact image that began the film. The meaning of this provocative story is ambiguous. It is clear, however, that eating the egg acts out oophagy or perhaps embryophagy. The cyclical narrative structure duplicates the visual metamorphosis: cells reproduce, die (or are destroyed), and reproduce again.

Muto (Blu, 2007 and 2008) is an animated graffiti pageant of swallowing, regurgitation, and cannibalism. It's a film made of paintings on walls, sidewalks, and streets that have been photographed, overpainted, and rephotographed to animate them. We don't see the artist at work with ladders and paint rollers—the performance *of* animation—only the animated result of hundreds of paintings and repaintings, each change leaving behind visible streaks and pentimenti. Blu pushes the bodies of his grotesque beings through never-ending metamorphoses based on cycles of parthenogenesis and reincarnation. Humanoid, insectivorous, and protoplasmic beings eat each other, copulate, divide, and issue monstrous copies of themselves. Rapidly evolving forms swallow their kin and autoingest. In one sequence a head opens its mouth, regurgitates a similar head that opens its mouth and regurgitates, and so on. Eventually a child-man emerges from the cycle. As he crawls along the sidewalk, large hands reach down and crack him open like a peanut shell to extract a diamond, whose facets unfold into a mechanical man, which leads to the next sequence. In one segment reminiscent of the cannibal scene in *Fantasmagorie,* a giant plucks a man's head off his body and swallows it.[46] A "zoom" into a close-up of the giant's head shows him ripping open his own skull to birth a clone. This action repeats until, instead of a head, a house emerges. From its windows an insect with a human head crawls out. Men open their chests to give birth to their clones. In the final scene a man spews from his mouth ravenous black beetles that swarm over a head and strip it to the skull. The animation stops and the sun sets on the wall with its painted death's head graffito, creating a natural fade to black. Because of the narrative's diurnal structure, though, we may assume that tomorrow the creatures will come out again.

Allegories of orality like this stretch and distend the human form. As if it weren't enough to twist, turn, and rubberize bodies, such films turn them inside out and pass through them, glorying in their intimate cavities and their work of apparent self-reproduction. Heather Crow's remarks on animation in general are pertinent to Blu's film. "The bodies constructed cinematically, graphically, and sculpturally through animation techniques unsettle conventional notions of a stable, bounded, coherent body. Animated film is characterized by shapeshifting bodies: bodies squashed and stretched, organs that jump out of the skin, human figures that transform into animal or objects."[47] *Muto* creates a nightmare vision of a zombie-like food chain feeding upon itself in a starved metropolis. Passersby (like the oblivious ones caught in single frames) see nothing but the ubiquitous graffiti of their environment. It's only in viewing *Muto* as a projected film that the performance *in* the animation may be seen, when these monsters of the city enact their macabre feedings.

The smack of cannibalism is ever-present in Švankmajer's films. Some, like *Food* (1992), readily lend themselves to allegorical political analyses, appropriate for work done under the eye of a repressive state. Structured as three bizarre meals and combining non-animated and animated acting, it seems to allude to competition among the classes for nourishment. At "Breakfast," each man retrieves a plate of sausage and fries from the man across the table and the cycle repeats. This seems like a never-ending ritual until, in the last shot, we see a long line of people waiting their turn to join in the rotation. In "Lunch," a bourgeois-looking middle-aged man in a business suit and a young bohemian-styled student devour everything in their environment. They eat utensils, tables, chairs, and their clothing. The scene fades out just as they're on the verge of cannibalism.

Dimensions of Dialogue (*Moznosti dialogu,* 1982), Švankmajer's best-known short film, is a tour de force of animated everyday objects and clay. In part one, "Exhaustive Discussion," two heads composed of organic matter, bits of cast-off hardware, and implements of writing and filmmaking chew each other in successive shots into an ever-finer paste, regurgitate, and then restart the process. Ultimately the digestive breakdown results in complete mutual consumption. The clay lovers in the "Passionate Discourse" section meld and incorporate each other, extracting passion from the physical violence of the coupling. Hands dig into clay "flesh" and mouths intimately engulf and swallow the blending bodies (Plate 14). The physically all-consuming, mutually cannibalizing sex act leaves behind a little residue, an embryonic clay offspring. Each of the lovers denies responsibility for the progeny, which turns out to be the seed of their destruction. Now their formerly passionate embrace is deadly. They claw each other into formless shapes, disembody themselves, and return to amorphous clay.

The third section, "Factual Conversation," presents two realistically rendered male heads on a table that are locked in an otherworldly staring contest. The men confront each other by producing unexpected objects from their mouths. With dueling tongues (claimed to be real ones from a butcher shop) they thrust out non sequiturs such as tubes of toothpaste, shoes with writhing laces, pencils and sharpeners, and bread, butter, and knives. There is no clear winner because the heads wind up as flaccid, panting lumps of clay.

To spice up its depiction of alimentation, *A Game with Stones* (*Hra s kameny,* Jan Švankmajer, 1965) adds cannibalism and defecation. First, the stone performers reproduce themselves through mitosis, then they refigure themselves as foodstuffs. Next, anthropomorphic pebble faces consume each other and vomit, followed by images of excreting rocks. An actual game is the subject of *Manly Games* (*Muzné hry,* Jan Švankmajer, 1988), in which a sports fan eats and drinks beer—lots of beer—while watching football (soccer) on TV. A folk festival of violent cannibalism has invaded the athletic-televisual spectacle. The carnage on the field mounts as the players (animated photograph cutouts) fight literally tooth and nail. Since all the performers are animated photographs or clay models of the same actor, the game is both homicidal and suicidal. Referees intermittently halt the match to carry off the mangled bodies in coffins, and then the game resumes. The violence only increases the TV viewer's immersion until the metaleptic illusion becomes real and the viewer is *in* the game. He is oblivious when the players storm into his apartment and dismember each other behind his back. The cannibalism theme continues as cookies are endowed with blinking human eyes and players' heads are ground into sausage, after which they crawl into the earth as wormlike strands (Figure 61).

Extraordinary soundtracks magnify the organic quality of the performances. Švankmajer utilizes very literal music scores, but he also syncs organic sounds of squishing, grinding, chomping, slurping, and grating to emphasize the violence of the body invasions, the dismemberments, engorgements, and the disgustingness of the animated schmutz. The sound effects seem to emanate from the objects and therefore naturalize the images, contributing to the impression that normally inanimate objects are performing for us. At the same time, the sounds are distancing effects. Such patently inanimate things could not moan, gnash, or grunt like these things, thus drawing attention to the films as constructed performances.

Little Otik (*Otesánek*, Jan Švankmajer, 2000) is a feature-length film structured around cannibalism and monstrous ingestions.[48] The plot is based on a nineteenth-century Czech folk tale, but it is also reminiscent of McCay's *The Pet*. A farmer tries to placate his wife, who is pleading for a baby. He presents an anthropomorphically shaped root he's dug up to her as an infant. As she suckles and swaddles it, it comes to life. Eventually it cannibalizes the adoptive parents and eats almost everything else in the village. Švankmajer's films share with many fairy tales the re-performance of the repressed horror of being eaten. Such motifs revive folk humor with its emphasis on over-the-top situations involving the body and grotesque realism. As Michael Nottingham observes, "Otik eats nearly everything and everyone over the course of the film, and as such might be read as an embodiment of the primal force of hunger—Bakhtin's material bodily lower stratum."[49] Like many of Švankmajer's works, *Little Otik* lends itself to allegorical analysis. Zipes sees it as "a dark comedy about how the Czechs stumbled into

FIGURE 61. *Manly Games* (1988). Grinding the opponent's head into sausage is fair play in this macho vision of football. Original in color. Courtesy of Athanor Ltd. Film Production Company, Jaromir Kallista, and Jan Švankmajer.

global capitalism that may swallow them alive. . . . [I]t is about unrestrained consumerism in post-1989 Czechoslovakia in which consumption is related to cannibalism and barbarianism."[50] Actually, it may be that most artists' depictions of the lower strata, like folk-festive activities in general, may be read as distorted re-performances of their quotidian, rational, and authoritative practices, so that all their bodies are ideological. As Crow observes, "The animated body has political, social, and cultural implications, challenging corporeal normativity, rendering the boundaries between bodies and environments (as well as between bodies and other bodies) malleable and elastic."[51]

Cannibalism as an animated spectacle may be a gesture of defiance to lure moviegoers into a strange space to enchant or intentionally repel them. These filmmakers' interest in images of digestion is one shared by contemporary performance artists.[52] Consider again the aforementioned Evaristti. For one of his pieces he served his dinner guests plates of pasta with meatballs made from his own liposuctioned body fat. Evaristti emphasized the performative component of his gesture: "The question of whether or not to eat human flesh is more important than the result. . . . You are not a cannibal if you eat art." The procedure produced enough fat for forty meatballs, which he canned and sold for a thousand dollars apiece.[53]

EATING THE ANIMATOR, AND VICE VERSA

The final segment of Švankmajer's *Food* is "Dinner." After the movie's episodes of pica and the run-up to cannibalism, it somehow seems logical that the next diners would devour their own limbs, breasts, and genitals, all of which are appetizingly plated. Švankmajer's actors perform their self-cannibalism at one of Western civilization's most ritualized performance sites, the fine restaurant. The imagery is disconcerting for many reasons, principally because the act of eating oneself fragments the expected integrity of the body metaphysically as well as physically. In Ruzante's sixteenth-century comedy *Most Facetious Dialogue,* the title of which strangely anticipates the sections of Švankmajer's *Dimensions of Dialogue,* the protagonist decides to eat himself to solve two problems at once: he will both spite his unfaithful lover and fill his belly. "I shall kill myself," recites Menego, "and it will be even better, because I myself shall eat me, and so I shall die well-nourished, in defiance of the famine." Camporesi notes, "The grotesque effect is surprisingly successful and of an irresistible humour (at least for us); except that the weighing and the interpretation could be modified, keeping in mind that episodes of this sort—here only imagined for the amusement of the noble listeners—were actually taking place outside the theatre."[54] *Food* is similarly instrumental because of its allegorical derision of the failed social programs of the politicians. When considered from the perspective of performance, however, animated representations of cannibalism and self-eating—sometimes humorous, sometimes aggressively disgusting—also evidence the tendency of animation to re-perform the processes and concepts by which the films were made.

The thing being eaten is the animators' handiwork, which in these films serves as a representation of (that is, an avatar of) the animator in the film, the animator as a proxy for ordinary individuals or artists in society, or of animation as a mode of film production. Therefore, when the animators attack, kill, or eat their avatars and other products of their own creation, they are turning the self-destruction of their work into autophagic performances. The filmmakers create their Tooniverse only to consume it. Applying this line of thinking to *Food,* the instances of cannibalization become increasingly outlandish, but we tolerate them as parody. By the third episode, though, the content is so over-the-top that some viewers might find the vignettes more abhorrent than comic, which might have been Švankmajer's intention. If the first sections are political satire, the scenes of a man fashioning a crude wooden prosthesis to hold a fork in order to eat his "real" hand and the man preparing to feast on his own privates (who, seemingly embarrassed, pushes the camera away from the plate) may distract us from whatever metaphoric instrumentality the film might have had. Švankmajer exploits the uncanny valley effect too, since, although it's obvious that the lifelike body parts are painted clay, their realistic appearance is too convincing for comfort. Referring to the "indexical" nature of cinematic representation, which Švankmajer seems to be exploiting and parodying, Thomas Lamarre has written, "This is what I think of as a 'consummated world'. It is a world that is consummated in the sense of completed. It is also consummated in the sense of consumed; it is already swallowed and digested, or always read for consumption. Of course, if cinema can be seen as a consummated world, it is partly because it has for so long been a staple for consumers."[55] *Food* constructs its allegories of engorgement and self-consumption as metaphors of his "consummated" society, certainly. Furthermore, however, his films reflect how animators habitually create works that consume the worlds they have created and to which they belong.

Stepping back further, if the scenes of food preparation and consumption around these restaurant tables are parallels to the work of the animation business, then showing it as pointless and self-destructive is a different level of autophagous performance. Sometimes autoingestion is a formal device, as in the sequences of visual metamorphoses showing objects transforming from one to another. Sometimes it's the narrative structure turning back on itself that signals self-cancellation, as in Out of the Inkwell, where each film ends as it began, back in the inkwell.

Metamorphosis is autophagic in two fundamental ways. Set in motion by the animators—or their primordial hand—the forms come into being by swallowing up the ones before them and cease to exist when they are eaten by their successors. And, to the extent that the on-screen bodies represent the animators' creative processes, their termination reflects the demise of the filmmaker. This was apparent in Cohl's distinctive style of graphic narration, a James Joycean (or Freudian) stream of consciousness visualized with flowing unstable pictures and lines. *Brains Repaired* (*Le retapeur de cervelles*, Emile Cohl/Pathé Frères, 1910) illustrates this magnificently convoluted idea of animated self-cannibalism. Cohl's plots often used a monstrator figure (one who

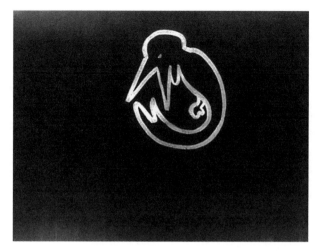

FIGURE 62. *Brains Repaired* (1910). The parasite forms itself into a bird that consumes itself, tail first.

shows us something, readily seen as the animator's avatar), such as a magician, scientist, clown, or artist who conjures up the animated imagery. Here it is a doctor who employs a fanciful X-ray-like device to peer into a patient's brain. Amid the thoughts dancing through the cerebral cortex—literally in the case of a Russian dancer—the doctor finds a ravenous parasite. The white worm's physical shape becomes a white line in Cohl's animation when he spins out his incoherent metamorphoses.

The nightmarish imagery and bizarre transformations within the patient's brain are every bit as awful as the shifting shapes in *Muto,* especially since they are being produced by the brain worm as it consumes its cerebral host. But of course the worm/lines are direct visualizations of the man's thoughts; so his consciousness is destroying itself. As if to emblematize this, in one metamorphosis a bird eats itself Ouroboros-style (Figure 62). In another, a man's mouth consumes his own face (Figure 63). A nutcracker or Polichinelle character transforms into a house and a man emerges from its window. The house morphs into a smiling face and chews up the man with satisfaction—and so on it goes. These bodies are contingent, dialectical, and organic, each serving as an intermediary image connecting the ones before and after it. Plympton's *Your Face* (1987), which is a nearly continuous metamorphosis of body violations and self-ingestions centered on a man's insipidly smiling face

FIGURE 63. *Brains Repaired* (1910). A face eats itself.

(Figure 64), carries on the autophagous performances until the final shot—and beyond. There the earth swallows the oft-eaten face, followed by a postcredits belch.

There clearly are parallels between cinematic metamorphosis and digestion. Nottingham's thoughts about the performativity of food also apply to the filmic process. It "represents the negotiations between self and other, interior and exterior, through its uneasy relationship to excrement. Food is ultimately transformed into excrement, which in turn will fertilize the soil for the production of more food. Excrement is the underworld, the lower, meeting the sunlight from above to form the life that inhabits an intermediary reality."[56] Whether in cultural practices, religious services, or social interactions or as an artistic act, eating food is still an important component of the performance of everyday life, though it is generally less orgiastic than in the olden days of Rabelais and Ruzante. In animation, these self-consuming images demonstrate how the work enlists and exhausts its creative processes.

Powerful themes of self-ingestion run throughout McCay's graphic and cinematic work. For the prologue of his first film, *Little Nemo* (Winsor McCay/Vitagraph, 1911), the cartoonist chose not to re-create his vaudeville stage presentation where the footage was first used.[57] Instead, he dramatized a fictitious dinner for a gathering of fellow Hearst cartoonists, integrating his performance within an established social ritual. The high point in the animated segment occurs when the protagonists,

FIGURE 64. *Your Face* (1987). A face consumes and regenerates itself in endless metamorphoses. Original in color. Courtesy of Bill Plympton.

Nemo and the Princess, enter the seat of a chariot that turns out to be mouth of a living dragon (Figure 65), which is perhaps patterned on the Dragon's Gorge, a "scenic railway" built at Luna Park, Coney Island. Visitors on that ride entered through the monster's mouth. The cartoon dragon transports Nemo and the Princess out of the frame. This would have ended the film except for the coda, in which Dr. Pill and the cannibal Impy return—only to have their bodies blown to bits.

Gertie was infused with ritual eating. In the filmed prologue, it is not the context of the vaudeville show but rather another dinner party that sets the scene for the cartoon dinosaur's prodigious appetite. The movie gathering echoes the extravagant dinners at which the 1914 film had its initial performances. "The newspaper artists of this city," according to the *Times* account, "met for a beefsteak supper at midnight last night at Reisenweber's Restaurant, Seventh Avenue and Fifty-eighth Street. Some 200 illustrators were present, representing most of the newspapers published in New York. A vaudeville performance was given while supper was served, one feature of which was the comic 'movies' drawn by Winsor McCay."[58] So there were nested gustatory performances in this original presentation: a film about eating was set within the filmed framing story of a banquet, projected at just such a banquet, with the artist performing his work "live" at the banquet, performing it filmed within the film of the banquet, and performing as an animated self-drawing

FIGURE 65. *Little Nemo* (1911). Nemo and the Princess enter the dragon-chariot's mouth. Original in color.

within the film—in which his drawing of a dinosaur takes his avatar into its mouth.

As the cartoonists at Reisenweber's and those in the fictional dinner party feasted on their multicourse dinners (was rarebit on the menu?), the dinosaur in the film demonstrates its own gluttonous pica, gulping down whole trees and drinking a lake, its monumental abdomen swelling as the water is ingested. As though offering himself to Gertie as dessert, McCay steps into the dinosaur's mouth to exit, reprising the scene in which Nemo entered the dragon's mouth (Figure 66). Gertie, like McCay's Impy, the dragon, and Steve, are lovable monsters—sympathetic, even adorable, but also fearsome, capable of killing and eating humans.

Flip's Circus (McCay, 1918–21) survives only as unedited fragments, yet it is one of McCay's most intriguing autophagous performances. Flip, the character from Slumberland whom we met in *Little Nemo*, now re-performs McCay's roles in *Gertie* as a trainer and as McCay's avatar. Flip brings Baby Wiffenpoof onto the stage within the film.[59] In contrast to Gertie, this huge critter is a good-natured dullard. Unlike McCay's verbal coaxing of Gertie, Flip pounds on his exhibit with a large club. Mimicking a lion tamer, Flip attempts to perform the old head-in-the-mouth trick. Baby promptly swallows him (Figure 67). Flip manages to get himself regurgitated and gives his "pet" another sound beating.

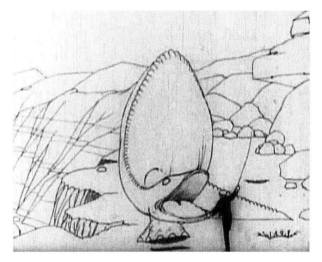

FIGURE 66. *Gertie* (1914). The dinosaur scoops McCay's avatar into her mouth.

Although *Dream of the Rarebit Fiend: Bug Vaudeville* (with Robert McCay, 1921) is one of McCay's least interesting films from the point of view of cinematic and animation technique, it does astonish at the end. An overeating hobo falls asleep and dreams he is in the front row of an insect vaudeville show.[60] For the grand finale of its act, the giant spider suddenly seizes the hobo by the head and begins to eat him, which causes the man to wake up. Understandably, he swears off cakes. McCay uses the dream of the catastrophic demise of the protagonist to provide a suitably autophagous moral: he who gorges may dream of being gorged upon. Furthermore, the liveness of the spider performer is hazardous to the viewers for whom the hobo is also an avatar. If the spider were to transgress the theatrical space of the screen as it had crossed the metaleptic boundary of the stage in the film, it might eat the movie audience too.

Autophagy is emblematic of the power structures in the animator-animated relationship in the films of McCay and others. By giving their toons the need and capability to eat, cartoonists embody their characters' liveness. By making the objects they feast upon impossibly outrageous, they also insist on their status as constructed beings. Having them eat the animator confirms the hierarchical relationships often deployed in animated performances; indeed, it's the power arrangement of the hand of the artist motif. As described in chapter 2, it's a competition

FIGURE 67. *Flip's Circus* (1918–21). Baby Wiffenpoof eats Flip and then regurgitates him.

for agency. The toons are created by the animators, become independent beings, and then rebel or threaten the creators, in these cases rationalized as digestive and cannibalistic motifs.[61]

Films with such imagery and narratives are self-begetting because they incorporate into their performances the circular mechanisms by which they came into being, whether sequential images on paper or a cursor on a computer screen. "This device of a narrative which is in effect a record of its own genesis," writes Steven G. Kellman of the analogous self-begetting novel, "is a happy fusion of form and content. We are at once confronted with both process and product, quest and goal, parent and child."[62] The animated figures' freethinking, their volition, and their very being has been brought about by means of a technology that has been specially designed to produce this cunning replay of its own conditions of existence.

In a quintessential example, Ko-Ko turns the tables on Sketcher Max, who has been torturing him in *Invisible Ink* (Dave Fleischer/Out of the Inkwell Films, 1921). Ko-Ko, here as Max's avatar (as well as Director Dave's), rebels against him by spraying him with ink, thus inking the inker. Then the clown "directs" Max, as a movie director does an actor, by drawing a chalk line that Max is obliged to follow out of the studio and into the neighborhood of New York City tenements.[63] Ko-Ko next becomes an animator, replicating his own image in dozens

FIGURE 68. *Invisible Ink* (1921). Eating the animation: Ko-Ko dives into Max's mouth.

of self-portraits on animation sheets. Finally, Ko-Ko plunges into Max's mouth (Figure 68). Instead of descending into his intestines, as Cohl's protagonist did, or leaving the film, as McCay did in *Gertie,* Ko-Ko stays in Max's head a bit until he emerges from his ear (rather as in *Your Face).* This is an act of autophagy, then, because Max eats his avatar Ko-Ko to thwart him from hijacking the film, thus ending the avatar's rebellion and also the cartoon.

Take *Jumping Beans* (Dave Fleischer/Out of the Inkwell Films, 1922), in which Sketcher Max, again the malicious animator, torments Ko-Ko with Mexican jumping beans. Ko-Ko swears, "I'll fix you for this," devises a rubber stamp that allows him to take on the animator function, and prints dozens of replicas of himself. The clone army of drawings springs into life and leaves the sketchpad to attack Max. The animated beings steal the animation from the avatar (Max) by immobilizing him.[64] This performance, like the one in *Brains Repaired,* enacts a fundamental anxiety: can the products of our imagination, meant to entertain, turn on us and do us harm? The Fleischers' series constructed a cosmology in which the creative force is matched by the ever-present threat of extinction. Kellman cites Out of the Inkwell as an example of the circular narrative device: "The self-begetting novel, like Fleischer's cartoons, projects the illusion of art creating itself. Truly *samizdat,* in the original sense of 'self-publishing,' it is an account, usually first-person, of the development of a character to the point at which he is

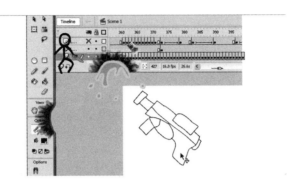

FIGURE 69. *Animator vs. Animation* (2006). Figures made with Flash animation use the Flash tools on the desktop to attack the animator. Original in color. Courtesy of Alan Becker.

able to take up his pen and compose the novel we have just finished reading."[65]

The self-begetting and -ending narrative has been updated in Blu's films and in *Animator vs. Animation* (Alan Becker, 2006).[66] The animator is again unseen, but its puppet master–like agency appears as the cursor on the computer screen, a modern form of the hand of the artist. Rather than ink, the tools used to create the animation are the controls and formatting palette of the software Adobe Flash. The animator draws a simple stick figure in a box, labels it "Victim," and pokes, spins, and torments it. The figure escapes, fights back, and turns the desktop into a battleground. It successfully neutralizes the animator's fanciful weapons and, at one point, grabs the "eraser" from the tool bar and wipes out the "delete" function to save itself. As did Ko-Ko, this figure is able to replicate itself, this time using Flash's library function (Figure 69). The clones destroy the software that was the means of their own production and attempt to obliterate the victimizer-animator as well. In place of the inkwell, always the site of the end of Ko-Ko's transient existence (to be followed by a new beginning in the next film), here there is the "exit" command. The stick figures may not leave the screen to enter the animator's world, though, and finally the animator reasserts control by ending the session and opting not to save the file. However rebellious the animation, and however successful the little rebels' on-screen efforts to kill their creator, the animator as the constructive agent ultimately has the power *of* the performance.

In Plympton's *Eat*, we first see circles metamorphosing in abstract patterns, which are eventually revealed to be rain falling in a puddle. A

FIGURE 70. *Eat* (2000). The animator's avatar, a diner, eats his spaghetti, which is also his outline, which is also the animator's line drawing. Original in color. Courtesy of Bill Plympton.

diner enters a restaurant and his imagination weaves a voluptuous female dining companion out of a plate of spaghetti. After some funny and disgusting eating scenes, the film ends with the diner sucking the strands of pasta into his mouth. He keeps going until he finishes the spaghetti woman and then the table. Finally he consumes his own outline, thus eating himself into oblivion (Figure 70). The narrative tells of the creation of the narrative out of the avatar's musings and ends by eating itself . . . and him.

Discussing his film *The Big Upgrade* (2007), writer-director James Dick touched upon the anxiety induced by the industry's changeover from traditional cel techniques to computer design: "In 2004 Disney announced that *Home on the Range* [Will Finn and John Sanford/Disney, 2004] would be their last hand drawn film. The field in which we were entering, computer animation, was no longer complementing the art of cel animation, as was the case with *Aladdin* or *The Lion King,* it had conquered it. Animation's autophagy caused a deep ambivalence towards my future career."[67]

Dick's film is a parable of how CGI animation consumes not only technology but also traditional animation themes (such as the hand of the artist) and generic practices (like Acme animation techniques and mickey-mousing music). He cynically addresses the resulting obsolescence of character embodiment as well as alienating technology after the "upgrade" to digital compositing and animation. The title of the film is reminiscent of *The Big Sleep* and, similarly, a euphemism for death. We see a pseudo-Mickey named Rickey the Rat, whom we may assume is an avatar of the traditional cel-based animator, enter a sleek foyer decorated with menacing lobby art suggestive of computer-animated box office hits like *Finding Nemo*. Rickey is rather the worse for wear, sporting a bitten-off ear, threadbare gloves, and worn-out shoes. Floyd, his old manager, greets him, prompting a flood of nostalgia (for "The Sorcerer's Apprentice") from Rickey: "Remember those brooms? And all that water? . . . And that steamboat sure was swell." He whistles "Steamboat Bill" from *Steamboat Willie*. Floyd quashes Rickey's peppy reminiscences and leads him into the darkened former animation studio: "Rickey, you've got to realize . . . this business, it's changed a lot." As dust motes drift in the gloom, Rickey is startled to meet Miss Harrington, executive producer of new projects, and her companion, an anthropomorphic Luxo light, Pixar's corporate logo appearing in a cameo role. Rickey gives his old magic wand a flick, producing a little pixie dust à la Tinkerbelle, but it doesn't impress the new regime. An old animation stand attacks Rickey and presses him into his aboriginal form on a cel. Until this point the toon has been rendered as a three-dimensional character, but now he's a lifeless two-dimensional drawing (Plate 15). Floyd discards the cel into a box with others. *The Big Upgrade* illustrates a common attitude about new media that Lamarre summarizes (before critiquing it), "The basic problem remains. How can the replication or simulation of something dead result in life? To become animated (or reanimated), cinema must be seen as dead or at least completely motionless."[68] The developing mythology of New Media seems to be that advancing technology must define itself by consuming or destroying its rivals.

ANIMATION IN THE BLENDER OF THEORY

Imagining the inside of the body as a performance space where digestion, gestation, and so on are showcased, using eating and its associations as subject matter, depicting cannibalism and autophagy literally or allusively, and creating self-generating, self-consuming narratives have become bound up with animation film stories. Sometimes they symbolically narrate their films' and animators' own creative annihilation. Like horror films, cartoons fascinate while they appall.

Animators have repeatedly used these performances to parallel the processing of food and artistic production. This is one of Švankmajer's tactics. He shows food as having its own animism, as susceptible to natural decay and thus putatively outside the control of the filmmaker.

Michael O'Pray has characterized this powerful vision as "transformational animation."[69] Like digestion, the films process raw materials into another form. The feature *Faust* (Jan Švankmajer, 1994), for example, is a self-begetting and -consuming narrative that orchestrates enigmatic recurring scenes: A red car repeatedly drives up to the protagonist and speeds away. A man is running off (we learn that he'll become the saga's next victim/protagonist). The current protagonist keeps seeing a furtive old man carrying a severed human leg. These foreboding incidents come together at the end when the red car collides with the protagonist and severs his leg, the old man steals it and runs away, and the story resets to the beginning. Along the way, Švankmajer seasons the plot with gratuitous culinary eccentricity (which the filmmaker describes *ludic,* that is, defining itself as play), including unsavory hints of pica, cannibalism, and autophagy. "The whole process of eating can thus be made intensely erotic," Švankmajer wrote, "or it can be translated into a cannibalistic and aggressive act through which accumulated misanthropy can be released. In any case such activity can become ludic, and as such is no longer perceived merely as an act of filling the belly."[70]

Performances that turn the body's processing of food, whatever the source, into symbols, metaphors, and rituals are essential components of the folk-festive mode. Such rituals connect food and the earth.[71] In this sense, many works by Cohl, the Fleischers and Blu and some Hollywood cartoons are also transformational. They muddle the metaphor of digestion with playful metamorphosis. But to what end? These films play with the possibility that animation may, during its conceptualization, also generate the cells of its own destruction. This critical motif of the morbidity of the form itself is encountered frequently in current animation theory. "The art of enabling the spectator to envision the dead as alive is a characteristic feature of animation," writes Richard Weihe. "In this respect animation film seems paradigmatic of film as such the premise of which is the spectator's willing acceptance of the moving image as a representation of 'life.' "[72]

Hervé Joubert-Laurencin writes about the morbid fixation on the human body in animation. Folding performance back on material form, he notes that this screen violence is emblematic of animation techniques' disruption of "normal" cinematography:

> The human "body" is strangely fetishized in animation. Jerry Mouse martyrs the body of Tom Cat; the Hand of Power or that of a vengeful God martyrs Trnka's potter's body [in *The Hand,* Jiřrí Trnka, 1965]. Toons are sliced, puppets are disjointed and modeling clay is tortured, from Will Vinton's

caricatures to Jan Švankmajer's aggressive surrealism, to the neighbors' appalling tooth and nail fight accompanied by McLaren's scratching on the optical sound track [in *Neighbours,* Norman McLaren, 1952], etc., etc. If this is a horrifying Punch and Judy, it's always in pieces. And isn't it a strange butchery when Norman McLaren arranges "the bones, the flesh and the blood" in the invisible interstices of the film, while telling us that these components have been organically reassembled, having been hidden by the "clothes" of images, these "vestments of meaning"?[73]

Joubert-Laurencin alludes to the two kinds of violence demonstrated in *Neighbours.* On one level, there is the on-screen mutual annihilation of the protagonists (who are animated human actors) as they hack at each other. (They are made up as "cannibals" at one point.) Creating such scenes demanded the filmmaker's physical assault on the filmed scene as he started and stopped the camera to expose the single frames required to animate the actors. Therefore, rephrasing Joubert-Laurencin in our terms, he distinguishes between the performances *in* the animation (the actors' behavior on the screen, their poses) and the filmmaker's performance *of* the animation (during the shooting, between the frames). He thus implies that the animated film itself is an organic body that lives or brings to life, paradoxically, only when cinematography "kills" what it is filming in real time.

The animator's ability to re-perform life logically makes death a spectacle. Alan Cholodenko has observed that there is a zombie complex at work preying on our fascination with the undead. According to him, "Animation always has something of the inanimate about it, that it is a certain inanimateness that both allows and disallows animation. Animation therefore could never be only animation. It is both and neither animation and nonanimation at the same time."[74]

Animator as creator and as death angel at once is gloomy to contemplate, yet it is consistent with the development of the medium's alimentary conceits. McCay's animation career began with intimations of divinity as he wagered he could reanimate long-dead beasts. But underlying his Faustian powers was also the intimation of the inevitable end. The animators of the 1930s who felt compelled to make instrumental narratives about coping with Depression hardships embodied optimistic personifications of harmony and communitas through labor in their pigs, bunnies, and hungry orphans, but they dematerialized them by suggesting the inevitability of their deaths.

But enough fatalism. Certainly these invocations of extreme eating were and are outside audiences' comfort zones, but then that's part of their morbid, possibly erotic, and therefore vorephilic attraction. Sado-masochism floats on the surface of the Fleischers' tormenting Ko-Ko the Clown, of the voracious competition among screen animals, and of *South Park*'s oft-killed Kenny. Digestion motifs and autophagy are often soaked in irony, like the modern art of the twentieth century that was made to be destroyed intentionally or that self-annihilated. One thinks of Man Ray's "Object to be Destroyed" (1923) or Jean Tinguely's hybrid of sculpture and performance piece, "Machine Designed to Self-Destruct" (1960). As in self-begetting literature, autophagic animation, and artworks that cancel their own existence, the pointlessness of the production is exactly the point. María Lorenzo Hernández has observed a similar irony in animation, "Visual metaphors and metonymies arise from any community of form or function, which creates rhetorical links. The discovery of a secondary meaning enables a double speech, operating through parallelism, substitution, or even euphemism."[75] Thus the preoccupation with autophagy and death in animation may, ironically, be life affirming too. These melancholic sides to animated films are certainly instrumental, warning us of rapacious wolves or repressive regimes, but they are also ludic and redemptive and provide playrooms for the game of "what if." True, animation implies counteranimation, but don't forget: unlike us, toons never die. Contemporary performance art goes even further, moving the site of meaning production away from content, the performance *in*, and toward the expressivity of the medium (performers' bodies, video, multimedia installations, etc.), that is, the performance *of* performance.

Now more than ever, we see the media and their publics obsessed with gastronomy and cuisine as performances. Cooking shows appear on two dedicated food cable channels. Several reality programs, including *Man v. Food Nation*,[76] show us nothing but competitive and extreme eating (of live bugs and reptiles, ten-pound burritos, and excessive spices, for example). Public food preparation and presentations abound, such as knife-flipping hibachi chefs at the Japanese restaurant, burger-flipping dads at the weekend barbecue party, and wedding-cake-smearing brides and grooms, to name just a few of the diverse manifestations of food as cultural performance. In the opinion of Kirshenblatt-Gimblett, "Food, and all that is associated with it, is already larger than life. It is already highly charged with meaning and affect. It is already performative and theatrical. An art of the concrete, food, like performance, is alive, fugitive and sensory."[77] From the enthusiastic gorgers at the pie-eating contest to the couple dining out on an intimate date, public consumption may be a ritual means to an end that has nothing at all to do with nutrition.[78]

In parthenogenetic and autophagic forms of animation, reflexive as always, scenes showing bodies' creation and destruction as well as scenes of performative eating may be symptomatic of animation's relation to its enveloping culture. As a place where these extremes may be pictured and imaginatively transmuted into entertainment, we see that such cinema is far from marginal; it functions at the core of society. Its presence is systemic, biological, reflecting how our society organizes itself to accommodate our physical needs and functions. It also may be instrumental, inoculating. These displays call attention to the impulse to gorge, to binge on junk food, to patronize fast-food establishments that serve fare inconducive to good health. Whatever the ramifications, all is fair game, of course, for animated witticism and self-parody. The idea of a snake eating its own tail may be fraught with much metaphysical symbolism, but it's also, after all, pretty funny.

Coda

The Shadow of a Mouse's Tail

This expedition through the solar system of animated performance has not touched all the possible planets, but we've gathered a lot of information and racked up plenty of speculations. The conjecturing about, if not the answering of, our initial questions will continue.

I've said that the performative is a galaxy of relationships. Now, at the end of this volume, it feels more like we've been on the organ-hopping trip through the human body in *Fantastic Voyage* (Richard Fleischer, 1966), which probably would have been an equally apt metaphor for our of journey of discovery. Although this book is in no way an effort to chronicle, to describe, or—heaven help us—to explain animation cinema of the past 110 years, certain modes of production, formal structures, modes of screen acting, and content leitmotivs have become apparent. Each of these aspects involves the performing human body in some way.

Early animation at first was a filmmaking technique. Only gradually did it differentiate itself with characteristic ideas, specialized subjects, and audience expectations to become an identifiable subcategory of cinema. Animation once shared cinematography's unrelenting interest in picturing the body moving in space, and it still does. McCay's *Little Nemo* characters expand, shrink, explode, float, and tumble in an ambiguous space suitable for weightless astronauts. I say *ambiguous* because the space in which the characters perform would have fascinated contemporaneous Cubist painters, being readable simultaneously as the artist's white paper and as the proxy space of the characters on the white screen. As in analogous modernist images, the "ground"—that is, the space—is as of much interest as the "figure."

When animation entered its industrialized phase in the 1920s, the filmmakers and engineers, both in tandem and independently, developed the mechanical tools necessary to automate the formerly manual labor of production. The films produced using these implements still showed evidence of the "hand of the artist," which we may now see as a performance that overtly or covertly drew attention to the filmmakers' agency and the work of their own creation. These tools—animation disks, stands, cels, and so forth—were engineered to facilitate the animators' own bodywork. The great schism between the animated image on cel and on background, when finally repaired by the animatographic apparatus (that is, after having been photographed and projected), enabled the filmmakers to energize their toon actors. Ironically, the highly restrictive, artificially bifurcated spatial system of animation technology enabled extraordinary performances that happened in kinetic worlds not to be seen or experienced anywhere before and not reproducible in "regular" filmmaking before the introduction of digital techniques. Classic animation production, with its Acme basis and its assembly-line division of labor, allowed the filmmakers to express their imagined somatic performances with all the ease enjoyed by their non-animation cinema colleagues, not to mention poets, painters, comic strip artists, and vaudeville gagsters.

In animation's first eighty or so years, it was the settled institutions that cultivated and satisfied the national curiosity about and adulation of performing bodies that informed animation. These included traveling circuses, athletic leagues, and exhibitions (both intellectual and burlesque), as well as, of course, vaudeville. (Like cinema, these entertainments were founded on a high-speed transportation system, locomotives that could whisk troupes, divas, teams, menageries, and cans of movie prints from town to town overnight.)

The persistence of vaudeville-like forms and content throughout animation's history seems puzzling until we realize that emulating vaudeville was one of the animators' many world-making strategies. Although it wasn't necessary to have direct knowledge about popular variety theater to make or enjoy the films, one nevertheless became aware that in many cartoons an external structure was in place, that the subjects of stories or the nature of the gags referenced some archetype. Vaudeville,

I have argued, was a handy imaginative world that animators could offer as a means of engaging moviegoers who were willing to accept it as reconstructed or synthesized memory. I freely admit that I have never attended a vaudeville performance except vicariously in my research and in the form of documentary films and movie re-creations, and yet I feel confident that I know its appeal as performance, at least partly—and infectiously, as it were—through my cartoon watching and those films' memory palaces.

Vaudeville was convenient, too, for a film form that delighted in endlessly repeating its bills, that is, re-performing its own past and its origins. That cyclical concept of the entertainment package enabled filmmakers to work within an existing archaeological genre, the vaudevillesque, much as a composer might sit down to compose a waltz rather than a fox-trot. Vaudeville was also the origin of some basic assumptions about the formation of cartoon space. The shallowness of the stage's apron and curtain often defined the performative world of vaude-villians, not unlike the world in certain animation shots where the action is restricted to the 2-D space of the cel in contrast to the deeper space of the background. Much of the interest in and immersiveness of animation comes from the flow of action across these spaces.

While non-animated cinema was stoking its audiences' affection for melodrama and comedy, many animators were aiming lower, for vaude-villian slapstick and gags, for the readymade populist content of comic strips, and for the nether stratum of human expression. This was the domain of comedy based on performative violence, ingestion, penetration, explosion, and expulsion. Of course, not all animation is completely Dionysian—*Playful Pluto* is perhaps about as Apollonian as it gets. Nevertheless, it now seems clear that as the genre developed, cartoons gravitated toward the tail end of the comedic animal.

It's true that Walt Disney publicly repudiated the kind of filmmaking that he and his rivals made before the mid-1930s, but a close look at his changeover from the figurative mode of acting to the embodied has revealed that the transition was never fully achieved. Disney pursued the ideal of embodied acting as the artistic benchmark of his films, closely basing his performances on Hollywood acting, especially that informed by Stanislavskian methods. While his animators were becoming extraordinarily proficient at that, other layout and background artists on the staff were pursuing a performativity based on dynamic shapes, light, color, and design—in other words, applying a system of representation deriving not so much from feature filmmaking as from the aesthetics of art school. The results were performances that are brilliant hybrids of classical composition, children's book illustration, and California watercolor. Furthermore, the filmmakers generally did not completely reject the figurative expressions of classic cartoons: caricaturing, metamorphosing, stretching, and squashing; addressing audiences by glances at the "camera"; and breaking the theatrical fourth wall. Disney's films therefore are filled with fascinating internal tensions.

The signature style of the Mouse began to transform in the 1940s. This happened not only for the purely political and economic reasons given in the standard studio histories, but also because audiences' tastes changed. Figurative performances of the sort seen in postwar Warner Bros. cartoons, Walter Lantz's Woody Woodpecker series, Tex Avery's MGM films, and, most notably, United Productions of America films, captured the public's imagination. Perhaps moviegoers just preferred their cartoon characters to have modern design flair and to embody their favorite toon performers with their own interests, narratives, and imaginations rather than the overwrought heroes and heroines of Disney. Of course, the Disney studio eventually rededicated itself to figurative expression, for example, by relying on recognizable characters that were already icons from American mythology. Johnny Appleseed, Casey Jones and Paul Bunyan, for example, exhibited simplified forms, inhabited uncomplicated spaces and gave figurative body performances, which audiences seemed to prefer.

Although it's not possible to generalize about the vast range of animated stories that have been produced, I have nevertheless tried to reach some conclusions about the philosophical questions of how the animated body differs from the inanimate, how and why the animated body has been so horrifically and hilariously deformed and mutilated in cartoons through the ages. Over time this violent struggle for agency in animation narratives has engendered ideologies of consumption, with metaphors mixing real and symbolic digestion, and life and death.

We may say that, yes, animated cartoon stars like Betty, Mickey, the Disney princesses, Pokémon, and the others are real.* And they are live.* The qualifying asterisks refer to the arguments in this book. Although I've jumped through some hoops to reach this conclusion, I claim that liveness in animation (and, I have to say, in cinema, stage drama, and perhaps all performances) comes down to everyday systems of belief. As participants and consumers, we develop degrees of trust about everything in the world around us. This includes what's real and live and what isn't. As Auslander has pointed out, some fans at a rock concert may not consider the performance to be "live," authentic, or even real if the show on the stage lacks the electronic interventions of the recording studio. We grant contingent existence, liveness, reality to such performances when it serves our current needs, conforms to our socially determined mores, or fits the patterns of behavior we bring to entertainment and/or to art. That's why "reality TV" is not an oxymoron; the real is not in the medium but in the viewer's volition. The same is true of toons. There is no frog alive in a real blender in "Frog in a Blender," any more than our favorite toon characters are alive. But their performances and our performances too are as real as we deem them to be. We navigate through our days according to various belief systems, some of them the mundane ones studied by cognitive psychologists, some that make up our *Matrix*-like existential worlds and the ideologies contained therein, and some that we hold just for fun.

This doesn't mean that we experience the Tooniverse in a lonely existential void. On the contrary, animation, especially in its classical theatrical phase, has been a communal activity, with parents and children, children and children, and moviegoers of all ages and persuasions participating in its reception. These films continue to provide us outlets for ecstasy, for getting happy and for looking at our world askance. They bring joyous, accusative, mirthful, and caustic experiences to our lives. There has also been a bond of expectation between the animators and their anticipated audiences as the filmmakers imagine the reaction of the viewers when their films are performed for them. Audiences expect certain patterns and ways of representing bodies in their cartoon entertainment. Even now, there are limited but lively interchanges of ideas and conversations about animated videos in the comments sections of online video websites, on blogs, and in the social media.

Paradoxically, animated films are often used as authorities about what is real. Their ability to reduce the optical world to its haptic essence has made animation a useful medium for films that are instructional (for instance, on how to load and clean rifles), educational (tutorials on how to keep teeth healthy), or medical (on how diseases spread in the body). In these cases, we trust the films to represent truth as a visual, moving abstraction—the unreal performing the real.

Performing the unreal, though, has been animation's stock-in-trade for most of its existence. Even Disney was outspoken about avoiding the too real, insisting on terms such as *illusion* and *caricature* to express his desire not to plunge into the uncanny valley of photorealism. Accordingly, we've seen that animators have been adept at generating proximal liveness, creating the impression that something is as close to being alive as it can be without magically being alive. Although illusionists populate their films, animators never claimed to be magicians themselves. They may be mediums or shamans, but they're metaphorical ones. In any case, they're facilitators for viewers who will consummate the performances by adding their own imaginative liveness to the animators' precursor bodies. Underlying this debate, it now appears, isn't simply the question of liveness but the issue of humanness, and how the representational media have clung to the human image that is at the center.

Animation may be symptomatic of the twentieth and possibly the twenty-first centuries' serious testing of anthropocentricity—from the heights of humanistic affirmation to the depths of posthuman malaise. Over and over, films have examined and tortured the integrity of the human form. We have grasped this performance as part of larger philosophical explorations. Although the equipment originally designed to make animated films was designed to extend the human body's agency, symbolized by the hand, after the big upgrade to computer animation there are no longer physical megamachines. The laptop has replaced the hulking metal monsters that Acme made. Now there are apps for palm-size smartphones that allow one to draw, shoot, edit, and disseminate animation. Talk about the hand of the artist!

It may be, then, that all animation performances are fundamentally figurative because they are symbols and metaphors of human behaviors. Furthermore, like all cultural expressions and artifacts, they reference the times in which they were made and are microcosmic images of the circumstances of their own production. This provides a possible response to questions that may arise about lacunae in my book. It might legitimately be asked, for example, where are the women? Although there have been many significant female animators in recent years, for most of the twentieth century there were precious few involved on the front end of animating. Their performances *in* animation during the classic period fell within a triangle whose corners were the princess (Snow White and her progeny), the showgirl (Betty Boop), and the paradoxically androgynous yet sexy (Olive Oyl).[1] These few figurations of femininity, maternity, objectivity, and marginality may have reflected society's prevailing view of women as absent necessities of the bourgeois family structure.

Behind the screen, however, animation was a woman's industry. We must consider the hundreds (thousands?) of female laborers who inked, painted, and did the countless other invisible but necessary chores to bring the animators' work to the screens. In a reflexive form such as animation, we should be able to locate their avatars. But we'd usually be looking in vain, since the female toon population (except maybe Betty Boop, whose situation is complicated) was represented with little agency. Perhaps all those cartoon assembly lines showing synchronized communities producing useful things (as, for example, in *Father Noah's Ark*), is the place to look. Those tireless toon workers figure the women's tedious, repetitive work, where the job is making films about laborers who whistle while they work at their tedious, repetitive jobs. In the film stories, these workers—usually cute furry mammals—put up no resistance to long hours with no pay.

Traditional animation plots have mapped out schematics of creative power since the earliest days. In the persistent "hand of the artist" motif, the figure of the animator might understandably be assumed to be masculine or paternal because the physical animators were males. But the motif alternatively might be seen as embodying maternal narrative forces that birthed the creations. The problematic gendering of the animator as male is theological. It was always God the Father who was the Animator with capital *A*. An argument can be made, however, for reconceiving the animator function as feminine. This animatrix model would resonate better with the medium's long-established parthenogenesis narratives. The toons, then, become truculent children who eventually return to domesticity with the expectation that in their next incarnation they too will be life givers. Since there are many cinesthetic bodies in animation, who is to say that their genders are fixed by a priori assumptions? As readily as we may change the default genders of our avatars in video games, in virtual worlds, and perhaps in our everyday imagination, so may we shift the authorship of animation performance between animators and animatrices. Thus seemingly simple cartoons contain complicated lessons about the real body's arbitrariness, malleability, contingency, and eventual incorporeity.

The Tooniverse, whether existing at the outer edge of consciousness, like the solar system, or inside the confines of somatic forms, is itself a proxy space, expanding or contracting as necessary to accommodate its cartoon inhabitants and us, their visitors. Like most films in the classical mode, animation sustains our predilection for world-making. Susan Orlean described this well in the context of Rin Tin Tin's reception. It seemed "that Rin Tin Tin existed within the film and outside of the film at the same time. Within the film, he was a cinematic character in some cinematic predicament, existing in some other place or time. Outside the

film, he was Rin Tin Tin, the famous actor dog. Fusing those two manifestations together highlighted the artifice of film and the self-referential
nature of art, the fluid relationship we have with those things we imagine and create."[2]

Although this describes all performances to some extent, the situation of animal actors and cartoon characters invariably calls attention
to the constructed universe of cinema and animation. Stardom, whether
of the human, dog, or cartoon variety, is part of that construction and
therefore not biologically attached to any personage or species. Rather,
producers, publicists, and cultural inhabitants co-manufacture these
"fluid relationships," and thus no star—animal, human or toon—is
more or less real than any other. Furthermore, all stars exemplify camp,
since they're always playacting as something they're not.

We may know that the German shepherd breed did not exist in the
1870s, but for the purposes of the story, that fact is unproblematic. We
assign Rinty to the timescape proposed by the filmmakers. Analogously,
we know that Betty is made of pen and ink, but that is part of her
charm, not a liability. Animation, like dog movies, enables us to be in
two places at once, concretely in the fiction as a cinesthetic body, yet
happy in the knowledge that our molecules will stay put in the seat.

I have emphasized the role of competition among studios and the
importance of innovations in teaching the arts and skills of animation
at Disney. Reconsidering Disney's vision from the present era, it appears
that his studio's accomplishments were consistent with his generation's
views that progress in science and technology was inevitable and that
ultimately it would benefit civilization. Here is Lewis Mumford:

> Some of our most characteristic mechanical instruments—the telephone, the
> phonograph, the motion picture—have grown out of our interest in the hu-
> man voice and the human eye and our knowledge of their physiology and
> anatomy. Can one detect, perhaps, the characteristic properties of this emer-
> gent order—its pattern, its planes, its angle of polarization, its color? Can
> one, in the process of crystallization, remove the turbid residues left behind
> by our earlier forms of technology? Can one distinguish and define the spe-
> cific properties of a technics directed toward the service of life: properties
> that distinguish it morally, socially, politically, esthetically from the cruder
> forms that preceded it? Let us make the attempt.[3]

Not only did Disney and his lieutenants seem to subscribe to this strain
of technological determinism, but such thinking also seemed to under-
pin the actions of filmmakers such as Preston Sturges, who sought the
same goals through infectious laughter. Mumford's fusion of technol-

ogy and ethics is made easy because he sees modern inventions as extensions—re-performances, we might say—of the body's senses. This way of thinking parallels Disney's emphasis on the presence of self-contained bodily forms in his films of the late 1930s. Their implied internal skeletons, their solid exteriors that cast shadows, and their personalities evidencing thinking minds and forms that moved of their own accord: these were predicated on a vast invisible technology. Like Mumford, Disney seemed to believe that his cinema would become a new era for art and a new humanism, since it implied a utopian reconstruction not only of toons as automatons, but of the human body as an ideal image as well.

Utopias, unfortunately, tend to peter out quickly in the real world. Perhaps the continuing production of films that focus on violence, sex, and the slippery, inchoate performance spaces inside our bodies were reactions by animators to the clean, rational spaces that developed in classical animation with the aim of embodying toons by cinematic and theatrical methods. We now experience in our daily lives competing media visions of what animation should be. The varieties of animation art reflect the multitude of those who create the works, as well as the numerous software applications available with which to do so. The off-putting squishiness of some of these performances and their filmmakers' fascination with exploding taboos are perhaps haptic reactions to the rational optical spaces that were appropriate for the relatively linear narratives of cinema-based classic cartoons created with Acme apparatuses of steel, glass, and electric motors.

It has become clear from this study of classic animation—and, I predict, it will become increasingly apparent as performance theory adapts to computer-generated imagery and the production and dissemination of new media—that the oft-repeated requirement that living human bodies must be in temporal-spatial synchronicity, producing and receiving a performance together for one to exist, is an unsustainable idea. Perhaps it was relevant for a world in which the theatrical apparatus consisted of prosceniums, curtains, incandescent lights, pulleys, and a ticket-buying audience. But such insistence doesn't pass the reality test of the performances that surround us now in our quotidian lives. Non-humans are already performing for us, albeit in fairly primitive and utilitarian ways, and machines not only communicate performances among us but are also beginning to make their own original compositions. In this area, performance theory has lagged behind actual developments not only in the arts, but also in science and engineering.

Perhaps the greatest irony of the motion picture is that it is no longer made of shadows. With the advent of digital displays, the light of the cinema, including animation, shines from screens, as it does from the sun, and no longer reflects, as from the moon. Our final conundrum is, if the animated images we see are formed by intensely radiant pixels instead of light escaping through the translucent emulsion of film stock and bouncing off a surface, will that affect the way that we model our lives around cinema and cartoons, and vice versa? As we watch them on our screens, how will we respond to and embody animated beings when it is the light of their toon bodies that generates our shadows?

Notes

PREFACE

1. Frank Cotham, "Two Barbarians and a Professor of Barbarian Studies," *The New Yorker* (September 1, 2003), www.newyorkerstore.com/Education/Two-Barbarians-and-a-Professor-of-Barbarian-Studies/invt/126562.

2. Carlson, *Performance,* p. ix.

3. When I say *animation* and *animated films,* I mean films that contain extensive footage made by the traditional single-frame exposure method and its variant techniques according to established content patterns. I prefer the term *non-animated film* instead of *live-action film* to refer to standard films of filmed human actors because both the human and cartoon characters may enjoy the same "live" properties, a proposition discussed later in this book. Of course, there is also the argument that all cinema is "animated"—that is, that mainstream movies are a subcategory of animation—in which case there would be no such thing as a non-animated film. This just further complicates things. I've discussed this idea elsewhere (Crafton, "Veiled Genealogies").

4. Furthermore, I am sensitive to alerts by David Bordwell and Noël Carroll about the perils of invoking a top-down grand theory, and to warnings by Steven Shaviro against the "objectifying scholarly tendency" in film theory (and, one may add, performance theory). According to Shaviro, such a tendency "seeks to reduce particulars to generals, bizarre exceptions to representative patterns, specific practices to the predictable regularities of genre" (*The Cinematic Body,* p. viii). To be clear, I don't wish to be normative, essentialist, or a universalist, but I do aim to organize some commonsense reflections about things that happened in history that fell into definite patterns (perhaps representative) based on approaches, assumptions, and attitudes displayed by animators, producers, exhibitors, and audiences. I also believe that the theatrical cartoons of the "classical" period, my primary subject here, constituted a distinct film genre.

5. "Performance has become a central lens for understanding events as disparate as the war in Iraq and Madonna's newest video," writes Peggy Phelan. "We have entered a realm of all-performance-all-the-time" (Phelan, "Performance, Live Culture and Things of the Heart," p. 292). Richard Schechner alerts us, "Performing is a mode of behavior that may characterize *any* activity. Thus performance is a 'quality' that can occur in any situation rather than a fenced-off genre." He adds, "From the vantage of the kind of performance theory I am propounding, every action is a performance" (Schechner, *Performance Studies,* pp. 22, 30).

6. Schechner compares the ways that cultures rely on what he calls restored behavior to a film director's use of a strip of film. There may be an attachment to the film image's audiovisual origin, but it is severed in editing when the filmmakers construct "a new process, a performance" (*Between Theater and Anthropology,* p. 35).

INTRODUCTION

Epigraph: Walt Disney, *New York Times* interview, March 1938, quoted in Barrier, *The Animated Man,* p. 132.

1. Bendazzi, *Cartoons: One Hundred Years of Cinema Animation.*

2. Hank Sartin's dissertation, "Drawing on Hollywood," specifically addresses the performance theories and templates underlying Warner Bros. animation. The same year his dissertation was completed, 1998, Paul Wells's important book *Understanding Animation* included a short section entitled "Acting and Performance" (pp. 104–10), but the topic runs throughout the comprehensive theory he developed. Barrier acknowledged the centrality of animation performance in the subsection "Cartoon Acting," which comprised the first half—about three hundred pages—of his *Hollywood Cartoons,* a fundamental history of the subject. He concentrated on how Disney cultivated acting by his animators during the making of *Snow White.*

1. PERFORMANCE *IN* AND *OF* ANIMATION

Epigraph: Brad Bird, foreword to Hooks, *Acting for Animators,* p. vi.

1. Alexander Sesonske, comments at a conference, quoted in Stanley Cavell's response in Cavell, *The World Viewed,* p. 168.

2. This includes autobiographical performances, in which characters play themselves or present an image of their ideal selves.

3. "What Makes and Breaks Personality: Measured by the Impression of a Spectator," Walt Disney Studios memorandum, September 13, 1935.

4. Stern and Henderson, *Performance: Texts and Contexts,* p. 16.

5. Schechner, *Performance Studies,* p. 22.

6. Carlson, *Performance,* pp. 2–3.

7. True, Betty's character originally was a dog, but . . . things evolve. The impermanent nature of toon bodies is one aspect of their embodiment.

8. The term *toon* as a reference to cartoon workers originated in the film's source, Gary K. Wolf's *Who Censored Roger Rabbit* (1982). The term for these marginalized and segregated beings has racial overtones. See also Susan Ohmer, "*Who Framed Roger Rabbit?* The Presence of the Past," in Canemaker, ed., *Storytelling in Animation,* pp. 97–104.

9. Gilles Deleuze's concept of the body is relevant here. "'Body' for Deleuze is defined as any whole composed of parts, where these parts stand in some definite relation to one another, and has a capacity for being affected by other bodies. The human body is just one example of such a body; the animal body is another, but a body can also be a body of work, a social body or collectivity, a linguistic corpus, a political party, or even an idea. A Body is not defined by either simple materiality, by its occupying space ('extension'), or by organic structure. It is defined by the relations of its parts (relations of relative motion and rest, speed and slowness), and by its actions and reactions with respect both to its environment or milieu and to its internal milieu" (Bruce Baugh, "Body," in Parr, *The Deleuze Dictionary,* pp. 30–31). It is this total contingency of embodiment that encourages us to discard actors' and drama theorists' colonization of "the body" as the exclusive preserve of living humans.

10. Not that this was necessarily a good thing, according to Ruskin. "An inspired writer, in full impetuosity of passion, may speak wisely and truly of 'raging waves of the sea, foaming out their own shame'; but it is only the basest writer who cannot speak of the sea without talking of 'raging waves,' 'remorseless floods,' 'ravenous billows,' &c.; and it is one of the signs of the highest power in a writer to check all such habits of thought and to keep his eyes fixed firmly on the *pure fact,* out of which if any feeling comes to him or his reader, he knows it must be a true one" (John Ruskin, "Of the Pathetic Fallacy," in Ruskin, *Modern Painters,* p. 160).

11. Thomas Lamarre uses the term *multilectical* to describe the different "signature layers" in films combining authors and technologies. It also could be useful to describe how opposing readings of the same character compete and are reconciled in all film experiences (Lamarre, "New Media Worlds," in Buchan, ed., *Animated "Worlds,"* p. 146.

12. Suzanne Buchan provides a "generous and encompassing" definition of animated worlds that is helpful: "realms of cinematic experience that are accessible to the spectator only through the techniques available in animation filmmaking" (Buchan, ed., *Animated "Worlds,"* p. vii). My use of "worlds" is perhaps even more generous, since I emphasize the moviegoers' world-making role as much as the techniques of animation.

13. Chuck Jones, interviewed by Jo Jürgens, in Furniss, ed., *Chuck Jones,* p. 184.

14. "All theatrical performance . . . involves a degree of ostensiveness that marks it off from quotidian behavior" (Naremore, *Acting in the Cinema,* p. 17). "At its most sophisticated, acting in theater or movies is an art devoted to the systematic ostentatious depiction of character, or to what seventeenth-century England described as 'personation'" (ibid., p. 23).

15. Gaudreault's discussion of modes of narrative corresponds roughly to the performative modes, *in* performance and *of* performance, that I am proposing: "There are two basic modes, two distinct systems of narrative communication: monstration and narration. The first is the product, at least in part, of characters in dramatic action (whether in the theatre or in the cinema). The second emerges from a higher level of abstraction and goes beyond the concreteness inherent in all cases of 'representations' " (Gaudreault, *From Plato to Lumière*, p. 37).

16. Gunning, "An Aesthetic of Astonishment," p. 86.

17. Eisenstein, *Eisenstein on Disney*, p. 21. Eisenstein's notion of the animated body as protean form defined environmentally rather than by a skeleton remarkably anticipates Antonin Artaud's "body without organs," introduced in a 1947 radio play. Artaud's image, in turn, became the basis for a central trope of "desiring-machines," schizophrenia, and a worldview in Deleuze and Guattari's *Anti-Oedipus:* "The full body without organs is the unproductive, the sterile, the unengendered, the unconsumable" (*Anti-Oedipus*, pp. 8–9).

18. Naremore, *Acting in the Cinema*, p. 77.

19. The gag might also be a reference to the stage manager's call for a doctor during the burlesque show in *Applause* (Rouben Mamoulian, 1929).

20. Leslie, *Hollywood Flatlands*, pp. 232–34.

21. Hendershot, "Secretary, Homemaker, and 'White' Woman," p. 117.

22. Bouldin, "The Body, Animation and The Real," p. 1.

23. Holberg, "Betty Boop: Yiddish Film Star." There are conflicting opinions regarding Betty's ethnicity. It seems that fluidity—her ability to "pass" as Jewish, German, Midwestern, a WASP, or even Japanese—is part of her toon identity.

24. Although Betty sings one of Kane's signature songs, "That's My Weakness Now" (Sam H. Stept and Bud Green, 1928), all visual references to that singer that had been featured in the source, *Stopping the Show* (Dave Fleischer/ Paramount, 1932), have been excised from *Rise to Fame* in response to Kane's lawsuit against the studio.

25. This sequence illustrates one of the performance types described by Naremore, people portraying themselves in films: "This suggests that people in a film can be regarded in at least three different senses: as actors playing theatrical personages, as public figures playing theatrical versions of themselves, and as documentary evidence. If the term *performance* is defined in its broadest sense, it covers the last category as much as the first" (*Acting in the Cinema*, p. 15). Betty would be an actor playing a theatrical personage, Max (known from his roles in *Out of the Inkwell* and as a radio celebrity) would be playing a theatrical version of himself, and the celebrity appearances of Brice and Chevalier would be documentary evidence of Betty's fame and quasi-human status.

26. For example, see the illustrations in Stebbins, *Delsarte System of Expression. See also* Brewster and Jacobs, *Theatre to Cinema*, pp. 81–82.

27. See, for example, the various "Layout Training" courses given at the Walt Disney studio by Ken Anderson from 1937 to 1938; Langer, "Institutional Power and the Fleischer Studios: The 'Standard Production Reference,' " p. 9; Naremore, *Acting in the Cinema*, pp. 51–67.

28. Other instances include *Pencil Mania* (John Foster and George Stallings/ Van Beuren, 1932). In this film, Van Beuren's Tom and Jerry are animated human characters that act like animators, drawing objects that change their dimensionality and come to life, like cartoons. *The Magic Pencil* (Volney White/ Terrytoons, 1940) has Gandy Goose in a similar plot. *I'm Just a Jitterbug* (Alex Lovy/Walter Lantz, 1941) is set in an animation studio at night where a live-action animator's hand is sketching a bug character. After midnight, the various cartoon creatures dance a jitterbug with the Acme animation equipment and paraphernalia from the animation desk in the background.

29. I generally use "embodiment" in the rather unspecialized sense used by Stanislavsky and his followers, including those at Disney. A related usage derives from the philosophy of Maurice Merleau-Ponty, especially in his development of the body-subject in *Phenomenology of Perception* (1945). Critical theorists, notably Sobchack, Shaviro, Pierre Bourdieu, and Mark B.N. Hansen, for example, analyze and apply these concepts of socially inflected and mediated gesture and embodiment, but not specifically to animation.

30. Sung to the tune of "The Teddy Bears' Picnic" (Victor Herbert): "We are creations from your pen./It's within your hands we lie./You've always managed for us to sin/Now by your own hands you'll die./We'll make you draw a very deep pit/And into it we'll make you fit. /The tables are turned and now you're in our clutches."

31. The character is possibly a self-caricature of Jack King (1895–1958), who had worked for Disney from 1929 to 1933 and would rejoin the studio from 1936 to 1948.

32. Schechner, *Between Theater and Anthropology*, p. 35.

33. The root of the English *repetition* is the French word for a play rehearsal, *répétition*.

34. Schechner, *Between Theater and Anthropology*, p. 52.

35. Ibid., pp. 35–36.

36. Everyday behaviors such as yawning and sneezing are not performances, for example. But Sleepy's yawns in *Snow White and the Seven Dwarfs* (David Hand/Disney, 1937) and Donald Duck's sneeze (which blows all the loot he'd just won back inside a carnival crane machine) in *A Good Time for a Dime* (Dick Lundy/Disney, 1941) are restored behaviors and thus performances.

37. The Royal Samoans were a popular "presentation act," that is, performers in live movie theater prologues. There are newspaper accounts of their performances in New York, Washington, D.C., and Los Angeles.

38. The rotoscoped drawings once again became the basis for Betty and Popeye's dance in *Popeye the Sailor* (Fleischer, 1933).

39. Graver, "The Actor's Bodies," p. 226.

40. Ibid., p. 229.

41. Bouldin, "The Body, Animation and The Real," p. 6.

42. For example, in the object animations of Charley Bowers, as in *It's a Bird* (Harold Muller/Educational Film Exchanges, 1930).

43. David Surman has emphasized that these theoretical worlds are built upon foundational realities: "To be in the 'world' of a novel, film or performance

suggests an experience with strong continuities with aspects of our real-world experience; an experience that is immersive and all-encompassing, without the kinds of reflexive punctuation that would destroy its holistic effect. A fictional world, then, is on one level a realist discourse since it deals with the construction of a naturalized space to be disavowed, and which is ancillary to the noteworthy things that happen, and the events [that] take place in that world. However, simultaneously one is able to look to the corners of that world and note that things are happening outside of the terms of a restricted narration, as part of a holistic 'sphere of activity' " (Surman, "Style, Consistency and Plausibility in the *Fable* Gameworld," in Buchan, ed., *Animated "Worlds,"* p. 154).

44. Schechner, *Performance Studies*, pp. 28–29.

45. Klein adds burlesque hall hoochie-coochie dancers and Kewpie dolls as elements of Betty's pop-culture pedigree. He notes the "earthy humor" of Fleischer's New York street kid animators. Klein, *Seven Minutes*, p. 60.

46. Donald Graham, "The New Art," in "The Art of Animation," pp. 34–36, 44–46.

47. The film had become studio lore in only three years, as these guidelines for animators suggested: "The close and logical dependence between the character and incidents of a changing situation is an important *touchstone* of a perfect construction of a story and building a character and actions. By means of contrast two frivolous pigs with the third wise pig, is driven home the philosophy of the story. Clarity, unity of conception, simplicity in variety, harmony of proportion of parts and perfect blending of visual and auditory, dramatic and comical devices—are earmarks of perfection. It is an *achievement of a high standard* of a great inspiration and hard work, not a good luck or happy coincidence as some people may comfortably say in order to find an excuse for not studying and not following this classical standard set by the Walt Disney Studio" ("What Makes and Breaks Personality," p. 3).

48. Chuck Jones, interviewed by Jo Jürgens, in Furniss, ed., *Chuck Jones*, p. 184.

49. Wilfred Jackson, interviewed by Steve Hulett, in Ghez, ed., *Walt's People, Volume 6*, p. 63. Gabler provides an excellent documented discussion of the turn to the new style of acting at the studio, concluding, "He [Walt] almost single-handedly broke the long-standing tradition, to which he himself had once subscribed, of self-reflexive cartoons in which one saw the animator's hand, in favor of a new aesthetic in which the cartoon world was presented as self-contained" (Gabler, *Walt Disney*, p. 173).

50. Thomas and Johnston, *Disney Animation*, pp. 324–25.

51. Experts disagree on the nuances of Stanislavskian theories. The editors of a recent anthology observe, "Some of the most interesting inconsistencies in the collection emerge from contributors' conflicting understandings of Stanislavsky, [Lev] Kuleshov, and [Bertolt] Brecht" (Baron, Carson, and Tomasulo, eds., *More Than a Method*, p. 10). Baron and Carnicke point out that Stanislavsky's "System" was open to many interpretations and that many of his followers, notably Lee Strasberg, developed adaptations that were contradictory (Baron and Carnicke, *Reframing Screen Performance*, pp. 25–26).

52. Acting teachers in the Hollywood studios were also teaching techniques "that were more compatible with the central principles of Stanislavsky's System" (Baron and Carnicke, *Reframing Screen Performance*, p. 27).

One Disney staffer's alleged association with the Moscow Art Theatre had far-reaching consequences. David Hilberman (1911–2007) began working at the Disney studio in 1936 and became a layout artist on the Silly Symphonies and *Bambi*. In the early 1930s he had studied briefly at the Leningrad Academy of Fine Art and worked as a stagehand at the Leningrad State People's Theater. Disney, testifying before the House Un-American Activities Committee in 1947, claimed that the 1941 animators' strike was Communist-led and "named" Hilberman: "I looked into his record and I found that, number 1, that he had no religion and, number 2, that he had spent considerable time at the Moscow Art Theatre studying art direction or something" (Robert E. Stripling and H.A. Smith, "The Testimony of Walter E. Disney before the House Committee on Un-American Activities," in Peary and Peary, *The American Animated Cartoon*, p. 97). After the Disney animators' strike, Hilberman went on to cofound the studio United Productions of America (Canemaker, "David Hilberman," pp. 18–19).

53. Stanislavsky, *An Actor Prepares*, p. 17.

54. Stanislavsky, *My Life in Art*, p. 210. See also Carnicke, *Stanislavsky in Focus*. Murray Smith describes this "pre-structural conception" of character as "a view in which characters should transcend the work in which they are produced and take on an independent, albeit merely imaginative, existence." He defines epiphenomenal characters as "figures of an illusory stability, effects of the underlying structures of fantasy" (Smith, *Engaging Characters*, pp. 18, 78).

55. Boleslavsky, *Acting: The First Six Lessons*. For Tytla, see Barrier, *Hollywood Cartoons*, p. 205. From 1931 to 1940, Strasberg and Adler taught Stanislavkian methods at The Group Theatre in New York, the forerunner of the renowned Actor's Studio. Butler, *Star Texts*, p. 42. Note that the names may also be transliterated as Stanislavski and Boleslavski.

56. Gloria Swanson and Joseph P. Kennedy had brought Boleslavksy out to Hollywood in 1930 to salvage their aborted feature *Queen Kelly*. Boleslavsky spent the remainder of his brief career there.

57. Barrier, *Hollywood Cartoons*, pp. 205, 223; Barrier, *The Animated Man*, p. 154. It's especially illuminating to compare the acting of the queen in *Snow White*'s early scenes with performances in Boleslavsky's feature films. Her performance is a hybrid. Several of her poses are closely modeled on Delsarte templates, but she also displays expressive facial acting, body movements, and hand motions very similar to those of Marlene Dietrich in *The Garden of Allah*, which was released on November 19, 1936.

58. Thomas and Johnston, *Disney Animation*, p. 245.

59. "What Makes and Breaks Personality."

60. Don Towsley, "Character Analysis Class: Discussion and Analysis of Donald Duck and Donna Duck," Walt Disney Studios transcript, August 1, 1936.

61. David Hand, "Action Analysis: Director's Relationship to the Picture and to the Animator," Walt Disney Studios transcript, February 26, 1936, p. 1.

62. Donald Graham, "The Art of Animation," pp. 16–17.

63. Mauss, "Techniques of the Body," p. 80.

64. Ibid. Although he confined most of his research to non-Western cultures, he went so far as to claim, "I think I can also recognize a girl who has been raised in a convent" based on the way she walked and carried herself. Mauss defined all the sets of learned and learnable techniques that identify a body as its *habitus*. This totalizing concept is pertinent for envisioning the experience of the "me ... not me" effect in animation because, as Nolan observes, "*Habitus* is well chosen, insofar as it captures the odd temporality of the gestural, that sudden ownership of a capacity that is both always virtually one's own (an innate faculty of the moving body) and, paradoxically, something one obtains *only through the intermediary of the other*" (Nolan, *Agency and Embodiment,* p. 24).

65. Graver, "The Actor's Bodies," p. 223.

66. "What Makes and Breaks Personality," p. 4. Graham emphasized that animators must conceptualize personality from the start, not only for a more successful personality animation, but also to save money: "In order to build a picture as Walt is trying to build pictures, it is absolutely essential that the feeling of character, charm, and intensity be built into the action right at the start, when the scene is first taken from the director. . . . If he builds character and personality from the very beginning, his chances of achieving a successful scene are very much better" (Donald Graham, "Action Analysis: Discussion of Hound Dance Team in 'Mickey's Review' in Relation to Similar Hound Characters to Be Used in Band in 'Mickey's Circus,'" Walt Disney Studios transcript, January 9, 1936).

67. Graham, "The Art of Animation," p. 27.

68. The research on the uncanny valley effect is summarized in Chin-Chang Ho and Karl F. MacDorman, "Revisiting the Uncanny Valley Theory," p. 1508.

69. "Special Sweatbox Session: *Mountain Climbing [Alpine Climbers],*" Walt Disney Studios transcript, March 10, 1936, n.p.

70. Walt Disney, quoted in Thomas, *Walt Disney, the Art of Animation,* p. 22.

71. Hooks, *Acting for Animators,* p. 16. The "Opera Picture" probably refers to *Mickey's Grand Opera* (Wilfred Jackson), which was in current release at the time of the sweatbox session. Clara Cluck's singing career began in *Orphan's Benefit* (Burt Gillett, 1934). She was voiced brilliantly by Florence Gill.

72. Bird, foreword to Hooks, *Acting for Animators,* pp. vi–vii.

73. Graham, "The Art of Animation," p. 12.

74. "What Makes and Breaks Personality," p. 3.

75. Graham, "The Art of Animation," p. 58.

76. Naremore, *Acting in the Cinema,* p. 36. Solomon draws on this distinction when he comments that variety theater and magic shows rely on presentational modes of performance "that accomplish or demonstrate something, often something wonderful or marvelous—and not on representational modes of performance like acting, which simulates the actions and interactions of characters" (Solomon, *Disappearing Tricks,* p. 8).

77. Michael Barrier, "David Hand: An Interview by Michael Barrier" [1973], http://michaelbarrier.com/Interviews/Hand/interview_david_hand.htm.

78. Graver, "The Actor's Bodies," p. 222.

79. As video performance artist Bill Viola explained, "Art has always been a whole-body, physical experience. This sensuality is the basis of its true concep-

tual and intellectual nature, and is inseparable from it." Viola, quoted in Karen Lang, "Performativity in the History of Art," in Jones and Stephenson, *Performing the Body/Performing the Text*, p. 28.

80. Schechner, *The Future of Ritual*, p. 40.

81. There are plenty of animated satires of this metalepsis between cinesthetic and "real" beings. In *Buddy's Theatre* (Ben Hardaway/Schlesinger, 1935), projectionist Buddy uses a reel of film to swing into the movie and rescue the movie heroine. *Popeye's Premiere* (director uncredited/Famous Studios, 1949) has Popeye and Olive attending the premier of *Aladdin and His Wonderful Lamp* (Fleischer/Paramount, 1939). Our hero gets so involved in the story that at one point he saves on-screen Popeye by handing him the lifesaving can of spinach.

82. Naremore's emphatic remarks that the screen "creates a boundary between audience and performer unlike any other in theatrical history" and that it's an "impenetrable barrier" (*Acting in the Cinema*, pp. 27, 30) are partially correct in the sense that cinema is a mediatized spectacle. We can't interact with the screen actors or toons in a physical way, say by going up and shaking their hands, or as in a puppet show. But his statements ignore the potential for imaginative permeability of the screen as the viewers insert themselves into and co-create the narrative and the spectacle.

83. Gunning, "An Aesthetic of Astonishment," p. 79.

84. Ibid., p. 91.

85. Erwin Feyersinger, "Diegetic Short Circuits," 281.

86. Buchan, ed., *Animated "Worlds,"* p. 25.

87. Sobchack, *Carnal Thoughts*, p. 72. Naremore attributed this sensation less to the audience than to a formal property of the movie screen, a barrier that "promotes a fetishistic dynamic in the spectator; the actor is manifestly *there* in the image, but *not there* in the room, 'present' in a more intimate way than even the *Kammerspiel* could provide, but also impervious and inaccessible" (*Acting in the Cinema*, p. 30).

88. Shaviro, *The Cinematic Body*, p. 45.

89. Jones, *Chuck Amuck*, p. 219. Jones, an erudite person, plays on the double-bodied concept of stardom when he puns on *fabulous*, meaning both extraordinary or celebrated and an imaginary being, as in a *fabulous creature*.

90. Hooks, *Acting for Animators*, p. 21.

91. Morris Carnovsky, "The Actor's Eye," quoted in Wojcik, ed., *Movie Acting*, p. 92.

92. Animators' premonitory visualization of their scenes is analogous to composers' or music performers' ability to "hear" a passage or even an entire piece without the need for a physical performance.

93. Citing Stephen Heath ("Body, Voice"), Baron and Carnicke disallow the "entrenched opposition between 'present' stage actors and 'absent' screen actors because it clarifies that in the cinema *performance details are present to audiences*, just as lighting, framing, and editing choices are present to audiences" (*Reframing Screen Performance*, pp. 77–78).

94. Hansen, *Cinema and Experience*, p. 192. She devotes an entire section to the intricacies and multivalences behind Benjamin's concept of the *Spiel-Raum* (Hansen, *Cinema and Experience*, p. 19).

95. Cavell, quoted in Wojcik, ed., *Movie Acting*, p. 29.

96. Shaviro, *The Cinematic Body*, p. 37.

97. Disney in particular had his eye on Hollywood acting style during the 1935 planning of *Snow White*. "By the midthirties," writes Barrier, "much [live-action] screen acting seemed far more natural; and it was acting of that kind that audiences would measure the animation in Disney's feature against" (Barrier, *Hollywood Cartoons*, p. 141).

98. Nolan, *Agency and Embodiment*, pp. 71–72.

99. Ibid., p. 72.

2. LIVE AND IN PERSON: TOONS!

1. *Betty Boop's Rise to Fame*, for example, was released on May 18, 1934, when the Motion Pictures Producers and Distributors Association was making substantial revisions to the Motion Picture Production Code. The new "Hays Code" was announced in June and went into effect on July 1, 1934. Had the film been released a few months later and not been a cartoon, Betty's hula might have violated the provision barring "naked and suggestive dances." Animated short films, however, were adjudicated on the basis of scripts submitted.

2. Andrew Gordon, quoted in Everett and Caldwell, *New Media*, p. 215. Everett and Caldwell implicitly distinguish between embodied performance—"Human actors study the motivating details of a character, then they might improvise the acting once they are 'in character'"—and CGI as a variety of figurative performance. They continue, "Computer animation characters, by contrast, are always in character. They were born in character. Animators need to finesse certain details and make the acting seem improvised, matter-of-fact, *natural*."

3. Carlson, *Performance*, p. 3.

4. Chris Wilbert, "Anti-This—Against-That: Resistances along a Human-Non-Human Axis," in Sharp, ed., *Entanglements of Power*, p. 238.

5. Burt, *Animals in Film*, p. 32.

6. "Just as 'sympathetic humans' are engaging in the sabotage of places that exploit animals, so we are told that animals are fighting back: 'fighting for their own liberations'" (Wilbert, "Anti-This—Against-That," p. 247).

7. Susan Orlean claims, without documentation, that the dog star was snubbed by the Oscars. "Rinty received the most votes for Best Actor. But members of the Academy, anxious to establish the new awards as serious and important, decided that giving an Oscar to a dog did not serve that end, so the votes were recalculated, and the award diverted to Emil Jannings" (Orlean, *Rin Tin Tin*, p. 88). According to Academy archivists, no records exist to support or deny the claim.

8. Basinger, *Silent Stars*, p. 463.

9. "Each animal was a specialist. One was used for attack scenes, another was trained to jump twelve-foot walls, a third was a gentle house dog, and so on" (Jack Warner interview, quoted in Orlean, *Rin Tin Tin*, p. 96).

10. Fan letters in the Lee Duncan Collection, Riverside Metropolitan Museum, Riverside, California, quoted in Orlean, *Rin Tin Tin*, pp. 76–77.

11. Philo and Wilbert, *Animal Spaces, Beastly Places*, p. 17.

12. These films were supposed to make us laugh, and maybe audiences found them funny in the 1930s. Now it's hard to forgive the sophomoric jokes, and we wince at the obvious discomfort of some of the players. We are more likely to contemplate the ethics of animal acting than to embody these mutts.

13. Burt, *Animals in Film*, p. 32. Animal performance is, of course, a contested academic terrain. See Paul Bouissac, "Behavior in Context: In What Sense Is a Circus Animal Performing?" and other essays in Sebeok and Rosenthal, eds., *The Clever Hans Phenomenon*.

14. Burt, *Animals in Film*, p. 32.

15. Cavell, *The World Viewed*, p. 170.

16. Wenceslao Moreno (1896–1999) created his character Johnny by drawing the face on his thumb and forefinger and using a doll's body, button eyes, and a little wig. Videos of his act can be found online.

17. In this section I am referring mainly to the "bourgeois" puppet shows presented primarily for children, not to "art" or avant-garde examples of puppetry, such as Alfred Jarry's production of *Ubu Roi*.

18. Maeterlinck, quoted in Brachear, "Maurice Maeterlinck and His 'Musée Grévin,'" pp. 347–51. Maeterlinck won the Nobel Prize in Literature in 1911 and is best known for his play *The Blue Bird* (1908), which was adapted for film by Maurice Tourneur in 1918. There is debate as to whether some of his plays from the 1890s were intended to be performed by marionettes, but the relevant point was that he wished to use actors as mouthpieces of the author, desiring that they bring nothing of themselves to the performance.

19. Craig, *On the Art of the Theatre*, p. 81. Craig is vague about the exact nature of the über-marionette. He may have had in mind a full-body puppet similar to Maeterlinck's *fantoche* (Le Bœuf, "On the Nature of Edward Gordon Craig's Über-Marionette," p. 102).

20. Craig, *On the Art of the Theatre*, pp. 84–85.

21. Olf, "The Man/Marionette Debate in Modern Theatre," pp. 488–94.

22. Later Hitchcock seemed to back away from this Craig-like stance, writing, "Silliest of all Hollywood arguments is between the school that claims to believe the actor is completely a puppet, putting into a role only the director's 'genius' (I am, God forgive me, charged with belonging to that school) and the equally asinine school of 'natural acting' in which the player is supposed to wander through the scenes at will, a self-propelling, floating, freewheeling, embodied inspiration" ("Actors Aren't *Really* Cattle," ghostwritten article quoted in McGilligan, *Alfred Hitchcock*, p. 140). Appropriately, it would seem, Hitchcock's interest in puppets was reflected in the theme song for his TV series *Alfred Hitchcock Presents*, "Funeral March of a Marionette" (Charles Gounod, 1882).

23. Filmed puppets routinely act without their puppeteers, as in *At the Races* (Joseph Henabery/Vitaphone, 1934). In one scene Charlie McCarthy sits on a fence speaking and gesturing "on his own," without the benefit of ventriloquist Edgar Bergen.

24. Puppeteer Tony Sarg (Anthony Frederick Sarg [1880–1942]) and shadow theater devotee Lotte Reiniger (Charlotte Reiniger [1899–1981]) are examples of filmmakers who combined silhouette puppetry with animation.

25. Richard Weihe, "The Strings of the Marionette," in Buchan, ed., *Animated "Worlds,"* p. 42.

26. Hillel Schwartz, *The Culture of the Copy,* p. 69. He is referring to mime performances, exemplified by Charles Deburau and his performance of Pierrot, in which "on stage there was little breach between the mime and his second body."

27. Kleist, "On the Marionette Theatre," p. 212.

28. Buchan, *Quay Brothers,* p. 104.

29. Frierson, *Clay Animation.* An interesting case for further research is the career of Bob Clampett (1913–84), the brilliant Warner Bros. animation director who, in 1949, developed his puppetry hobby into a television venture starring his hand-puppet characters Beany and Cecil.

30. Auerbach cautions that focusing too much on the similarity between old and new forms may limit our understanding of historical processes. "In so linking cinema to precursor cultural formations, turning to the past instead of assuming that film must anticipate its future, such projects have the tendency to overlook the process of transition itself: how one sort of cinema turned into another." His yellow flag is critical for studying animation history. Although speculating about animation's origins reveals some of its founding principles, it does not "explain" animation or exhaust its meaning. Auerbach, *Body Shots,* p. 87.

31. The word *fantoche* (in Italian, *fantoccino*) originally referred to a particular kind of puppet. The diminutive body with short arms and legs was worn around the actor's torso, suggesting a doll with a human head. (For an example, see the "Triplets" number in *The Band Wagon* [Vincente Minnelli, 1953]). Since the 1990s the word has been used as an homage to Emile Cohl and has become more widely applied. There is a Fantoche festival of animation, a band with that name, several songs by that title, and a remarkable film, *Fantoche,* by graffiti artist Blu, which he later incorporated into *Muto* (discussed in chapter 6).

32. Cohl's doll protagonists re-perform the popular operetta "Le Petit-Faust," a parody of Gounod's *Faust* first performed in 1869. Crafton, *Emile Cohl, Caricature, and Film,* p. 144.

33. Buchan, "The Animated Spectator: Watching the Quay Brothers' 'Worlds,' " in Buchan, ed., *Animated "Worlds,"* p. 21.

34. There is, for example, the CoPuppet project, which "explores the possibilities offered by multimodal and cooperative interaction, in which performers, or even audience members, are called to affect different parts of a puppet through gestures and voice. In particular, we exploit an existing architecture for the creation of multimodal interfaces to develop the CoPuppet framework for designing, deploying and interacting during performances in which virtual puppets are steered by multiple multimodal controls" (Paolo Bottoni et al., "CoPuppet: Collaborative Interaction in Virtual Puppetry," in Adams et al., eds., *Transdisciplinary Digital Art,* p. 326).

35. Schwartz, *The Culture of the Copy,* p. 66.

36. Hernández, "The *Double Sense* of Animated Images," p. 39.

37. Nor can they have sex with them. This is a theme in *Cool World* (Ralph Bakshi, 1996), in which a cartoonist enters the animated world of his creation and has an erotic encounter with his "doodle" protagonist.

38. Shaviro, *The Cinematic Body,* p. 50.

39. Phelan, *Unmarked*, p. 149.

40. Philip Auslander, "Against Ontology: Making Distinctions Between the Live and the Mediatized," in Gough and MacDonald, eds., *Performance Research*, pp. 54–55.

41. Auslander, *Liveness*, pp. 5, 2.

42. Shaviro aptly distinguishes between film illusions and films *of* illusions: "We neglect the basic tactility and viscerality of cinematic experience when we describe material processes and effects, such as the persistence of vision, merely as mental illusions. Cinema produces real effects *in* the viewer, rather than merely presenting phantasmic reflections *to* the viewer. The cinematic image is not an object for some (actual or ideal) spectator; instead, the spectator is drawn *into* the fragmented materiality and the 'depth without depth' (Blanchot . . .) of the image. In film, the old structure of aesthetic contemplation collapses" (Shaviro, *The Cinematic Body*, pp. 52–53).

43. Auslander, "At the Listening Post," p. 8.

44. Auslander, "Live from Cyberspace," p. 17. Auslander selected 1934 because that is the year that "live" was first mentioned in the *Oxford English Dictionary* in the media sense, referring to radio broadcasts. I suspect, though I haven't researched it, that one could find earlier mentions in media trade journals of the 1920s. Auslander's semantic argument assumes that naming an effect brings it into existence.

45. "The Singing Towers of the Low Countries," on the website of the Speelklok Museum, Utrecht, Netherlands. Images (and sounds) of the vast collection of self-playing and automatic instruments are displayed at www.muse umspeelklok.nl/?Language=en.

46. One of many competing automatic instruments, the Pianola brand player piano, invented by Edwin Votey in 1896 and commercially distributed by the Aeolian Company in 1897, dominated the market through the 1920s, when improved phonographs and radio displaced it.

47. Christie, *The Last Machine*, p. 32.

48. Ibid., p. 89.

49. Cartoons have a curious vestigial attachment to this semantic connection to life. Warner Bros. acquired one of the original American film companies, Vitagraph, in 1924. When it introduced its sound system in 1926, it christened the system "Vitaphone," connoting "life" plus "sound." This resonated with "telephone" to convey the idea that the sound films had the immediacy, intimacy, and being-there-ness—in short, the liveness—of the telephone. After Warners lost the exclusive rights to the sound system, they repurposed the corporate subsidiary to distribute its short subjects, including its cartoons. That's why all the Merrie Melodies and Looney Tunes films were copyrighted and released by the Vitaphone Corporation long after the name's associations with the telephone and early film liveness had dissipated.

50. Gunning, "The Ghost in the Machine," p. 4.

51. Craig Roell, cited in Durkin, "The Self-Playing Piano as a Site for Textual Criticism," p. 168. Altman gives 1898 as the date of the invention of Wurlitzer's coin-operated self-playing piano. The histories of the cinema and player piano were conjoined briefly during the nickelodeon era (1906 to about 1912). It's

probable that some of these "automatic pianos" were used in small movie theaters, but, as Altman points out, they were placed in the lobby to attract customers, not next to the screen as musical accompaniment (Altman, *Silent Film Sound*, pp. 128, 323–24).

52. Durkin, "The Self-Playing Piano," p. 170. Edison phonographs were exhibited as stage attractions soon after their invention in 1877, thereby augmenting or displacing "live" acts. Whether anyone articulated (as Auslander's thesis would predict) the recorded-live dichotomy back then is unknown, but it seems possible.

53. Ibid., pp. 175–78. Several modern composers created pieces for the Pianola. Selections by George Antheil, Igor Stravinsky, Paul Hindemith, and others are available on *Piano Music Without Limits*, MDG Scene, 2007, Cat. No. MDG 645 1404–2.

54. Auslander, "Live From Cyberspace," p. 20; "At the Listening Post," p. 7.

55. Carroll, *Theorizing the Moving Image*, p. 67.

56. Ibid., p. 69. His conclusion follows from an assertion that film performances may not be artworks: "If theatrical performances and film performances may both be said to be tokens, the tokens in the theatrical case are generated by interpretations, whereas the tokens in the film case are generated by templates [film reels, DVDs, etc.]. And this, in turn, yields a crucial aesthetic difference between the two. The theatrical performances are artworks in their own right that, thereby, can be objects of artistic evaluation, but the film performance itself is neither an artwork nor is it a legitimate candidate for artistic evaluation" (p. 67).

57. Langer, "A Note on the Film," p. 80.

58. One might say that the animation of drawings based on rotoscoped film footage, as with Betty's hula, is a token in Carroll's proposition. And in a general sense it is. In another sense, though, it's a re-performance that artistically translates the film frames into the drawings of the toon body and so is more accurately a re-performance, not an exact indexical copy of the original.

59. I'm bracketing here for a later discussion those animated performances that are based on reproducing prior "live" performances, such as ones produced by rotoscoping, motion capture, and CGI. In these special cases, the resulting transformed imagery is a re-performance of the original motion.

60. It is doubtful whether non-animated cinema performances are etchings of prior acting performances, since many film performances are constructed in ways not unlike animation, such as by using stunt doubles, body doubles, or digital simulations to create embodiments that rely on the viewers' willingness to accept these composited scenes as discrete, uninterrupted actions. As in animation, there are no "tokens" that the film passively records; the performances exist only when the film rolls.

61. Auslander, "At the Listening Post," p. 7.

62. This is true of documentary films that purport to re-present the past. Although the events were filmed in the past, and we embody the beings we see as living in the past, the performance of the documentary is still in the present.

63. Artis Wodehouse, quoted in Durkin, "The Self-Playing Piano," p. 177. A review of a concert by the Florida Orchestra featuring Gershwin playing his

1925 piano-roll version of "Rhapsody in Blue" illustrates the wild card that is audience response. Unlike Wodehouse, this reviewer had difficulty embodying the great composer and experienced only strangeness and tedium: "Most of the time the piano was playing away alone, a weird, rather boring experience to watch the keys and pedals move by themselves. I'd rather watch and hear a real live soloist" (John Fleming, *St. Petersburg Times,* March 6, 2010). The choice of the words "real live" is telling. Though it was Gershwin playing, this listener required bodily presence to acknowledge liveness, even if it required that another pianist play Gershwin's music. Also, the auditor's reliance on sight, not his musical acumen, was the cause of the breakdown of the illusion. Had he been blindfolded or had the playing taken place behind a curtain, would he have believed in the concert's liveness?

64. Spadoni, "The Uncanny Body of Early Sound Film," p. 12. He cites Freud's essay "The Uncanny" (1919). Spadoni's remarks are in the context of the introduction of sound in the late 1920s, but animation too provokes a crisis of an implied but physically absent body. This multiplies the uncanny effect when cartoon beings also talk and sing during the sound era.

65. Two film examples capture the uncanniness of the player piano. In *Jasper in the Haunted House* (George Pal/Paramount, 1942), a ghost plays a piano. We don't see this dead person's shade, only signs of his presence, such as his footprints in the dust. The piano keys move on their own, like those of a Pianola. In the non-animated film *Rules of the Game* (Jean Renoir, 1939), houseguests stare mesmerized at a player piano. In an appropriately ghostly fashion, the piano is playing "Danse Macabre" (Camille Saint-Saëns, 1874) as it accompanies dancers in skeleton costumes.

66. Auslander, "Live from Cyberspace," p. 20.

67. Herbert Blau, "The Human Nature of the Bot," pp. 23, 22.

68. Kevin Brown, "The Auslander Test," p. 185.

69. Ibid., p. 187.

70. White, *The Body and the Screen,* p. 20.

71. The Gertie Project, directed by David L. Nathan, M.D., is re-creating the film from the best surviving prints and original drawings. The curtain call sequence has been successfully "reanimated." See www.gertie.org/project.htm.

72. Disney, Interoffice Memo to Don Graham, December 23, 1935, quoted in Barrier, *The Animated Man,* p. 116.

73. Walt Disney, *New York Times* interview, March 1938, quoted in Barrier, *The Animated Man,* p. 132.

74. Disney may have been criticizing *Gulliver's Travels* (Dave Fleischer/Paramount, 1939). Many critics agreed that the Gulliver character, although he gave a highly mimetic body performance by means of rotoscoping, paradoxically gave a less fully embodied "live" performance than the cartoon-style characters made using drawings.

75. Thompson, "Implications of the Cel Animation Technique," lists a number of these simulations, including lens distortions, trucking, panning, and zooming.

76. Auslander, *Liveness,* pp. 50–51.

77. Dyer, *Heavenly Bodies.*

78. Another thorough case study of toon stardom is "Bugs Bunny Superstar," a chapter in Sartin's dissertation, "Drawing on Hollywood."

79. This is discussed throughout Crafton, "The View from Termite Terrace."

80. Paul Wells, "To Affinity and Beyond: Woody, Buzz and the New Authenticity," in Austin and Barker, eds., *Contemporary Hollywood Stardom*, p. 92.

81. Belton, *American Cinema, American Culture*, p. 90.

82. "Indeed, publicity surrounding screen actors has often actively suppressed information about training, preferring instead the myth of the born performer whose natural talents and genuine feelings are first captured by the camera and then presented on screen. Traditional ways of thinking about film and about acting have caused screen performances to be valued insofar as they appear truthful, sincere, and authentic. Performances by Hollywood stars in particular are prized not for their craftsmanship but as glimpses of idealized people. Film stars function as social hieroglyphs, objects of desire, and sites of identity construction. Screen narratives activate complex subjective processes insofar as they effectively circulate a culture's understanding of the human figure, countenance, and psyche" (Baron and Carnicke, *Reframing Screen Performance*, p. 18).

83. Wojcik, ed., *Movie Acting*, p. 185.

84. Barrier, *Hollywood Cartoons*, p. 208.

85. I am referring to ownership in the Stanislavskian sense, not to the material ownership of the rights to exploit the character commercially. Of course, Popeye may "own" other characters as an actor. In *Aladdin and His Wonderful Lamp* (Fleischer, 1939), he is cast in the hero's role in the film script Olive Oyl has written for them. Some films may show a toon playing his or her toon character on-screen, as in *Puttin on the Act* (discussed in chapter 3) or in Bugs Bunny's "biographical" cartoons.

86. Wells, "To Affinity and Beyond," p. 97.

87. Lovell expressed this well: "'Persona' and 'image' are the analytical terms most used in the discussion of stars, and they are used in confusing ways. . . . However, it is less important than the assumptions that underlie the use of these terms. Persona/image points to the fact that stars are more than their individual performances. The individual performances combine with each other and with personal biography, publicity, and general media exposure to create the persona/image. In analyzing a star, all of these should be considered" (Alan Lovell, "I Went in Search of Deborah Kerr, Jodie Foster, and Julianne Moore but Got Waylaid," in Austin and Barker, eds., *Contemporary Hollywood Stardom*, p. 265).

88. Sartin, "Drawing on Hollywood," p. 96.

89. Wills, *John Wayne's America*, p. 17.

90. DeCordova, *Picture Personalities*, p. 21.

91. Graver, "The Actor's Bodies," pp. 226–27.

92. In fact, she had always been an on-stage lead. See Faris, *Ginger Rogers: A Bio-Bibliography*, p. 4. For more on the creation of Rogers as a media entity, see Ohmer, *George Gallup in Hollywood*, pp. 141–56.

93. Wills, *John Wayne's America*, p. 14.

94. Ibid., p. 15. Of course, that there is a second private life behind the official off-screen private life leads to a never-ending circuit of further claims and

counterclaims, all of which stoke fan curiosity and add to the star's commercial capital.

95. A robust industry not authorized by the character's rights holders blossomed to satisfy consumers' demand for images and objects of Betty that facilitated fan-based embodiment. For example, a quick search of eBay has turned up Depression-era bisque Kewpie dolls of Betty and sheets of tattoo designs marked "Printed in Japan" that were clearly unlicensed.

96. A theme that runs through Naremore's treatise is that *all* acting is semiotic and we never have access to the performer's true emotions or self. "My real concern is with the ways persons and inanimate materials interact, so that we cannot tell where a face or body leaves off and a mask begins" (*Acting in the Cinema*, p. 83). Elsewhere he expresses a sort of performance pantheism that is pertinent to animation: "After all, only the most vulgar empiricism regards the objects around us as inanimate. Once those objects have entered into social relations and narrative actions, they are imbued with the same 'spirit' as the humans who touch them" (p. 87).

97. Langer, "Institutional Power."

98. Betty and Popeye are mentioned throughout Adelman, Spiegelman, and Merkin, *Tijuana Bibles*.

99. Graver, "The Actor's Bodies," p. 222.

100. Naremore, quoted in Wojcik, ed., *Movie Acting*, p. 100.

101. Graver, "The Actor's Bodies," p. 223.

102. Dyer, *Heavenly Bodies*, p. 2.

103. Dyer's argument is congruent with Auslander's when he contends that contemporary audiences for music prefer the sound of the recording studio product to the actual "live" performance, which logically leads to such practices as on-stage lip-synching, audio playback, and sweetening.

104. Sartin, "Subcultural Reading: Queer Bugs," in "Drawing on Hollywood," pp. 207–12.

105. Bronski, *Culture Clash*, p. 42.

106. Cohan, *Incongruous Entertainment*, p. 1.

107. Robertson [Wojcik], *Guilty Pleasures*, p. 12.

108. "Gender Parody, therefore, doesn't differ in structure from the activity of the masquerade but self-consciously theatricalizes masquerade's construction of gender identities" (ibid., p. 13).

109. Richard Dyer, "*A Star Is Born* and the Construction of Authenticity," in Gledhill, ed., *Stardom*, p. 133.

110. Naremore, *Acting in the Cinema*, pp. 2–3.

3. THE ACME OF VARIEGATED ENTERTAINMENT

1. Keaton (1895–1966) reminisced about *Gertie* when planning *Three Ages*: "I saw it in a nickelodeon when I was fourteen [sic]. I'll ride in on an animated cartoon" (quoted in Blesh, *Buster Keaton*, p. 220). The Fleischer Studio produced the animated dinosaur sequence (McPherson, *Buster Keaton*, p. 123). My fanciful narrative is based on a clipping that documents when Buster Keaton appeared with his parents, Joe and Myra, as The Three Keatons on the

Hammerstein's program with McCay and *Gertie* for the week of January 25, 1914 (*New York Times*, January 25, 1914, p. 75).

In the graphic novel *McCay 4: La quatrième dimension,* Smolderen takes the reader/viewer to one of the cartoonist's vaudeville shows. He "explains" McCay's astounding feat of prehistoric conjuring by taking us behind the screen just after McCay has ridden off on Gertie's back. He is still mounted—atop a real dinosaur! See www.editions-delcourt.fr/catalogue/bd/mccay_4_la_quatrieme _dimension.

2. Kirshenblatt-Gimblett, "Performance Studies," in Bial, ed., *The Performance Studies Reader,* p. 50.

3. Malraux argued that photography transformed the experience of art by detaching its formation of meaning within curated collections in physical museums to, instead, a *musée imaginaire* (*Museum Without Walls*).

4. Foucault, *L'Archéologie du Savoir,* pp. 14–15. The translation is mine.

5. J.B. Kaufman, "The Heir Apparent," in Goldmark and Keil, eds., *Funny Pictures,* p. 53.

6. Panofsky, "Reflections on Historical Time," pp. 691–701; Mikhail Bakhtin, "Forms of Time and of the Chronotope in the Novel: Notes toward a Historical Poetics," in *The Dialogic Imagination,* pp. 84–258; Lefebvre, *The Production of Space.* My "timescape" differs from Benjamin's "monad" in that his unit was a fragment or metonymy of a larger historical whole ("every idea contains the image of the world"), while "timescape," as I use it, is always a fiction, an imaginative projection of the present onto the past. See Peltonen, "Clues, Margins, and Monads," pp. 354–55.

7. See Robert Stam et al., "The Documentary Chronotope," pp. 56–61; Montgomery, *Carnivals and Commonplaces: Bakhtin's Chronotope, Cultural Studies, and Film;* Shohat and Stam, *Unthinking Eurocentrism;* Sobchack, "Lounge Time: Postwar Crises and the Chronotope of Film Noir," in Browne, ed., *Refiguring American Film Genres,* pp. 129–70. An essay that specifically gives a Bakhtinian reading of animation is Terrance R. Lindvall and J. Matthew Melton, "Towards a Post-Modern Animated Discourse: Bakhtin, Intertextuality and the Cartoon Carnival," in Pilling, ed., *A Reader in Animation Studies,* pp. 203–20.

8. When criticized for circumventing the "reality of historical time" in his novel *Timescape* (1992), author Benford responded, "Our notions about time are not firm, and chastising authors with a supposed hard-nosed reality may be merely naïve." Benford, "Death and the Textual Shadow of the SF Author, Again," p. 341.

9. Panofsky, "Reflections on Historical Time," p. 695.

10. Stam, *Subversive Pleasures,* p. 11.

11. One thing that is beyond the control of any filmmaker, of course, is reception. Moviegoers produced "unauthorized" readings and were offended by perceived Arab stereotypes in *Aladdin* (Ron Clements and John Musker/Walt Disney Pictures, 1992), for example.

12. Bakhtin, "Forms of Time and of the Chronotope in the Novel," p. 255.

13. Ibid., pp. 254–55.

14. Pertinent to Bakhtin's observations, science fiction, and the self-performance of the Fleischer brothers, Benford says about *Timescape,* "I appear

twice in the novel. The unnamed twins in 1963 are in fact myself and my brother, who were indeed at that place and time, even in the correct classes. Second, the character Gregory Markham has exactly my biography (except that he didn't write *Timescape!*)" (Benford, "Death and the Textual Shadow of the SF Author, Again," p. 341).

15. Feyersinger, "Diegetic Short Circuits," 281. The rhetorical figure of metalepsis resembles other ontological dyads, such as Schechner's "me . . . not me" paradox and my distinction between performance *in* and *of* animation, discussed in chapter 1.

16. For a taste of Friganza's rollicking stage act, see *Trixie Friganza in "Strong and Willing"* (director uncredited/Vitaphone, 1930). She also performed a knockabout duet with Buster Keaton in *Free and Easy* (Edward Sedgwick/MGM, 1930). Charlotte Greenwood's pliability is visible in *So Long Letty* (Lloyd Bacon/Warner Bros., 1929). Allen stresses that burlesque and vaudeville were quite separate institutions. Burlesque was "structured around the body of the burlesque performer, its size and display foregrounding sexual difference and marking it as the body of the low other. Without the performer's body, there was no burlesque. Vaudeville had no body." Instead, vaudeville was an aggregate of its entertainment modules, each of which had a different audience appeal and function on the program. It was a "performance machine" (Allen, *Horrible Prettiness,* p. 189).

17. B.F. Keith's Riverside Theatre, September 12, 1921, Oscar Hammerstein II Collection, Library of Congress. See www.loc.gov/exhibits/bobhope/images /s9.1.jpg. The cartoon replaced the traditional "dumb [i.e., wordless] act" in the program sequence, chosen so that patrons could return to their seats without interfering with the audibility of the stage performers.

18. Koko the Clown's name was changed to Ko-Ko the Clown in the mid-1920s.

19. A reviewer, who observed that "sometimes the added attractions at cinema theaters are more interesting than the features," noted that the Out of the Inkwell cartoon was "very interesting" (Kenneth Taylor, "Alice Gentle Sings," *Los Angeles Times,* August 11, 1924, p. A7).

20. *Vaudeville: An "American Masters" Special,* narrated by Ben Vereen, written by Greg Palmer, and produced by Rosemary Garner (1997). Extant playbills show that vaudeville acts often lasted more than seven minutes and sometimes as much as twenty. The point, however, is that the form relied on brief bursts of attention. This otherwise excellent television program makes one gaffe. Although it correctly concludes that the spirit of vaudeville influenced early animation and cites the example of Winsor McCay, unfortunately it features footage from the Bray Studio's remake of *Gertie the Dinosaur* instead of McCay's cartoon.

21. Langer observes, "The polyphonic and heterogeneous format of a newspaper page of comic strips or the mixed vaudeville bill were similar to the way in which silent Fleischer films were exhibited in theaters. This format was also internalized into the very structure of their movies." Mark Langer, "Polyphony and Heterogeneity in Early Fleischer Films," in Goldmark and Keil, eds., *Funny Pictures,* p. 44.

22. Lewis, *Traveling Show to Vaudeville,* p. 316.

23. As Jenkins writes, "Historical reconstruction of this now lost tradition is a necessary precondition for a full understanding of early sound comedy" (*What Made Pistachio Nuts?*, p. 60).

24. "In Vaudeville: A Short History of This Popular Character of Amusement," *Midway* 1 (October 1905): 27; reprinted in Lewis, *From Traveling Show to Vaudeville*, p. 321.

25. E. F. Albee, "E. F. Albee on Vaudeville." Edward Franklin Albee II (1857–1930) was the adoptive grandfather of Edward F. Albee III (b. 1928), the contemporary playwright.

26. Sergei M. Eisenstein, "The Montage of Attractions" [1923], in *Sergei Eisenstein: Selected Works*, p. 8. He praised the Proletkult program for "abolishing the very institution of theatre as such and replacing it by a showplace for achievements in the field at the *level of the everyday skills of the masses*" (p. 33).

27. Albee, "E. F. Albee on Vaudeville."

28. Allen, *Horrible Prettiness*, pp. 185–86.

29. Albee, "E. F. Albee on Vaudeville."

30. Jenkins, *What Made Pistachio Nuts?*, p. 77.

31. Ibid.

32. Keaton recalled the infamous Cherry Sisters at the Hammerstein, who sang so badly that the audience always threw rotten tomatoes at them (Robinson, *Buster Keaton*, p. 17). The management likely supplied the projectiles as part of the act.

33. Matthew Solomon, "Twenty-Five Heads under One Hat," in Sobchack, ed., *Meta Morphing*, pp. 5–6. For another cartoon quick change, see *Bugs' Bonnets* (Chuck Jones/Warner Bros., 1956). Every time a hat falls from the Acme Theatrical Hat Co. truck and lands on a character, his behavior and his personality change to fit the headgear. Mayhem ensues, with Elmer and Bugs ending up as bride and groom.

34. An incomplete list of cartoons that reference vaudeville (or vaudeville-like settings), excluding films discussed in the text, includes:

1914: *Hesanut at a Vaudeville Show* (Kalem Company)

1916: *Our National Vaudeville* (Harry S. Palmer/Gaumont Company), *Colonel Heeza Liar at the Vaudeville Show* (Walter Lantz/Bray Studios/Pathé Film Exchange)

1917: *Goodrich Dirt's Amateur Night* (Wallace A. Carlson/Bray)

1920: *The Circus* (Max and Dave Fleischer/Bray)

1922: *The Show* (Dave Fleischer/Out of the Inkwell Films)

1923: *The Contest* (Dave Fleischer/Out of the Inkwell Films)

1924: *The Artist's Model* (Earl Hurd); *Vacation* (Dave Fleischer/Out of the Inkwell Films)

1925: *Bobby Bumps and Company* (Earl Hurd/Famous Players–Lasky Corporation).

1926: *It's the Cats* (Dave Fleischer/Out of the Inkwell Films)

1927: *Ko-Ko Makes 'Em Laugh* (Dave Fleischer/Out of the Inkwell Films)

1928: *The Vaudeville Show* (Kinex Studios)

1931: *You Don't Know What You're Doin'* (Rudolf Ising/Schlesinger)

1933: *Boilesk* [in the Screen Song series] (Dave Fleischer/Fleischer Studios)

1935: *The Lady in Red* (Friz Freleng/Schlesinger), *Hollywood Capers* (Jack King/Schlesinger)

1936: *Betty Boop and the Little King* (Dave Fleischer/Paramount)

1938: *Love and Curses* (Cal Dalton and Ben Hardaway/Schlesinger), *The Penguin Parade* (Tex Avery/Schlesinger)

1939: *Hamateur Night* (Tex Avery/Schlesinger)

1946: *Willie the Operatic Whale* (Clyde Geronimi and Hamilton Luske/Walt Disney Productions)

1948: *Back Alley Oproar* (Friz Freleng/Warner Bros.)

1950: *Rabbit of Seville* (Chuck Jones/Warner Bros.)

1951: *Vegetable Vaudeville* (Isadore Sparber/Famous Studios)

1952: *Off to the Opera* (Connie Rasinski)

1957: *What's Opera, Doc?* (Chuck Jones/Warner Bros.)

The list doesn't include independent animation, such as *Asparagus* (Suzan Pitt, 1979) and *78 Tours* (Georges Schwizgebel, 1986), or contemporary films exploiting the vaudeville-cartoon timescape.

35. Watts, *The Magic Kingdom*, pp. 10, 19. Disney studio insiders gave the name "vaudevilles" to the omnibus features made by combining short cartoons, for example *Make Mine Music* (Robert Cormack et al./Disney, 1946). "Described by Ben Sharpsteen as 'vaudeville shows,' they tried to lure an audience by combining various kinds of entertainment and offering something for everyone" (p. 249).

36. Langer, "Polyphony and Heterogeneity," pp. 40–43.

37. Its cascading boxes, similar to the ones that flank the stage in the cartoon, distinguished the interior of the Palace. In November 1932, three months after the release of *Stopping the Show,* the Palace was converted into a full-time movie theater, an action that was often taken as a symbol of the death of vaudeville. The Palace now operates as a venue for large-scale stage productions. See http://cinematreasures.org/theater/6635/.

38. The Paramount Newsreel described itself as the "Eyes and Ears of the World" (Raymond Fielding, *The American Newsreel,* p. 97). As a pun, Paramouse Noose is intriguing. In addition to corrupting the newsreel's name, it also evokes images of a mouse and a noose. Is this a morbid reflection on Mickey? Or is *para-* being used as a prefix, rendering the meaning "about or around the mouse"? It also sounds like *Paramus,* the city in New Jersey, which is just funny.

39. Quoted in Antelyes, "Haim Afen Range," p. 25. Betty softens the lyrics' Jewish inflection when she sings "uh, oh" instead of "oy, oy" and "Indian squaw" instead of "Yiddishe squaw."

40. Allen, *Horrible Prettiness,* p. 282. This oxymoron supplied the title for Allen's superb study of burlesque.

41. Jenkins, *What Made Pistachio Nuts?*, p. 67.

42. Lehman, *The Colored Cartoon*, p. 1.

43. Arthur Knight, *Disintegrating the Musical*, p. 32.

44. Sambo was an African boy in *The Story of Little Black Sambo,* a nineteenth-century illustrated children's book. It became the basis for the early twentieth-century comics *Sambo and His Funny Noises,* by William Marriner, and *Sammy Johnsin,* by Pat Sullivan, who had illustrated Marriner's strip. Sullivan's character Felix the Cat retained many of Sambo/Sammy's qualities. See Lehman, *The Colored Cartoon,* pp. 9–11.

45. Zip Coon figures appeared contemporaneously in feature films, notably in the characters played by Stepin Fetchit (Lincoln Theodore Monroe Andrew Perry, 1902–85). See the website of the Museum of Racist Memorabilia, at Ferris State University, at www.ferris.edu/jimcrow/coon/. In a Tom Mix western, *Hello, Cheyenne* (Eugene Forde/Fox Film Corporation, 1928), white comedian Al St. John plays a character named Zip Coon.

Although Ising later denied that Bosko was "a little colored boy," he also revealed that the actors who voiced Bosko and Honey "did wear blackface makeup, but that was part of our recording process. We shot them in live action at the same time we recorded the dialogue, then we studied the footage on a Moviola" (Rudolf Ising quoted in Solomon, *Enchanted Drawings,* p. 100).

46. The Fleischers' cartoons that encapsulated filmed performances by jazz legends Louis Armstrong and Cab Calloway are legendary. See "Jazz and the Urban Scene: The Fleischer Studio," in Goldmark, *Tunes for 'Toons,* pp. 84–93.

47. *A Language All My Own* was made to be shown at the opening of a Paramount theater in Tokyo.

48. During the "Mammy" shot, the image reprises the famous poster of Jolson in *The Jazz Singer.* Mickey's actual enunciation of "Mammy" has been edited out of some video versions.

49. For the character (which was usually performed in drag) and the song, "Miss Lucy Long," see Knapp, *The American Musical and the Formation of National Identity,* p. 53 ff.

50. There is a possible connection between *Blue Rhythm* and one of the icons of blues music. Born Lizzie Douglas (1897–1973), Memphis Minnie was a prolific composer, a recording artist, and an innovator of the electric guitar as a blues instrument. She and her husband and accompanist, Joe McCoy, received their professional names in the summer of 1929, when their first Columbia Records contracts were being drawn up. According to her biographers, "a Columbia A and R [artists and repertoire] man named Minnie and Joe 'Memphis Minnie' and 'Kansas Joe'" (Garon and Garon, *Woman with Guitar,* p. 24). This event coincided with the release, on June 26, 1929, of *Mickey's Follies,* in which Carl Stalling's sing-along version of Mickey's theme song, "Minnie's Yoo Hoo," christened Mickey's new girlfriend. Minnie was being promoted to launch the Mickey Mouse clubs in theaters.

Minnie Mouse's publicity may well have inspired the Columbia representative. Indeed, this is the opinion of pioneer blues researcher Mike Leadbitter, but the idea is doubted by the Garons, who write, "The suggestions *[sic]* that Minnie's name was derived from the cartoon character, Minnie Mouse is attributed to Mike Leadbitter by Herzhaft, in 'Memphis Minnie Revisited,' but, Leadbitter does not mention Minnie Mouse [in his biography of Memphis Minnie]. The 'Minnie Mouse' theory is pure speculation, although the Disney character did debut around the time of Minnie's first session" (Garon and Garon, *Memphis Minnie*, p. 288, n. 45; citing Gérard Herzhaft, "Memphis Minnie Revisited," *Soul Bag* 97 [January/February 1984]: 8–9). It is also possible that Minnie Mouse was named after Memphis Minnie.

Fast-forwarding to 1938, Memphis Minnie records one of her two hundred blues compositions, "I Hate to See the Sun Go Down," on Columbia's Vocalion label. Though the song is obviously based on "St. Louis Blues," Memphis Minnie's delivery is remarkably similar to Minnie Mouse's in *Blue Rhythm*. (The song is available on *Memphis Minnie: Hoodoo Lady, 1933–1937* [Legacy/Columbia/Sony CD, 1991].) The lyrics in the Minnie Mouse and Memphis Minnie performances are identical in the first bars but diverge after that. The piano work on Memphis Minnie's recording follows the tempo and style of Mickey's accompaniment in the cartoon.

So we are left with a mystery: Did a central figure in American vernacular music take her name from Minnie Mouse and later cover one of her namesake's cartoon performances?

51. Lehman, *The Colored Cartoon*, p. 22. He is referencing the use of the song in an earlier cartoon, *Dixie Days* (Mannie Davis and John Foster/Paul Terry, 1930).

52. Knight, *Disintegrating the Musical*, pp. 40–47. Mickey resembles the interlocutor of the minstrel show who "could be seen as white, black, or a mixture of both" (p. 44).

53. Lewis, *Traveling Show to Vaudeville*, p. 317.

54. Goldmark, *Tunes for 'Toons*, p. 86.

55. Albee, "E. F. Albee on Vaudeville."

56. DeCordova, *Picture Personalities*, p. 98.

57. Leslie Bishko, "The Uses and Abuses of Cartoon Style in Animation," p. 24. Bishko uses the terminology of Laban Movement Analysis, a twentieth-century system of dance and movement notation, to analyze the principles that animators employed to connote "authenticity" in cartoons from the early 1930s onward. ("LMA offers us a framework of movement constructs that excel at delineating the elements of expressive style in movement" [p. 30]). This approach is very useful because it acknowledges that authenticity is a constructed performance. One of her three criteria for evaluating authenticity is especially pertinent for our study: "alignment of style with content, as opposed to adoption of style without connecting it to its subject" (p. 25).

58. Solomon, *Disappearing Tricks*, pp. 64–65.

59. Mumford, *Technics and Civilization*, pp. 40–41.

60. Gunning, "An Aesthetic of Astonishment," p. 80.

61. Méliès both gained and lost by converting to cinema. On the one hand, the tricks were perfectly executed on film as instantaneous transformations, and once he filmed a trick, he never had to worry that a live slipup would spoil the illusion. He could also reach a lot more people to monetize his performance either directly (through ticket sales) or indirectly (through distribution). On the other hand, as

Gunning observed in "An Aesthetic of Astonishment," it relocated the magic of the event from the magician to the film apparatus. The awesome experience of witnessing transformations of objects and bodies in front of us in real time and in the shared physical space of his theater could only be re-performed on film as a new—cinematic—performance. As one of the initiators of the mediatization of theater, Méliès was also among the first to create nostalgia for "live" magic.

62. Chuck Jones, interviewed by Mary Harrington Hall (1989), in Furniss, ed., *Chuck Jones,* p. 6.

63. Draw: 1. To make a drawing; 2. To attract an audience to a show; 3. To attract flies or vermin through an odor.

64. Jenkins, *What Made Pistachio Nuts?,* p. 79.

65. Solomon, *Disappearing Tricks,* pp. 2–3.

66. Ibid., p. 6. He references early cinema here, but the parallel to these cartoons about magic is noteworthy.

67. Feyersinger, "Diegetic Short Circuits," p. 282.

68. These reflexive jokes include: Wilfred Jaxon Feed and Fuel, Walter D's "Hats That Please," Riley Livery Stable, Breezy Allen's Haberdashery, The Famous T. Hee Shoes, McFlanigan Coffee, Gen. J. Sharpsteen Dentist, R.B. Martch Guns, and Professor Churchill's Piano Tuning. One of the featured acts is "Fred and Ward, Two Clever Boys from Illinois," presumably referring to animators Fred Moore and Ward Kimball.

69. Chanan, "The Documentary Chronotope," n.p.

70. A partial list includes *For Me and My* Gal (Busby Berkeley/MGM, 1942), *The Dolly Sisters* (Irving Cummings/Twentieth Century-Fox, 1945), *Mother Wore Tights* (Walter Lang/Twentieth Century-Fox, 1947), *Give My Regards to Broadway* (Lloyd Bacon/Twentieth Century-Fox, 1948), *Look for the Silver Lining* (David Butler/Warner Bros., 1949), and *Singin' in the Rain* (Gene Kelly and Stanley Donen/MGM, 1952).

71. The showgirl was an important figure for Freud. As it turns out, beginning in 1889, he corresponded with Yvette Guilbert, one of Paris's noted chanteuses. Werman and Guilbert, "Freud, Yvette Guilbert, and the Psychology of Performance," pp. 399–412. *Piano Tooners* holds some sort of distinction as a cartoon in which the protagonist uses a toilet.

72. The opportunity to make a self-referential in-joke was, as usual, not missed. One attraction is "Clampett's Trained Seals," a reference to Warner Bros. director Bob Clampett—and his animation staff?

73. Studio head Jack Warner and animator Otto Messmer were born in 1892—but in December and May, respectively, not April. Since there is nothing arbitrary or accidental in Maltese and Jones's films, it is likely that the date held some personal or professional significance.

For an authoritative and suitably tongue-in-cheek account of the Los Angeles architecture in *One Froggy Evening,* see the article "Hello My Ragtime Pile of Rubble" at www.onbunkerhill.org/SonsoftheRevolution.

74. In the (unconfirmed) lore of animation, the inspiration for Maltese's story was Old Rip, a horny toad that the burg of Eastland, Texas, entombed alive in its courthouse cornerstone in 1897. When the building was demolished and the cornerstone reopened in 1928, the critter was still clinging to life. Since

the horned lizard *(Phrynosoma coronatum)* lives only five to eight years in the wild and even less in captivity, this story is suspicious. Nevertheless, the animal's owner, Will M. Wood, took his specimen on tour accompanied by a delegation of Texas politicians. One stop included a fifteen-minute stint on President Calvin Coolidge's desk. There are no reports of dancing or singing. Old Rip died on January 20, 1929. His mummified remains (or some horned lizard's remains) are still on display at the Eastland Court House. See "Coolidge Sees Texas Toad That Was Entombed 31 Years," *New York Times,* May 4, 1928, p. 1; "Old Rip to Rest on Bed of Fame," *Los Angeles Times,* January 21, 1929, p. 2; www.eastlandvisitor.com/oldRipHistory.html.

75. As Goldmark has remarked, some are authentic, some new (DVD commentary, "It Hopped One Night: The Story Behind *One Froggy Evening,*" New Wave Entertainment/Warner Home Video, 2004).

76. The site of the original Hippodrome was 6th Avenue between 43rd and 44th Streets. Now it's an office building at 1120 Avenue of the Americas.

77. All the national newspapers carried Barrymore's death notice, but I have not identified one with the headline in the Jones film: "Lionel Barrymore Heiress Tells of His Big, Soft Heart." The closest candidate is syndicated columnist Hedda Hopper's tribute, "Barrymore Extolled as Gruff but Gentle," which carries the subhead "Big Heart." Hedda Hopper, "Barrymore Extolled as Gruff but Gentle," *Los Angeles Times,* November 18, 1954, p. A12.

78. Cartoon buffs know that Tregoweth "Treg" Brown was the editor and sound effects technician for Warner Bros. cartoons and that the Gribbroek Theatrical Shoes storefront refers to Robert Gribbroek, the layout artist. But who was J.C. Wilber? Because the other names are identifiable as Warner Bros. crew members, it seems likely that Wilber also worked for the studio. However, the only Wilber I have uncovered in animation is the pet cat of Honey in the original Warner Bros. Bosko series. Perhaps they have an obscure common namesake.

Another remote possibility is that J.C. Wilber is a reference to actor, screenwriter, and director Crane Wilbur, although his surname isn't spelled the same and his first name was Irwin (or Erwin). Born in 1886, he would have been six when the *Froggy* cornerstone was laid, so the 1892 date isn't Wilbur's birthday. Setting aside for the moment this overwhelming counterevidence and entertaining the unlikely possibility that this is the reference, why? Wilbur had an extraordinarily lengthy career as an actor, Broadway playwright, Hollywood screenwriter, and film director. During the 1950s, Wilbur worked for independent producers and at Warner Bros., where he was a "king of the Bs," penning prison films, some now-respected films noir, and the Vincent Price 3-D classics *House of Wax* (André De Toth/Warner Bros., 1953) and *The Mad Magician* (John Brahm/Columbia Pictures, 1954). That Jones and Wilbur might have known each other is suggested in *He Walked by Night* (Alfred Werker and Anthony Mann/Eagle-Lion Films, 1948), in which screenwriter Wilbur created a character named "Chuck Jones." Was J.C. Wilber Jones's witty but obscure payback for a compliment?

Like the frog, Crane Wilbur might have seemed to Jones and Maltese like an anomaly from vaudeville and the early days of cinema that just wouldn't quit performing. They could have admired his Old Rip–like tenacity as a survivor. The plots of Wilbur's Price films about obsessive madness might also have appealed to them.

79. The frog continues to live as a media re-performance as a denizen of cable channel cartoons and as erstwhile corporate mascot for Warner Bros. He made a startling cameo as a hideous alien that emerges from a human body in *Spaceballs* (Mel Brooks, 1987), high-stepping to the "Michigan Rag."

80. Barrier, *Hollywood Cartoons*, p. 486.

4. SHADOW OF A MOUSE: ANIMATION PERFORMANCE SPACES

Epigraphs: Focillon, *The Life of Forms in Art*, pp. 162–63; "Notes on Jean Charlot Lectures [to the animation staff]," Walt Disney Studios transcript, April 19, 1938, pp. 1–2. This chapter is dedicated to Kristin and Antonia.

1. Sergei Eisenstein, "From Lectures on Music and Colour in *Ivan The Terrible*," in *Sergei Eisenstein: Selected Works*, p. 336.

2. Graham, "The Art of Animation," pp. 10–11.

3. Langer, "Polyphony and Heterogeneity," in Goldmark and Keil, eds., *Funny Pictures*, pp. 31–35.

4. Crowther, "Figure, Plane, and Frame," in *Phenomenology of the Visual Arts (even the frame)*, p. 42.

5. Barrier, *Hollywood Cartoons*, p. 79.

6. Canemaker, "Disney Design 1928–1979," p. 102.

7. [Vladimir] Bill Tytla, "Class on Action Analysis: Discussion of Sequence 4-D of Feature from Point of View of Drawing; Also Continuation of Discussion of Preceding Session of Form versus Force in Animation," Walt Disney Studios transcript, June 28, 1937, p. 5.

8. Disney, "Growing Pains," p. 106.

9. Wells, *Understanding Animation*, p. 23.

10. Langer, "Regionalism in Disney Animation," pp. 305–6.

11. Donald Graham, "The New Art," in "The Art of Animation," pp. 34–36, 44–46.

12. David R. Smith, "New Dimensions: Beginnings of the Disney Multiplane Camera," in Canemaker, *Storytelling in Animation*, p. 40.

13. This passion is recounted in detail by Mark Langer in "The Disney-Fleischer Dilemma: Product Differentiation and Technological Innovation."

14. Merritt and Kaufman, *Walt Disney's Silly Symphonies*, pp. 94–95.

15. A similar scene appears in *Big Bang Big Boom* (Blu, 2010), a mural animation painted on the side of a cylindrical oil tank. A soldier launches a grenade to the right. We follow its flight around the tank until it kills the men standing behind (i.e., to the left of) the soldier who fired. See http://blublu.org /sito/video/video.htm.

16. Donald W. Graham (1903–76) was born in Fort Williams, Ontario. He had studied engineering at Stanford, was among the first graduates of Chouinard Art Institute, and taught there from 1924 to 1965. The studio art school that Disney organized, which was on Hyperion Avenue, had Graham, Phil Dike,

and James Patrick as instructors. The school was discontinued in 1941, but Graham continued to consult and lecture occasionally at Disney's studio ("Donald W. Graham, Former Disney Art School Teacher, Dies," press release, Walt Disney Productions, October 22, 1976; Neupert, "Color, Lines and Nudes," p. 77). Perine has a somewhat different account. He writes that Herbert Jepson taught the first fifteen Disney students enrolled at the studio school, in 1929, with Graham taking over in the fall of 1930 (Perine, *Chouinard*, p. 25).

17. Langer, "Polyphony and Heterogeneity," pp. 31–35; "Regionalism in Disney Animation," pp. 305–6.

18. Walt Disney, Interoffice Memo to Don Graham, December 23, 1935.

19. Mumford, *Technics and Civilization*, pp. 341, 218.

20. Graham, *Composing Pictures*, p. 382.

21. Graham, "The Art of Animation," pp. 7–8.

22. Graham, *Composing Pictures*, p. 149.

23. Ibid., p. 325.

24. Ken Anderson, "Layout Training Course: Second Lecture," Walt Disney Studios transcript, November 27, 1938, pp. 12–13.

25. Disney, "Growing Pains," p. 107.

26. Allan, *Walt Disney and Europe*, p. 32.

27. Arthur Millier, quoted in McClelland, *Millard Sheets*, p. 43. See also MacAdam, *Coastline to Skyline*, p. 12; Janet Blake Dominik, "The California Water Color Society: Genesis of an American Style," in Westphal and Dominik, eds., *American Scene Painting: California 1930s and 1940s*, www.tfaoi.com/aa/3aa/3aa50.htm; and the Smithsonian exhibition "1934: A New Deal for Artists," http://americanart.si.edu/exhibitions/archive/2009/1934/.

28. Nancy Dustin Wall Moure, quoted in Perine, *Chouinard*, p. 113. The CWCS became the National Watercolor Society in 1973. At least the first ten presidents of the CWCS were "Chouinard people" (p. 113).

29. This painting can be viewed at www.californiawatercolor.com/paintings/millard_sheets/migratory_camp_near_nipomo_1936/. To get a sense of the Sheets's vigorous command of perspective and shadow, view *Tenement Flats* (1933–34), at the Smithsonian American Art Museum. Millard Sheets's most famous and visible picture by far is *Word of Life* (1964), better known as *Touchdown Jesus*, the mosaic that adorns the fourteen-story Hesburgh Library at the University of Notre Dame. See www.library.nd.edu/about/history/mosaic.shtml.

30. Skolnick, *Paintings of California*, p. 118.

31. Don Graham quoted in Finch, *The Art of Walt Disney*, p. 138.

32. This painting can be viewed at www.californiawatercolor.com/paintings/phil_dike/grape_harvest_c_1930s/?ret=%2Fpaintings%2Fphil_dike%2F.

33. Dike's other Disney credits include *Fantasia* (Algar/Disney, 1940; story development on "Night on Bald Mountain/Ave Maria" and "Toccata and Fugue in D Minor") and *The Three Caballeros* (Norman Ferguson/Disney, 1944; color consultant on live-action sequences). Dike recalled, "So mine was a learning process—nobody else knew anything about it, and I didn't have any of the technical and scientific knowledge of the medium of Technicolor. The only thing

I could say was that I felt that it was too light or too dark or too red or too yellow or too pink and etcetera" (quoted in Perine, *Chouinard*, p. 25).

34. Blair's "Sunbathing on the Rooftops" (1930s) shows his keen sense of linear perspective and shadows. It can be seen at www.californiawatercolor .com/paintings/lee_blair/sunbathing_on_the_rooftops_c_1930_s/. For Blair's animation work for Avery, see Place-Verghnes, *Tex Avery*, p. 107.

35. McClelland, *Millard Sheets*, p. 106. Lee Blair's expertise was called upon while he was working at the Harman-Ising studio: "Disney's rights to the three-color process ran out and we were able to switch to Technicolor [in 1936]. When we did, they naturally said, 'Hey, Lee is a great watercolor painter, he's the president of the California Watercolor Society. Why doesn't he do some scenes for us, in terms of color-keying?' So I started on the side doing all their color sketches and laid the thing out color-wise with real broad strokes, and we began really slapping all over the place" (Lee Blair interviewed by Robin Allan, in Ghez, ed., *Walt's People, Volume 3*, pp. 169–70).

36. Lee and Mary Blair were both art supervisors on *Saludos Amigos*. For a sample of Mary Blair's early watercolor style, see *Chicken Coops* (1935) at www.californiawatercolor.com/paintings/mary_blair/chicken_coops_1935/. For details on all three Blairs, see Canemaker, *The Art and Flair of Mary Blair*.

37. Although the watercolorist sensibility dominated Chouinard in the 1930s, this altered late in the decade. Graham remained an influential teacher there until he retired in 1970, but the school's emphasis shifted to design from the fine arts (Amidi, *Cartoon Modern,* p. 18). A vivid example of this change is Maurice Noble's career. Having begun on scholarship at Chouinard in the early 1930s, he dropped out to design windows at a Los Angeles department store. He was recruited to Disney and worked on backgrounds for *Snow White,* on "The Rite of Spring" sequence of *Fantasia*, and as color coordinator on *Dumbo.* In the army he designed backgrounds for the Private Snafu series. In 1950 he joined Chuck Jones at Warner Bros., where he began his distinctive semiabstract backgrounds, "a type of accessible modernism that resonated with mainstream audiences," according to Amidi (pp. 173–75).

38. It was not only through the teachers that this aesthetic influenced Disney; it also came from Chouinard students who worked there, such as Hardie Gramatky (1907–79). He began as a comic strip artist at Disney in 1929 and gradually worked his way up to animator on *The Robber Kitten* (David Hand/Disney, 1935), *Who Killed Cock Robin* (David Hand/Disney, 1935), and *Through the Mirror* (David Hand/Disney, 1936). Gramatky left the studio in 1936 to pursue a career writing and illustrating children's books. Disney adapted his 1939 *Little Toot* as a segment of *Melody Time* (Clyde Geronimi et al./Disney, 1948). A statement by Gramatky suggests that not only did the watercolorists influence the Disney aesthetic, but animation informed him as a watercolorist as well: "I think that the movement and action in my watercolors stem primarily from that early work with animation" (Linda Gramatky Smith, "Memories of Hardie Gramatky by His Daughter," www.gramatky.com/story.asp).

39. Thompson, "Implications of the Cel Animation Technique," p. 113.

40. Friedberg, *The Virtual Window,* p. 60.

41. Tom Codrick, "Layout Lecture," Walt Disney Studios transcript, May 19, 1938 (Supplement: "The Layout Man's Approach to Scene Planning," p. 1).

42. The slash system used an opaque sheet of paper or cardboard with a background drawn around the edges of a central blank space. An opening was torn or "slashed" out of the center. The animation drawings were on separate sheets of paper, not cels. When the slashed background overlay was placed atop each drawing during photography, the animation drawings underneath appeared in the opening and created the illusion that the movement was in the foreground (Crafton, *Before Mickey*, p. 194). The Fleischers' *Vaudeville* is an example of a slash system animation.

43. The immortal Acme name is part of animation mythology, but we've lost sight of Acme's origins as an actual company and product line. Adolph Furer operated the modest machine shop on San Fernando Road from 1927 to 1939, when he sold it to Edward "Bud" Kiel, whose descendants still manage the company. Now it is Photo-Sonics, Inc., a diversified designer and manufacturer of optical tracking cameras and other specialized photographic instruments.

Gradually, Acme products became ubiquitous in Los Angeles animation shops. This is said to have annoyed Disney, who gradually cut back his dependence on Acme and started his own machine shop. Disney's engineers designed the 1937 multiplane camera, but the precision parts were still milled, assembled, and maintained by Acme, which temporarily assigned an employee to provide technical support for the camera at the studio. When the Disney studio moved to Burbank, Acme followed. Among its many contributions to the film business was the Acme Optical Printer, which won an Academy Award in 1980. I am grateful to John Kiel, Philip Kiel, Arthur Stroud, and Graham Jones of Photo-Sonics for their interviews on March 17, 2010.

When Ub Iwerks set up his MGM studio in 1930, he adopted the Acme system and used their supplies. He felt, though, that his needs were not Acme's highest priority, so he outfitted his own machine shop (Iwerks and Kenworthy, *The Hand Behind the Mouse*, p. 111).

The hegemony of Acme as a supplier to the trade waned after World War II, when the company began to diversify into other product lines and a competitor, the Oxberry animation system, began making inroads in the 1950s. At that time Acme changed its name to Producers Service Co.

44. There are fleeting references to the Acme brand in cartoons from the 1930s and '40s, but Chuck Jones's Road Runner series, which commenced in 1949, made the products from the semifictitious company a household name. The luckless Wile E. Coyote depends on their mail-order catalogue to supply the tools for his never-ending quest to eat the speedy little bird. Jones may have sensed the irony inherent in the highfalutin brand name, meaning a state of perfection, and the utilitarian ordinariness of all these contraptions lying around the animation shop. Leslie Iwerks and John Kenworthy wondered "how the Acme Tool Company came to inhabit Chuck Jones's consciousness during his second stint at the Iwerks Studio. As low man on the Iwerks totem pole at the time, he would no doubt have had intimate dealings with Acme. It is all too easy to imagine the young Jones receiving the parcels of animation equipment

with the fervor of his future alter ego, Wile E. Coyote" (Iwerks and Kenworthy, *The Hand Behind the Mouse,* pp. 112–13).

45. "Cels" refer to the sheets of cellulose nitrate that were in wide use until the 1940s, despite their color tinge and flammability. Clear cellulose acetate became the nonflammable alternative. In some literature, e.g., Falk, *How to Make Animated Cartoons,* the word is spelled "cell." One finds both spellings in Disney studio documents.

46. Crowther, "Figure, Plane, and Frame," p. 42.

47. Some animators drew on animation paper and cels with the perforations on top, while others preferred the perforations at the bottom of the sheet. The choice seems to have been specific to each studio. Warner Bros. animators used top pegs, while Disney animators used the bottom ones (Williams, *The Animator's Survival Kit,* pp. 80–83; Thomas, *Walt Disney, the Art of Animation,* p. 139).

48. Robert D. Feild, *The Art of Walt Disney,* p. 272. Disney converted to a 16-field size for the production of *Snow White* (Gabler, *Walt Disney,* p. 257). These papers and cels are 16 inches by 13.5 inches. Disney also switched from the standard Acme peg and perfs to an in-house standard using five holes instead of three.

49. The reframing indications are clearly visible as concentric rectangles drawn on storyboard sketches. See the illustrations in Finch, *The Art of Walt Disney,* p. 80; Canemaker, *Treasures of Disney Animation Art,* pp. 42–44.

50. Mique Nelson, "Condensed Version of Lecture on Mechanics of Background and Light," Walt Disney Studios transcript, July 17, 1938. "So, since we cannot control this point of grief, give us [background artists], if possible, sky, blank wall or undetailed grass or ground when getting below a 4 field" (p. 2). Philippi warned, "Within the boundaries of the 5-field you can move around in different field sizes, but you cannot go outside the boundaries of the 5-field, of course" (Charles Philippi, "Layout Training Course: Third Lecture," Walt Disney Studios transcript, December 3, 1936, p. 2).

51. An excellent example of how this looked are the pencil tests for an unrealized "soup slurping" segment of *Snow White,* presented as a DVD extra on *Snow White and the Seven Dwarfs.* The animators' figure drawings in pencil were photographed with a sketch of the background under each drawing.

52. The Disney studio, in fact, began laying out complex movements as choreographic plans. In *The Art of Walt Disney,* Feild reproduces ones from *Bambi* (p. 207) and *Fantasia* (p. 219). Leslie Bishko has shown that it may be productive to apply Laban Movement Analysis to animation. See http://labanforani mators.wordpress.com/leslie-bishko/.

53. Feild, *The Art of Walt Disney,* p. 268.

54. Sam Armstrong, "Lecture on Mechanics of Background and Layout," Walt Disney Studios transcript, June 29, 1938, p. 4.

55. Thompson, "Implications of the Cel Animation Technique," 112–13.

56. Anderson, "Layout Training Course: Second Lecture," p. 2.

57. See Lutz's diagram reproduced in Crafton, *Before Mickey,* p. 203. The eight-drawing module was based on silent film projection speed, which was approximately sixteen frames per second. It was assumed that each drawing would be shot twice ("on the twos," that is, eight drawings per second of pro-

jection) to save the animator (or, more likely, the assistant animator or in-betweener) time and effort. After the conversion to sound, according to Shamus Culhane, the Disney studio normally used twelve-frame modules and photographed the drawings on the twos (i.e., twelve drawings per second). When especially smooth motion was desired, twenty to twenty-four drawings per second would be made (Culhane, *Talking Animals,* p. 156). In a memo to the staff, Disney encouraged them to animate on the twos, to use sliding (top) cels, and to limit retracing whenever practical:

> Economize on drawings as much as possible within a reasonable limit or to the extent that such economy will not detract from the quality of the work.
> For instance, some action looks as good on twos as on ones. Sometimes a sliding cell will save your animating an inanimate prop; and many times a held cell will save calling for trace-backs for fee on as many as ten to one hundred drawings, or more (Anonymous on behalf of Walt Disney, "Attention Animators," pp. 1–2).

58. Walt Disney, recorded remarks included in John Canemaker's DVD commentary on *Snow White and the Seven Dwarfs.*

59. A variant on this technique makes it easy to create reflections in mirrors or on water by flipping the original drawings upside down before tracing.

60. The Disney studio began referring to the creation of a scene's background layouts as "staging." "The layout man evolved as the creator who actually stages the scenes. He is responsible for how the picture looks, just as the art director decides the appearance of a live-action movie or a designer the appearance of a stage play" (Thomas, *Walt Disney, the Art of Animation,* p. 118).

61. Crowther, *Phenomenology of the Visual Arts (even the frame),* p. 50.

62. Graham, "The Art of Animation," pp. 6–8.

63. The use of "setting" rather than "background" seems to have been common in the New York studios. In *Betty Boop's Rise to Fame,* Max refers to Betty's "sets." Falk's *How to Make Animated Cartoons* also calls them "sets" (p. 46.)

64. A cel setup with a 3-pan background for *The Tortoise and the Hare* (Wilfred Jackson/Disney, 1935) is illustrated in Merritt and Kaufman, *Walt Disney's Silly Symphonies,* p. 152. A 16-field 3-pan background is 46.5 by 13.5 inches.

65. There was a comparable non-animated cinema technique, borrowed from theater, for filming a running actor with a static camera. The Keystone studio built a stage with a treadmill on which the actors ran. Behind them an enormous cyclorama background painting revolved on a sort of carousel. This may be seen during chase scenes, for example, in *Teddy at the Throttle* (Clarence Badger/Keystone, 1917). The two planes of action anticipate cartoon space: the treadmill allowed the runner to go only left or right, not into depth. The revolving drum is a continuous cylindrical space that repeated every revolution.

66. "The story-men and the layout men must have a clear idea of the physical environment within which action will take place. . . . These considerations are self-evident when one realizes the need for action-control of the characters to the minutest detail. There can be nothing vague about their environment" (Feild, *The Art of Walt Disney,* p. 146).

67. Anderson, "Layout Training Course," p. 2. In the same lecture transcript, layout artist Philippi reiterated, "It is really up to the layout man to feel

responsible for the looks of the picture on the screen. The director has certain ideas that he will give the layout man; he will then depend on the layout man to go further, to improve, to enhance the idea if he can in executing it" (p. 16).

68. A working Acme animation stand is on display at the Museum of Cartoon Art in San Francisco. Thanks to Andrew Farago.

69. Philippi, "Layout Training Class," pp. 1–2. Feild gives an illustrated description of the process using a scene from *Fantasia* (*The Art of Walt Disney*, pp. 278–79).

70. Adapted from "Animation Tech Notes #1: Of Peg Bars and Field Charts, Tools of the Trade," RMIT Centre for Animation and Interactive Media, http://minyos.its.rmit.cdu.au/aim/a_notes/tools_of_trade.html.

71. Philippi, "Layout Training Course," p. 17.

72. Illustrated in Crafton, *Before Mickey*, Figure 130, p. 340. Another example from silent cartoons is *Barnyard Olympics* (Paul Terry/Pathé Exchange, 1924), in which the cat has a bit of a noonday shadow while jumping rope but does not have one through most of the film. The Phantom in *Slick Sleuths* (Charles Bowers/Bud Fisher Film Corp., 1926) casts an ominous shadow, but Mutt and Jeff do not, even when they are with the Phantom in the same scene. There are no shadows in *Alice the Whaler* (Ub Iwerks/Disney, 1927).

73. The Fleischer film *A Car-Tune Portrait* (Dave Fleischer/Paramount, 1936) appears to use transparent shadows in the spotlight that illuminates the lion orchestra conductor. There is also a transparent white light effect when we see the musicians through the beam of the spotlight. The musicians in much of the first part of the film perform in silhouette, a treatment that reappears in *Fantasia* (James Algar et al./Disney, 1940).

74. The same anomaly appears in *Katnip Kollege*. Because the shadows were painted on the cels in gray, when the characters appear on a dark background, as in the nocturnal song performance, the shadows appear brighter than their surroundings.

75. Merritt and Kaufman illustrate a frame from *Music Land* (Jackson/Disney, 1935) in which an interior space is rendered darkly confining using double-exposed shadows (*Walt Disney's Silly Symphonies*, pp. 45, 164).

76. By 1938 the Background Department at Disney had become an autonomous entity in the studio's Taylorized organization. It described itself as primarily a "research laboratory for the study and use of color" (Walt Disney Studios, *An Introduction to the Walt Disney Studios*, a.k.a. *Artist Try-Out Book* [1938], ASIFA Animation Archive, www.animationarchive.org/2007/02/history-disneys-artist-tryout-book.html, p. 9).

77. Anonymous on behalf of Walt Disney, "Attention Animators," p. 2.

78. Scene instruction sheet for *The Country Cousin* (Wilfred Jackson/Disney, 1936), Art Babbitt Papers in the Cowan Collection, courtesy of Bob Cowan.

79. Walter E. Disney, "Art of Animation," US Patent 2,201,689, May 21, 1940.

80. Bob Martsch, "Supplement to Lecture on Effects," Walt Disney Studio transcript, June 15, 1938, p. 2.

81. Marc Davis recalled seeing *Nosferatu* as one of the films screened for the animators during their regular Wednesday evening shows (Canemaker's DVD commentary on *Snow White and the Seven Dwarfs*).

82. Compare to "Yosemite Valley" (1868) by Albert Bierstadt, at http://library.artstor.org.

83. Feild, *The Art of Walt Disney,* p. 271.

84. By the 1960s, zoom lenses were standard on the Acme animation stand. Other features included sophisticated film-handling mechanisms in the camera, the capability to make matte shots in-camera, movement tracking to .001 inch, automatic dissolving, autofocus, a movable camera, a vacuum platen that pressed cels against backgrounds with forty pounds of pressure per square inch, and multiple peg sets, "making it possible to get the illusion of depth" (Photo-Sonics, Inc., "Equipment Catalogue," ca. 1968).

85. "Another nonpictorial cue that provides valuable information for calculating the location of objects in three-dimensional space is *motion parallax....* Motion parallax helps animals with limited binocular visual fields [as it does, for example, movie spectators, who see only a monocular image on the screen even when they watch with two eyes] to see depth.... Depth judgments based on motion parallax are almost as accurate as those based on binocular disparity.... This is not surprising because motion parallax produces large image displacements on the retina that are equivalent to those produced by disparity" (Steinman et al., *Foundations of Binocular Vision,* pp. 180–81).

86. See John Krantz, "Motion Parallax," http://psych.hanover.edu/krantz/MotionParallax/MotionParallax.html, for an animated illustration.

87. Walt Disney, "Tricks of Our Trade," *Disneyland* episode, February 13, 1957, on *Behind the Scenes at the Walt Disney Studio* DVD.

88. Shamus Culhane, *Talking Animals and Other People,* p. 157.

89. Jean Charlot, *Art from the Mayans to Disney,* p. 188. Three hundred images by Charlot are available at http://artstor.org/news/n-html/an-110111-charlot.shtml.

90. Richard Neupert, "Colour, Lines, and Nudes," p. 78.

91. Ibid.

92. As Eric Goldberg points out *(A Dream Walking* DVD commentary, *Popeye the Sailor: 1933–1938, Vol. I),* designing the movements was the work of the animators, who were Seymour Kneitel, Roland "Doc" Crandall, and William Henning on this film, but the tedious work of redrawing the orthogonal lines to their correct vanishing points on each sheet would have fallen to the anonymous staff of in-betweeners.

93. Graham, "Animation," p. 10.

94. Graham, *Composing Pictures,* p. 152.

95. There is ample evidence in the anecdotes told by animators and recorded in a few of the transcripts of the action analysis classes that some of the animators disagreed with Graham's principles.

96. Graham, "Animation," p. 10.

97. Smith, "New Dimensions," p. 40.

98. Ibid., p. 41.

99. For an illustration of the setback from the Max Fleischer and John E. Burks patent, see Harvey Deneroff, "Willis O'Brien, Iwerks' Multiplane Camera and Fleischer's Stereoptical Process," http://deneroff.com/blog/2008/03/04/willis-obrien-iwerks-multiplane-camera-and-fleischers-stereoptical-process/.

Deneroff speculates that Iwerks's multiplane system might have been inspired by Willis O'Brien's miniature *King Kong* sets. The original patent (no. 2,054,414, "Art of Making Motion Picture Cartoons") is available on Google Scholar. The patent was filed in 1933 and granted on September 15, 1936.

100. For more information, see Maltin and Beck, *Of Mice and Magic,* pp. 339–41; Lenburg, *The Great Cartoon Directors,* pp. 36, 201.

101. One of the studio's three multiplane systems is on permanent display at the Walt Disney Family Museum, San Francisco.

102. Disney, "Tricks of Our Trade."

103. Smith, "New Dimensions," p. 47.

104. Disney, "Growing Pains," p. 140. The studio joined the 3-D craze in 1953 with two shorts, *Melody (Adventures in Music)* (Ward Kimball and Charles Nichols/Disney, 1953) and *Working for Peanuts* (Jack Hannah/Disney, 1953). Disney showed no particular passion for the 3-D process. "How many we make depends on how long the theaters run them," he stated at the time. "If the novelty holds up, we'll make more" (quoted in Robert Tieman, *The Disney Keepsakes,* pp. 36–37).

105. Not every film used the carnivalesque opening shot. *Flowers and Trees* (Gillett, 1932), for example, does not have one. *The Three Little Pigs* (Burt Gillett/Disney, 1933) begins with three separate openings, each showing its respective porker in long shot, then refielding for a closer view.

106. Don Graham, "Action Analysis: Discussion of Hound Dance Team in 'Mickey's Review' in Relation to Similar Hound Characters to Be Used in Band in 'Mickey's Circus,'" Walt Disney Studios transcript, January 9, 1936, p. 1.

107. Don Graham quoted in Canemaker, "Disney Design 1928–1979," p. 106.

108. Antonia Lant, "The Curse of the Pharaoh, or How Cinema Contracted Egyptomania," in Bernstein and Studlar, eds., *Visions of the East,* pp. 69–98.

109. Lant, "Haptical Cinema," pp. 45–73.

110. Focillon, *The Life of Forms in Art,* p. 162.

111. Walt Disney Studio, "Notes on Jean Charlot Lectures," Walt Disney Studios transcript. April 19, 1938, p. 7.

112. Ibid., p. 13.

113. Graham, *Composing Pictures,* p. 356. Graham called the "quantitative degree of space to volume the *space matrix.*"

114. David Hockney, *Secret Knowledge.* See also Friedberg's comments in *The Virtual Window,* pp. 63–64.

115. Norman M. Klein, "Animation and Animorphs: A Brief Disappearing Act," in Sobchack, ed., *Meta Morphing,* p. 25.

116. Graham, "The Art of Animation," p. 8.

117. Nelson, "Condensed Version of Lecture," p. 3.

118. Arnheim, *Film As Art,* pp. 199–233.

119. Robert Sklar warned against the allure of technological determinism. "To say that later is better than earlier," he wrote, "is to ignore a more fundamental kind of change. In the early Mickey Mouse and Silly Symphony films, Disney and his animators created one kind of fantasy world. Then they gave it up, putting in its place not a fantasy but an idealized world. A preference for the flatter over the

earlier cartoon shorts should be recognized as an aesthetic and cultural as well as a technological judgment" (Robert Sklar, "The Making of Cultural Myths—Walt Disney," in Peary and Peary, eds., *The American Animated Cartoon*, p. 58).

120. John Hubley, quoted in Amidi, *Cartoon Modern*, p. 13. According to Amidi, "Though [Ward] Kimball had spent his entire career at Disney, he remained a graphic iconoclast within the studio and displayed a sympathy for modern art shared by few of the studio's other animators" (p. 149).

121. Friedberg, *The Virtual Window*, p. 63.

5. INFECTIOUS LAUGHTER

Epigraphs: Leo Tolstoy, *What Is Art?*, p. 38; Walt Disney, narration on "Tricks of Our Trade," *Disneyland* episode, February 13, 1957, on *Behind the Scenes at the Walt Disney Studio* DVD. This chapter is dedicated to Miriam.

1. Watts, *The Magic Kingdom*, p. 65.

2. Ibid., p. 77. For a survey of criticism, see Gregory A. Waller, "Mickey, Walt and Film Criticism from *Steamboat Willie* to *Bambi*," in Peary and Peary, *The American Animated Cartoon*, pp. 49–57.

3. Waller, "Mickey, Walt and Film Criticism," p. 51.

4. Kaufman, "*Three Little Pigs*—Big Little Picture," p. 39. The revenue the film took in became a minor obsession with the press. One estimate placed the projected two-year revenue of the cartoon at $1.5 million (John Scott, "Three Little Pigs and Big Bad Wolf Clean up Millions," *Los Angeles Times*, October 8, 1933, p. A1). This would have been about one hundred times the film's negative cost of $15,720 (Merritt and Kaufman, *Walt Disney's Silly Symphonies*, p. 126). Disney responded to such stories by claiming that he did not expect his net profit on the film to exceed $25,000 over a two-year period ("Before the Cameras and the Microphones," *New York Times*, November 26, 1933, p. X5). All the journalists concluded that whatever the film's profits were, they were minuscule in comparison to the franchise's merchandising and licensing revenue.

5. For a concise survey of humor theories and their practical application, see the introduction to Goldstein, *Laughter Out of Place*, pp. 1–17. Theories of comedy specifically in relation to media are woven throughout Jenkins, *What Made Pistachio Nuts?*

6. Bergson, *Laughter*, pp. 6–8.

7. Freud, "The Joke and the Varieties of the Comic," in *The Joke and Its Relation to the Unconscious*, p. 183.

8. Sigmund Freud, letter to Max Shiller, March 26, 1931, in Ernst Freud, Lucie Freud, and Ilse Grubrich-Simitis, *Sigmund Freud: His Life in Pictures and Words*, quoted in Werman and Guilbert, "Freud, Yvette Guilbert, and the Psychology of Performance," pp. 405–6.

9. Grafly, "America's Youngest Art," p. 137.

10. Maltby, *Harmless Entertainment*, p. 55. "Shirts" refers to the story that the sale of men's undergarments was affected by Clark Gable's removal of his shirt and revelation of a bare chest in *It Happened One Night* (Frank Capra, 1934).

11. Schechner, *Performance Studies*, p. 77.

12. Berger, *Redeeming Laughter,* p. 114.

13. Ibid., p. 99.

14. *Stand Up and Cheer!* is the film with the backflipping senators routine, a line from which inspired the title of Jenkins's *What Made Pistachio Nuts?*

15. Franklin D. Roosevelt, first inaugural address, 1932, available at www .archives.gov/education/lessons/fdr-inaugural/.

16. Jenkins, *What Made Pistachio Nuts?,* p. 1.

17. Martin Rubin, "Movies and the New Deal in Entertainment," in Hark, ed., *American Cinema of the 1930s,* p. 94. "Happy Days Are Here Again" may be heard in pre-FDR-era films like *Chasing Rainbows* (Charles Reisner/Paramount, 1930) and *Rain or Shine* (Frank Capra/Columbia, 1930) and in the post–New Deal *Thanks a Million* (Roy Del Ruth/Twentieth Century-Fox, 1935).

"Infectious music" was a distinctive feature of early 1930s Hollywood musicals. In *Monte Carlo* (Ernst Lubitsch, 1930), when Jeanette MacDonald lilts "Beyond the Blue Horizon" (Franke Harling, Leo Robin, and Richard Whiting, 1930), her voice floats from her compartment on a speeding locomotive out to the peasants in a passing vineyard, who join in the refrain. In *Love Me Tonight* (Rouben Mamoulian/Paramount, 1932), Rouben Mamoulian satirized infectiousness—while brilliantly exploiting it—in "Isn't It Romantic?" (Lorenz Hart and Richard Rodgers, 1932). Tailor Maurice Chevalier hums the tune in Paris and—after it works its way through a customer, a taxi driver, a musician, a platoon of marching soldiers, and a band of gypsies—it alights on MacDonald's country estate balcony, where her waiting lips pick it up without missing a beat.

18. Originally the characters had no names. The third pig was named Practical Pig in publicity for the sequel, *The Big Bad Wolf* (Burt Gillett/Disney, 1934). The others became Fiddler Pig and Fife Pig.

19. Walt Disney to Roy Disney, quoted in Thomas, *Walt Disney, the Art of Animation,* p. 48.

20. Watts, *The Magic Kingdom,* p. 80.

21. That the wolf figure had come to stand for the Depression at the time of the production of *Three Little Pigs* is amply documented in a surprising archival source. Hoover had been a great fan of political cartoons—especially those that referenced him, whether positively or critically. Long before his presidency and continuing through the 1930s, he used a clipping service to collect these published drawings, which are now preserved at the Herbert Hoover Presidential Library in West Branch, Iowa. There are many wolves at doors in these cartoons satirizing politics, politicians, and the Depression in general, some drawn in styles anticipating Disney's. See www.hoover.archives.gov/index.html.

22. Mitts-Smith, *Picturing the Wolf in Children's Literature,* pp. 1, 3.

23. Thomas Nast, "Tilden's Wolf at the Door," *Harper's Weekly,* September 16, 1876, pp. 756–57. The caption read, "The public-school system is the bulwark of the American republic and for its security the application of public funds to sectarian purposes should be forbidden—Republican declaration" (Olmsted, "The Cigar-Box Papers," pp. 256–69).

24. George Bernard Shaw, "The Living Wage Keeps the Wolf from the Door," *The New Leader* 13, no. 83 (October 13, 1926). See the illustration in the Corbis Library, item no. 42–18592190, www.corbisimages.com.

25. "The Big Bad Wolf," p. 88.

26. Mordaunt Hall, "Joe E. Brown and Patricia Ellis in a Film of a Baseball Comedy by Ring Lardner," *New York Times,* May 26, 1933, p. 24. In fairness, it should be said that for a cartoon to receive any notice in a major publication was a distinction.

27. Mayme Ober Peak, "Who's Afraid of Big Bad Wolf!," *Daily Boston Globe,* October 29, 1933, p. B5. I am grateful to Susan Ohmer for access to this and other items in her Disney research files.

28. Bloomingdale's display ad, *New York Times,* October 13, 1933, p. 7. Though a caption says that it was "suggested by" the film, there is no indication that the studio approved of or participated in the production of the advertisement.

29. "The Mechanical Mouse," p. 252.

30. Schickel, *The Disney Version,* p. 143.

31. Nelson B. Bell, "About the Show Shops," *Washington Post,* June 5, 1933, p. 7. He hinted at superficiality when he observed, "Coating its bitter lesson is a sugary layer of whimsical humor and flawlessly synchronized melody." Bell disliked the final scene of the wolf's scalded bottom, but not because of its violence. He concluded, "Too bad it has the vulgar touch at the finish."

32. Herbert Hoover, second state of the union address, December 2, 1930; http://en.wikisource.org/wiki/Herbert_Hoover%27s_Second_State_of_the _Union_Address.

33. Kyvig, *Daily Life in the United States, 1920–1940,* p. 237.

34. Eliot, *Walt Disney,* p. 75.

35. Merritt and Kaufman, *Walt Disney's Silly Symphonies,* p. 124. Ben Sharpsteen kept a copy of Disney's story idea, dated December 1932, that the boss had circulated. Disney also passed around Andrew Lang's compendium of fairy tales, *The Green Fairy Book.* Disney apolitically noted, "These little pig characters look as if they would work up very cute and we should be able to develop quite a bit of personality in them" (Sharpsteen papers, quoted in Barrier, *The Animated Man,* p. 94). Another story is that Mary Pickford, upon hearing an impromptu rendition of the theme song during a studio visit, told Disney, "If you don't make this cartoon about the pigs, I'll never speak to you again" (Thomas, *Walt Disney, the Art of Animation,* p. 48).

36. On Disney's early politics, see Watts, *The Magic Kingdom,* pp. 81–82; Gabler, *Walt Disney,* p. 185; Schickel, *The Disney Version,* p. 154.

37. Peak, "Who's Afraid of Big Bad Wolf!," p. B5. At the time of Disney's reference to it, *Abie's Irish Rose* (Anne Nichols, 1922), a schmaltzy interfaith romance, had been the longest-running play on Broadway and held the same record as a touring show.

38. Schickel, *The Disney Version,* p. 156. "Gagging" has two meanings, of course, making gags and choking on something stuck in the throat.

39. [Attributed to] Walt Disney, "The Cartoon's Contribution to Children," *Overland Monthly and Out West Magazine* 91, no. 8 (October 1933): 138. It is interesting, nonetheless, that although he sought to deny that political content seeped into his films, Disney echoed Roosevelt on the role of money. In his inaugural address, FDR had said, "Happiness lies not in the mere possession of

money; it lies in the joy of achievement, in the thrill of creative effort. The joy and moral stimulation of work no longer must be forgotten in the mad chase of evanescent profits." The sentiment emerged when Disney told an interviewer, "I'm not interested in money, except for what I can do with it to advance my work. Work is the real adventure in life. Money is merely a means to make more work possible" (Disney, interviewed by Alice T. Tildedsley, "A Silly Symphony Becomes America's Slogan," *Star-Journal* [Lincoln, Nebraska], December 24, 1933, quoted in Watts, *The Magic Kingdom*, p. 72). This was also the moral of the only Silly Symphony that Disney personally directed, *The Golden Touch* (Disney/Disney, 1935). The story of Midas concludes with the king finding happiness not in his gold but by having been granted his wish for a hamburger—with onions.

Disney's statement may have been part of the studio's concerted response to accusations of the studio's corporate greed and charges that United Artists was gouging exhibitors, allegedly charging more rent for the cartoon than for feature film rentals. See Kaufman, *"Three Little Pigs,"* pp. 41–42.

40. Sklar, "The Making of Cultural Myths," p. 64.

41. King Vidor, "Rubber Stamp Movies," *New Theatre*, September 1934, in Koszarski, ed., *Hollywood Directors, 1914–1940*, p. 278.

42. Schwab, "The Communalistic Art of Walt Disney," p. 150.

43. Eisenstein, *Eisenstein on Disney*, p. 4.

44. Otis Ferguson, "Extra Added Attractions," *New Republic,* August 7, 1935, p. 363.

45. Jack Zipes, *The Enchanted Screen*, p. 28.

46. George Shaffer, "Silly Symphony Feature Signed for Big Movie," *Chicago Daily Tribune,* September 29, 1933, p. 20.

47. Argus, "On the Screen," *Literary Digest*, October 14, 1933, p. 29.

48. Mollie Merrick, "Hollywood in Person," *Atlanta Constitution,* September 29, 1933, p. 18.

49. The studio was on Hyperion Avenue in Los Angeles. In the parking lot Disney built gatehouses designed like the pigs' houses of sticks, straw, and brick. After the studio moved to Burbank, the little brick house had an afterlife as a Kodak drive-up one-hour film processing station. Thanks to David Shepard for pointing this out to me long ago on a drive through historic Hollywood. Today the site is a Gelson's supermarket and Los Angeles Historic-Cultural Monument no. 163. See http://bigorangelandmarks.blogspot.com/2008/07/no -163-site-of-first-official-walt.html. Alas, the house of brick (and Kodachrome) is no more.

50. Charles Darwin, *The Expression of the Emotions in Man and Animals* (1872), quoted in Hösle, *Woody Allen*, p. 10.

51. For other industry reactions to the Depression, see Crafton, *The Talkies*, p. 190.

52. Zipes, *Happily Ever After*, pp. 3–4.

53. Roland Barthes, "The Reality Effect," pp. 142 ff. Barthes argued that it was the extraneous, nonnarrative details of description that made a written scene "real" for the reader.

54. Maltby, *Harmless Entertainment*, p. 155.

55. The prominent display of the Tanglefoot label is significant. This company, which was acquired by Contech in 2009, had become synonymous with its principal product, Tanglefoot brand flypaper. Although it was commonly used from the 1880s onward, its use declined in the 1920s, reflecting urbanization, the replacement of horses (and their attendant fly-breeding manure) with motorcars, and higher sanitation standards in the food industry. More convenient products, including spray insecticides such as Flit, were challenging Tanglefoot's business by the mid-1930s.

56. The Fleischers poked fun at the policy in *We Aim to Please* (Dave Fleischer/Paramount, 1934). After Wimpy, the first customer at Popeye's new diner, enters, Popeye shakes Olive's hand and proclaims, "New Deal, New Deal." Betty starred in *The New Deal Show* (Dave Fleischer/Paramount, 1937), but by that late date the New Deal had apparently become synonymous with handouts—in this case, to pets. Regardless, her dance number with a hen is sublime.

57. Muscio, *Hollywood's New Deal*, p. 102.

58. Keezer, "The Consumer under the National Recovery Administration," p. 89.

59. Billington, "The New Deal Is a Joke," p. 17.

60. Jacobs, *Pocketbook Politics*, p. 128; Edsforth, *The New Deal*, p. 185.

61. The underlying pessimism evident in this film is even more apparent in *Betty Boop for President* (Fleischer, 1932), in which she cynically echoes Hoover's promise of prosperity in fantastic campaign promises. In one scene she becomes a caricature of Hoover's face.

62. Sito, *Drawing the Line*, pp. 83–84. See also Deneroff, "Popeye the Union Man."

63. Zipes, *The Enchanted Screen*, p. 274. A cinema precedent might have been Jean Renoir's celebrated short film *La petite marchande d'allumettes* (1928). An animated version that preserved the story's original ending was made as *The Little Match Girl* (Arthur Davis and Sid Marcus/Columbia Pictures, 1937). Zipes discusses Michael Sporn's adaptation (Italtoons, 1990) in his chapter "Andersen's Cinematic Legacy" (pp. 276–77).

64. Preston Sturges, quoted in Curtis, *Between Flops*, p. 157.

65. The film abounds in in-jokes. Director Sullivan perhaps is a reference to King Vidor, a director of social dramas in the early 1930s. LeBrand is an arch pun on the name of Paramount's William LeBaron, who executive produced Sturges's *Christmas in July* (1940), *The Great McGinty* (1940), and *The Lady Eve* (1941).

66. James Sully, *An Essay on Laughter*, cited in Jenkins, *What Made Pistachio Nuts?*, p. 288.

67. This interpretation of *Sullivan's Travels* is by no means unambiguous, laced as the film is with Sturges's own antagonism toward Hollywood's politics, his sardonic humor, and his guilty conscious for participating in the system he was ridiculing. For a discussion of the film that is quite different from mine, see Moran and Rogin, "What's the Matter with Capra?"

68. The use of *Playful Pluto* in Sturges's film was serendipitous. Originally he had wanted a Charlie Chaplin short for the scene, but Chaplin declined to give permission (Diane Jacobs, *Christmas in July: The Life and Art of Preston Sturges,* cited in Moran and Rogin, "What's the Matter with Capra?"). Wells

noticed a similarity between the use of animated sequences in *Sullivan's Travels* and *The Blackboard Jungle* (Richard Brooks/MGM, 1955): "Both . . . foreground the animated film as the vehicle by which significant moments of revelation and understanding take place. Both films thus invest the animated film with a specific ability to communicate complex, and sometimes contradictory, ideas within the framework of an apparently accessible, yet taken for granted, form" (Wells, *Understanding Animation,* p. 6).

69. Jahn, "The Aesthetic Theory of Leo Tolstoy's *What Is Art?*," p. 61. This essay is a concise analysis of the strengths and weaknesses of Tolstoy's aesthetic theory, especially as it relates to his moral theory of art. I disagree with Jahn when he writes, "If Tolstoy had written in English he might have employed the term 'expression' and 'impression,' thus establishing a verbal connection similar to that of the Russian" (p. 65). It seems to me that Tolstoy meant the viral metaphor to evoke the involuntary spread and absorption of emotions, which could be benign or malignant.

70. Mounce, *Tolstoy on Aesthetics,* p. 27.

71. *Redemption* (MGM, 1930, based on *The Living Corpse*); *Resurrection* (Universal, 1931); *Resurrección* (Universal, 1931, a Spanish-language remake of the English version); *We Live Again* (Goldwyn/United Artists, 1934, based on *Resurrection*); and *Anna Karenina* (MGM, 1935).

72. Tolstoy, *What Is Art?,* p. 44.

73. Caldwell has characterized the viral nature of contemporary film marketing: "Each multimedia platform (the Web site and the DVD with extras) serves as a 'host body' for the studio/network's mutating content, and various forms of industrial reflexivity (behind-the-scenes, making-ofs, bonus tracks, and interactively negotiated production knowledge) serve as the fuel that drives the endless mutation of this content across proprietary host bodies within the conglomerated world. As a form of constant textual renegotiation, onscreen critical analysis (whether from scholars, publicists, show-biz reports, or industrial marketing departments) facilitates the process of repurposing and mutation" ("Welcome to the Viral Future of Cinema [Television]," pp. 94–95).

Note that Tolstoy does not attribute negative qualities to infection, which he sees as neutral. This is distinct from Brophy's use of the term *infection* to describe the musical establishment's view of folk/popular music as a disease (Philip Brophy, "The Animation of Sound," in Cholodenko, ed., *The Illusion of Life,* p. 97).

74. Tolstoy, *What Is Art?,* p. 38. This view of an aestheticized space between the artist and the audience resonates later in the writings of Eisenstein, Kuleshov, Stanislavsky, and Godard. Indeed, film theorists may recognize traces of Tolstoy in the famous film experiment that led to the naming of the Kuleshov effect, perhaps by way of Marxist theorist and politician Nikolai Bukharin. Tolstoy's stories and novels were the sources of many Russian and Soviet film adaptations. See Bordwell, *The Cinema of Eisenstein,* p. 116; Kenez, *Cinema and Soviet Society, 1917–1953,* p. 33.

75. Kracauer, "Preston Sturges or Laughter Betrayed," p. 47.

76. While Kracauer's image of the masses absorbing an individual's identity is a bit like a virulent strain of Tolstoy's infection model, the immediate and irresistible spread of this influence via laughter also has some similarity to the

observations of Max Scheler (1874–1928) about empathy. In his view, profound emotions such as sympathy and anger spread directly and unthinkingly among people. Cutting, "Scheler, Phenomenology, and Psychopathology," p. 156. Thanks to Vittorio Hösle for his comments.

77. Kracauer, "Cult of Distraction," p. 93.

78. Hansen, "Of Mice and Ducks," p. 54. I follow Hansen's literal translation of the essay's title and the mouse's German name.

79. For a detailed study of the Frankfurt School's love-hate relationship with animation, see the chapter "Micky-Maus" in Hansen's *Cinema and Experience,* pp. 163–82. See also Esther Leslie's discussion of the Frankfurt School in "Mickey Mouse, Utopia and Walter Benjamin," in *Hollywood Flatlands,* pp. 80–122.

80. Walter Benjamin, "To Mickey Mouse" (1931), p. 144, cited in Leslie, *Hollywood Flatlands,* p. 83.

81. Benjamin, quoted in and translated by Hansen, "Of Mice and Ducks," p. 30. The following paragraphs are indebted to Hansen's research on Benjamin and Adorno (pp. 30–33).

82. Benjamin, quoted in Hansen, "With Skin and Hair," p. 460, n. 37. For slightly different translations, see Walter Benjamin, "The Work of Art in the Age of Its Technological Reproducibility: Second Version," in Jennings et al., eds., *The Work of Art,* p. 38; Leslie, *Hollywood Flatlands,* pp. 110–11.

83. Hansen, "Of Mice and Ducks," p. 32; ellipsis in original.

84. Theodor Adorno and Max Horkheimer, *Dialectic of Enlightenment,* quoted in Hansen, "Of Mice and Ducks," p. 34.

85. Adorno, "Chaplin in Malibu," pp. 60–61. See also Leslie, *Hollywood Flatlands,* p. 196.

86. Hansen, "Of Mice and Ducks," p. 39.

87. Tolstoy, *What Is Art?,* p. 82.

88. Rachel Kearney, "The Joyous Reception: Animated Worlds and the Romantic Imagination," in Buchan, ed., *Animated "Worlds,"* p. 12.

89. Hansen, *Cinema and Experience,* p. 291, n. 72.

90. Ferriano, "Did He Write That?," p. 10; Ewen, *Panorama of American Popular Music,* p. 295. Koehler, the lyricist who produced cabaret shows, was a future "legend of jazz" songsmith. For example, he wrote "Stormy Weather," also with Arlen.

91. See Cohen, *Forbidden Animation;* Goldmark, *Tunes for 'Toons,* especially the chapter "Jungle Jive: Animation, Jazz Music, and Swing Culture," pp. 77–106.

92. James Standifer, "Musical Behaviors of Black People in American Society," p. 52.

93. Berger, *Redeeming Laughter,* p. 205.

94. Maltby, *Harmless Entertainment,* p. 182.

95. Hösle, *Woody Allen,* pp. 84–85.

6. ANIMATION AND AUTOPHAGY

1. According to Bakhtin, "Laughter at the feast of fools was not, of course, an abstract and purely negative mockery of the Christian ritual and the Church's

hierarchy. The negative derisive element was deeply immersed in the triumphant theme of bodily regeneration and renewal. It was 'man's second nature' that was laughing, the lower bodily stratum which could not express itself in official cult and ideology" (Bakhtin, *Rabelais and His World*, p. 75).

2. There are many similar images in contemporary popular culture. Halloran has written about how TV and popular literature have specularized extreme eating in televisual spectacles (e.g., *Fear Factor*), which include food-eating contests, fetish eating, and eating stunts (Halloran, "Biting Reality," pp. 24–42).

3. Camporesi, *Bread of Dreams*, pp. 36–37.

4. Kyvig, *Daily Life in the United States, 1920–1940*, pp. 118–19; Children's Bureau data, quoted in Mintz and Kellogg, "Domestic Revolutions," pp. 136–37.

5. Andrew Lang, "The Three Little Pigs," in *The Green Fairy Book,* n.p.

6. Joseph Jacobs, "The Story of the Three Little Pigs," pp. 68–72. Although the Lang version is usually cited as Disney's source, the cartoon version is much closer to Jacobs's version. In the Jacobs story, the villain is a wolf, not a fox, and the pigs build their houses of straw, furze sticks, and bricks, not mud, cabbages, and bricks, as in the Lang. The Jacobs version also contains the immortal dialogue that recurs in the Disney version: "Little pig, little pig, let me come in.";/"No, no, by the hair of my chinny chin chin.";/"Then I'll huff, and I'll puff, and I'll blow your house in." In the Jacobs version, the wolf eats the first two pigs and the third pig eats the wolf. For other variants, see D.L. Ashliman, "Three Little Pigs and Other Folktales of Aarne-Thompson-Uther Type 124," www.pitt.edu/~dash/type0124.html.

7. Zipes, *The Trials and Tribulations of Little Red Riding Hood*, pp. 2, 55. Zipes sees the swallowing motif as "an obvious sexual act." The voracious wolf represented for Freud repressed memories of the father's violence; for Jung, the "wolf is the father, and the fear of being swallowed concerns fear of intercourse and conception" (p. 59, n. 2).

8. Merritt shows how the eating threat transferred from the sources in folk and fairy tales. Merritt, "Lost on Pleasure Islands," p. 14.

9. There are, however, a surprising number of instances of "vore" in Disney's films. The *Pinocchio* heroes' encampment within the diluvial mouth of Monstro the whale comes to mind, and the Red Chief in *Peter Pan* has a fearsome red mouth, complete with a pendulous uvula. Then there's the ultimate vorephobe, Captain Hook and his personal "fear factor," the crocodile that ate his hand.

10. One speculates that the scene may have inadvertently set off audience coperformance, since what kid could resist throwing popcorn at the wolf as he makes his howling exit? Also, the way in which the popcorn trails from the wolf's breeches definitely has an excremental connotation.

11. Don Marquis, "the big bad wolf," in *archy does his part*, pp. 9–10.

12. Mitts-Smith notes that in the Aesop's fable "The Lamb and the Wolf," the lamb opts to be killed by humans rather than to be eaten by the wolf: "It would be better for me to be sacrificed in the temple than to be eaten by you." In a predecessor of the Three Little Pigs story, "Pigweeney the Wise" (1830), the mother sow lets the three piglets know that they are doomed to be eaten by humans. "It is, of course, the irony of most of these stories that the wolf is de-

picted as wicked for doing what humans do: kill and eat other animals" (Mitts-Smith, *Picturing the Wolf in Children's Literature*, p. 39).

13. Marquis, "the big bad wolf," p. 10.

14. Ibid., p. 11.

15. Mitts-Smith, *Picturing the Wolf in Children's Literature*, pp. 15–16.

16. Kaufman, "*Three Little Pigs*—Big Little Picture," p. 43. The accented dialogue was left intact in the 1948 revision. Later it was replaced with the wolf saying he's the Fuller Brush man. This third version is the one on the *Walt Disney Treasures: Silly Symphonies* DVD. A brief clip of the original version appears in Leonard Maltin's introduction in the "Leonard's Picks" chapter on that disc. A fourth version, which was available on YouTube at the time of this writing, has the original artwork with the wolf as a heavily bearded Jew, but it uses the newer Fuller Brush man dialogue.

The wolf's penchant for disguise also associates him with the racist stereotype of African Americans as tricksters. Mitts-Smith argues:

> From taking on female voices and dress to adopting more docile and refined behavior, the wolf uses aspects of the female and feminine (gentle, *gentile*, civilized, refined, and nurturing) to disguise not only his wolfishness but also his masculine traits. . . .
>
> Embedded in Disney's characterizations and slapstick humor are racial and ethnic stereotypes. The wolf in *Three Little Pigs* and *Bag Bad Wolf* appears to be a slow-witted Southerner, his black fur suggesting an African American background. (Mitts-Smith, *Picturing the Wolf in Children's Literature*, pp. 34, 73)

17. Mitts-Smith, *Picturing the Wolf in Children's Literature*, p. 19.

18. Merritt, "Lost on Pleasure Islands," p. 14.

19. The fear of being eaten was exploited again in *Toy Story 3* (Lee Unkrich/Pixar-Disney, 2010) in a scene in which Buzz Lightyear is about to be swallowed by a boy with a really large mouth and a uvula to match.

20. Freud had an explanation for such scary tales. He wrote, apropos of the vorephobic patient he called the Wolfman, that as a boy his father "may more than once, as he caressed the little boy or played with him have threatened in fun to 'gobble him up'" (Sigmund Freud, "The Occurrence in Dreams of Material from Fairy Tales," quoted in Mitts-Smith, *Picturing the Wolf in Children's Literature*, p. 7).

21. Zipes, *The Trials and Tribulations of Little Red Riding Hood*, p. 2. Folklorists call these stories *Schreckmärchen* or *Warnmärchen*.

22. Vorephilia is the fetish of desiring to swallow or be swallowed by another person. Posting videos of one's or a friend's uvula has become quite trendy on YouTube.

23. A frame enlargement from this film is on the cover of Zipes's *The Enchanted Screen*.

24. Visitors to Disneyland in the 1950s had the opportunity to peer up close into a giant replica of Monstro's maw (images are available online). A sought-after Disney collectible is the Pinocchio and Monstro snow globe showing the whale swallowing the puppet. Do these court vorephilia, vorephobia, or both?

25. Wilbert, "Anti-This—Against-That: Resistances along a Human-Non-Human Axis," in Sharp, ed., *Entanglements of Power*, p. 238.

26. Quoted in Christie, *The Last Machine*, p. 99.

27. The performance is wonderfully complicated, involving two actors outside screen space: the photographer, whose presence becomes visible only after he's been eaten, and the cinematographer, whom we never see but who becomes implicated in the plot nonetheless. It therefore establishes a shifting point of view for the cinematic narrator. Almost as in Cubism, the scene fluidly alternates between the still photographer's optical point of view (or, more precisely, the view through his apparatus), the movie cameraman's view (through his viewfinder), and the point of view of the master narrator (who is not necessarily the cinematographer in the scene). McMahon has analyzed graphically how the film slips among these competing narrators. The scene typifies the developing senses of (literal) immersion and engagement sought by early filmmakers and audiences. "Immersiveness and engagement are therefore invoked by the same point-of-view shot. At first we see the photographic subject from the cameraman's point-of-view, but once he is swallowed we occupy an imaginary position" (Alison McMahan, "Chez le Photographe c'est chez moi: Relationship of Actor and Filmed Subject to Camera in Early Film and Virtual Reality Spaces," in Strauven, ed., *The Cinema of Attractions Reloaded*, p. 299).

28. My thanks to Tom Gunning, who cited *The Big Swallow* in his comments made at the presentation of an early version of this chapter at the University of Chicago on January 11, 2008. He singled out the satisfaction with which the man rubs his stomach after his indulgence as socially transgressive. Elsewhere he observed that early trick films like this "play in similar ways with unity of point of view within a nontheatrical framing. It is the framing itself, its marking the act of display, that remains primary. The spectator is directly addressed, even confronted, by these plays with framing" (Gunning, "'Primitive' Cinema," p. 9).

29. Gunning, "An Aesthetic of Astonishment," p. 86.

30. Le Pétomane was the stage name of Joseph Pujol (1857–1945). The character appears in *Moulin Rouge* (Baz Luhrmann, 2001). See Caradec, *Le Pétomane*.

31. "I was sitting close to [Hadji Ali] and saw him drink six quarts. He was then able, while in an erect position, to expel all the water forcibly and without any apparent effort for a distance of from 4 to 6 feet" (R.C. Thackery, M.D., "Queries and Minor Notes," *Journal of the American Medical Association*, February 16, 1929, p. 580). See also Cullen et al., *Vaudeville Old and New*, p. 413. Skeptical readers may view Mr. Ali's feats, including the signature kerosene-spewing act, as filmed for *Politiquerías* (James Horne, 1931), a Laurel and Hardy Spanish-language film. For frame grabs, see http://billpriceweb.com/hadjiali.html. For the clip, see http://thehumanmarvels.com/?p=964.

32. Greg Bjerg, "Hadji Ali and the Regurgitators," www.damninteresting.com/. For Waldo and other "freak acts," see www.thehumanmarvels.com.

33. Merkl, ed., *The Complete "Dream of the Rarebit Fiend" (1904–1913)*.

34. See www.eating-disorder-info.com/Pica.html.

35. A tip o' the hat to Kawarda Taylor Hightower for her insightful reference to Mr. Creosote.

36. McCrea, "Explosive, Expulsive, Extraordinary," p. 18.

37. Also known as "Frog Blender" and "Frog Bender," it is viewable at http://www.youtube.com/playlist?list=PLD48707BE85CC27C1. A number of sequels have appeared, including "Octomom in a Blender" (2009) and "Ahmadinejad in a Blender" (2009).

38. "A Life in Plastic More Frazzled Than Fantastic," *Copenhagen Post Online*, January 7, 2010, www.cphpost.dk/in-a-out/157-event-calendar/47909-kill-me-marco-everistti.html.

39. It is said to be a three-dimensional adaptation of Giuseppe Arcimboldo's painting of a female similarly composed of spring vegetation, *Flora* (ca. 1591). Actually, however, Švankmajer's reclining figure much more closely resembles Arcimboldo's *Summer* (1580).

40. The ending of the music video *Don't Come Around Here No More* (Jeff Stein, 1985) resembles *Flora*. The actor portraying Carroll's Alice becomes a cake with a realistically frosted body. Tom Petty, as the Mad Hatter, cuts slices out of her torso and serves the cake/body to guests. Alice is last seen disappearing down Petty's throat.

41. Cannibalism performances have been institutionalized in non-animated feature film plots and, of course, horror flicks. The keyword *cannibalism* yields more than 250 titles on the Internet Movie Database (www.imdb.com). There are even a dozen titles for *auto-cannibalism*. A few Hollywood cartoons featuring cannibals not discussed in this volume are *Felix Follows the Swallows* (Otto Messmer/Pat Sullivan Productions, 1925), *Felix Dopes It Out* (Otto Messmer/Pat Sullivan Productions, 1925), *Alice Cans the Cannibals* (Ub Iwerks/Disney, 1925), *Cannibal Capers* (Burt Gillett/Disney, 1930), *Bosko Shipwrecked* (Hugh Harman/Schlesinger, 1931), *I'll Be Glad When You're Dead You Rascal You* (Dave Fleischer/Paramount, 1932), *Plane Dumb* (John Foster and George Rufle/Van Beuren, 1932), *Mickey's Man Friday* (David Hand/Disney, 1933), *I've Got to Sing a Torch Song* (Tom Palmer/Schlesinger, 1933), *Pop-Pie a la Mode* (Isadore Sparber/Famous Studios, 1945), and *Swiss Cheese Family Robinson* (Manny Davis/Paul Terry, 1947).

42. In the unrestored footage I viewed at the Cinémathèque Gaumont in the 1970s, the Indian goes behind the bush briefly. By means of an edit, two actors (and the cannibal) emerge from the same bush, implying that defecation has occurred. This scene does not appear in the 2008 DVD version of the film distributed by Gaumont.

43. For illustrations, see Crafton, *Emile Cohl, Caricature, and Film,* pp. 301–2.

44. For example, there are few if any Hollywood films about the Donner Pass incident. A notable exception to portraying cannibals as black or (rarely) Native American is the English film adaptation of the play *Sweeney Todd: The Demon Barber of Fleet Street* (George King/MGM, 1936). Here, as everyone familiar with the subsequent musical and film versions knows, the cannibalism is treated as Grand Guignol spectacle and displaced using black humor. I'm not counting "documentary" productions such as *Across the World with Mr. and Mrs. Johnson* (James Leo Meehan/Talking Picture Epics, 1930), which purported to show headhunters and cannibals in their native environments.

45. Blu's films and public works are viewable at http://blublu.org. The films are also available on the main online video sites.

46. The first part of the film, made in Baden in 2007, was originally called *Fantoche,* perhaps in homage to Emile Cohl's animated characters. The second part was filmed in Buenos Aires in 2008.

47. Heather Crow, "Gesturing toward Olympia," in Buchan, ed., *Animated "Worlds,"* p. 51.

48. The film was also distributed under the title *Greedy Guts.*

49. Nottingham, "Downing the Folk-Festive," p. 145.

50. Zipes, *The Enchanted Screen,* pp. 352–53.

51. Crow, "Gesturing toward Olympia," p. 51.

52. Richard Schechner cites John Pfeiffer's ethnographic analysis of rituals involving eating: "Meat meant survival, and people did everything in their power, and more, to assure success in the hunt. Above all, they killed animals ritually by drawing them on cave walls and piercing them with spears and arrows" (Pfeiffer, *The Creative Explosion,* quoted in Schechner, *Performance Studies,* p. 49). In Schechner's performance piece "Faust/Gastronome," participants passed chewed food from mouth to mouth (cited in Kirshenblatt-Gimblett, "Playing to the Senses," p. 1).

53. "Meal Fried in Artist's Own Body Fat," News.com.au, January 13, 2007, www.news.com.au/weird-true-freaky/meal-fried-in-artists-own-body-fat/story -e6frflri-1111112825543. For Evaristii's more recent performance work, "Kill Me," see "A Life in Plastic More Frazzled Than Fantastic."

54. Camporesi, *Bread of Dreams,* p. 38.

55. Thomas Lamarre, "New Media Worlds," in Buchan, ed., *Animated "Worlds,"* p. 137.

56. Nottingham, "Downing the Folk-Festive," p. 138.

57. The title of the film was *Winsor McCay, the Famous Cartoonist of the N.Y. Herald and His Moving Comics,* though it is usually identified by the name of its subject, Little Nemo.

58. "Newspaper Artists Feast," *New York Times,* February 22, 1914, p. 11.

59. The Wiffenpoof had been a character in the musical *Little Nemo in Slumberland.* In 1909 the Yale glee club took its name (with modified spelling) from the show: "It was Goat Fowler who suggested we call ourselves The Whiffenpoofs. He had been tickled by the patter of one of the characters in a Victor Herbert musical comedy called 'Little Nemo' which [had] recently been running on Broadway." The famous "Whiffenpoof Song" came a bit later but was unrelated to the McCay show (Reverend James M. Howard, "An Authentic Account of the Founding of the Whiffenpoofs," ca. 1959, www.yale.edu /whiffenpoofs/history/).

60. Irresistibly, one thinks of Avery's use of the device of the silhouette of audience members before the movie screen, for instance, in *Thugs with Dirty Mugs* (Tex Avery/Schlesinger, 1939).

61. Rebellious characters retaliating by autoingesting their comic strip are shown brilliantly in the *Little Nemo in Slumberland* strip of December 1, 1907 (illustrated in Crafton, *Before Mickey,* p. 133). As Flip, Nemo, and Impy eat the

letters of the Slumberland title, Flip says, "It'll teach the fellow who draws us a lesson."

62. Kellman, *The Self-Begetting Novel*, p. 3.

63. The scene is a good example of what Klein calls the endemic "streetwise paranoia" that "is very evident in the mordant edge of Fleischer cartoons" (Norman Klein, "Animation and Animorphs," in Sobchack, ed., *Meta Morphing*, p. 30).

64. The image of a man being held at bay by tiny animated figures anticipates the scene in the feature *Gulliver's Travels* (Dave Fleischer/Paramount, 1939) in which Gulliver is tied up by the Lilliputians.

65. Kellman, *The Self-Begetting Novel*, p. 3.

66. The film is viewable online at http://alanbecker.deviantart.com/art/Animator-vs-Animation-34244097.

67. James Dick, *"The Big Upgrade,"* comments for the Woods Hole Film Festival, 2008, http://woodshole.bside.com/2008/films/thebigupgrade_woodshole2008.

68. Lamarre, "New Media Worlds," p. 135.

69. Michael O'Pray, "Jan Švankmajer: A Bohemian Surrealist," in Švankmajer and Švankmajerova, *The Communication of Dreams*, p. 13.

70. Švankmajer quoted in Michael O'Pray, "Jan Švankmajer: A Mannerist Surrealist," in Hames, ed., *Dark Alchemy*, p. 71.

71. Stern and Henderson described Bakhtin's carnivalesque function of food rituals: "In the antics, usually the clown or the populace is king for the day, and those holding real power play the fool. These powerful inversions also affect the rite of eating. Many of the games and feasts are not adorned by a wealth of rich food but offer pigs' bladders, the pope's nose, or actual excrement as the just fare for those who have abused their powers" (Stern and Henderson, *Performance*, p. 89).

72. Weihe, "The Strings of the Marionette," p. 42.

73. Hervé Joubert-Laurencin, *La lettre volante*, p. 316. The translation is mine. The original text uses *Guignol* rather than *Punch and Judy*, which may refer to the French puppet theater generically or to the traditional protagonist in the plays.

74. Cholodenko, "Introduction," *The Illusion of Life*, p. 28.

75. Hernández, "The *Double Sense* of Animated Images," p. 38.

76. Based on an earlier incarnation of the show, *Man v. Food* (Sony DSC/Travel Channel, 2008–11), *Man v. Food Nation* is hosted by "food enthusiast" Adam Richman. According to the website for the program, "as Adam samples the local flavor of every location he visits, he'll look for fans to walk in his shoes. Is it for the glory? Is it for the honor? Adam and his Man v. Food Nation are doing it for the love of the game, as they work together to defeat these edible 'beasts' and celebrate the community that created them" (www.travelchannel.com/tv-shows/man-v-food/articles/man-v-food-nation).

77. Kirshenblatt-Gimblett, "Playing to the Senses," p. 1.

78. "You are not only 'what you eat' or what you make, consume, or collect, but you are also, and especially, what you desire. As with sexuality, with art you

desire what you imagine the 'desire' of the object itself to be—'what it wants to be.' Consumption as the quintessential modernist performance" (Donald Preziosi, "Performing Modernity," in Jones and Stephenson, *Performing the Body/Performing the Text*, p. 36).

CODA

1. For assorted case studies, refer to Pilling's *Women and Animation.*
2. Orlean, *Rin Tin Tin,* p. 238.
3. Mumford, *Technics and Civilization,* pp. 6–7.

Bibliography

NOTE ON VIDEO SOURCES FOR THE FILMS

With very few exceptions, all of the films mentioned in this book are available in various video formats and as online resources (for example, on YouTube. com, Vimeo.com, DailyMotion.com, and ShortFilmCentral.com). The individual entries in the Big Cartoon DataBase (www.bcdb.com), a comprehensive research tool, often have embedded links to the films. Of course, print quality, digital transfers, and completeness vary greatly.

Adams, Randy, et al., eds. *Transdisciplinary Digital Art: Sound, Vision and the New Screen*. Berlin: Springer, 2008.

Adamson, Joe. *The Walter Lantz Story with Woody Woodpecker & Friends*. New York: G.P. Putnam's Sons, 1985.

Adelman, Bob, Art Spiegelman, and Richard Merkin. *Tijuana Bibles: Art and Wit in America's Forbidden Funnies, 1930s–1950s*. New York: Simon & Schuster, 2004.

Adorno, Theodor W. "Chaplin in Malibu [1964]," in "Chaplin Times Two." Trans. John MacKay. *Yale Journal of Criticism* 9, no. 1 (1996): 58–61.

Adorno, Theodor W., and Max Horkheimer. *Dialectic of Enlightenment*. London: Verso, 1989.

Albee, Edward F. "E.F. Albee on Vaudeville." *Variety* 72, no. 3 (September 6, 1923): 1.

Allan, Robin. *Walt Disney and Europe: European Influences on the Animated Feature Films of Walt Disney*. Bloomington: Indiana University Press, 1999.

Allen, Robert C. *Horrible Prettiness: Burlesque and American Culture*. Chapel Hill: University of North Carolina Press, 1991.

Altman, Rick. *Silent Film Sound*. New York: Columbia University Press, 2004.

———, ed. *Sound Theory/Sound Practice*. New York: Routledge, 1992.

Amidi, Amid. *Cartoon Modern: Style and Design in Fifties Animation.* San Francisco: Chronicle Books, 2006.

Anonymous on behalf of Walt Disney. "Attention Animators: Notes and Suggestions for Animators and Assistants." Intraoffice memo, Walt Disney Productions, April 22, 1935, 1–2.

Antelyes, Peter. "'Haim Afen Range': The Jewish Indian and the Redface Western." *Melus* 34, no. 3 (Fall 2009): 15–42.

Arnheim, Rudolf. *Film As Art.* Berkeley: University of California Press, 2006.

Auerbach, Jonathan. *Body Shots: Early Cinema's Incarnations.* Berkeley: University of California Press, 2007.

Auslander, Philip. "At the Listening Post, or, Do Machines Perform?" *International Journal of Performance Arts and Digital Media* 1, no. 1 (2005): 5–10.

———. "Live from Cyberspace: Or, I Was Sitting at My Computer This Guy Appeared He Thought I Was a Bot." *PAJ: A Journal of Performance and Art* 24, no. 1 (January 2002): 16–21.

———. *Liveness: Performance in a Mediatized Culture.* New York: Routledge, 1999.

Austin, Thomas, and Martin Barker, eds. *Contemporary Hollywood Stardom:* New York: Oxford University Press, 2003.

Bakhtin, Mikhail M. *The Dialogic Imagination: Four Essays by M.M. Bakhtin.* Ed. Michael Holquist. Austin: University of Texas Press, 1981.

———. *Rabelais and His World.* Trans. Hélène Iswolsky. Bloomington: Indiana University Press, 1984.

Balio, Tino, ed. *Grand Design: Hollywood as a Modern Business Enterprise 1930–1939.* Berkeley: University of California Press, 1995.

Barbera, Joseph. *My Life in 'Toons: From Flatbush to Bedrock in Under a Century.* Atlanta: Turner Publishing, 1994.

Barker, Martin. "*Crash,* Theatre Audiences, and the Idea of 'Liveness.'" *Studies in Theatre and Performance* 23, no. 1 (2003): 21–39.

Baron, Cynthia, and Sharon Marie Carnicke. *Reframing Screen Performance.* Ann Arbor: University of Michigan Press, 2008.

Baron, Cynthia, Diane Carson, and Frank P. Tomasulo. *More Than a Method.* Detroit, MI: Wayne State University Press, 2004.

Barrier, Michael. *The Animated Man: A Life of Walt Disney.* Berkeley: University of California Press, 2008.

———. *Hollywood Cartoons: American Animation in Its Golden Age.* New York: Oxford University Press, 2003.

Barthes, Roland. "The Reality Effect." In *The Rustle of Language.* Trans. Richard Howard, 141–48. Berkeley: University of California Press, 1989.

Basinger, Jeanine. *Silent Stars.* Middletown, CT: Wesleyan University Press, 2000.

Belington, Monroe. "The New Deal Was a Joke: Political Humor during the Great Depression." *Journal of American Culture* 5, no. 33 (Fall 1982): 15–21.

Belton, John. *American Cinema, American Culture.* New York: McGraw Hill, 1994.

Bendazzi, Giannalberto. *Cartoons: One Hundred Years of Cinema Animation.* Bloomington: University of Indiana Press, 1994.

Benford, Gregory. "Death and the Textual Shadow of the SF Author, Again." *Science Fiction Studies* 9, no. 3 (November 1982): 341.

———. *Timescape*. New York: Random House, 1992.

Benjamin, Walter. *The Work of Art in the Age of Its Technological Reproducibility and Other Writings on Media*. Ed. Michael W. Jennings et al. Trans. Edmund Jephcott and Harry Zohn. Cambridge, MA: Harvard University Press, 2008.

Berger, Peter. *Redeeming Laughter: The Comic Dimension of Human Experience*. New York: Walter De Gruyter, 1997.

Bergson, Henri. *Laughter: An Essay on the Meaning of the Comic* (1904). Trans. Cloudesley Brereton and Fred Rothwell. New York: Macmillan and Co., 1911.

Bernstein, Matthew, and Gaylyn Studlar, eds. *Visions of the East: Orientalism in Film*. New Brunswick, NJ: Rutgers University Press, 1997.

Bial, Henry, ed. *The Performance Studies Reader*. New York: Psychology Press, 2004.

"The Big Bad Wolf." *Fortune* (November 1934), 88–95, 142–48.

Bishko, Leslie. "The Uses and Abuses of Cartoon Style in Animation." *Animation Studies* 2 (2007).

Blau, Herbert. "The Human Nature of the Bot: A Response to Philip Auslander." *PAJ: A Journal of Performance and Art* 24, no. 1 (January 2002): 22–24.

Blesh, Rudi. *Buster Keaton*. New York: Macmillan, 1966.

Boleslavsky, Richard. *Acting: The First Six Lessons*. New York: Taylor & Francis, 1933.

Bordwell, David. *The Cinema of Eisenstein*. New York: Routledge, 2005.

Bordwell, David, and Kristin Thompson. *Film Art: An Introduction*. New York: McGraw-Hill, 2004.

Bouldin, Joanna. "The Body, Animation and The Real: Race, Reality and the Rotoscope in Betty Boop." In *Conference Proceedings for Affective Encounters: Rethinking Embodiment in Feminist Media Studies,* ed. Anu Koivunen and Susanna Paasonen. E-book published by the University of Turku School of Art, Literature and Music and the Finnish Society for Cinema Studies.

Brachear, Robert. "Maurice Maeterlinck and His 'Musée Grévin.'" *French Review* 40, no. 3 (December 1966): 347–51.

Braun, V. "Conceptualizing the Body." *Feminism and Psychology* 10, part 4 (2000): 511–18.

Brewster, Ben, and Lea Jacobs. *Theatre to Cinema: Stage Pictorialism and the Early Feature Film*. New York: Oxford University Press, 1997.

Broido, Lucy. *The Posters of Jules Chéret*. New York: Dover, 1992.

Bronski, Michael. *Culture Clash: The Making of Gay Sensibility*. New York: South End Press, 1984.

Brown, Kevin. "The Auslander Test: Or, 'Of Bots and Humans.'" *International Journal of Performance Arts and Digital Media* 4, nos. 2 and 3 (2008): 181–88.

Browne, Nick, ed. *Refiguring American Film Genres: Theory and History*. Berkeley: University of California Press, 1998.

Bryman, Alan. "Animating the Pioneer versus Late Entrant Debate: An Historical Case Study." *Journal of Management Studies* 34, no. 3 (May 1997): 415–38.

Buchan, Suzanne. *Quay Brothers: Into a Metaphysical Playroom.* Minneapolis: University of Minnesota Press, 2010.

———, ed. *Animated "Worlds."* London: John Libbey, 2006.

Burke, Edmund. *On the Sublime and Beautiful* . Harvard Classics, vol. 24, part 2. New York: P.F. Collier & Son, 1909–14.

Burt, Jonathan. *Animals in Film.* London: Reaktion Books, 2002.

Butler, Jeremy G. *Star Texts: Image and Performance in Film and Television.* Detroit, MI: Wayne State University Press, 1991.

Cabarga, Leslie. *The Fleischer Story.* Rev. ed. New York: DaCapo Press, 1988.

Caldwell, John T. "Welcome to the Viral Future of Cinema (Television)." *Cinema Journal* 45, no. 1 (Fall 2005): 90–97.

Callahan, David. "Cel Animation: Mass Production and Marginalization in the Animated Film Industry." *Film History* 2, no. 3 (1988): 223–28.

Camporesi, Piero. *Bread of Dreams: Food and Fantasy in Early Modern Europe.* Trans. David Gentilcore. Chicago: University of Chicago Press, 1989.

Canemaker, John. *The Art and Flair of Mary Blair.* New York: Disney Editions, 2003.

———. "David Hilberman." *Cartoonist Profiles* 48 (December 1980): 17–21.

———. "Disney Design 1928–1979: How the Disney Studio Changed the Look of the Animated Cartoon." *Millimeter,* February 1979, 102–9.

———. *Felix: The Twisted Tale of the World's Most Famous Cat.* New York: Pantheon Books, 1991.

———, ed. *Storytelling in Animation: The Art of the Animated Image.* Los Angeles: American Film Institute, 1988.

———. *Treasures of Disney Animation Art.* New York: Abbeville Press, 1982.

Capra, Frank. *The Name above the Title: An Autobiography.* New York: Macmillan, 1971.

Caradec, François. *Le Pétomane.* Trans. Warren Tute. London: Sphere, 1971.

Carlson, Marvin. *Performance: A Critical Introduction.* 2nd ed. London: Routledge, 2004.

Carnicke, Sharon. *Stanislavsky in Focus: An Acting Master for the Twenty-First Century.* 2nd ed. London: Taylor & Francis, 2008.

Carroll, Noël. *Comedy Incarnate: Buster Keaton, Physical Humor, and Bodily Coping.* Malden, MA: Blackwell, 2007.

———. *Theorizing the Moving Image.* Cambridge: Cambridge University Press, 1996.

Carroll, Noël, and Jinhee Choi, eds. *Philosophy of Film and Motion Pictures: An Anthology.* Malden, MA: Blackwell, 2006.

Cavell, Stanley. *The World Viewed: Reflections on the Ontology of Film, Enlarged Edition.* Cambridge, MA: Harvard University Press, 1979.

Chanan, Michael. "The Documentary Chronotope." *Jump Cut* 43 (2000): 56–61.

Charlot, Jean. *Art from the Mayans to Disney.* New York: Sheed & Ward, 1939.

Cholodenko, Alan, ed. *The Illusion of Life: Essays on Animation.* Sydney: Power Publications, 1991.

Christie, Ian. *The Last Machine: Early Cinema and the Birth of the Modern World.* London: British Film Institute, 1994.

Cohan, Steven. *Incongruous Entertainment: Camp, Cultural Value, and the MGM Musical.* Durham, NC: Duke University Press, 2005.

Cohen, Karl F. *Forbidden Animation: Censored Cartoons and Blacklisted Animators in America.* Jefferson, NC: McFarland, 1997.

Crafton, Donald. *Before Mickey: The Animated Film, 1898–1928.* Chicago: University of Chicago Press, 1993.

————. *Emile Cohl, Caricature, and Film.* Princeton, NJ: Princeton University Press, 1990.

————. *The Talkies: American Cinema's Transition to Sound, 1926–1931.* Berkeley: University of California Press, 1999.

————. "The Veiled Genealogies of Animation and Cinema." *Animation: An Interdisciplinary Journal* 6, no. 2 (July 2011): 93–10.

————. "The View from Termite Terrace: Caricature and Parody in Warner Bros Animation." *Film History* 5, no. 2 (1993): 204–30

Craig, Edward Gordon. *On the Art of the Theatre* (1905). Chicago: Brown's Bookstore, 1911.

Crowther, Paul. *Phenomenology of the Visual Arts (even the frame).* Stanford, CA: Stanford University Press, 2005.

Culhane, Shamus. *Talking Animals and Other People.* New York: St. Martin's Press, 1981.

Cullen, Frank, et al. *Vaudeville Old and New: An Encyclopedia of Variety Performers in America.* New York: Routledge, 2007.

Curtis, James. *Between Flops: A Biography of Preston Sturges.* New York: Harcourt, Brace, Jovanovich, 1982.

Curtis, Scott. "The Sound of the Early Warner Bros. Cartoons." In *Sound Theory/Sound Practice,* ed. Rick Altman, 191–203. New York: Routledge, 1992.

Cutting, John. "Scheler, Phenomenology, and Psychopathology." *Philosophy, Psychiatry, & Psychology* 16, no. 2 (June 2009): 143–59.

Dailey, Sheron J., ed. *The Future of Performance Studies: Visions and Revisions.* Annandale, VA: National Communication Association, 1998.

DeCordova, Richard. *Picture Personalities: The Emergence of the Star System in America.* Champaign: University of Illinois Press, 2001.

Deleuze, Gilles, and Felix Guattari. *Anti-Oedipus: Capitalism and Schizophrenia.* New York: Continuum International Publishing Group, 2004.

Deneroff, Harvey Raphael. "Popeye the Union Man: A Historical Study of the Fleischer Strike." Ph.D. diss., University of Southern California, Los Angeles, 1985.

Disney, Walt. "Growing Pains." *American Cinematographer* 22, no. 3 (March 1941): 106–7, 139–42.

Durkin, Andrew. "The Self-Playing Piano as a Site for Textual Criticism." *Text* 12 (1999): 167–88.

Dyer, Richard. *Heavenly Bodies: Film Stars and Society.* London: Routledge, 2004.

Edsforth, Ronald. *The New Deal: America's Response to the Great Depression.* Malden, MA: Blackwell, 2000.

Eisenstein, Sergei. *Eisenstein on Disney.* Ed. and trans. Jay Leyda. London: Methuen, 1988.

———. *Sergei Eisenstein: Selected Works, Vol. III, Writings, 1934–47.* Ed. Richard Taylor. New York: Palgrave Macmillan, 2010.

Eliot, Marc. *Walt Disney: Hollywood's Dark Prince.* Secaucus, NJ: Birch Lane Press, 1993.

Everett, Anna, and John Caldwell. *New Media: Theories and Practices of Digitextuality.* New York: Routledge, 2007.

Ewen, David. *Panorama of American Popular Music: The Story of Our National Ballads and Folk Songs, the Songs of Tin Pan Alley, Broadway and Hollywood, New Orleans Jazz, Swing, and Symphonic Jazz.* Englewood Cliffs, N.J.: PrenticeHall. 1957.

Falk, Nat. *How to Make Animated Cartoons: The History and Technique.* New York: Foundation Books, 1941.

Faris, Jocelyn. *Ginger Rogers: A Bio-Bibliography.* Westport, CT: Greenwood Press, 1994.

Feild, Robert D. *The Art of Walt Disney.* New York: Macmillan, 1942.

Ferguson, Otis. "Extra Added Attractions." *New Republic,* August 7, 1935, 363.

Ferriano, Frank. "Did He Write That? America's Great Unknown Song Writer, Harold Arlen." *Tracking [Journal of Popular Music Studies]* 3, no. 1 (December 1990): 8–17.

Feyersinger, Erwin. "Diegetic Short Circuits: Metalepsis in Animation." *Animation* 5, no. 3 (2010): 279–94.

Fielding, Raymond. *The American Newsreel, 1911–1967.* Norman: University of Oklahoma Press, 1972.

Finch, Christopher. *The Art of Walt Disney: From Mickey Mouse to the Magic Kingdoms.* New York: Abrams, 1973.

Focillon, Henri. *The Life of Forms in Art.* Trans. C.B. Hogan and George Kubler. London: Zone, 1989.

Foucault, Michel. *L'Archéologie du Savoir.* Paris: Gallimard, 1969.

Freleng, Friz, with David Weber. *Animation: The Art of Friz Freleng.* Newport Beach, CA: Donovan Publishing, 1994.

Freud, Sigmund. *The Joke and Its Relation to the Unconscious.* Trans. Joyce Crick. New York: Penguin, 2003.

Friedberg, Anne. *The Virtual Window: From Alberti to Microsoft.* Cambridge, MA: MIT Press, 2006.

Frierson, Michael. *Clay Animation: American Highlights 1908 to the Present.* New York: Twayne, 1994.

Furniss, Maureen, ed. *Chuck Jones: Conversations.* Jackson: University Press of Mississippi, 2005.

Gabler, Neil. *Walt Disney: The Triumph of the American Imagination.* New York: Knopf, 2006.

Garon, Paul, and Beth Garon. *Woman with Guitar: Memphis Minnie's Blues.* New York: Da Capo Press, 1992.

Gaudreault, André. *From Plato to Lumière: Narration and Monstration in Literature and Cinema.* Trans. Timothy Barnard. Toronto: University of Toronto Press, 2009.

Ghez, Didier, ed. *Walt's People, Volume 1: Talking Disney with the Artists Who Knew Him*. Bloomington, IN: Xlibris, 2005.

———, ed. *Walt's People, Volume 3: Talking Disney with the Artists Who Knew Him*. Bloomington, IN: Xlibris, 2006.

———, ed. *Walt's People, Volume 6: Talking Disney with the Artists Who Knew Him*. Bloomington, IN: Xlibris, 2008.

Gill, Pat. "Taking It Personally: Male Suffering in *8mm*." *Camera Obscura* 18, no. 1 (2003): 157–87.

Gledhill, Christine, ed. *Stardom: Industry of Desire*. London: Routledge, 1991.

Goffman, Ervin. *The Presentation of Self in Everyday Life*. Garden City, NJ: Doubleday, 1959.

Goldmark, Daniel. *Tunes for 'Toons*. Berkeley: University of California Press, 2005.

Goldmark, Daniel, and Charlie Keil, eds. *Funny Pictures: Animation and Comedy in Studio-Era Hollywood*. Berkeley: University of California Press, 2011.

Goldstein, Donna M. *Laughter Out of Place: Race, Class, Violence, and Sexuality in a Rio Shantytown*. Berkeley: University of California Press, 2003.

Gomery, Douglas. *The Hollywood Studio System*. New York: St. Martin's Press, 1986.

Gough, Richard, and Claire MacDonald, eds. *Performance Research* 2, no. 3 (1998).

Gould, Stephen Jay. "A Biological Homage to Mickey Mouse." In *The Panda's Thumb: More Reflections in Natural History*, 95–107. New York: W.W. Norton & Company, 1992.

Gourley, Catherine. *Rosie and Mrs. America: Perceptions of Women in the 1930s and 1940s*. Minneapolis, MN: Twenty-First Century Books, 2008.

Grafly, Dorothy. "America's Youngest Art." *American Magazine of Art* 26 (July 1933): 336–42.

Graham, Donald W. "Animation: Art Acquires a New Dimension." *American Artist* (December 1940): 10.

———. "The Art of Animation." Unpublished manuscript dated July 20, 1955, held at Walt Disney Studios.

———. *Composing Pictures*. New York: Van Nostrand Reinhold, 1970.

Graver, David. "The Actor's Bodies." *Text and Performance Quarterly* 17, no. 3 (July 1997): 221–35.

Gunning, Tom. "An Aesthetic of Astonishment: Early Film and the (In)credulous Spectator" (1989). In *Film Theory: Critical Concepts in Media and Cultural Studies, Volume 3*, ed. Philip Simpson and Karen J. Shepherdson, 78–95. London: Taylor & Francis, 2004.

———. "The Ghost in the Machine: Animated Pictures at the Haunted Hotel of Early Cinema." *Living Pictures* 1, no. 1 (2001): 3–17.

———. "'Primitive' Cinema: A Frame-up? Or the Trick's on Us." *Cinema Journal* 28, no. 2 (Winter, 1989): 3–12.

Halas, John, and Roger Manville. *The Technique of Film Animation*. Rev. ed. New York: Focal Press, 1976.

Halloran, Vivian Nun. "Biting Reality: Extreme Eating and the Fascination with the Gustatory Abject." *Iowa Journal of Cultural Studies* 4 (Spring 2004): 24–42.

Hames, Peter, ed. *Dark Alchemy: The Films of Jan Švankmajer.* Westport, CT: Greenwood Press, 1995.

Hansen, Miriam Bratu. *Cinema and Experience: Siegfried Kracauer, Walter Benjamin, and Theodor W. Adorno.* Berkeley: University of California Press, 2012.

———. "Of Mice and Ducks: Benjamin and Adorno on Disney." *South Atlantic Quarterly* 92, no. 1 (Winter 1993): 27–61.

———. "With Skin and Hair: Kracauer's Theory of Film, Marseille 1940." *Critical Inquiry* 19, no. 3 (Spring, 1993): 437–69.

Hark, Ina Rae, ed. *American Cinema of the 1930s.* New Brunswick, NJ: Rutgers University Press, 2007.

Harrison, Paul Carter, and Gus Edwards, eds. *Black Theatre: Ritual Performance in the African Diaspora.* Philadelphia: Temple University Press, 2002.

Hayes-Roth, Barbara, and Robert van Gent. "Improvisational Puppets, Actors, and Avatars." *Agents '97: Proceedings of the First International conference on Autonomous Agents.* New York: Association for Computing Machinery, 1997.

Heath, Stephen. "Body, Voice." In *Questions of Cinema,* 176–93. Bloomington: University of Indiana Press, 1981.

Hendershot, Heather. "Secretary, Homemaker, and 'White' Woman: Industrial Censorship and Betty Boop's Shifting Design." *Journal of Design History* 8, no. 2 (1995): 117–30.

Hernández, María Lorenzo. "The *Double Sense* of Animated Images: A View on the Paradoxes of Animation as a Visual Language." *Animation Studies* 2 (2007): 36–44.

Ho, Chin-Chang, and Karl F. MacDorman. "Revisiting the Uncanny Valley Theory: Developing and Validating an Alternative to the Godspeed Indices." *Computers in Human Behavior* 26, no. 6 (November 2010): 1508–18.

Hockney, David. *Secret Knowledge: Rediscovering the Lost Techniques of the Old Masters.* New York: Viking Penguin, 2001.

Holberg, Amelia S. "Betty Boop: Yiddish Film Star." *American Jewish History* 87, no. 4 (December1999): 291–312.

Hooks, Ed. *Acting for Animators: A Complete Guide to Performance Animation.* Portsmouth, NH: Heinemann, 2000.

Hösle, Vittorio. *Woody Allen: An Essay on the Nature of the Comical.* Notre Dame, IN: University of Notre Dame Press, 2007.

Huizinga, Johan. *Homo Ludens: A Study of the Play-Element in Culture.* New York: Beacon, 1955.

Iwerks, Leslie, and John Kenworthy. *The Hand Behind the Mouse.* New York: Disney Editions, 2001.

Jacobs, Joseph. "The Story of the Three Little Pigs." In *English Fairy Tales.* London: David Nutt, 1890.

Jacobs, Meg. *Pocketbook Politics: Economic Citizenship in Twentieth-Century America.* Princeton, NJ: Princeton University Press, 2005.

Jahn, Gary R. "The Aesthetic Theory of Leo Tolstoy's *What Is Art?" Journal of Aesthetics and Art Criticism* 34, no. 1 (Autumn, 1975): 59–65.

Jenkins, Henry. *What Made Pistachio Nuts? Early Sound Comedy and the Vaudeville Aesthetic.* New York: Columbia University Press, 1992.

Jennings, Michael J., et al., eds. *The Work of Art in the Age of Its Technological Reproducibility, and Other Writings on Media.* Cambridge, MA: Harvard University Press, 2008.

Jones, Amelia, and Andrew Stephenson. *Performing the Body/Performing the Text.* New York: Routledge, 1999.

Jones, Chuck. *Chuck Amuck: The Life and Times of an Animated Cartoonist.* New York: Macmillan, 1999.

Joubert-Laurencin, Hervé. *La lettre volante: Quatre essais sur le cinéma d'animation.* Paris: Presses de la Sorbonne Nouvelle, 1997.

Kanfer, Stefan. *Serious Business: The Art and Commerce of Animation in America from Betty Boop to Toy Story.* New York: DaCapo Press, 2000.

Kaufman, J.B. "*Three Little Pigs*—Big Little Picture." *American Cinematographer* 69 (November 1988): 38–44.

———. "The Transcontinental Making of *The Barn Dance.*" *Animation Journal* 5, no. 2 (Spring 1997): 36–44.

Keezer, Dexter M. "The Consumer under the National Recovery Administration." *Annals of the American Academy of Political and Social Science* 172 (March 1934): 88–97.

Kellman, Steven G. *The Self-Begetting Novel.* New York: Columbia University Press, 1980.

Kenez, Peter. *Cinema and Soviet Society: From the Revolution to the Death of Stalin.* London: I.B. Tauris, 2001.

Lasseter, John. "Principles of Traditional Animation Applied to 3D Computer Animation." *Computer Graphics* 21:, no. 4 (July 1987): 35–44.

Le Bœuf, Patrick. "On the Nature of Edward Gordon Craig's Über-Marionette." *New Theatre Quarterly* 26 (2010): 102–14.

Lefebvre, Henri. *The Production of Space.* Trans. Donald Nicholson-Smith. London: Blackwell Publishing, 1991.

Lehman, Christopher P. *The Colored Cartoon: Black Representation in American Animated Short Films, 1907–1954.* Amherst: University of Massachusetts Press, 2007.

Lenburg, Jeff. *The Great Cartoon Directors.* New York: Da Capo Press, 1993.

———. *Who's Who in Animated Cartoons: An International Guide to Film & Television's Award-Winning and Legendary Animators.* Milwaukee, WI: Hal Leonard Corporation, 2006.

Leslie, Esther. *Hollywood Flatlands: Animation, Critical Theory and the Avant-Garde.* New York: Verso, 2004.

Levin, Bob. *The Air Pirates and the Mouse: Disney's War against the Underground.* San Francisco, CA: Fantagraphics, 2003.

Lewis, Robert M. *Traveling Show to Vaudeville: Theatrical Spectacle in America, 1830–1910.* Baltimore, MD: Johns Hopkins University Press, 2003.

Lutz, Edwin G. *Animated Cartoons: How They Are Made, Their Origin and Development.* New York: Scribner's, 1920.

MacAdam, Barbara. *Coastline to Skyline: The Philip H. Green Gift of California Watercolors, 1930–1960.* Hanover, NH: Hood Museum of Art, Dartmouth College, 2008.

Malraux, André. *Museum Without Walls.* New York: Pantheon, 1949.

Maltby, Richard. *Harmless Entertainment: Hollywood and the Ideology of Consensus.* Metuchen, NJ: Scarecrow Press, 1983.

Maltin, Leonard, and Jerry Beck. *Of Mice and Magic: A History of American Animated Cartoons.* New York: Plume, 1987.

Mann, Arthur. "Mickey Mouse's Financial Career." *Harper's,* May 1934, 714–21.

Marquis, Don. *archy does his part.* New York: Doubleday, Doran, 1935.

Mauss, Marcel. "Techniques of the Body" (1935). In *Techniques, Technology and Civilization,* ed. Nathan Schlanger. Trans. Ben Brewster, 77–95. New York: Berghahn Books, 2006.

Mayer, David. *Stagestruck Filmmaker: D. W. Griffith and the American Theatre.* Iowa City: University of Iowa Press, 2009.

McClelland, Gordon T. *Millard Sheets: The Early Years (1926–1944).* Newport Beach, CA: The California Regionalist Art Information Center, 2010.

McCord, David Frederick. "Is Walt Disney a Menace to Our Children?" *Photoplay* 45, no. 5 (April 1934): 30–32, 103.

McCrea, Christian. "Explosive, Expulsive, Extraordinary: The Dimensional Excess of Animated Bodies." *Animation: An Interdisciplinary Journal* 3, no. 1 (March 2008): 9–24.

McGilligan, Patrick. *Alfred Hitchcock: A Life in Darkness and Light.* New York: Harper Collins, 2004.

McPherson, Edward. *Buster Keaton: Tempest in a Flat Hat.* New York: Newmarket Press, 2005.

"The Mechanical Mouse." *Saturday Review of Literature* 10 (November 11, 1933): 252.

Merkl, Ulrich, ed. *The Complete "Dream of the Rarebit Fiend" (1904–1913) by Winsor McCay "Silas."* Self-published by rarebit-fiend-book.com, 2007.

Merlock Jackson, Kathy. *Walt Disney: A Bio-Bibliography.* Westport, CT: Greenwood Press, 1993.

Merritt, Russell. "Lost on Pleasure Islands: Storytelling in Disney's 'Silly Symphonies.'" *Film Quarterly,* 59, no. 11 (Autumn 2005): 4–17.

Merritt, Russell, and J.B. Kaufman. *Walt Disney's Silly Symphonies: A Companion to the Classic Cartoon Series.* Udine, Italy: La Cineteca del Friuli, 2006.

———. *Walt in Wonderland: The Silent Films of Walt Disney.* Baltimore, MD: Johns Hopkins University Press, 1993.

"Mickey Mouse and the Bankers." *Fortune,* November 1934, 94.

Mintz, Steven, and Susan Kellogg. *Domestic Revolutions: A Social History of American Family Life.* New York: Simon and Schuster, 1989.

Mitts-Smith, Debra. *Picturing the Wolf in Children's Literature.* New York: Routledge, 2010.

Montgomery, Michael V. *Carnivals and Commonplaces: Bakhtin's Chronotope, Cultural Studies, and Film.* New York: Peter Lang, 1993.

Moran, Kathleen and Michael Rogin. "'What's the Matter with Capra?': *Sullivan's Travels* and the Popular Front." *Representations* 71 (Summer 2000): 106–34.

Mounce, H.O. *Tolstoy on Aesthetics: What Is Art?* Aldershot, UK: Ashgate, 2001.

Mumford, Lewis. *Technics and Civilization* (1934). Chicago: University of Chicago Press, 2010.

Muscio, Giuliana. *Hollywood's New Deal.* Philadelphia, PA: Temple University Press, 1996.

Naremore, James. *Acting in the Cinema.* Berkeley: University of California Press, 1988.

Neupert, Richard. "Colour, Lines, and Nudes: Teaching Disney's Animators." *Film History* 11, no. 1 (1999): 77–84.

Nolan, Carrie. *Agency and Embodiment: Performing Gestures/Producing Culture.* Cambridge, MA: Harvard University Press, 2009.

Nottingham, Michael. "Downing the Folk-Festive: Menacing Meals in the Films of Jan Švankmajer." *EnterText* 4, no. 1 (Winter 2004–5): 126–50.

Ohmer, Susan. *George Gallup in Hollywood.* New York: Columbia University Press, 2006.

Olf, Julian. "The Man/Marionette Debate in Modern Theatre." *Educational Theatre Journal* 26, no. 4 (December 1974): 488–94.

Olmsted, Roger. "The Cigar-Box Papers: A Local View of the Centennial Electoral Scandals." *California Historical Quarterly* 55, no. 3 (Fall 1976): 256–69.

Orlean, Susan. *Rin Tin Tin: The Life and the Legend.* New York: Simon & Schuster, 2011.

Pan, Da'an. "Tasting the Good and the Beautiful: The Aestheticization of Eating and Drinking in Traditional Chinese Culture." *Journal of Interdisciplinary Studies* 16 (Fall 2003): 67–76.

Panofsky, Erwin. "Reflections on Historical Time." Trans. Johanna Bauman. *Critical Inquiry* 30 (Summer 2004): 691–701.

Parr, Adrian. *The Deleuze Dictionary.* New York: Columbia University Press, 2005.

Peary, Danny, and Gerald Peary. *The American Animated Cartoon: A Critical Anthology.* New York: E.P. Dutton, 1980.

Peltonen, Matti. "Clues, Margins, and Monads: The Micro-Macro Link in Historical Research." *History and Theory* 40, no. 3 (October 2001): 347–59.

Perine, Robert. *Chouinard: An Art Vision Betrayed, the Story of the Chouinard Art Institute, 1921–1972.* Encinitas, CA: Artra Publishing, 1985.

Perniola, Mario. *Enigmas: The Egyptian Moment in Society and Art.* Trans. Christopher Woodall. London: Verso, 1995.

Phelan, Peggy. "Performance, Live Culture and Things of the Heart." *Journal of Visual Culture* 2, no. 3 (2003): 291–302.

———. *Unmarked: The Politics of Performance.* New York: Routledge, 1993.

Philo, Chris, and Chris Wilbert. *Animal Spaces, Beastly Places.* New York: Routledge, 2000.

Pilling, Jayne. *A Reader in Animation Studies.* London: John Libbey, 1997.

———. *Women and Animation: A Compendium*. London: British Film Institute, 1992.

Place-Verghnes, Floriane. *Tex Avery: A Unique Legacy, 1942–1955*. Bloomington: Indiana University Press, 2006.

Pudovkin, V.I. *Film Acting: A Course of Lectures Delivered at the State Institute of Cinematography*. Trans. Ivor Montagu. New York: Grove Press, 1976.

Rickel, Jeff, and W. Lewis Johnson. "Animated Agents for Procedural Training in Virtual Reality: Perception, Cognition, and Motor Control." *Applied Artificial Intelligence* 13 (1999): 343–82.

Robertson [Wojcik], Pamela. *Guilty Pleasures: Feminist Camp from Mae West to Madonna*. Durham, NC: Duke University Press, 1996.

Robinson, David. *Buster Keaton*. Bloomington: Indiana University Press, 1969.

Rogin, Michael. *Blackface, White Noise: Jewish Immigrants in the Hollywood Melting Pot*. Berkeley: University of California Press, 1996.

Ruskin, John. *Modern Painters*. Vol. 3, Part 4. New York: John Wiley & Sons, 1885.

Sandler, Kevin S. *Reading the Rabbit: Explorations in Warner Bros. Animation*. New Brunswick, NJ: Rutgers University Press, 1998.

Sartin, Hank. "Drawing on Hollywood: Warner Bros. Cartoons and Hollywood, 1930–1960." PhD diss., University of Chicago, Chicago, 1998.

Schechner, Richard. *Between Theater and Anthropology*. 3rd ed. Philadelphia: University of Pennsylvania Press, 1987.

———. *Performance Studies: An Introduction*. New York: Routledge, 2006.

———. *The Future of Ritual: Writings on Culture and Performance*. New York: Psychology Press, 1993.

Schickel, Richard. *The Disney Version: The Life, Times, Art, and Commerce of Walt Disney*. New York: Simon and Schuster, 1968.

Schwab, Mack W. "The Communalistic Art of Walt Disney." *Cinema Quarterly* (Edinburgh) 2, no. 3 (Spring 1934): 150–54.

Schwartz, Hillel. *The Culture of the Copy: Striking Likenesses, Unreasonable Facsimiles*. New York: Zone Books, 1996.

Sebeok, Thomas, and Robert Rosenthal, eds. *The Clever Hans Phenomenon: Communication with Horses, Whales, Apes and People*. New York: New York Academy of Sciences, 1981.

Sharp, Joanne P. *Entanglements of Power: Geographies of Domination/Resistance*. New York: Psychology Press, 2000.

Shaviro, Steven. *The Cinematic Body*. Minneapolis: University of Minnesota Press, 1993.

Shohat, Ella, and Robert Stam. *Unthinking Eurocentrism: Multiculturalism and the Media*. New York: Routledge, 1994.

Simpson, Philip, and Karen J. Shepherdson. *Film Theory: Critical Concepts in Media and Cultural Studies, Volume 3*. London: Taylor & Francis, 2004.

Sito, Tom. *Drawing the Line: The Untold Story of the Animation Unions from Bosko to Bart Simpson*. Lexington: University Press of Kentucky, 2006.

Skolnick, Arnold. *Paintings of California*. Berkeley: University of California Press, 1997.

Smith, Jeff. *The Sounds of Commerce: Marketing Popular Film Music.* New York: Columbia University Press, 1998.

Smith, Murray. *Engaging Characters: Fiction, Emotion, and the Cinema.* Oxford: Oxford University Press, 1995.

Smolderen, Thierry, and Jean-Philippe Bramanti. *McCay 4: La quatrième dimension.* Paris: Editions Delcourt, 2006.

Smoodin, Eric. *Disney Discourse: Producing the Magic Kingdom.* New York: Routledge, 1994.

Snyder, Sharon L., and David T. Mitchell, "Re-engaging the Body: Disability Studies and the Resistance to Embodiment." *Public Culture* 13, no. 3 (2001): 367–89.

Sobchack, Vivian. *Carnal Thoughts: Embodiment and Moving Image Culture.* Berkeley: University of California Press, 2004.

———, ed. *Meta Morphing: Visual Transformation and The Culture of Quick-Change.* Minneapolis: University of Minnesota Press, 2000.

Solomon, Charles. *Enchanted Drawings: The History of Animation.* New York: Knopf, 1989.

———, ed. *The Art of the Animated Image: An Anthology.* Los Angeles: American Film Institute, 1987.

Solomon, Matthew. *Disappearing Tricks: Silent Film, Houdini, and the New Magic of the Twentieth Century.* Urbana: University of Illinois Press, 2010.

Spadoni, Robert. "The Uncanny Body of Early Sound Film." *Velvet Light Trap* 51 (Spring 2003): 4–16.

Stam, Robert. *Subversive Pleasures: Bakhtin, Cultural Criticism, and Film.* Baltimore, MD: Johns Hopkins University Press, 1992.

Stam, Robert, Paula Massood, Terry Lindvall, and Michael Chanan. "The Documentary Chronotope." *Jump Cut* 43 (July 2000): 56–61.

Standifer, James. "Musical Behaviors of Black People in American Society." *Black Music Research Journal* 1 (1980): 51–62.

Stanislavsky, Konstantin. *An Actor Prepares.* New York: Taylor & Francis, 1989.

———. *My Life in Art.* New York: Taylor & Francis, 1948.

Stebbins, Genevieve. *Delsarte System of Expression.* New York: Edgar S. Werner, 1887.

Steinman, Scott B., Barbara A. Steinman, and Ralph Philip Garzia. *Foundations of Binocular Vision: A Clinical Perspective.* New York: McGraw-Hill Professional, 2000.

Stern, Carol Simpson, and Bruce Henderson. *Performance: Texts and Contexts.* New York: Longman, 1993.

Strauven, Wanda, ed. *The Cinema of Attractions Reloaded.* Amsterdam: Amsterdam University Press, 2006.

Sully, James. *An Essay on Laughter: Its Forms, Its Causes, Its Development and Its Value.* London: Longmans, Green, and Co., 1902.

Švankmajer, Jan, and Eva Švankmajerova. *The Communication of Dreams.* Exhibition catalogue. Cardiff: Welsh Arts Council, 1992.

Thomas, Bob. *Walt Disney: An American Original.* New York: Simon and Schuster, 1976.

———. *Walt Disney, the Art of Animation: The Story of the Disney Studio Contribution to a New Art.* New York: Simon and Schuster, 1958.

Thomas, Frank, and Ollie Johnston. *Disney Animation: The Illusion of Life.* New York: Abbeville Press, 1984.

Thompson, Kristin. "Implications of the Cel Animation Technique." In *The Cinematic Apparatus,* ed. Teresa de Lauretis and Stephen Heath. New York: St. Martin's Press, 1980.

Tieman, Robert. *The Disney Keepsakes.* New York: Disney Editions, 2005.

Tolstoy, Leo. *What Is Art?* Trans. Aylmer Maude. New York: Thomas Y. Crowell Co., 1899.

———. *What Is Art?* Trans. Richard Pevear and Larissa Volokhonsky. Harmondsworth, UK: Penguin Books, 1995.

Tomasovic, Dick. *Le corps en abîme: Sur la figurine et le cinéma d'animation.* Paris: Editions Rouge Profond, 2006.

Turner, Victor. *From Ritual to Theatre.* New York: PAJ Publications, 1982.

Watts, Steven. *The Magic Kingdom: Walt Disney and the American Way of Life.* New York: Houghton Mifflin Co., 1997.

Weis, Elisabeth, and John Belton, eds. *Film Sound: Theory and Practice.* New York: Columbia University Press, 1985.

Wells, Paul. *Understanding Animation.* London: Routledge, 1998.

Werman, D.S., and Y. Guilbert. "Freud, Yvette Guilbert, and the Psychology of Performance." *Psychoanalytic Review* 85 (1998): 399–412.

White, Michele. *The Body and the Screen: Theories of Internet Spectatorship.* Cambridge, MA: MIT Press, 2006.

Williams, Linda. "Film Bodies: Gender, Genre and Excess." *Film Quarterly* 44, no. 4 (Summer 1991): 2–13.

Williams, Richard. *The Animator's Survival Kit.* London: Faber and Faber, 2001.

Wills, Garry. *John Wayne's America: The Politics of Celebrity.* New York: Touchstone, 1998.

Wojcik, Pamela Robertson, ed. *Movie Acting: The Film Reader.* New York: Routledge, 2004.

Wolf, Gary K. *Who Censored Roger Rabbit?* New York: Ballantine Books, 1982.

Worthen, W.B. "Disciplines of the Text/Sites of Performance." *TDR* 39, no. 1 (Spring 1995): 13–28.

Zipes, Jack. *The Enchanted Screen: The Unknown History of Fairy-Tale Films.* New York: Routledge, 2010.

———. *Happily Ever After: Fairy Tales, Children, and the Culture Industry.* New York: Routledge, 1997.

———. *The Trials and Tribulations of Little Red Riding Hood: Versions of the Tale in Sociocultural Context.* South Hadley, MA: Bergin & Garvey, 1983.

Index